Jawaharlal Nehru

Jawaharlal Nehru

Edited by
Shiv Gajrani
S. Ram

Commonwealth

Jawaharlal Nehru

Edition : 2027

ISBN 978-81-311-0182-7

Published by :
COMMONWEALTH PUBLISHERS (P) LTD.
4831/24, Govind Lane,
Ansari Road, Darya Ganj,.
New Delhi - 110002
Ph. : 23272541, 23242541
e-mail : commonwealthpublishers2016@gmail.com

Distributed by :
ARJUN PUBLISHING HOUSE
4831/24, Govind Lane,
Ansari Road, Darya Ganj,
New Delhi - 110002
Ph. : 23272541, 23242541
e-mail : arjunbooks2001@grnail.com

Laser Typesetting by :
Dimple Computers
Delhi

Printed at :
Milan Enterprises
Delhi

Preface

Jawaharlal Nehru was one of the greatest figures of our times wrote Dr. Radhakrishnan. He was an outstanding statesman whose services to the cause of human freedom are unforgettable. His life and work performally influenced our mental make up, social structure and intellectual development. His ideas of freedom, democracy, secularism and socialism had world wide appeal.

New researchers and great man continue to prophet different aspects of the vast and deep impact that Nehru left on his age.

Aim of this book is to provide to our readers some of the lesser known, more important and innovative material on the life and times of this great son of India.

We record our indebtedness and acknowledgments to the authorities on the subject and librarians and their staff members to help and kindness.

Last but not the least my publisher deserves a word of praise for making this such material for wider intellectual pursuits.

Authors

Contents

1

Introduction

Jawaharlal Nehru was one of the greatest figures of our generation, an outstanding statesman whose services to the cause of human freedom are unforgettable. As a fighter for freedom he was illustrious, as a maker of modern India his services were unparalleled. His life and work have had a profound influence on our mental make-up, social structure and intellectual development. It will be difficult to reconcile ourselves to the image of India without Nehru's active and all-pervasive leadership. An epoch in our country's history has come to a close.

As a man Nehru combined a fine sensitivity of mind, a rare delicacy of feeling, with large and generous impulses. To the weak and the frustrated his heart went out in profound sympathy. He was an author of distinction. His *Autobiography,* which tells the story of his life and struggle without a touch of self-pity or moral superiority, is one of the most remarkable books of our time.

Nehru held the office of the Prime Minister of our country ever since the dawn of independence; and in the long years of his premiership tried to put our country on a progressive, scientific, dynamic and noncommunal basis. His steadfast loyalty to certain fundamental principles of liberalism gave direction to our thought and life. We can understand the endless surprises of his attitudes and actions; all these fall into place if we remember his faith in democracy and freedom. He used the existing social and political institutions and breathed into them a new spirit, a new vitality.

Nehru by his series of public utterances educated our people to an appreciation of the values he had cherished. He fought for a high level of human life and burnt his ideals into the understanding of the common people. By his own powerful and vibrant voice, which we will not hear any more, he created, moulded, inspired and kindled a whole generation of Indians to a loyalty to the first principles which he held so dear. It is not enough to have great ideals; we have to work for their achievement. Time is the essence of the situation, and Nehru had a great regard for the sanctity of time. The pitiless exactions of time take no denial, and so the great leader has fallen.

Though nurtured in a life of sheltered ease and comfort, he drew himself into the national struggle and became a great leader second only to Gandhi. The part that he played in the national struggle and in the final settlement of the Indian question in 1947 are part of recent Indian history.

Nehru realized, even before the advent of freedom, that our economic regeneration, our progressive modern lives, cannot be achieved unless there is concerted planning. After the transfer of power, as the Chairman of the Planning Commission, it was he who gave dynamism and power to the various plans which are now being implemented.

The path of Nehru as a nation builder in the early years of India's freedom was beset with fantastic difficulties and formidable challenges. The partition of the country—resulting in the exodus of millions of people from one part of the subcontinent to the other amidst scenes of appalling riots, looting and arson—brought in its wake problems, political and economic, which defied easy solution. We have outbreaks of communal violence here and there in our country even now. This must have seemed to Nehru a terrific disillusionment of his great work, inherited from Gandhi and developed by himself.

Nehru always had a conviction that India cannot be viewed in isolation from other States of the world. Even before the advent of freedom, he was pleading that the Indian question was a part of the large movement of the oppressed people fighting against colonialism. He had a love of liberty, not merely for his own people, but for all people of the world. He therefore expressed sympathy and support for all liberation movements in Africa, Asia and South America. He believed in the liberty of all without distinction of class, creed or country.

Nehru was a great believer in world peace and the concept of one world community. No one had shown greater faith and allegiance to the Charter of the United Nations than Nehru. He realised that in a thermonuclear age, war would mean the extinction of all civilised values. That is why he was convinced that the true role of a statesman in this distracted world lay in the way of lessening tensions and conflicts and bringing about a climate of understanding and mutual accommodation, with a view to settlement of international differences without resort to the horrors of war. On several international questions such as Korea, Laos, the Congo and Vietnam, his was the voice of peace and friendship, and his voice was always heard with respect.

His courage, wisdom and personality have held this country together. It is these qualities which should be cherished if we are to hold on. Our thought today go out to him as a great emancipator of the human race, one who gave all his life and energy to the freeing of men's minds from political bondage, economic slavery, social oppression and cultural stagnation.

Those of us who are left behind to mourn his loss could do no better than work for the ideals he cherished. That is the best tribute we can pay to our departed leader.

S. Radhakrishnan

2

Early Years

The broad details of the early life of Jawaharlal Nehru are by now well known. He was born at 11.30 p.m. on 14 November 1889 at Allahabad, to which place his father, Motilal Nehru, had moved three years earlier from Kanpur. A pampered child surrounded by luxury, with a private swimming pool and tennis court, Jawaharlal ran the risk of being smothered by devotion and affluence. The mother's influence ensured an Indian environment. The atmosphere of Hindu custom and folklore was not lacking in the Nehru home; and Jawaharlal picked up a great deal of legend from the women and indulged in temple-going and Ganga-bathing. But the Nehru family was never fully integrated into the high-caste Hindu society of Allahabad, for not only was Motilal a relative newcomer but he had been excommunicated in 1899 for his refusal to make atonement for having travelled overseas. This insulated the Nehrus from the revivalism then rampant in Hindu orthodox circles in Allahabad, and even cut them off from the more orthodox sections among the Kashmiri Pandits.

However, the Kashmiri Pandit community derived certain incidental advantages which distinguished it from the other Hindus. Among the Hindus of Kashmir there were no castes below the Brahmins; and so while the Pandits were very conscious of their status, inter-caste antagonisms did not enter deeply into their lives. There was also, among the Kashmiri Pandits, often little feeling of separateness from the Muslims. Motilal himself was, like his ancestors, more fluent in Arabic and Persian and in Urdu than in any other Indian language.

The fortunes of the Nehrus had for generations been tied to Muslim patrons. Raj Kaul came to Delhi, and gradually the Kauls assumed the double-barrelled name of Kaul-Nehrus, because, it is said, their house was situated on the banks of a canal *(nahar* in Urdu).[1] Then, after the revolt of 1857 and the final collapse of the Moghuls, the Kaul-Nehrus moved to Agra. The Nehrus—the Kaul part of the name gradually dropped out—were one of the many Indian families which took advantage of the conditions and opportunities created by the raj. Ganga Dhar Nehru, Motilal's father, died in 1861, three months before the birth of Motilal, but the two older brothers, who themselves had taken service directly under the British or in a neighbouring Indian state, saw to it that Motilal received a proper education in the English language. He was a bright pupil, though he never graduated, and set up legal practice, first in Kanpur and then in Allahabad, where he soon became one of the leaders of the Bar.

Though Motilal had been born poor, had acquired many responsibilities at an early age as head of a large Hindu joint family, and was professionally equipped rather than generally educated, he had no complexes. A cheerful extrovert, full of the confidence and inner'balance that come from self-made success, he set about living the life of an English gentleman. Even the fact that his country was under alien rule did not subdue him. He was too busy making money, and enjoying what money could buy. Like most members of the educated Indian elite, he took an interest in politics and dutifully attended as many sessions of the Indian National Congress as he could. But these were the years when the Congress was a loyalist organization, interested not in subverting British rule, nor even in extracting concessions from it, but in pleading for greater opportunities for service.

So it was but natural that Motilal should want for his son the best that British education could offer. He first engaged two English governesses, and then sent his son for a few months to a local convent and finally decided on private instruction at home. The great Sanskrit scholar Pandit

Ganganatha Jha tried, with no noticeable success, to teach Jawaharlal Sanskrit.[2] But the main emphasis was on a British tutor. A young and ardent Irish-French theosophist, F.T. Brooks, who had been recommended by Mrs Annie Besant, was in charge of Jawaharlal's education from 1901 to 1904. He introduced Jawaharlal to English poetry and literature and developed in him an interest in science by improvising a tiny laboratory in his rooms. He also, by allowing Jawaharlal to be present at his regular discourses on theosophy, planted in the boy's mind the idea that there might be more in religion than myth and miracle. The concept of ethics is what Jawaharlal perhaps rather vaguely comprehended when, at Brooks's instance, he read the not-too-easy Upanishads and the Bhagavad Gita.

Dissatisfied with private tuition, and in particular with Brooks, in May 1905 Motilal took his family to Britain and secured admission for his son at Harrow. Jawaharlal was now a boy of fifteen. Not very tall, and slightly built, he was handsome, with a fair skin, clear features and well-brushed black hair which was, however, never very thick. He was good at his school work and impressed his teachers. He never fulfilled academically, in later years at Cambridge or the Bar, the promise he showed at Harrow. The reason was that he was not very keen, did not share his father's ambition for such prizes as the senior wranglership and did well at school merely because there was at this time very little else that interested him. Only the Officers Training Corps roused any enthusiasm.

Jawaharlal's arrival at Harrow coincided with startling events in India and outside, and it was now that he began, for the first time, to take an interest in politics and world affairs. In 1905 the viceroy, Lord Curzon, had, by his heavy-handed partitioning of the province of Bengal, forced the transition in India from the era of supplication to that of pressure. The broad-based agitation in Bengal found vigorous support in every other part of India because the partition was regarded not as a minor administrative reform but as a deliberate attempt to weaken the growing forces of Indian nationalism. Jawaharlal was avid for news, and asked his father to mail Indian newspapers to him regularly.

The course of the agitation against partition accentuated division opinion within the Congress, between the Extremists who believed in methods of agitation and the Moderates who were committed to constitutional processes. Jawaharlal found himself in sympathy with the Extremists, and Tilak seemed to him the embodiment of Indian nationalism struggling for freedom.[3] But it was a vague sympathy. The ideas were unformed and the emotion imprecise.

However, it was not only developments in India that excited Jawaharlal's interest. On the day Jawaharlal landed in Britain, news came of Japan's decisive naval victory over Russia at Tshushima. Feeling relatively a stranger in a British public school, and with his mind full of reports of the growing estrangement between the British rulers and the Indian people, he thrilled to this evidence of the new strength of an Asian nation.

Bored with Harrow, Jawaharlal sat for the entrance examinations to Cambridge in the spring of 1907 and went up to Trinity that October. In the intervening summer he had spent a few weeks in Ireland. He missed the rioting in Belfast and was disappointed that Dublin was quiet during his stay. But he had felt, first-hand, the force of nationalist agitation and was impressed by the Sinn Fein movement. The parallel in India was, of course, obvious, and Jawaharlal's visit to Ireland and his understanding of her politics seem to have strengthened his Extremist sympathies. The result was that he became more critical of his father's attitude in politics. He accused Motilal of being 'immoderately moderate',[4] and a later light-hearted reference to the government demonstrating their satisfaction with 'the insulting offer of a Rai Bahadurship' hurt Motilal so deeply that Jawaharlal had to apologize.[5]

The extremism, however, was confined to his letters to his father. Jawaharlal did not plunge into the student politics of Cambridge. His extremist opinions, it should be added, were still not deep-seated or transforming his whole outlook. They were but a natural part of the general posture of dilettantism which Jawaharlal deliberately cultivated. Though he told no one but his father of these views, the occasional assertion doubtless gave him inner satisfaction. But that was all. There was no greater hint of the rebel about him or about his view of his own future. He showed at this time no real signs of any sort of fire or distinction, and did not stand put among his generation. He accepted the values and ambitions of his class, and was quite at ease in the vapid society of Indian middle-class convention. He did not, despite his epistolary extremism, resist the hopes which his father had nurtured from the start of entombing him in the Indian Civil Service. In fact, it was Motilal who, early in 1910, abandoned the idea of Jawaharlal sitting for the ICS examination, mainly because he could not brook the prospect of his only son serving for long years in remote districts away from home, and had a growing feeling that the examiners were biased against Indian candidates. But neither father nor—more startlingly in the light of later events—son resented the thought of serving the British rulers. They had not yet recognized the necessity of freedom.

The impression Jawaharlal gives as an undergraduate is of a man only half-awakened and waiting for further experience and comprehension. But Jawaharlal was, as we know, interested in William Morris, and bought a full set of his collected works, which began to be issued from 1910.[6] The revolt of Morris against the ugliness of industrial capitalism and its impoverished human relationships had led on to a frontal attack on class exploitation and the evils of imperialism. The life of Morris was the story of the evolution of a revolutionary, the progress from aestheticism to the basic question of class power; and Jawaharlal may have been, in his own context, moving in the same direction. His moral sensibility and fastidiousness were beginning to develop in the social context.

Looking back on these years, Jawaharlal described his primary mood as a vague kind of Cyrenaicism.[7] But even the assiduous cultivation of pleasure seems to have been only half-hearted. Cambridge in those days was an exciting place, but Jawaharlal never got into its full swing. He took as his subjects chemistry, geology and physics, but soon gave up physics for botany, and in the final tripos was placed in the second half of the second class. This was an achievement well below the level of his talent, but Jawaharlal was not by temperament an academic, and appears to have done very little work.

Outside the laboratories and lecture rooms Jawaharlal led a busy life, even if it was unspectacular. He played tennis, rode a great deal and applied for admission to the University Mounted Infantry. He was summoned to a riding test but did not go, ostensibly for lack of time but probably because he knew that as an Indian he would be rejected. He joined the Trinity Boat Club and, being only 8 st. 4 lb. in weight, was made cox. He had not looked forward to this, but proved efficient enough.

Jawaharlal had many acquaintances but no small intimate social circle, no close friendships without reserve; nor does he seem to have known any women. His public school background helped him to do without them. But, as he confessed to his father, at times he was 'almost overpowered by the sense of my solitary condition.'[8] Where, then, was the successful pursuit of egoistic hedonism, the deliberate achievement of sensation? It was obviously a pose to cover an emptiness in his life. Jawaharlal had opinions but needed a cause; there stretched before him a future secure but with no purpose.

Even before his final tripos examination, Jawaharlal had joined the Inner Temple, and the fond father believed that the son had followed his aptitude. Motilal was confident of Jawaharlal's success. He had failed to realize that Jawaharlal had no enthusiasm for the law and joining the Inner Temple was merely part of his general policy, at this time, of drift. Being forced to do what he disliked resulted, as was to be expected, in Jawaharlal leading a life of idleness. But before that he had nearly succeeded in killing himself. On a holiday in Norway with a friend, while trekking somewhere north of Bergen, he plunged into an ice-cold fjord for a bath and became numb.[9] His foot slipped and he was swept away by the current. His companion pulled him out on the brink of a waterfall. But Jawaharlal was always a man of physical courage, and proximity to death pleased rather than sobered him.

For the next two years Jawaharlal was caught up in the whirl of London life. Renewing contact with some old school acquaintances, he was very much the man of fashion. Never overloaded with money, Jawaharlal now found himself often in debt, was forced to pawn his watch and chain, sometimes had no money even for bus or tube fares, and more and more frequently approached his father for supplementary grants. He never in his life had any money sense.

Motilal was alarmed. Far from carrying off the scholarships and prizes at the Bar examinations, Jawaharlal just managed to pass. He had done all the things he had been told to do, but with no great enthusiasm. His deep attachment to his father had the defect that it made him almost passive. He was willing to conform and to leave the major decisions of his life to be made by his father. He had emerged from seven years in England, having passed through the mill of a traditional education, with no confidence in himself or interest in the world. But his mind and character had been trained not for a profession but for the call which was to come in the years ahead. Others might have been disappointed that he had not fulfilled the promise of Harrow and carried off the academic spoils, but Jawaharlal himself saw no reason to regret or repent. He returned to India with a nurtured mind and imagination.

In addition, he brought back with him attachments to Britain, and the values he considered British, which were never to leave him. They moulded his outlook, sustained him in his struggles and influenced his policies in the days of his power.

Throughout his life, Britain was a country with which Jawaharlal identified extensively in the personal sense. Indeed, he felt that his reaction to foreign rule would be that, in similar circumstances, of any average Englishman uncontaminated by imperialism.

Life Gets Meaning

Back in India, Jawaharlal slipped without resistance into the vacuous, parasitic life of upper-middle-class Indian society in Allahabad. He joined his father's chambers and Motilal saw to it that work came his way. Jawaharlal toiled fairly hard and had the advantages of his father's sponsorship and of social contacts with judges, eminent lawyers and the leading landlords and industrialists of the UP. But he could whip up no enthusiasm for the law, was shy of speaking, and found the work tedious.

Apart from professional work, Jawaharlal continued in Allahabad the life of a man-about-town which he had led in his last years in London. He enjoyed the lavish entertainments of his father; and there are, in addition, reports of his own late-night parties and revels. The casual sympathy with Extremist politics which he had shown in Cambridge did not inhibit him from participating in the formal rounds of Anglo-Indian society.

However, the great event of that year was his marriage on 8 February 1916. This question had been worrying Motilal and his wife ever since their son went to Harrow. For, even though their son was then only a boy of fifteen, Motilal was concerned lest Jawaharlal begin to show interest in women, particularly in view of the entanglement of one of his friends. Motilal had no cause for worry. With an odd detachment Jawaharlal wanted his father to settle his engagement and preclude further discussion.

After years of search, in 1912, just before Jawaharlal's return to India, Motilal chose Kamala Kaul, a young girl of thirteen belonging to a Kashmiri Brahmin middle-class family who ran a flour mill in Delhi. She had been educated at home and spoke Hindi and Urdu; and after the engagement she was brought to Allahabad for training in deportment. When she was seventeen the marriage was celebrated in Delhi on a munificent scale, with special trains carrying the guests to the 'Nehru marriage camp'.

That summer Jawaharlal spent in Kashmir. He went in pursuit of bear and shot one as well as a large number of pigeons and marmots. Trying to hop across a crevasse, Jawaharlal slipped and fell in, and was pulled out by the rope. As there were many other such crevasses and it was still snowing, the party turned back.[10]

Along with high life and shikar, there was the usual ostentatious public service. For three or four years Jawaharlal served as one of the provincial secretaries of the St John Ambulance Association. He was also one of the joint secretaries of the UP South Africa Committee for the collection of funds for Gandhi's passive resisters in South Africa, but this was not an anti-government activity, for the Government of India had frequently expressed their support for the Indian community in South Africa. He was willing in June 1917 to join the Indian Defence Force, constituted on the lines of the territorial army, and encourage other young Indians to do the same.

Within a week, however, the situation underwent a marked change. Tilak and Mrs Besant, failing to secure the readmission of the Extremists into the Congress, had set up Home Rule leagues. They were intended to be primarily educative—to argue the case for Home Rule, hold classes and seminars, circulate literature, collect funds and organize social work. But the government feared Mrs Besant's influence. She was first expelled from Bombay and then from the Central Provinces and finally, in June 1917, interned at a hill station by the Madras government. This panicky step caused resentment throughout India; and among those roused to annoyance was Jawaharlal. He was, at long last, beginning to find his role. The meeting for considering the expansion of the Indian Defence Force was promptly cancelled;[11] and Jawaharlal withdrew his own application for enlistment. A Home Rule League was formed in the UP with Motilal as president and Jawaharlal as one of the joint secretaries. Mere protest meetings and representations were the politics of cowards and opium-eaters : what was now needed was non-co-operation with the government till they reversed their folly.[12]

Such vehemence showed that despite the superficiality of his way of living, his spirit was not dead and he was keen on action. But what action should be taken, what form non-co-operation should be given, was not clear to him. He had no startling ideas of his own. Neither the Anglo-Saxon approach of Mrs Besant nor the orthodox extremism of Tilak had any great appeal for him, and, while he spoke in terms of Home Rulers capturing the Congress,[13] he had given no thought as to what should be done once that organization had been taken over. In fact, his mind, for lack of anything better, fell into Moderate grooves, and he objected to the refusal by the government to permit deputations to proceed to England to plead the cause of Home Rule.[14]

So Jawaharlal, even in his late twenties, was a man who had yet to know his mind, discontented with his lot of comfort and affluence, dissatisfied with merely helping to run *The Independent,* the newspaper started by his father in February 1919 to give voice in the UP to the viewpoint of the Congress, and groping for some form of action which would provide mental and emotional satisfaction. When, therefore, the call of Gandhi came he could respond to it not merely at a political but at a human level. Long after, looking back on these fallow years, he remarked that it was the acceptance of Gandhi's leadership, and the civil disobedience and jail-going which had followed, that had made a man of him.[15] Life now had meaning in the service of a cause.

REFERENCES

1. This was Motilal's theory, to which Jawaharlal gave currency in his *Autobiography;* but, on the other hand, it has to be remembered that there were Nehrus even in Kashmir.

2. See Jawaharlal's message on the death of Amaranatha Jha, 19 September 1955.

3. See his message on Tilak, 18 June 1956.

4. Letter, 20 December 1907, *Selected Works of Jawaharlal* (hereafter SW), vol. 1 (Delhi, 1972), p. 39.

5. Letter, 30 January 1908, SW, vol. 1, p. 44.

6. See His letter to E. P. Thompson, written in 1955, Nehru papers.

7. *Autobiography* (Indian edition, 1962), p. 20.

8. Letter, 29 October 1908, SW, vol. 1, p. 59.

9. Jawaharlal could not remember the exact place; letter to Judge Andren, 11 October 1954, Nehru papers.

10. Diary entries from 24 August to 7 September 1916; letter to S.S. Khera, 1 July 1958, Nehru papers.

11. Letter to the editor, 20 June 1917, *The Leader,* 22 June 1917.

12. Letter to the editor, *The Leader,* 21 June 1917.

13. See his letter to A.M. Khwaja, 12 December 1917.

14. Resolution moved by Jawaharlal at the UP political conference, *The Leader,* 16 October 1918.

15. Narendra Deva, 'Favourite of Fortune', in *Nehru Abhinandan Granth* (New Delhi, 1949), p. 108.

3

Politics

The Independent began its career with severe criticism of the Rowlatt bills, whereby the Government of India established summary procedures for dealing with political agitation; and Jawaharlal did not rule out the possibility of his arrest. This did not happen. Jawaharlal was one of the signatories of the satyagraha vow, formulated by Gandhi, pledging refusal to obey certain laws and a member of the committee "formed at Allahabad to organize satyagraha in that district and to get in touch with other districts to constitute a provincial committee.[1] After the massacre at Amritsar he assisted the Congress Inquiry Committee, and visited Amritsar and the Punjab to take depositions and collect material for the speeches in the assembly of his father and Pandit Malaviya, a moderate Congress leader, about the actual firing, the atrocities under martial law and the 'general misbehaviour of tommies'.[2] He also helped in relief work, though the government believed that any distinction between such humanitarian effort and political agitation was fanciful.[3] The Allahabad Seva Samiti (relief organization) raised over a lakh of rupees for the work and Jawaharlal took some volunteers with him to the Punjab to help in organizing such relief.[4]

Yet, as in the case of Mahatma Gandhi and many others in India, it was not the happenings at Amritsar and the attitude of Dyer at the time and later, before the official commission of inquiry, which upset Jawaharlal as much as the reaction in England to these events. Till now he had been in the stream of the Indian moderate tradition, expecting favours from the benign British rulers; and his conversion was part of the general realization that freedom could never be a gift but only the achievement of struggle and resistance.

Motilal, however, disliked greatly the idea of boycott of the councils and, not expecting that the Congress would accept this programme of Gandhi for non-co-operation, planned the election campaign in the United Provinces for the Congress against the Moderates. Jawaharlal helped in drafting the election manifesto,[5] and Motilal was seriously considering the choice of a suitable constituency for his son. He finally decided on Fatehpur and was disappointed that Jawaharlal turned it down, preferring to follow Gandhi's lead. He knew that his destiny and that of his son were scrambled together, but he did not always relish it. Austerity and puritanism did not come naturally to him, and watching Jawaharlal embrace Gandhian rigours caused him intense pain. When Jawaharlal sought permission to transfer his war bonds worth Rs. 10,000 to the Tilak Swaraj Fund and meantime announced it as an anonymous donation in *The Independent,* Motilal in great irritation replied that he was planning to resume practice. And, he added brutally, stressing that it was his affluence that made possible Jawaharlal's political involvement : 'You cannot have it both ways: Insist on my having no money and yet expect me to pay you money.'[6]

These financial worries, however, Jawaharlal left to his father. Gandhi had at last given India a lead in action, and Jawaharlal was enthusiastic. His main preoccupation was the task of organizing non-co-operation in the UP, and he was soon among its recognized leaders. To introduce some discipline into the movement, he organized drill for the volunteers and had plans for linking up the various local organizations. He was elected president of the Etah district Congress conference; and though the government banned the procession and sought to prevent the conference, Jawaharlal was welcomed by large crowds at every wayside station and he delivered his address as scheduled.[7]

The hold which Gandhi had acquired on Jawaharlal and which he was never to lose is, at first view, incongruous.

Gandhi was Christ-like in his seizure of men; but his conversion of Jawaharlal is capable of rational explanation. What appealed to the younger man was Gandhi's strength, his rock-like commitment to India's freedom, the way in which he had perfected his character and personality so as to make himself an effective instrument of political change in India. He was above all a man of action, of enormous restlessness and energy, with a will to power and a touch of ruthlessness. He repeatedly stressed that God appears not in person but in action.

Jawaharlal's first direct clash with the government, however, came about in an entirely fortuitous way and had nothing to do with Gandhi. In the summer of 1920 he had taken the family up to Mussoorie, a hill station. An Afghan delegation was staying at the same hotel and the authorities knew well that Jawaharlal had, during the period of over a fortnight when he was there, not seen anything of them. Yet suddenly the local superintendent of police called on him and asked him either to furnish a positive undertaking not to get into touch with the Afghan delegation or to leave Mussoorie on his own. The police official was, in fact, carrying out a decision of the Government of India.

Jawaharlal, faced with this unnecessary provocation, refused to bind himself not to meet the Afghans or to leave Mussoorie on his own. However, he departed after an explusion order had been served on him. He made no effort to resist expulsion, nor, on his return to the plains, did he seek to break the order and return to Mussoorie. It is hard to believe that the Jawaharlal of later years would have so mildly complied with such an 'insensate' order and been, satisfied with a mere refusal to give an undertaking.[8] Even at this time, when there was a deterioration in his mother's health he might have returned to Mussoorie in defiance of the order and courted arrest, had not the UP government, genteel as ever with drawn the order in view, as they said, of the health of the ladies of the family.

REFERENCES

1. *The Leader,* 3 April 1919. 'Satyagraha' ('truth-force') was Gandhi's name for passive resistance.

2. *Notes on the Occurrences in the Punjab,* April-June 1919, SW, vol. 1, pp. 130-40. At Amritsar, General Dyer, dealing with civil disorder, had opened fire without warning on a large crowd that had inadequate means of dispersal, ordered that Indians could only crawl on their stomachs along a street in which an Englishwoman had been attacked, and had some persons whom he suspected of defiance of this order summarily whipped.

3. Report on the political and economic situation in the Punjab for the fortnight ending 15 September 1919, home dept. political deposit, October 1919, proceeding 59.

4. Note of the UP criminal investigation dept., 18 December 1919, home dept. pol. A., June 1921, proceedings 248-62.

5. See Motilal to Gandhi, 25 April 1920, Gandhi papers, Gandhi Smarak Sangrahalaya, serial no. 7163.

6. Motilal to Jawaharlal, 27 June 1921.

7. *The Independent,* 1 October 1920.

8. *The Independent,* 19 May 1920.

4

Among The Peasants

More crucial to Jawaharlal's development than his expulsion was his involvement in the peasant unrest in the United Provinces. The special cause of agrarian distress in Avadh (Oudh) was the inelastic Rent Act of 1886 which forbade landlords to enhance rents by more than one anna in the rupee once every seven years.[1] Clearly, with the great rise in prices of consumer goods, landlords would try to circumvent the rigidity of the statute by demanding payment of other dues; and the lack of occupancy rights enabled them to collect these dues by holding out the threat of eviction. Actual evictions were frequent, both because landlords saw an advantage, with the rising price of foodgrains, in cultivating the land themselves and enforcing their customary right to free or ill-paid labour, and because, with the apparent imminence of an amendment of the law granting fixity of tenure, it appeared worthwhile to terminate tenancy of any duration. But more often the threat to evict was utilized to compel the tenant to pay higher cesses or *nazarana* in addition to the rent; and this had become a regular form of income to the landlords. Tenants could only secure renewals of their leases by borrowing heavily from moneylenders or from their relatives—or from the landlords themselves—in order to pay nazarana. But these *kisans* (peasants), never wholly lacking in some form of power in at least some estates, were no longer unaware of anything better; and there was a growing resentment at working for, and paying heavy cesses to, distant and unknown landowners at the bidding of foul-mouthed middle-men. Nor was there much faith left in the efficacy of the law courts as a means of obtaining redress.

The situation was particularly critical in Pratabgarh district. The population here was unusually dense; on the other hand, large tracts of land in the district were barren. So there was a keen competition for land, and this enabled the landlords, who were in this district a particularly poor lot, to demand exorbitant nazarana. The social composition of the district was also somewhat uncommon; 11.3 per cent of the population was composed of Kurmis, a low caste which could not muster the resistance to the exactions of landlords which the high-caste tenantry were generally able to do. They had to pay a higher rental than Brahmin or Kshatriya tenants.[2] Nor were there under-proprietors to act as a breakwater between the landlords and these low-caste tenants.

If the repression of the tenants was more severe in Pratabgarh than in other districts of Avadh, there were other balancing reasons which made a peasant outbreak more probable here than elsewhere. The Kurmis had a tradition of defiance, and they had never lost their social coherence and capacity for organization. It was of course easier to organize concerted action within a caste, however low, than to draw tenants of high and low caste together. Moreover, the Kurmi peasants of Pratabgarh could not fail to notice the occupancy rights enjoyed by the tillers, after twelve years of continuous cultivation, in the neighbouring districts of Allahabad and Jaunpur (which were part of the Agra division); and their kinsmen in these districts were reluctant to enter into marriage relations with persons who might overnight be reduced to the level of beggars at the whim of their landlord.[3] The proximity of Allahabad city was also a source of strength, for the tenants of Pratabgarh could derive leadership and advice from urban politicians, who had by now begun to realize the value to them of peasant support.

Trouble began in Pratabgarh from April 1920, the beginning of the season of notices of eviction and of ejectment. At first the leadership of the Kurmis of Pratabgarh was assumed by a millenarian figure of shadowy antecedents, Baba Ram Chandra, who addressed large crowds, calling on them to stand up for their rights and resist the landlords, to pay their rents but not illegal cesses. He then, in June 1920, led about 500 of his followers to Allahabad in the hope of meeting Gandhi. They failed to find Gandhi, but instead met Jawaharlal, who happened to be there because of his expulsion from Mussoorie, and persuaded him to return with them to Pratabgarh. So casual circumstance thrust Jawaharlal into the problem of the Indian peasantry and gave a new and permanent dimension to his outlook. The tranquil firmness of these men, living often below the margin of subsistence but never being overcome, impressed him profoundly.

Jawaharlal now gave publicity to the grievances of the kisans. But in Pratabgarh itself, where he was accompanied by Gauri Shankar Misra, more conservative even than the Jawaharlal of those days, the general effect of their presence was, as the commissioner acknowledged, 'to bring a number of vague demands into a coherent shape and to a certain extent to moderate it.'[4] They encouraged the peasants to organize themselves into village kisan sabhas and to formulate their demands for restrictions on evictions and forced labour, leases for fourteen years, payment of cesses at only customary rates, cessation of fines and free access to landlords—demands which could hardly be regarded as extreme. When the authorities arrested a few kisans for 'highhandedness', Jawaharlal and another colleague from Allahabad, Purushottam Das Tandon, met the deputy commissioner and, while not approving of the conduct of the men arrested, suggested that the cases be withdrawn so that the relations between zamindars and tenants might not worsen.[5]

By now, however, with the non-co-operation movement in full swing, Jawaharlal began to feel that some of his colleagues were taking their moderation too far. What, in fact, Jawaharlal hoped for was to link kisan discontent with nationalist politics. He had made no study of economic and land problems and he had no clear ideas about peasant participation. It was not his intention to provide a revolutionary dimension to Indian nationalism. But this contact with the kisans was satisfying psychologically, as it gave him the feeling that he was re-Indianizing himself and functioning in a wholly Indian situation; and politically it was important, for it provided an opportunity to do in his own province what Gandhi had done elsewhere, harnessing peasant strength in the interests of the Congress.

Pratabgarh and Rae Bareli were more suited for Jawaharlal's effort than Allahabad district itself, for there the presence of many Muslim landlords would give communal overtones to any kisan agitation, and this was hardly to be desired while the Khilafat agitation was at its height. At a meeting held in Pratabgarh in October to federate the numerous village sabhas into an Oudh Kisan Sabha, the objectives were defined in a harmless enough manner; but the deputy commissioner was obliged to walk out when Jawaharlal advised his kisan audience to boycott elections to the councils and stressed that the only moral to be drawn from the Punjab and Khilafat events was that the government was an utterly unjust one which cared little for the lives, honour and even the religion of the Indian people.

Throughout the winter months of 1920-1 the efforts to harness tenant power to the non-co-operation movement continued. Jawaharlal spoke to large kisan audiences and was struck above all by their discipline.[6] Gandhi himself visited Pratabgarh in November. The Kisan Congress, meeting at Fyzabad in December, attracted more persons from a few districts than the National Congress, meeting at Nagpur, attracted from the whole of India. The landlords also helped by utilizing what they believed was their last opportunity to push through a rush of enhancements. This enraged the lower tenantry, which was now joined by landless labourers, suddenly caught by the rise in prices and diminished prospects of employment.[7]

The distress which, as even discerning officials realized, was genuine and very great, began to assume political overtones. It was still, however, not the Congress nor their own strength but the government whom the kisans looked to for an improvement of their condition.[8] Their discontent was entirely with the landlords and was not in any way anti-British or anti-government. But the UP government threw away their chance and, by their reckless handling of the situation, gave a strong fillip to the movement, so that throughout the year 1921 many districts in Avadh were shaken by explosions of agrarian unrest.

Early in January local ruffians in Rae Bareli district took advantage of the tension to burn crops grown on the *sir* (personal) lands of the zamindars and to loot shops in the bazaars; and there was probably some ground for the belief that a few of these miscreants had been encouraged by the zamindars themselves in order to bring the kisans and their organizations into disrepute. On the 5th three of the kisan leaders were arrested, and a large crowd began to drift towards Rae Bareli town in the hope of seeing these leaders. Encouragement for this move was provided by the deputy commissioner's assurance to the kisans that he would listen at Rae Bareli to their grievances which had been heightened by the failure of the *kharif* (autumn) harvest and the holding off of the winter rains. However, on the 6th the police opened fire on a crowd at Fursatganj, ten miles to the east of Rae Bareli, killing between four and six people; and the next day there was heavy firing at Munshiganj, two miles south of the town, with at least nine dead and a large number wounded.

On both occasions the authorities had clearly panicked. But to the public it was pretended that the firings alone had saved the whole of the south of Rae Bareli district from widespread looting and the rapid attainment of a state of anarchy. To many officials the differences between dacoits, kisans and non-co-operators were becoming increasingly blurred. This confusion in the official outlook suited the talukdars; but it worried the kisan representatives, some of whom came to see Jawaharlal at Allahabad on the 5th and requested him to visit the Rae Bareli district. Jawaharlal was reluctant, as he had just returned from the Congress session at Nagpur; nor was he willing to see the Congress and kisan organizations associated with the looting that had occurred. But on hearing from a well-known citizen of Rae Bareli the next day that the situation was serious, and knowing that the local kisans had no capable leader, Jawaharlal left by the night train, reaching Rae Bareli at 2 p.m. on the 7th. He then heard of the firing at Fursatganj the previous day, and of the confrontation between the officials and the large kisan crowd at Munshiganj. He promptly went to the scene with the intention of directing the crowd to disperse, and told the kisans he met on the way to go home. But meantime he received a pencilled note from the deputy commissioner : 'Pt Jawaharlal Nehru. You are hereby informed that your presence in this district is not desired—you are directed to leave by the next train.' Jawaharlal sent his reply on the back of the slip : 'I should like to know if this is a formal order or a mere request. If it is the former then it should be drawn up in a formal manner mentioning the section etc. Until such an order is served on me I propose to remain here.' Stopped by policemen from crossing a bridge on the other side of which the firing was taking place, Jawaharlal addressed such of the kisans as he came across, impressing on them the need to be both non-violent and fearless. It was obviously a deep experience for Jawaharlal :

> They behaved as brave men, calm and unruffled in the face of danger. I do not know how they felt but I know what my feelings were. For a moment my blood was up, non-violence was almost forgotten—but for a moment only. The thought of the great leader, who by God's goodness has been sent to lead us to victory, came to me, and I saw the kisans seated and standing near me, less excited, more peaceful than I was—and the moment of weakness passed. I spoke to them in all humility on nonviolence—I who needed the lesson more than they—and they heeded me and peacefully dispersed. On the other side of the river, however, men lay dead and dying. It was a similar crowd with a similar object. Yet they poured their hearts' blood before they would disperse.[9]

The deputy commissioner, who had by now come back across the bridge, sent for Jawaharlal and informed him that meetings were prohibited. Though aware that Jawaharlal was using his influence against violent agitation, the officials were unwilling to let him speak to the crowd; for, as they said to him, they were not there to increase his prestige.[10] Jawaharlal, abiding by this order, dissolved the meeting after addressing it for a few minutes.

Joined by his father the next day, Jawaharlal visited the wounded in hospital and then left for Allahabad. His dispatches, signed and unsigned, to *The Independent,* were sharply critical of the government and the local talukdar; but his conduct at Rae Bareli itself far from being that of a 'firebrand', as the deputy commissioner had expected before his arrival.[11] His whole influence was thrown the side of moderation, in urging the kisans to be quiet and peaceful, to abide by whatever orders were issued by the local officials and to go back to their homes. A few days later, when disturbances began in Fyzabad division, where too, as in Pratabgarh, the small tenants were low-caste men employed by Brahmin zamindars, he went to Unchahar to call off the meeting, which had been announced long before to inform the kisans of the decisions of the Nagpur Congress, and persuaded the kisans who had collected from various parts of Avadh to disperse.[12]

Then, when news came in of sporadic renewal of looting, Jawaharlal was asked by local leaders to visit Fyzabad district; and he addressed large meetings exhorting kisans, if they were serious and earnest about swaraj', to take a pledge not to resort to violence or looting.[13] Often, after he had spoken, men got up to confess to looting, knowing well that this would lead to their arrest. Jawaharlal glamorized the kisans and saw them as brave men uncontaminated by city life or textbook education; but he was not deeply moved by their economic wretchedness. He saw in them a sturdy peasantry which would be the backbone of a successful nationalist movement, and he wished to enlist them wholly for the political struggle as it was being waged by the Congress; but he did not envisage the coordination of these scattered outbursts against local misery and the development of a large-scale peasant revolt and even perhaps a revolution. He agreed with Gandhi and the other leaders of the Congress that the kisans should pay their rents and devote their full attention to the non-violent struggle for swaraj. Indeed, later Jawaharlal even preached kisan-zamindar unity;[14] and on the issue of ejectment, which, more than any other, agitated the kisans of the UP, all he could say was that this was but a minor part of the major issue of ejectment of the British from India.[15]

At this time Jawaharlal had not considered carefully whether economic and social change should be part of, or even parallel to, the political revolution; and he was willing to accept without thought the suggestion that economic issues should not be allowed to hinder political activity. His idea of freedom was purely political—ridding the British of their control over finance, the army and the police. Freedom was spinning, the wearing of hand-spun cloth, justice, prohibition, removal of untouchability and all such moral virtues; and foreign rule was the opposite of these.[16] There was very little economic connotation. But even this concept of 'politics in command' was narrow and limited. Jawaharlal's political ideas in these years were a curious, unformed mixture of anarchism and village government, of Gandhi and Bertrand Russell. Representative institutions and democracy as found in Western countries had proved failures, and the problem was to free democracy from the malign influences of capital, property, militarism and an overgrown bureaucracy. Orthodox socialism also did not give much hope, and the war had shown that an all-powerful state was no lover of individual liberty. Life under socialism would be a joyless and a soulless thing, regulated to the minutest detail by bureaucratic rules and orders. Jawaharlal was at this time a great believer in devolution and as little centralization as possible. Swaraj was to him *panchayat raj* and he favoured giving these village councils considerable powers even in civil and criminal matters.[17] But all this lay in the future. It did not strike him to take any immediate steps such as setting up village schools and cooperatives or demanding even the minimum redressal of tenant wrong.

Whether Jawaharlal was aware of it or not, his attitudes at this time implied informal collaboration with the government in the maintenance of law and order; and the UP government were shrewd enough to realize this. In February 1921, when Baba Ram Chandra was arrested, a serious riot broke out. Gandhi and Jawaharlal were then in Banaras, and Jawaharlal urged the excited crowd to obey Gandhi and allow Ram Chandra to be arrested quietly.[18] The UP government now prohibited public meetings the five districts of Avadh and decided to prosecute three local agitators and the officials of village panchayats—though not Jawaharlal or any other prominent leader. The situation was, from the government's point of view, deepening into a crisis. Kisan unrest was widespread and, in part of the Fyzabad district, embraced the bulk of the rural population. In the affected areas, few were now on the side of the government. It was believed by the officials that the leaders of the non-co-operation party had built up an enormous organization which they could start working whenever they pleased, and that they were steadily using their influence to instil hatred of Europeans and Indian officials. The suspicion, though baseless, made the government all the more anxious that the leadership of this movement should remain with men like Gandhi and Jawaharlal, who advised the tenants to pay rents, rather than that it should pass to the itinerant sadhus who ordered the cultivators to pay nothing. The arrest of these agitators cleared the way for the strengthening of Congress influence over the kisans. The government were relieved to find that though the leaders of the Congress formally recorded their protest at these arrests, they placed less emphasis on inflammatory propaganda and concentrated their efforts on organization and the collection of funds.

Motilal Nehru drafted a leaflet for distribution to the kisans, urging them to join the Congress, take up spinning, settle disputes in their own panchayats and not in the law courts, subscribe to the swaraj fund and promote caste and communal harmony. Nothing was said about rents or evictions, and a positive directive was given to avoid gatherings in districts where public meetings had been prohibited. Those instructions, far from being revolutionary, were to the benefit of the authorities. Yet the government arrested six young men who were distributing the pamphlet and sentenced them to jail for six months on the ground that the pamphlet attempted to excite disaffection and to bring the government into hatred and contempt. The harsh action was clearly meant to proclaim that the government had recovered their nerve, and intended no longer to tolerate intervention by Congressmen in kisan affairs. The pamphlet itself was later proscribed; but significantly no action was taken against its author, Motilal Nehru, or against Jawaharlal who distributed the pamphlet in the court room itself and wrote formally to the magistrate that he would continue to give the widest possible publicity to the pamphlet which gave expression to his views.[19]

The failure to be arrested, at a time when his followers were receiving savage sentences for carrying out his orders, acutely embarrassed Jawaharlal. In November 1921 the AICC permitted full civil disobedience, including non-payment of taxes (but not of rents); and though the Congress had little to do with the Eka Movement in Hardoi, Sitapur and Lucknow, which was a revival of kisan agitation in a new form, the Eka associations soon began to pass political resolutions. But Jawaharlal himself took little part in this kisan resurgence, being preoccupied elsewhere.

REFERENCES

1. At this time there were 16 annas in the rupee.
2. M.H. Siddiqi, 'The Peasant Movement in Pratabgarh, 1920', *Indian Economic and Social History Review*, September 1972, pp. 316-17.
3. Commissioner, Fyzabad division to chief secretary UP, 25 November 1920, revenue dept. file 753 of 1920, UP archives.

4. H.R.C. Hailey to M. Keane, 26 November 1920, revenue dept. file 753 of 1920. UP archives.
5. Report of V.N. Mehta, *ibid.*
6. Many years later he recounted an incident that occurred at this time. While speaking, he noticed people pushing and elbowing each other, though still remaining seated. Irritated by this behaviour, he asked that section of the crowd what was worrying them and they replied, 'There is a snake here, but we dare not stand up, because the organizers have ordered us not to do so while you are speaking.' Speech at Calcutta, reported in the *Free Press Journal* (Bombay), 12 November 1956.
7. C.A. Bayly, 'The Development of Political Organization in the Allahabad Locality 1880-1925', Oxford D. Phil, thesis, 1970, pp. 369-70. A revised version of this has been published as *The Local Roots of Indian Politics : Allahabad 1880-1920* (Oxford 1975).
8. Report of the director, intelligence bureau, 11 January 1921, home dept. pol. deposit, January 1921, no. 75; Sir H. Butler's speech to UP legislative council, *The Leader,* 24 January 1921. This is a common feature of peasant revolts.
9. 'The Rae Bareli Tragedy', *The Independent,* 22 January 1921.
10. See Jawaharlal's article in *The Independent,* 23 January 1921.
11. *The Independent,* 11 January 1921.
12. *The Independent,* 18 January 1921.
13. *The Independent,* 26 January 1921.
14. Speech at Tanda, 5 March 1923.
15. Speech at Pratabgarh, 22 April 1923.
16. See his Hindi pamphlet 'Where are You?', published in 1922.
17. Incomplete review of Russell's *Roads to Freedom,* written sometime after April 1919, and letter to Sir Sita Ram, 11 May 1920, SW, vol. 1, pp. 140-4 and 160, respectively.
18. Sri Prakasa's article in *1921 Movement: Reminiscences* (Delhi, 1971), p. 199,
19. *The Independent,* 30 April 1921.

5

Disciple of Gandhi

Jawaharlal had by now begun to take an interest in all-India affairs. But he gave close attention to the development of the non-co-operation campaign in his own province, and this afforded him no great satisfaction. He appealed to students to leave government schools and colleges and to serve as volunteers or go out to assist the kisans : 'But if the flesh is weak and the conditions appear hard, then there is one service which all can do—the turning of the spinning wheel.'[1] He proposed that at least 50,000 persons in the district should be registered as members of the Congress, special efforts being made to enlist women.[2] But Jawaharlal was not prepared to recommend a no-tax campaign in Allahabad city without consultation with its leaders until the other items in the non-co-operation campaign had been completed, as he did not believe this could be properly carried out.[3] He then undertook a tour of the districts of the UP to strengthen the Congress and Khilafat movements. He travelled by train, car and *ekka* (horse carriage), and even on one occasion ran between two places—precedents for the election campaigns he was to undertake years later in all parts of India.[4] Once he reached a railway station too late and missed the train. The station master, an official but a patriot, provided him with a trolley to cover the twenty or thirty miles to the next junction, and was dismissed for his pains.[5] Yet, despite all this energetic effort of Jawaharlal and his colleagues, the non-co-operation campaign failed to gather impetus in the United Provinces. So the government could relax, and even the Congress acknowledged that a distinct change was noticeable in official policy from the end of August.[6]

Jawaharlal was now an ardent advocate of swadeshi and of the campaign for boycott of foreign cloth. In Allahabad city he was one of those who went round from house to house collecting foreign clothes.[7] At the UP political conference in October 1921 he moved the resolution on swadeshi. At this time an unqualified Gandhian, he argued that as the attainment of swaraj depended on the use of swadeshi cloth, the people should be asked to discard, burn or export foreign cloth and use home-made cloth instead. He was as impatient to drive out the English from India as anyone else, but he had not till now discovered any new method of doing so except swadeshi. He did not agree with those who advocated the use of the sword. In the last resort they would all come to the conclusion that they could win and retain swaraj only by the use of swadeshi cloth.[8]

Jawaharlal was also very careful at this time to abide by the various orders of the government. There was little defiance in his mood. At Shikarpur, for example, when an order prohibiting a meeting was served on him while he was speaking, he immediately stopped and turned his attention to the collection of foreign clothes and subscriptions for the swaraj fund.[9] When a similar order was served on him at Bhiti, he marched with the whole audience of about a thousand to the next district four and a half miles away and held the meeting there.

However, for some time the UP government had been collecting material for taking action against *The Independent* for its articles, and against Jawaharlal for seditious speeches. Opinion at Simla was in favour of giving *The Independent* an opportunity to express regret; and the UP government, although (excepting one minister) of the view that there was no alternative to taking proceedings, decided to give a similar opportunity to Jawaharlal.[10] So, on 16 June 1921, Jawaharlal was informed that no proceedings would be taken against him if he undertook not to deliver speeches directly or indirectly inciting violence or calculated to create an atmosphere of readiness for violence. Similar notices were sent the same day to the editor and printer of *The Independent*.

In his reply, drafted by him and revised by his father, Jawaharlal questioned the accuracy of police reporting of his speeches and refused any apology or undertaking; if he had erred by saying anything which was untrue or exaggerated or had produced the impression that he was condemning the whole British people, he would apologize, but only to the public.[11] At Simla the home member and his department agreed with the UP government that Jawaharlal should now be prosecuted.[12] The viceroy, as Motilal had expected, viewed this in the all-India context and, as part of the delaying tactics he was employing against the Congress, decided to ignore Jawaharlal. But by November 1921 the Government of India were ready to take drastic action against the non-co-operation campaign, which was now developing new manifestations and frequently erupting in violence. Among other measures it was decided to strike down the volunteer movement in the UP. So the volunteer organization in the UP was declared unlawful, and Jawaharlal, the convener and secretary of the UP volunteer board, his father were arrested on 5 December for their connection with this activity.

Motilal was delighted to go to jail with his son, and departed in a mood of exaltation. Jawaharlal too was happy to secure, as the accolade of patriotism, a sentence of six months' simple imprisonment and a fine of Rs. 100 or a further month in jail. Father and son and a few others, who were being treated better than the rank and I file of Congress prisoners, wrote to the jail superintendent declining these special privileges. Jawaharlal continued to direct from jail the work of the UP Congress, and drew up plans to ensure both that it did not cease to function despite official suppression and that it demonstrated its authority by filling the jails.[13]

Because of some technical defect in his sentence Jawaharlal, to his own surprise, was released in March 1922 when he had only served half his term. By now Gandhi had called off the civil disobedience campaign because of the increasing violence. Jawaharlal, like most others, was bitterly disappointed, especially as the campaign in his own province had been mustering strength. Gandhi's action enabled the government to relax and made Jawaharlal's task in sustaining the morale of Congressmen so much the harder. He attended Gandhi's trial at Ahmedabad, and then returned to organize spinning, boycott and picketing in the United Provinces.

As the government recognized, 'quiet propaganda work' organized by Jawaharlal from Allahabad was widespread.[14] He addressed public meetings in the city and elsewhere and circulated Hindi pamphlets. The voice throughout was Gandhian. But he began to feel that concentration on constructive work was becoming almost impossible because of official oppression and terrorism. So it might be necessary to start individual civil disobedience again of some kind.[15] The organization should therefore be perfected, tours planned and efforts made to visit all important towns and rouse the people. The government reacted and on 5 May the Congress offices and Anand Bhawan were searched. Clearly, arrest was imminent, and Jawaharlal issued another circular to Congress committees, written while the search was being conducted, 'almost in the shadow of the police'. The people had shown enthusiasm and courage, and only organization was necessary to achieve success. Non-co-operation had gained India a new status in the eyes of the world.

A week later, on 12 May, Jawaharlal was arrested on a charge of organizing picketing and advocating it in his writings and speeches. As a non-co-operator he refused to plead, cross-examine the witnesses or offer any defence, but he made a long statement. He pointed out that though he was being tried for criminal intimidation and extortion the prosecution could not produce any witness to suggest that the picketing had not been peaceful. On the other hand, it was the government which had, throughout the province, been guilty of intimidation and terrorism. However, he was grateful to the authorities for framing this particular charge, for it gave publicity to the boycott of foreign cloth.

Jawaharlal also referred to the wider issue of British rule. Fond as he was of England—and perhaps because of his fondness—he had now become a rebel and all his activities had but one end in view :

> Jail has indeed become a heaven for us, a holy place of pilgrimage since our saintly and beloved leader was sentenced... I marvel at my good fortune. To serve India in the battle of freedom is honour enough. To serve her under a leader like Mahatma Gandhi is doubly fortunate. But to suffer for the dear country! What greater good fortune could befall an Indian, unless it be death for the cause or the full realization of our glorious dream.

The government were deluding themselves with the belief that, while the cloth-dealer witnesses had respectfully saluted the accused, the case had attracted little public attention.[16] Jawaharlal had in mind a wider audience, and the first of his trial statements secured for him a national audience and became the manifesto of the educated youth of India.

Jawaharlal had expected and hoped for a long sentence; he had been some what galled by his earlier premature release, especially as his father was still in jail : 'One feels almost lonely outside the jail, and selfishness prompts a quick return.' He was not disappointed, the sentence being eighteen months' rigorous imprisonment and a fine of Rs. 100, and 3 months' further imprisonment in case of default. He was placed in Lucknow district jail. Because the jail superintendent and warders harassed visitors and subjected them to petty indignities, Jawaharlal and his companions for some months gave up interviews and saw no friendly face from outside. He did not even visit other barracks during this period. But on the whole Jawaharlal was content with his existence. The mere fact of being confine boosted his, self-respect. He hoped too that jail life, with its privations, would harden him, and enjoyed his enforced leisure to the full. Apart from physical exercise—walking and running—and regular daily spinning, he spent most of his time reading. His special interests were history, travel and romantic poetry. There is, in all his letters of this time, the glow of virginal suffering and a complacent absence of reflection. Jawaharlal was so excited by the situation in which he found himself, so much in love with sacrifice and hardship, and so self-conscious about the immediate context that he gave no thought to the way or the goal. He had made a cradle of emotional nationalism, and rocked himself in it.

Selfishness, Jawaharlal had written, would hardly favour a quick discharge.[17] However, once again he was released before serving his full sentence. He was set free on 31 January 1923, as part of a general amnesty declared by the UP government without consulting the Government of India, in order to give effect to a resolution of the Provincial Legislative Council recommending such a measure.[18] What gave him great concern on coming out was the sharp difference of opinion within the Congress itself. With Gandhi in jail, the Congress leadership was almost equally split on the issue of entry into councils. The predicament of Jawaharlal was that, while he was emotionally attached to the leaders of the Swaraj party, his mind was inclined to agree with those opposed to entering the councils. In his first speech after his release, he declared that he still stuck to his conviction that non-co-operation was the only path which could lead them to self-government. They should continue their fight and indeed further intensify it till their object had been attained. On the specific move of council entry he declined to express his opinion on the ground that he was not in touch with current politics; but he emphasized that the destination and road of both groups were the same, though their conveyances might differ.[19] It worried him too that the differences within the Congress might weaken the organization as a whole. So he, with a few others, sought not so much a compromise—the positions were irreconcilable—as 'an atmosphere of charity and goodwill' in which both sides could function.[20] At the session of the AICC in Allahabad towards the end of February, he and Maulana Azad persuaded the two groups to suspend all propaganda till the end of April. He himself spent this period of truce touring some of the districts of the United Provinces, collecting funds for the Congress and urging , discipline and the wearing of *khaddar*. But there was little heart in his speeches, and even the UP authorities were satisfied that his utterances, were mild.[21]

Jawaharlal was at this time, in fact, rudderless, with no clear ideas as to what he should do. He himself, he wrote in a public letter, was a bit of a missionary in his own way; but he was a missionary without a mission.[22] Congress politics too were once again heading to a collision; the truce was over, and in the first days of May both sides issued manifestos drawing up the lines of battle. Jawaharlal was concerned to, avoid this clash, if only to save the Congress, which seemed to him to have practically ceased, during the past four months, to function. The solution favoured by Jawaharlal was one which would give the Swaraj party the substance and its opponents only the shadow. The decision taken by the Congress in December 1922 against council entry would still hold, but no propaganda should be done in its favour; in other words, its operation would be suspended, and those who wished to contest the elections would be free to do so. This formula deceived nobody; but it was accepted by the UP Congress committee, and then by the AICC at Bombay in the last week of May.[23] Six members of the working committee who were opposed to council entry promptly resigned. Jawaharlal, whose purpose was to fend off final decisions while allowing the Swarajists to have their way, suggested that these resignations be not accepted; his resolution was carried by a large majority but the no-changers were firm. In the circumstances, it was agreed that the party executive be manned by those uncommitted to either side, such as Jawaharlal.

This was Jawaharlal's achievement—one which even he had not expected.[24] It was the first time he had functioned decisively on the national plane. However, the hollow compromise fashioned by Jawaharlal soon crumbled. In Nagpur in July the AICC rejected by a majority of two votes Jawaharlal's resolution advocating disciplinary action against those provincial Congress committees which had defied the compromise resolution of May. Thereupon Jawaharlal, along with his colleagues, resigned from the working committee and he is reported to have expressed a desire to retire from the AICC as well.[25] He had already, on 30 June, resigned his secretaryship of the UP provincial Congress committee.

REFERENCES

1. Letter to the Editor, *The Leader,* 25 April 1921.
2. *The Independent,* 13 May 1921.
3. Report of speech in Allahabad, *The Independent,* 7 May 1921.
4. Jawaharlal in *The Independent,* 25 May 1921.
5. Jawaharlal to Bhai Parmanand, 26 November 1933.
6. Report of the UP Congress on government repression in UP. *The Independent,* 27 November 1921.
7. *The Independent,* 12 August 1921.
8. *The Leader,* 26 October 1921.
9. *The Independent,* 25 September 1921.
10. Chief secretary, UP, to home secretary, Government of India, no. 1543, dated 9 July 1921, home dept. pol. 1922, file 112, nos. 1-8.
11. Jawaharlal to chief secretary, UP, 4 July 1921.
12. Notes of H.D, Craik, 13 July 1921, home dept. pol. 1922, file 112, nos. 1-8.
13. See note traced by CID and said to have been written by him in jail between 9 and 12 December 1921, home dept. pol. 1922, file 767.
14. Chief secretary, UP, to home secretary, 3 May 1922, home dept. pol. 1922, file 18.
15. Circular letter of UP provincial Congress committee, 25 April 1922.
16. Chief secretary, UP, to home dept., 4 June 1922, home dept. pol. 1922, file 18.
17. To his father, 15 November 1922.
18. See home dept. pol., 1923, file 56.

19. Speech at Allahabad, 1 February 1923, reported in *The Leader,* 4 February 1923.

20. Jawaharlal's telegram to 'Swarajya', Madras, *The Bombay Chronicle,* 24 February 1923.

21. See, for example, UP intelligence reports on his speeches at Sitapur, 18 March, and Gorakhpur towards the end of March 1923.

22. *The Leader,* 13 May 1923.

23. *Ibid.,* 16 May 1923.

24. See Jawaharlal to A.M. Khwaja, 6 June 1923, SW, vol. 1, pp. 358-60.

25. *The Leader,* 14 July 1923.

6

In Jail

Jawaharlal was now, therefore, a free man, relieved of the tussles within the party which had filled him with such distaste. His attention was given wholly to such opportunities for 'cold-blooded action' as came his way.[1] He recognized that mass civil disobedience was out of the question for the time being, but he helped to organize the satyagraha campaign that developed in Nagpur over the refusal of the district magistrate to allow a Congress procession to carry the national flag. Volunteer squads from different parts of the country were sent to reinforce the local workers till the authorities gave way and permitted a Congress procession with the flag to pass. Again in need of some issue to occupy him, Jawaharlal went to Nabha for a first-hand view of the Akali agitation.

The Sikhs had for long been a group favoured by the British government. They were encouraged to remain a separate community and not to merge in the general Hindu fold. The 1919 reforms extended separate representation to Sikhs. However, at the end of the First World War, certain sections of the Sikh community wished to reform the management of the Sikh temples *(gurdwaras),* and the reformers sought to take over the shrines. The Punjab government saw in this Akali movement a threat to law and order, and the resistance that the Akalis encountered led to their efforts developing into a widespread mass movement. A plan for religious reform had been converted, despite itself, into a political campaign. A semi-military organization, the Akali Dal, was formed, not merely to evict the corrupt managers of the Sikh shrines but also to accept the challenge of the government.

It was natural that the Akali movement should, at this stage, evoke the interest of the National Congress. Influenced by Gandhi's leadership of the non-co-operation campaign, the Sikhs had pledged themselves to non-violence; and they abode by their pledge despite severe provocation. The movement was of special interest to Jawaharlal, for he attached importance to discipline, and was impressed by the organization of the Akali Dal, which maintained order among its recruits and provided for the upkeep of the families of those injured or arrested. He attended conferences, at Lahore and Amritsar in June and July 1923, of Congress, Khilafat and Sikh League workers; and urged them not to be distracted by such sterile issues as communal representation on district boards and municipalities. The Congress regarded the principle as essentially evil, and local bodies were not of any importance, but if agreement could be reached on the basis of such a principle in the Punjab, the Congress might be prepared to approve it so as to enable the immediate success of the struggle against the bureaucracy.[2] And in September, when in Delhi for the special Congress session, Jawaharlal heard that Sikh *jathas* (squads) were daily proceeding to Nabha state, the deposition of whose maharaja in July for maladministration was strongly resented by the Sikhs; and he decided to go there to see for himself the Akalis in action.

On the night of 19 September, Jawaharlal, with two companions, Gidwani and Santanam, left Delhi for Muktesar, an Akali centre, and after addressing a meeting there on the 20th, commending the Akali struggle, he entered Nabha state on the morning of the 21st, along with a Sikh jatha, at Jaito.[3] There he and his two friends sat down under a tree to watch proceedings and intended to return to Delhi by the evening train. So Jawaharlal was well within the state before the order was served on him not to enter Nabha on the ground that he and some of his companions were members of the AICC and their presence was likely to lead to a disturbance of the peace. Jawaharlal replied that he had already entered Nabha and could not vanish into thin air, but that he had no intention of leaving the state; and he and his two friends, on whom an oral order had been served, moved into a rest-house near by. A prohibitory order incapable of enforcement was *ipso facto* invalid, and an oral order was of no worth at all; but clearly the Nabha government, even though now headed by a British official, attached no importance to legality. Although the presence of Jawaharlal had led to no disturbance, he and his companions were arrested, handcuffed and chained together, and marched to the railway station. They were brought by the night train, in a crowded third-class compartment, to Nabha town, and the chains and handcuffs were only removed twenty hours after, by noon the next day, after they were locked up in Nabha jail.

The conditions in this jail were, even by official admission, 'horrible'.[4] The prisoners were prevented from seeing or communicating with persons outside, denied all books and papers, and for two days not even allowed to bathe or change. Their trial was held in *camera* by a magistrate who knew no English and openly referred every issue for decision to the British administrator. The latter " had by now realized that, even in Nabha, Jawaharlal could not be convicted for entering the state before he had been prohibited from doing so, and decided to alter the charge to one of being in the company of an Akali jatha, and therefore of being a member of an unlawful assembly.[5] On the 24th fresh proceedings were casually started before another magistrate, and Jawaharlal and the others were charged with being members of the jatha and forcibly resisting dispersal.

On the 27th Motilal saw his son in jail. The interview, lasting over two hours, was not a success. Jawaharlal showed his irritation at his father's intervention, and Motilal, deeply upset, left Nabha. Meantime, the case dragged on. The Government of India directed that sentence should be passed on Jawaharlal but it should be announced at the same time that the Nabha government had suspended its execution without condition, and Jawaharlal should be expelled from the state. This would meet the probable contingency of the convicted persons declining to accept any conditions; but if they returned to the state the suspension would be cancelled. So Jawaharlal and his two companions were each sentenced to thirty months rigorous imprisonment; but these sentences were suspended and they were ordered to leave the state and not to return. They all left Nabha the same night.

It was not, however, disclosed that the sentences would be operative if they returned to Nabha; and Jawaharlal had no reason to believe that the suspension was conditional. In fact, the next year, when Gidwani returned to Nabha, he was thrown into prison, and Jawaharlal challenged the administrator to let him have a copy of the suspension order and to inform him as to whether he too would be arrested if he returned to Nabha.[6] The administrator replied that the sentence had only been suspended and not remitted, to which Jawaharlal retorted that the suspension had been unconditional.[7]

As Jawaharlal recognized years later in his *Autobiography,* probably the bold step to have taken, especially as Gidwani had been imprisoned again, would have been for him to return to Nabha : 'As often with us all, discretion was preferred to valour.'[8] On his return to Allahabad, where he received a hero's welcome, he had developed typhoid with high fever and confessed that he had not felt quite so feeble physically for a long time.[9] And his father too made sure that he did not involve himself in Nabha affairs again. So the Government of India, who had encouraged the administrator of Nabha to act arbitrarily, were not embarrassed by any further challenge.

REFERENCES

1. Interview in *Aaj,* 19 June 1923.
2. Report of Jawaharlal's speech in *The Tribune,* 4 July 1923.
3. Home dept. pol. 1924, file 1 KW.
4. Note of special commissioner on conditions in Nabha jails, 14 June 1923, home dept. pol., file 401 of 1924.

5. Administrator, Nabha state, to agent, governor-general, Punjab, 22 September 1923, *ibid.*

6. Jawaharlal's letters to the administrator, 24 May and 19 June 1924, reprinted in *The Leader,* 29 May and 23 June 1924, respectively.

7. Administrator, Nabha, to Jawaharlal, 25 June, and his reply, reproduced *in The Leader,* 27 July 1924.

8. *Autobiography,* p. 116.

9. To Sri Prakasa, 7 October 1923.

7

Congress Work

Free again after a fortnight in jail, but now a sick man, Jawaharlal could do little more for a while than write speeches. In his presidential address to the UP provincial conference in October, which was read in his absence, he deplored the loss of the faith and confidence which had inspired the Congress in 1920 and 1921. The Congress session at Delhi had marked a retreat from direct action. But non-violent non-co-operation could not die, and it was the duty of those like him to fight on while the main army rested or was engaged in peaceful pursuits. Till the time came for launching another mighty campaign of civil disobedience, they should keep the practice and ideal of direct action and peaceful revolution before the people. He was still very much a Gandhian : 'The choice for us is between Lenin and Mussolini on the one side and Gandhi on the other. Can there be any doubt as to who represents the soul of India today?' Political freedom was bound to come before long, if not entirely through their strength then through the weakness of Europe and England.

Two months later, at the Kakinada session of the Congress, he again emphasized, in Gandhian terms, that there was not really much in common between Indian volunteers and any Western counterparts, and an Indian volunteer organization must have non-violence as its basic principle. What India needed was nonviolent, disciplined soldiers. To Jawaharlal non-violent non-cooperation was a positive programme, and its exponent above all a man of action.

He himself, however, could at this stage engage in no

thrilling action and had to consume his energies in a variety of administrative duties. He was already president of the Allahabad town Congress committee and heavily involved in provincial Congress work, and at Kakinada the president, Maulana Mohamed Ali, insisted on Jawaharlal becoming one of the general secretaries of the Congress. This added considerably to Jawaharlal's work, he being the most active of the three secretaries. Because of the direct interest which Jawaharlal had shown in the Akali campaign and his excursion to Nabha, the Congress had appointed him one of the liaison officers to keep in touch with the defiant Sikhs; and as general secretary it was his responsibility to implement the Congress resolution to render all possible assistance, including the dispatch of men and money. The Congress had little money to provide, and Jawaharlal thought that the best assistance it could render was to perfect its own organization and throw in its whole weight at the moment of crisis, and till then to give full publicity to Akali activities, keeping the political side of it and the side affecting other communities well in the forefront.[1] Jawaharlal felt that the Congress could also help in rallying Hindus and Muslims behind the campaign, which should be regarded as part of the general movement for freedom.

All these activities kept Jawaharlal busy, and enabled him to ignore the malaise afflicting Congress. He had even hoped to return to jail, even though on a false issue, for at one time it seemed probable that the government would arrest him for defying, along with Pandit Malaviya, the injunction against bathing in the Sangam at Allahabad during the Kumbh Mela festival in January. But the government refrained from action.

However, he was soon glad to be unconfined, for on 5 February 1924 Gandhi was released on grounds of health. After seeing Gandhi at Poona, Jawaharlal spent a few weeks at Juhu. Some months later, in September 1924, to check the growing communal rancour, Gandhi began a fast for twenty-one days. When Jawaharlal, who had been visiting the riot-stricken area of Sambhal, received 'the shattering news whose consequences are terrible to contemplate', he called upon each town and village in the United Provinces to hold immediately its conference of leaders of all communities and parties to find means of unity. Jawaharlal, on his return from the Unity Conference at Delhi which had passed a series of platitudinous resolutions but could not persuade Gandhi to terminate his fast earlier than scheduled, himself went down with fever; but he sent Gandhi long reports on the disturbances in Allahabad itself. Speaking with this first-hand knowledge of communal animosity, he told the UP political conference that whatever pride he had had in the national strength and awakening had been shattered, and he was now not only humiliated but ashamed. They themselves had done more harm to their country than any foreigner.[2] An all-parties conference, meeting in January 1925, proved a failure, and Jawaharlal found its discussions painful to listen to.[3] All that there was to do, therefore, seemed to be the preaching of unity and of non-violence, spinning and the wearing of khaddar. This communal problem was such a wasteful diversion from the main campaign against the British, and it revolved round what seemed to him such unreal issues, that he could not bring himself to take energetic measures to deal with it.

These were also to Jawaharlal months of great personal stress and depression. In November 1924 his wife lost a child after premature birth and soon after began to show signs of tuberculosis. Then, in March 1925, he himself had to undergo a minor operation, performed by Dr. Ansari at Delhi. The deep commitment to Gandhi and known dislike of Swarajist policy had caused friction in his relations with his father, and Gandhi had sought to intervene.

These differences with Motilal made Jawaharlal acutely conscious of his dependence on his father for money. Gandhi had offered to arrange for some remunerative work, either as a press correspondent or as a college professor, but nothing had come of this.[4] Gandhi later suggested that Jawaharlal be paid as general secretary by the Congress or that personal friends be permitted to find funds for retaining his services :

'I will not mind even if you decided to do some business. I want your mental peace. I know that you will serve the country even as manager of a business.'[5] The Bombay firm of Tata's offered to employ him, and Motilal strongly recommended to his son that he proceed to Bombay and call on Tata.[6] But this again did not materialize, probably because Jawaharlal showed no keenness to serve in a commercial firm. Finally, to earn the money required to pay for the trip to Europe which he and Kamala were planning, he had to return to the distasteful practice of law; and for preparing a brief Motilal secured for him the large fee of Rs. 10,000—an amount which the client doubtless paid to ensure that Motilal would handle the case.

However, there was one sphere of activity which in these years provided Jawaharlal with some satisfaction. For two years, from April 1923 to April 1925, he was chairman of the Allahabad municipal board; and this phase in his life is of interest as marking his first experience of official administration. It is also of some significance, because many of the traits which marked his prime ministership can be discerned here in embryo—his domination of his colleagues, his desire for efficiency, his loyalty to his competent subordinates, his efforts to push forward in all directions with new ideas. Even officials had to recognize that he had brought a fresh impetus to municipal administration and that his management of Allahabad affairs was marked by both constructiveness and competence.

Jawaharlal was a most unwilling chairman. To him the primary task was the fight for swaraj, and he decided to continue as secretary of the provincial Congress committee, a post which he regarded as more important than the chairmanship of the municipal board and which, he declared, he was prouder to hold :

> My mentality is revolutionary... I do not forget the history and agony of India during the last few years and I am not going to spend most of my time in any office while my beloved leader lies in jail. I shall give battle

> whenever I can. I shall fight and hit hard whenever I may. That is my main function till swaraj is attained. All else is training and preparation.[7]

Invited by the collector of Allahabad to come and discuss the possibility of keeping general politics outside the municipal sphere, he replied that he would try to carry out the policies of the Congress, and would resign if he disagreed with the board on any matter of principle or if the Congress committee so desired it. Repeatedly during the next two years, till his resignation was finally accepted by the government, Jawaharlal offered to relinquish office, and he never allowed it to hamper his activities in the wider world and even courted arrest, as at Nabha.

However, though Jawaharlal's priorities never wavered, his distaste for municipal affairs gradually weakened, and he found himself enjoying the work. Himself regular in attendance, whenever he was in Allahabad, at meetings which were held at least twice a week, he deplored the tendency of the members to look to their own convenience and urged them to sacrifice their own professional work, if need be, for the sake of the municipality.[8] Indeed, he almost coerced his colleagues to work as hard as he did, and rather than adjourn meetings for lack of a quorum, he directed members to wait so that they were driven to send for their truant colleagues. Soon after taking over as chairman, he issued a public statement rebuking some members for idleness; this had its effect, so that later he could agree to refrain from such public criticism.[9] Chairmen and members of standing committees were told that, in addition to their routine work, they should inspect their departments periodically and introduce efficiency. But he soon won the confidence of all groups on the board and was able to direct the proceedings on the lines he desired.

The secret of Jawaharlal's influence was his manifest integrity. While he did not conceal his views on major issues, he never permitted the Congress majority to push matters to extremes, and in minor matters he voted, as was expected from a chairman, against any change. He turned down the request of the municipal employees that they be allowed to suspend work on Jallianwala Bagh day, for he knew that they were only interested in a holiday. He secured the rejection of the proposal of a member belonging to the Congress party that the board dispense with chairs and conduct proceedings while sitting on the floor, by pointing out that this had nothing to do with swadeshi.[10] He encouraged the wearing of khaddar by municipal employees and the use of Hindi or Urdu in official transactions but was not for making these obligatory.[11] He supported the passing of a resolution deploring the treatment of Indians in the United States and the British colonies, but did not accept suggestions for retaliation such as doubling municipal taxes on Englishmen and Americans or debarring them from buying land.[12]

From the municipal officials he expected efficiency but was loyal to those who served him well—and those who were surprised by his support of members of the Indian Civil Service after 1947 would have done well to study his attitude years earlier as municipal chairman. He had no illusions about civil servants. But he was willing, in the conduct of municipal affairs, to co-operate with government servants so long as the public interests and the principles of the Congress were not jeopardized.[13] He instructed the heads of departments to get rid of incompetent subordinates with all speed and without mercy.[14] But those officials who worked well received the chairman's full support even in face of public criticism and satyagraha.[15]

Most important of all, Jawaharlal was clearly above sectarian prejudices. His guidance enabled the board unanimously to reject the suggestion to prohibit the slaughter of cattle;[16] and the next week he reminded the members that while Christian missionaries had originally certainly come to India to convert Indians, at the same time their object was also to benefit India as far as possible.[17]

Such moderation and impartiality gave Jawaharlal a commanding influence. He first turned his attention to formulating a scheme for widening the municipal franchise and ensuring fair elections. But electoral reform being beyond the purview of the municipal board, Jawaharlal had to content himself with introducing, whenever possible, the spirit of nationalism in municipal administration and implementing the constructive, nation-building programme of the Congress. The singing of Iqbal's Hindustan Hamara (Our Hindustan) was made a part of the school curriculum. Tilak Day (1 August), the anniversary of the death of Tilak, and Gandhi Day (18 March), the anniversary of the day when Gandhi was sentenced to jail, were added to the list of public holidays, while Empire Day was omitted. The release of Gandhi in February 1924 was celebrated by the illumination of municipal buildings. Civic addresses were presented to Congress leaders. The United Provinces government sought to prevent such defiance by directing that civic addresses should be presented only to the viceroy and the governor of the province, but Jawaharlal secured the unanimous rejection by the board of this directive, which he termed 'an insult and impertinence'. In other words, even the nominated and non-Congress members supported his assertion of the board's independence on such matters.[18] Jawaharlal made it clear to his colleagues that they should be prepared for the consequences of their disobedience; but in fact it was the provincial government which had to withdraw from their position.[19] This was soon followed by the board's decision to ignore a viceregal visit to Allahabad.

Jawaharlal also secured the introduction of spinning and weaving in schools, and rejected the objection of the commissioner of Allahabad division to what seemed to the latter to be a Congress measure. Most of the teachers and the boys and girls dressed in khaddar.

Jawaharlal was eager to improve the quality of instruction imparted in the municipal schools, to raise the salaries of teachers, to make education compulsory and to train children to be good citizens who neither cringed nor boasted. Scouting was introduced for boys and a day's outing was arranged every month for all children nature study. But as government declined to give further grants for education which was directed to encouraging the 'new spirit', it could only be given low priority by the board, after the maintenance of the basic municipal services—sanitation, water supply and the upkeep of roads. Unwilling to raise money at the expense of the poorer classes, he rejected the suggestion of an octroi duty on cycles and exempted houses with a low rental value from payment of water rates.[20] He also terminated the practice whereby octroi was levied on foreign goods at the 'invoice' rate, while Indian goods were charged at the market rate, which often was higher, with the result that Indian goods paid more. It was laid down that the market rate should be the wholesale and not the retail rate, although this meant a loss in income. Jawaharlal urged that a heavier rate be charged on foreign goods so as to encourage Indian manufacturers,[21] but the board resolved on a complete boycott of British goods unless they were not manufactured elsewhere in the world or were not available in India.[22]

Jawaharlal's work attracted wide public attention because, apart from his general standing, he issued a fortnightly municipal gazette reporting the proceedings of the board and its committees and, in addition to the annual report, gave a detailed account of municipal activities once every three months. There were also Hindi and Urdu editions of the gazette. For the first time, too, the average citizen of Allahabad felt that he had a municipal chairman who was accessible and concerned with his welfare.

Jawaharlal had also, from the start, kept in close touch and exchanged ideas with the ten other Congress chairmen of municipal boards in the United Provinces,[23] and he was elected chairman of the United Provinces municipal conference that met at Aligarh in December 1924. This provincial conference accepted Jawaharlal's proposals that training as scouts should be made part of physical education in schools, adult franchise introduced for municipal elections and the autonomy of municipal boards protected. These recommendations were in line with his view that municipalities could become minor arenas for national education and for constructive national and political work. But at the Congress session in December 1924 presided over by Gandhi he opposed a resolution advocating the capture by Congressmen, whenever possible, of local boards and municipalities. His own experience, he said, had convinced him that Congressmen in these boards were so restricted that the effort was futile; and on his return from the Belgaum Congress he resigned both his chairmanship and membership of the board, ostensibly on the ground that he had little time to devote to municipal work.

His two years in municipal office could not have given Jawaharlal much cause for satisfaction. For a man who believed that a municipality should not confine itself to such matters as housing and sanitation but should regard social welfare in its widest sense as its primary concern, the disappointment could not be glossed over. But it was astonishing how much he had succeeded in achieving, despite the inherent limitations of the post and the demands of his wider interests. Even the commissioner was compelled to record reluctantly his impression that 'the improvement in the administration was largely due to the chairman, Pandit Jawaharlal Nehru, and a few public spirited members of the Board.'[24] The comment of the UP government at the time of Jawaharlal's relinquishment of the chairmanship is also worth mention : 'Pandit Kapildeo Malaviya', they wrote in April 1925, 'was elected chairman of the Allahabad Municipal Board by [a majority of] two votes, in succession to Jawaharlal Nehru, who strove to show that a swarajist could be an administrator and a gentleman, and the Commissioner thinks that the newcomer's position will be very difficult.'[25]

REFERENCES

1. To A.T. Gidwani, 25 January 1924; to K. M. Panikkar, 27 March 1924, AICC file 4 of 1924.

2. *The Leader,* 6 November 1924.

3. To Syed Mahmud, 3 February 1925.

4. Letter to Jawaharlal, 15 September 1924, *Collected Works*, vol. 25, pp. 148-9.
5. *Idem*, 30 September 1925.
6. Motilal to Jawaharlal, 9 November 1925.
7. Circular letter of Jawaharlal as secretary, provincial Congress committee, to all district, town and *tehsil* Congress committees and members of provincial Congress committees, 5 April 1923.
8. Meeting of 26 April 1923, reported in *The Leader*, 28 April 1923.
9. *The Leader*, 16 June 1923.
10. Report in *The Leader*, 3 May 1923.
11. Report in *The Leader*, 7 July 1923 : *The Allahabad Municipal Gazette*, 16 December 1923.
12. Proceedings of the board, 9 October 1923.
13. Speech at Ballia, 9 April, reported in *The Leader*, 11 April 1924.
14. Jawaharlal's note on municipal work, April-May 1923, dated 10 June 1923. *The Leader*, 16 June 1923.
15. Jawaharlal's letter to the editor, 18 April, published in *The Leader*, 21 April 1924.
16. Proceedings, 29 June 1923, reported in *The Leader*, 2 July 1923.
17. Proceedings, 3 July 1923, reported in *The Leader*, 7 July 1923.
18. *The Leader*, 29 June 1923.
19. *The Leader*, 2 July and 10 September 1923.
20. *The Leader*, 7 July 1923; annual administration report of the Allahabad municipal board, 30 May 1924.
21. Jawaharlal's notes on municipal work, June-August 1923 and September-November 1923, *Allahabad Municipal Gazettes Extraordinary*, 15 September 1923 and 21 December 1923, respectively.

22. "Proceedings of the meeting, 25 October 1923, reported in *The Leader*, 27 October 1923.
23. See Allahabad municipality, file 22.
24. *The Tribune*, 24 August 1924.
25. Fortnightly report on the political situation in the United Provinces for the second half of March 1925, home dept. pol., 1925, file 112.

8

European Experience and Campaign for Independence

On 1 March 1926 Jawaharlal sailed with his wife and child for Europe. The trip was undertaken primarily in the cause of his wife's health. It was hoped that a long stay in Switzerland would help her to shake off the tuberculosis that was still in an incipient stage, while her husband would spend his time in study and travel. But these two years, while they did Kamala little good, were to have a profound effect on Jawaharlal's mental development. Till now he had been one of the ordinary run of conforming nationalists, an unquestioning follower of the Mahatma. But it was this spell in Europe, and not the earlier years at Harrow and Cambridge, that was to provide Jawaharlal with his real political education.

In leaving India, Jawaharlal felt somewhat of a deserter. But it was a sense of relief which grew as the months passed. Indian politics at this time were in a low and grim condition. The Congress was riven with dissension, and even within the Swaraj party Motilal was fighting a losing battle against opportunism. Communal tension was rising, and many old Congressmen were reacting to events more as Hindus and Muslims than as nationalists. Gandhi had not lost heart, but even he was reconciled to the situation getting much worse before it began to improve.

Settled in Geneva in cheap lodgings, Jawaharlal's principal occupations now, besides nursing his wife and escorting his daughter to school and back, were learning French, reading widely and attending various courses and lectures. The news from India of communal rioting depressed him, but he was convinced that the only remedy was to scotch this so-called religion, secularize at least the intelligentsia and proceed on secular lines in politics : 'How long that will take I cannot say but religion in India will kill that country and its peoples if it is not subdued.' Europe, as Jawaharlal saw it, had got rid of religion by mass education which had followed industrialism, with the result that conflicts were now not religious but economic; and the same process was bound to be repeated in India.[1] This was, of course, too easy and hopeful a solution, based on a somewhat simplistic understanding of European developments. But Jawaharlal was still optimist enough to believe that religious differences in India would be automatically dissolved by economic advance, and therefore gave no serious thought to it.

By the end of the year it was clear that Kamala had benefited little. Jawaharlal was beginning to feel restive, for the wider world and for India. He could not as yet return to India; his wife was still far from well and Motilal was planning a trip to the West. So the family started their wanderings round Europe. The real significance of these travels was that Jawaharlal now came into contact with European political workers and movements, and these gave a new depth to his thinking and activities. The discursive reading undertaken in Switzerland had ploughed up his mind; it was ready for new seeds but had not yet received them. The turning-point in Jawaharlal's mental development was the invitation to help in organizing—and to participate as the representative of the Indian National Congress in—the International Congress against Colonial Oppression and Imperialism to be held at Brussels in February 1927. The Soviet Union kept severely aloof and no one from that country attended the conference, though, as Jawaharlal realized even at the time, the objectives of the conference were wholly in accordance with Soviet foreign policy and were intended to bring together the forces of anti-colonialism and organized labour against imperialism, especially British imperialism.[2] This did not frighten Jawaharlal and he suggested that a large delegation, including an economist and an expert on military matters, be sent from India by the Congress,[3] but in fact he was the only delegate.

Clearly, at such a conference where the prime target was British imperialism, the official representative of the Indian Congress would be an important figure; and Jawaharlal was appointed one of the member; of the presidium. He arrived at Brussels on 6 February, took part in all the informal meetings, presided over one of the formal sessions and played a leading role in the drafting of many of the resolutions. Jawaharlal could not but be influenced by some of the men and women he met here and his fallow mind was receptive to Marxist and radical ideas.

In his first statement to the press, Jawaharlal merely emphasized the common element in the struggles against imperialism in various parts of the world. Indian nationalism was based on the most intense internationalism, just as the problem of Indian freedom was a world problem; as in the past, so in the future, other countries and peoples would be vitally affected by the condition of India. But his speech at the inaugural session of the conference was at a deeper level. Jawaharlal pointed out that India was the prime example of imperialism. It was the policy of the British to create differences among Indians or, where they already existed, to increase them, to maintain the feudal princes in power, to support the rich landowners and to promote an unholy alliance of British and Indian capitalists. 'Naturally, therefore', concluded Jawaharlal, introducing into his articulated thought a consciousness of the interlinking of economics and politics, 'from their capitalist and imperialist point of view they wanted to do everything in their power to hold on to India.' For the first time, instead of merely condemning British imperialism, Jawaharlal had tried to understand the motives, manner and methods of its functioning. His mind had taken a big step forward.

The resolution on India, drafted by Jawaharlal, accorded the warm support of the conference to the liberation of India from foreign domination and all kinds of exploitation as an essential step in the full emancipation of the peoples of the world. The peoples and workers of other countries should fully co-operate in this task and in particular take effective steps to prevent both the dispatch of foreign troops to India and the retention there of an army of occupation. This was really meant by Jawaharlal for his audience in India, to weaken 'the extraordinary mentality which clings on to the British connection in spite of everything' and took the presence of British troops for granted. Similarly, to goad the Indian National Congress into looking beyond political freedom, Jawaharlal, in the last paragraph of the resolution, expressed the hope of the conference that the Indian national movement would base its programme on the full emancipation of the peasants and workers of India, 'without which there can be no real freedom', and would co-operate with the movements for emancipation in other parts of the world.

Apart from India, the chief planks of the conference were China and Mexico. A joint declaration of the Indian and Chinese delegations, clearly drafted by Jawaharlal, bears the marks of an outlook which was to remain unchanged for over thirty years. It recalled the close cultural ties between the peoples of India and China for over three thousand years and blamed the British for fostering ill-will against India in China by utilizing Indian mercenary troops 'in support of British capitalist brigandage'. It was therefore urgent and essential that the Indian people should be educated regarding China, and British imperialism should be simultaneously engaged on two of its most vital fronts.

The Chinese delegation was keen on promoting contacts between the Kuomintang and the Indian Congress and on educating Indian opinion on the Chinese question. Jawaharlal realized that the British government could prevent exchange of visits at any level, but he felt that the effort should be made. What he had in mind was the dispatch of an ambulance unit of twenty to twenty-five volunteers.[4] This was intended not only to encourage cordial relations between India and China;

Jawaharlal was also anxious to widen the vision of Indian nationalism. He saw too the importance to the world of the future of China, especially as at this time the Kuomintang and the Chinese Communist party were acting in alliance. What was happening in China, therefore, was not merely an assault on foreign imperialism but a direct attack on the capitalist system.

> A victory for the Chinese means the creation of a great Soviet republic in the East closely allied with Russia and together with it gradually dominating the whole of Asia and Europe. This does not mean that the Chinese Republic will be fashioned wholly on the lines laid down by Marx. Even Soviet Russia, owing to the pressure of the peasantry, has had to give up part of its communism, and in China where the small peasant is the deciding factor, the departure from pure communism will be all the greater.[5]

This prescience, the realization that if the alliance of Chinese parties held it would be the Communists and not the much larger Kuomintang which would determine the lines of the future, and the recognition that there would be a large indigenous element in Chinese communism, can only be regarded as astounding—especially as at this time Stalin's agents were dominating the Chinese Communist party. But this was not all. Jawaharlal proceeded to point out that Britain, even with the aid of other European countries, would be unable to do much injury to the great continental bloc of Russia and China : 'What is more likely is that England in order to save herself from extinction will become a satellite of the United States and incite the imperialism and capitalism of America to fight by her side.' It was at Brussels that Jawaharlal for the first time, perhaps because of his meeting with the delegates from Mexico and other countries of America, discerned that Britain was fast losing its leadership to the United States.

Jawaharlal's forecasts did not come immediately true, if only because the Kuomintang fell out with its Communist partner. But more than twenty years after this report was written, with the triumph of the Communists in China, the conclusion of a Sino-Soviet alliance, the formulation of a Chinese pattern of Communism and the evolution of Britain's 'special relationship' with the United States, Jawaharlal was to be proved one of the most far-seeing prophets in world affairs in our age.

The Brussels conference concluded with the issue of a manifesto based on the Marxist-Leninist theory of imperialism. It was asserted that European capitalism had battened on the exploitation of countries in Asia, Africa and America. In its latest phase of finance capitalism a few countries, and in them a few individuals, controlled the world. But the world war and its consequences had clearly shown that imperialist capitalism was its own grave-digger. A huge wave of the movement for national emancipation was passing over the world, and had received a mighty push forward from the Russian revolution and the formation of the Soviet Union. But the imperialists would not easily give up their booty. So the Brussels conference decided to found the League against Imperialism and for National Independence, to organize co-operation between nationalist movements in the colonial countries and labour and anti-imperialist movements in the exploiting countries.

Jawaharlal does not seem to have taken an active part in drafting this manifesto, originally written in French, and resented the way in which it was rushed through the conference. But by this time he had no very great objection to its sentiments. He had come round to the Marxist viewpoint in its broad essentials. He agreed that imperialism and capitalism went hand in hand and neither would disappear until both were put down. As against this, the forces opposing imperialism and capitalism should be co-ordinated so, as to strengthen each other. In colonial countries, nationalism automatically and rightly took precedence over all other ideologies, but such nationalism should have a broad basis, derive its strength from the masses and work specially for them.

Jawaharlal was appointed an honorary president of the League as well as a member of the executive committee, though he declined appointment as one of the secretaries on the grounds that he would be away in India. But during his stay in Europe for the rest of the year he attended regularly the meetings of the executive committee. Though the Communists were only a minority in this body, they sought to dominate it, and Jawaharlal was one of the leaders of an effective resistance. Often irritated, but never angry,[6] he made it clear that while he accepted in its fundamentals the socialist theory of the state, he had 'the strongest objection to being led by the nose by the Russians or by anybody else.'[7] But he did not think there was much danger of this, and, so long as the Soviet Union tried to utilize the League on unobjectionable lines, he saw no harm in co-operating with her against British imperialism. So he recommended to the Working Committee that the Congress might become an associate member of the League. External contacts might not provide help from abroad; but it would enable self-improvement. Association would also enable the Congress to utilize the League as its vehicle for propaganda abroad without committing it to the adoption of a socialist programme or limiting its freedom of action in India or elsewhere. Moreover, the League could be used by the Asian members to keep in close touch.

However, it was the Soviet Union that now dominated Jawaharlal's mind, just as it had, an unseen presence, dominated the Brussels conference. He read all that he could lay hands on, books both by partisans and by critics, about developments and conditions in that country, and found much to admire. He believed that whatever the tradition of hostility between Britain and Russia, to a free India she would be no threat; and even if India were wholly opposed to Communism she could have friendly relations with Russia. Jawaharlal, far-seeing as ever, recognized that as she grew in power Soviet Russia might develop a new type of imperialism; but he thought there was little chance of this for a long time to come, and for the moment, for reasons of self-interest, Russia was befriending all oppressed nationalities.[8] It seemed logical, therefore, that he should visit the Soviet Union before returning to India; and the opportunity came, after Motilal's arrival in Europe in the autumn, when father and son were invited to the decennial celebrations of the 1917 revolution.

They were in Russia for only a few days, but the articles which Jawaharlal wrote covering this visit show the deep impression made on him by 'this strange Eurasian country of the hammer and sickle, where workers and peasants sit on the thrones of the mighty and upset the best-laid schemes of mice and men.'[9] He knew that they were on a conducted tour, seeing only what they were allowed to see; he knew too that conditions in the sprawling provinces hardly came up to what was to be found in Moscow and its environs. Yet he was convinced that the Soviet Union had made rapid progress in agriculture, prison reform, the eradication of illiteracy, the treatment of women, the handling of the problem of minorities and the removal of the sharp contrasts between luxury and poverty and of the hierarchy of class. He was sure too that the Soviet Union had much to teach India, which also was a large agricultural country with a poor and illiterate population.

Jawaharlal saw the Soviet Union in the last days of its first, halcyon period. If his reaction was idealistic, it was partly because there was still some idealism in the air. The grounding in Marxism, which he had received at the Brussels conference and after, was followed by a near-conversion to Communism by practical testimony. Jawaharlal had been particularly impressed by Lenin's leadership, by his realism and resilience, and above all by his insistence on professional, full-time revolutionaries. The need for such workers in India was obviously even greater, and it was as one such that Jawaharlal now doubtless saw himself. He who had sailed from India as a dedicated disciple of Gandhi returned a self-conscious revolutionary radical. Although always to be deeply influenced by Gandhi, he was never again to be wholly a prisoner in the Gandhian mould. But it is significant that the change was wrought not by the revolutionary situation in India but by what he saw and heard and read in Europe. Jawaharlal was always a radical in the European tradition, seeking to apply and adapt its doctrine to his own country. This could be both a strength and a weakness.

REFERENCES

1. To Syed Mahmud, 24 May, 15 July and 11 August 1926, and 14 July 1927, SW, vol. 2, pp. 232-6, 240-41 and 328-29.
2. See his confidential report to the working committee, 19 February 1927, SW, vol. 2, pp. 278-97.
3. To his father, 16 November 1926, SW, vol. 2, pp. 250-51.
4. Letter to N.S. Hardikar, 3 March 1927, SW, vol. 2, p. 304. See also his article in *The Volunteer,* April 1927, on 'The Situation in China and India's Duty', *ibid.,* pp. 326-28.
5. Confidential report to the working committee, 19 February 1927, SW, vol. 2, p. 281.
6. Roger Baldwin's recollections, recorded in 1967, NMML.
7. Confidential report to the working committee, SW., vol. 2, p. 289.
8. A note on foreign policy for India, 13 September 1927, SW, vol. 2, pp. 348-64.
9. *Soviet Russia; Some Random Sketches and Impressions* (Allahabad 1928).

9

The Campaign for Independence

It was in this mood, not as before of novelettish romanticism but of thoughtful commitment to revolutionary change, that Jawaharlal returned to India. He was itching for action. For this, the first step seemed to him to be the acceptance of full independence as the objective. Jawaharlal had been thinking about this for a long time and had now finally come round to the view that the Congress should commit itself firmly to the goal of independence. He could not accept the usual argument that there was no real difference between Dominion Status and independence because the former carried with it the right to secede. Theoretically this was so, but in fact Dominion Status implied the maintenance of a connection with Britain and allowing her dominance in every major field. But independence need not mean enmity with Britain. Though there could be no friendship within the empire, once India was out of the imperial stranglehold she could co-operate with Britain as an equal.

Even more important to Jawaharlal than the political and economic implications of independence were the psychological consequences of a commitment to such an uncompromising policy. The assent to Dominion Status as the objective was in itself an indication of India's mental degradation, for behind it lay an unquestioning acceptance of the inevitability of a British presence in India. But once the Congress made independence its goal, it would shake off the defeatism and weariness that had followed the non-co-operation movement, sweep away Swarajist temporizings, gain a new strength and again pull in the masses.

Jawaharlal, therefore, was eager for wholehearted combat, with no quarter sought or given. His new radical ideas affirmed rather than diverted his enthusiasm for political action. Even the arrest of capitalist exploitation and a lightening of India's poverty required the termination of imperialist rule. But the mirage of Dominion Status weakened resistance in India to the British and generally strengthened reformist as against revolutionary forces. The real strength of the British in India lay in the submissive attitude of Indians to the status quo—to the raj, to established ideas, to old customs and traditions. So, as he complained to Gandhi, 'it passes my comprehension how a national organization can have as its ideal and goal dominion status. The very idea suffocates and strangles me.'[1]

It was Gandhi, of course, who was the main hurdle. He was not, present at the sessions of the Madras Congress when Jawaharlal secured the passage of a resolution committing the Congress to independence. But the followers of Gandhi had been there in sufficient numbers to secure the removal of the parts of the resolution which clarified independence to mean full control of defence, finance and economic and foreign policy, and demanded that this be implemented immediately, in particular by the complete withdrawal of the British army of occupation. So all that the party accepted was a general adherence to the goal of complete national independence; and even this was not incorporated into the constitution of the Congress. That still proclaimed the objective to be swaraj, and thus enabled those who did not believe in independence and a total severance from Britain, and had no wish to see the British army withdraw at once, continue to be members of the party.

So Jawaharlal's resolution, as he himself recognized, was not really taken seriously and was meant primarily to humour him.[2] But Gandhi did not conceal his disdain for what seemed to him mock heroics. He also warned Jawaharlal privately that he was proceeding too fast.[3] When Jawaharlal replied stiffly that he had a large measure of support, that Gandhi's leadership was now hesitant and ineffective, and that their ideals were very different, Gandhi offered to publish the correspondence.[4] In other words, he was prepared for an open break. The relationship had not yet developed to the extent that to the older man it was in any way indispensable. But Jawaharlal drew back. The firmness of his views was not to him incompatible with emotional dependence, and he was eager to remain, in Gandhi's phrase, 'under stupefaction'.[5]

So, without breaking away completely from Gandhi and the old leadership, Jawaharlal campaigned for independence as the ultimate objective. It was a circumscribed revolt. The issue came up again at the All-Parties Conference and at the proceedings of the committee set up by it, with Motilal Nehru as the chairman, to draw up a constitution. Jawaharlal spoke repeatedly against the acceptance of Dominion Status and often had to engage in public debate with his father. He knew, however, that he had no chance of getting the decision reversed, and fell back on keeping alive. the commitment of the Congress to independence. The fact that it was a party to the Nehru Report need not mean that it had abandoned its own preference.

It was for this purpose that he organized the Independence for India League as, in the first instance, a pressure group within the Congress. Knowing that Gandhi and other leading Congressmen disapproved of independence and all that it implied, Jawaharlal resigned the general secretaryship; but the working committee declined to accept it.[6] Ostensibly this was because the resolution of the Madras Congress gave legitimacy to propaganda for independence; but in fact it was because the general run of Congressmen attached little importance to Jawaharlal's efforts. To them the only value which the demand for independence now had was that it enabled them to bargain for Dominion Status. Had there been any danger of the Independence for India League altering the general direction of the Congress, it would doubtless have been hastily stifled. For the League was intended to keep alive not only the objective of political independence but also the concomitant ideals of republicanism and socialism. To Jawaharlal independence was not a purely political issue. Severance of the British connection implied also an attack on the vested interests supported by the British in India; indeed, the basis of the struggle was economic. The future republican government of India would be based not on the exploitation of the masses but on social equality.[7] The object of the Independence for India League was therefore both to achieve independence and to reconstruct Indian society by changing its capitalist and feudal basis. Instead of a few individuals amassing huge fortunes by the exploitation of others, the state should be organized on a vast co-operative basis for the benefit of all, and this in turn should lead on to 'a great world co-operative commonwealth'.[8]

Independence, therefore, was a composite ideal, and for its attainment Jawaharlal looked far beyond the Congress. The League should be both an active element within the parent party and a general catalyst in the nation. The Congress might head the political campaign and take the lead in drafting constitutions, but economic and social changes could be effected only by the sanction provided by the exploited classes. For this a revolutionary atmosphere would have to be created in the country and the people organized on a large scale.[9] But this required an economic programme. Gandhi had drawn the masses into the political struggle in a way in which no one else could have done, and this to Jawaharlal made his leadership indispensable. But they could only be kept in this struggle by providing an economic content to swaraj—something which Gandhi had never done. Gandhi claimed not to object to this on principle, but thought the effort was premature. However, Jawahariai went ahead and formulated a precise programme. Though he had a grand design of socialism, he wanted a very modest beginning. In the UP in particular there seemed to be no alternative to the abolition of landlordism, but this should be done with the payment of partial compensation and replaced by small holdings owned by individual peasant proprietors with no right of alienation.

There would be not nationalization but socialization of land, and the most that the state would manage would be model farms. Agricultural debts should be written off but after part payment. The state should gradually acquire key industries, ensure a minimum living wage and impose sharply graduated direct taxes, an inheritance tax and a tax on agricultural income.[10]

Jawaharlal was aware that such a programme would inevitably, at some stage or other, raise issues of the class struggle and bring about clashes of interests between labour and capitalists and between landlords and tenants; but these could not be shirked. It was no wisdom to refuse to recognize or face conflict where it existed. Such conflicts would have to be fought and overcome. Pushed to it, Jawaharlal was willing to concede both that violence was not objectionable in itself and that the final goal, the resolution of the struggle, might well be Communism. If India were convinced that she could become free through violence, she would undoubtedly have the right to indulge in it as other countries had done. He stood for intensive non-violent non-co-operation, only because in India's condition mass violence was impracticable while individual acts of terrorism had a counter-revolutionary effect and injured the national cause.

For the work of organization Jawaharlal looked to the young men and women of India. Within a few months of his return he wrote to the press, calling on those who were for independence and who detested the growing influence of religion in politics as well as desired the removal of inequalities of class, caste and wealth, to get in touch with each other and with him.[11] But revolutionary battalions do not spring into existence on the mere writing of letters to the editor, and Jawaharlal's appeal was significant only as indicative of his own aspirations. Throughout the year he gave the greatest importance to youth leagues and conferences, and was prepared to sacrifice all other work to the organization of youth. But an all-India corps dedicated to 'full-blooded socialism' and carrying the fight to various parts of the country never came into being.

Nor did the Independence for India League, as Jawaharlal sadly recognized soon enough, fulfil the hopes of its creator. It consisted of a few politicians who either were disgruntled with Gandhi and Motilal or hoped to draw on the growing popularity of Jawaharlal for their own advantage. Indeed, often people joined the League with the intention of smothering it.[12] The result was that the Independence for India League never became the spearhead of revolution, well-knit in its organization and clear-cut in its ideology. Rather, for a year it struggled on in a state of suspended animation till it ceased to have a *raison d'etre* in the beginning of 1929, with the Congress as a whole committed, in certain circumstances, to the goal of independence.

II

However, if at this time Jawaharlal failed to create an instrument to mobilize the country for a long-term revolution, he was more successful in helping to plan demonstrations all over the country as a reply to the insult proffered to it by the announcement in 1927 of a commission consisting solely of British members of Parliament to consider whether India was ready for a further instalment of constitutional reforms. To Jawaharlal the failure to nominate 'any Indian to membership of the commission seemed but a minor incident of imperial rule; what should be boycotted was not only the Simon Commission but the whole conception behind it, that India would be for ever a part of the British empire and the British Parliament had the right to give India what it wished and deny her what it liked.[13] But at least the affront of the Simon Commission could be used as an occasion for united action, to bring together members of various parties in a common cause. The chance of hitting back had almost a therapeutic effect on Jawaharlal, and he set about, as general secretary of the Congress, organizing the boycott on a country-wide scale.

The national hartal was a greater success than Jawaharlal had anticipated, and thereafter, throughout the year, wherever the commission went, demonstrations ending in police charges and firing took place.[14] At Lahore the leading Congressman of the Punjab, Lajpat Rai, was severely beaten. Jawaharlal and his colleagues now awaited the arrival of the commission in the United Provinces. The provincial government at first decided to adopt an accommodating attitude and to allow processions, provided the organizers asked for permission and agreed to follow the route laid down by the police; and processions were taken out with permission on 23 and 24 November. Jawaharlal arrived in Lucknow on the 25th and the tempo immediately rose. News of the death of Lajpat Rai on 18 November had already inflamed tempers throughout India and Jawaharlal called on the youth of Lucknow to answer this challenge.[15]

When the boycott committee sought permission for a procession on the 28th, it was granted on condition that the route was changed to avoid the European shopping area, where the governor was that day attending a garden party.[16] The organizers of the procession replied that it was too late to alter the route, and when the procession started to move it was lathi-charged by mounted police. Jawaharlal had by this time, probably expecting no major confrontation, left Lucknow; but on hearing of the lathi-charge he returned to the city on the 29th. The police, who believed that the defiance of the boycott committee on the 28th had been on Jawaharlal's orders, refused to permit any more processions.[17] They stopped a small group of twelve led by Jawaharlal and Govind Ballabh Pant, which was on its way to a public meeting, and asked them if they had secured a licence for a procession. Jawaharlal replied that in view of the behaviour of the police the previous day he was not prepared to have any further dealings with them, and the police thereupon broke up the group with lathis. Jawaharlal himself received two blows. Despite this, the group refused to disperse. Meantime a large crowd had gathered, and the officials were compelled to permit Jawaharlal and his companions to proceed along their chosen route to the meeting with, in fact, the police riding in front as a vanguard.[18]

The next morning the commission arrived in Lucknow.

A large procession, led by Jawaharlal, reached the station, and sought to take up a position nearer to the route of the commission than the one allotted to them. This was near an open space, and the police carried out a cavalry charge, using both lathis and spears, on a crowd of over 30,000 for two or three furlongs. Though hundreds were beaten and many trampled down, the large crowd generally stood its ground, neither retreating nor retaliating, till the police, once the commission had passed, fell back. Jawaharlal, after receiving half a dozen lathi blows on his back, shoulders and legs, was surrounded by students who shielded him from further attack.[19] Just then a young man, ostensibly a student but later discovered to be a police agent, offered to provide Jawaharlal with two revolvers.[20] The offer was politely declined, but the incident is suggestive of an effort to aggravate the situation and seriously incriminate Jawaharlal. It strengthens Jawaharlal's accusation that the police, angry at their loss of prestige on the two previous days, were out on this occasion for vengeance, and primarily against Jawaharlal.

The news of the lathi-charges on the 29th and 30th and of the injuries inflicted on Jawaharlal roused widespread anger in India. Apart from the impact on the development of the national resistance to British rule, they confirmed Jawaharlal's national standing. He was no longer merely a politician of the United Provinces; throughout India his popularity leapt, and he was firmly established as one of the front-runners of his generation. Gandhi realized and welcomed this : 'My love to you. It was all done bravely. You have braver things to do. May God spare you for many a long year to come and make you his chosen instrument for freeing India from [the] yoke.'[21]

III

The government's reaction to the growing popularity of Jawaharlal was to consider his arrest, but finally they decided to await the decisions of the National Congress which was to meet in its annual session in a few days at Calcutta. The hope of Motilal at Calcutta was to secure the adoption by the Congress of the Nehru Report and the acceptance of Dominion

Status without prejudice to the ultimate goal of complete independence. Jawaharlal was in a difficult position. The psychology behind the Nehru Report was alien to him. But if such a break occurred, Gandhi and his father would be on the other side; and, as so often in his public life, affection prevailed over logic. He opposed Dominion Status in the severest terms. But he toned down independence to mean severance of all connection not with the British but only with British imperialism; and he commended the Nehru Report without prejudice to the independence resolution of the Madras Congress. This suggested both a desire to find common ground and a willingness to face both ways.

Gandhi was as anxious to avoid a break. He recommended that if the government did not accept and act upon the Nehru Report within two years, the Congress should revert to full independence. Such flexibility of approach involved no long-term compromise on ideals and, especially as no one seriously expected the government to accept the Nehru Report, made a concession only to the ear. As a further step to placate Jawaharlal, the time-limit was reduced in discussions to one year. So Jàwaharlal and his friends could accept the resolution; but to mark his disapproval of even the paper concession, Jawaharlal stayed away from the final session when the resolution was passed.

IV

So the Congress gave its support to the Nehru Report and the demand for Dominion Status for one year, after which it would again resort to non-co-operation as the means for securing independence. As there was obviously no chance of the government responding to this resolution in any satisfactory way, 1929 was clearly to be a year of preparation. It was in that spirit that Jawaharlal carried out his duties as general secretary of the Congress. He himself was short of money, but spent as much as he could out of his own pocket on Congress work.[22] He secured authorization from the working committee to inspect, personally or by representatives chosen by him, the offices of the provincial committees and to make recommendations for their improved working. He also arranged for auditors to visit these offices and examine the accounts. Almost all the provincial headquarters were inspected and suggestions made for their improvement, and their finances were put in order.

Jawaharlal also gave considerable attention to the Congress volunteer corps, the Hindustani Seva Dal, youth leagues and student organizations. What he wanted was dedicated young men and women who would organize the peasants and workers and create a mass consciousness in preparation for the coming struggle. He planned an Indian National Service, at both all-India and provincial levels, and collected funds for building up a cadre of whole-time workers in the United Provinces. He also sought to reactivate the Independence for India League.

The government attached greater significance at this time to these efforts of Jawaharlal and his colleagues to rouse the masses and particularly, as they thought, the peasants and the students, to destroy the raj, than to the Communist programme to stir up a movement. The government recognized that the two movements had points of contact and in some respects were closely linked: 'There is a tendency for the political and the Communist revolutionaries to join hands, and Pandit Jawaharlal Nehru, an extreme nationalist who is at the same time genuinely attracted by some of the Communist doctrines, stands about at the the meeting point.'[23]

At first, it was intended merely to prosecute Jawaharlal; but then the government decided to move on the other front and deal first with the Communists.[24] The trial of the Communist leaders was staged at Meerut, chosen as the venue in order to avoid a jury, which might jeopardize the chance of a conviction. The Congress, though on principle it did not believe in defence in British courts, promptly formed a defence committee, of which Jawaharlal was a member; and this committee engaged lawyers to appear for the defence. For the first time, and as a very special case, the Congress sanctioned Rs 1500 for the defence, while Jawaharlal sought financial and other assistance from abroad. Indeed for months there was a widespread belief among the public, shared by both Motilal and Jawaharlal, that Jawaharlal himself would soon be arrested.[25] The lack of direct evidence and the desire to isolate the Communists from the general nationalist movement would seem to be the real reasons for the government's obvious reluctance to drag Jawaharlal into the net. Though attracted by the ideology of Communism, Jawaharlal was not, involved in the activities of the Communist party. Not, as was clear from the names of quite a few who had been arrested, that the government had any qualms about involving the innocent. As Jawaharlal is reported to have remarked on his first visit to Meerut jail, 'How little do these accused persons know about the Communist International. I know a lot more than they.'[26]

V

It was in this context that Jawaharlal found himself pitchforked by Gandhi and his father into the presidency of the Congress. In 1929, ten Congress committees voted for Gandhi, five for Vallabhbhai Patel and only three for Jawaharlal.[27] The general feeling was that he was still unseasoned for the presidency. Jawaharlal himself was unwilling. But Gandhi wrung consent out of him and then announced that the crown should be worn by Jawaharlal. Older men had had their innings, and it was but right that the young should be led into battle by one of themselves. Gandhi added, with a candour that was not flattering to his victim, that his relations with the younger man were such that the latter's being in the chair was as good as he himself being in it.[28] Again Jawaharlal begged Gandhi not to press his name,[29] while Motilal, much as he desired his son's election, pointed out to Gandhi that forcing Jawaharlal on the country against its will was unfair to both Jawaharlal and the country.[30] But Gandhi had made up his mind, and on 29 September 1929 the AICC reluctantly elected Jawaharlal to preside over the next session at Lahore in December.

From the viewpoint of the older leaders, there was a great advantage in having in the chair the malleable founder of the independence movement; his opinions underwrote the genuineness of their intention to start civil disobedience, even while they could be confident that he would be amenable, if need be, to Gandhi's persuasion. On the other hand, Jawaharlal's colleagues in the League against Imperialism expected that he would use his position to split the Congress and carry the country with a fully revolutionary programme.[31] Only Jawaharlal knew his predicament, that he would be torn between his loyalty to Gandhi and the Congress organization on the one side, and his ideological leanings on the other.

The testing time was not long in coming. Jawaharlal was getting ready for civil disobedience and fought hard, if he could not secure rejection of the viceroy's proposals to negotiate, at least to stiffen the response of the Congress; but he failed, and then, to the surprise of his friends, agreed to go along with Gandhi. It was urged that as a member of the working committee and general secretary he was bound to carry out the wishes of the majority of the members. But having done so, he resigned both his membership and the secretaryship, and seriously considered abdicating from the presidency.[32]

However, Gandhi, Motilal, Ansari and others persuaded Jawaharlal to hold his hand, mainly on the ground that he could rely on the British not to accept the terms stipulated by the Congress;[33] and on 19 November the working committee, while confirming the Congress offer, revised Gandhi's draft resolution to say, obviously to placate Jawaharlal, that it should be clearly understood that this confirmation would only hold till the next session of the Congress.[34] There was, in fact, no common ground between the government and the Congress, and the focus of attention shifted to Lahore.

VI

Jawaharlal had, therefore, been vindicated. He had had his way by yielding in the first instance. But though Jawaharlal's nationalist followers in India now had no grievance, he had still to contend with his radical friends abroad. Convinced by the frequent references to the League against Imperialism in the Central Assembly during the debates on the Public Safety Bill and by the proceedings at Meerut that the government was making a dead set against the League, Jawaharlal took much trouble during the summer of 1929 to prove to the public that the League was not a Communist organization, even though many Communists belonged to it, but rather an association to establish contacts between all movements throughout the world which supported the struggle against imperialism. If a broader and more international vision was gradually animating the Congress, this was the direct consequence of its association with the League.

This confidence of Jawaharlal was shaken by the end of the year when he heard that the Communists had taken over the central apparatus of the League and muzzled non-Communists. Clearly, he himself would have no place in the League and the organization as, he had conceived it—the grand all-party alliance between the forces of national freedom and social equality—had collapsed. So it caused him no great concern that those now in charge of the League disapproved of his behaviour.

So the decks were clear, and Jawaharlal was free to act as he chose, neither held back by his moderate colleagues nor pushed off course by his erstwhile friends of the left. In the last week of November, before his gamble had paid off, he presided at Nagpur over the annual session of the All-India Trade Union Congress. Jawaharlal's address was true to himself. He placed the responsibility for the miserable condition of the Indian worker on the system which was the natural outcome of capitalism and imperialism, and called on labour to join the national movement in its fight against imperialism, even while it sought to recruit nationalists in its own struggle against capitalism. The real problem was the conquest of power, the overthrow of both the foreign ruler and the exploiting employer, and the goal was a socialist order of society in which the interests of the workers were supreme and the sources of wealth owned by the community, not by individuals. He criticized the methods of the Communists but sat silent at the meetings of the executive committee while resolutions were passed rejecting the Nehru Report, condemning the Congress offer to the government, favouring independence as against Dominion Status, demanding the establishment of a workers' republic and calling for affiliation with the League against Imperialism. The fact that he and the Congress were still committed to negotiations for Dominion Status does not seem to have bothered him, while his inner hesitations about the League found no expression. It was not so much that Jawaharlal saw his role as president to be akin to that of a figurehead as that, whatever his public posture, he privately approved of most of these decisions. He also made no strong effort to prevent the secession of the moderates and the formation of a separate All-India Trade Union Federation.

If at Nagpur Jawaharlal had to connive at the rejection of policies to which he was still officially committed, at Lahore at the end of the year he was utterly unshackled. Riding, with his sense of theatre, on a white charger in the Congress procession, he fitted to perfection, as Gandhi had prophesied, the role of the young Galahad of revolt. The Congress was by now committed to independence and to civil disobedience. Jawaharlal's speech was attuned to this atmosphere of defiance and rebellion. He had begun to draft his presidential address about the tenth of December, but even then he could write with the full knowledge that the talks with the viceroy had no prospect of success.[35]

Jawaharlal put the Indian problem in its international context. It appeared to be a dissolving period of history, when the world was in labour, and out of her travail would give birth to a new order. In this Asia and even India would play a determining part, for the brief day of European domination was already approaching its end and the future lay with America and Asia. But if India had a message to give to the world, she had also much to learn and receive from other peoples.

Then, reverting to India, Jawaharlal pointed out that though her social structure had proved to be wonderfully stable, it had failed in one vital particular: it had found no solution for the problem of equality and in fact had deliberately based itself on inequality. But a solution based on the genius of the Indian people and on India's thought and culture had to be found if the political and social structure was to have any stability and if the discords between the various communities were to disappear. And this led Jawaharlal to plead for the faith and generosity which would remove fear and suspicion between the communities.

The British army of occupation, Jawaharlal went on, held India in its iron grip, and the whip of the master was ever ready to come down on the best of them who raised their heads. The answer to the Calcutta resolution had been clear and definite. Now they had but one goal—independence, complete freedom from British domination, which alone could lead to world co-operation and an international community of equals. 'I must frankly confess', Jawaharlal continued, 'that I am a Socialist and a republican, and am no believer in kings and princes, or in the order which produces the modern kings of industry, who have greater power over the lives and fortunes of men than even the kings of old, and whose methods are as predatory as those of the old feudal aristocracy.' He acknowledged that the Congress, as it was then constituted, might not be able to adopt a full socialistic programme, but the philosophy of socialism had gradually permeated the entire structure of society the world over, and almost the only points in dispute were the pace and the methods of advance. India too would have to go that way if she wished to end poverty and inequality, though methods and adapt the ideal to her own genius.

On the two particular problems of India, the minorities and the states, Jawaharlal had little that was startlingly new to say. He wanted the minorities to be given the fullest assurances that their culture and traditions would be safe. The princes were the products of a vicious system which would ultimately have to go. But, as regards the problem of peasantry and labour, Jawaharlal asked the Congress to commit itself to ending the domination of any one class over another, and to draw up a programme of such changes as could be immediately put into operation. Paternalism and trusteeship were both equally barren theories. The least that every worker in field or factory was entitled to was a minimum wage and humane hours of labour; and in the long term the Congress should strive for workers' control of industry on a co-operative basis and for a system of peasant proprietorship.

The immediate problem, however, was the conquest of power, and the forging of sanctions to enforce the national will. The Congress had not the material or the training for organized violence, and individual and sporadic violence was a confession of despair. The basic idea of non-co-operation must remain, but Jawaharlal did not think it wise to declare a boycott of schools and law courts at the very start. The programme should be one of political and economic boycott, the reduction of all points of contact with the British government. This would release energy and direct attention to the real struggle, which should take the shape of non-payment of taxes and, where possible, general strikes. It was now an Open Conspiracy, which everyone should join, to free the country from foreign rule.

The presidential address shows both the strength and the weakness of Jawaharlal at this stage. His impatient and full-blooded eagerness for freedom was manifest. He had no use for political compromise. He wished to eject the British from India and thereafter cut his country off from the British empire. In the campaign of civil disobedience which was to begin he accepted the leadership of Gandhi, but made it clear that he accepted non-violence as a technique rather than as a moral end in itself, and did not rule out the adoption of violent methods at any future time. With courage he announced that he was a socialist and a republican, but it was courage tinged with apology. The socialism which he envisaged was clearly of a mild and timid variety, and he spoke of India evolving her own methods and adjusting it to her traditions. Similarly, while he realized that the basic problem in India was an economic one and communal troubles were artificial, he spoke of finding an interim solution which would be typically Indian. The confusion of thought was probably the result of a dislike of precise choice, an instinctive reluctance to abandon Indian ways even while his mind turned away from them, and the feeling of a lack of immediacy about these matters. They all had to give way to the achievement of independence, and for this the Congress was the obvious instrument. He added almost in the same breath as his assertion of his personal credo that he did not expect the Congress, with its predominantly middle-class composition, to agree with him or to adopt a revolutionary programme. His loyalty to the Congress being unreserved, this could only mean that, while he would not abandon his principles, he would be willing to keep them in abeyance. To Jawaharlal discipline was more important than revolution, and political freedom took priority over economic and social change. There was little to fear from a man whom Gandhi described as a confirmed socialist who wanted for his country only what it could manage, a practical statesman who tempered his ideals to suit his surroundings.[36] On the other hand, it was worth having in the chair a figure of glamour and integrity who would keep captive within the Congress his wide following among the students and the intelligentsia. During the next ten years, no single individual did more to build in the Congress an awareness of economic issues; but Jawaharlal was also the best shield of the Congress against left-wing groups and organizations.

REFERENCES

1. 11 January 1928.
2. *Autobiography,* p. 167.
3. 4 January 1928; J. Nehru, *A Bunch of Old Letters* (Delhi, 1958), pp. 55-6.
4. 11 January 1928.

5. 17 January 1928, *Collected Works,* vol. 32 (New Delhi 1969), pp. 468-9.
6. *The Bombay Chronicle,* 4 September 1928.
7. Presidential address at the first session of the Republican Congress, *The Hindu,* 29 December 1927.
8. Circular letter to Congressmen, 5 April 1928, SW, vol. 3, p. 184.
9. See speech at Banaras, 17 January, *The Bombay Chronicle,* 18 January 1928.
10. Presidential address to the UP provincial conference, 27 October 1928, SW, vol. 3. pp. 255-63; Programme of the Independence for India League. UP branch. April 1929, SW. vol. 3. p. 287.
11. Letter to the press, 20 March 1928.
12. See Jawaharlal's letter to G.S. Vidyarthi, 2 October 1928.
13. Speech at Allahabad, 10 January, *The Leader,* 12 January 1928.
14. See his letter to the editor, 3 February, *The Leader,* 6 February 1928, and interview at Bombay, *The Bombay Chronicle,* 1 February 1928.
15. See his circular 'They have dared!', AICC file, G 73 of 1928.
16. Report of Deputy Commissioner, Lucknow, 5 December 1928, home dept. pol., file 130 of 1929.
17. *Ibid.*
18. Report in *The Tribune,* 1 December 1928; press statements of Jawaharlal, 1 and 4 December 1928, SW, vol. 3, pp. 108-15 and 119.
19. Press statements of Jawaharlal, 30 November and 1 December 1928; report in *The Tribune,* 2 December 1928; Gandhi in Navajivan, 9 December 1928, *Collected Works,* vol. 38, p. 184.
20. Jawaharlal's letter to Gandhi, quoted by him in *Young India,* 13 December 1928, *Collected Works,* vol. 38, p. 209.
21. 3 December 1928, *A Bunch of Old Letters,* p. 68.

22. See Sri Prakasa's article in R. Zakaria, *A Study of Nehru* (Bombay, 1959), pp. 328-9.

23. Home Secretary to all local govts., 21 February 1929, home dept. pol., file 168 of 1929.

24. Note of H.G. Haig, 4 January 1929, home dept., file 179/29 of 1929.

25. See Jawaharlal to A.C.N. Nambiar, 11 July 1929, AICC file, FD 20, part II, 1929.

26. Muzaffar Ahmad's introduction in *Communists Challenge Imperialism from the Dock* (Calcutta, 1967).

27. See AICC file, G 100 for 1929-30.

28. Article in Young India, 1 August 1929, reprinted in *Collected Works,* vol. 41, pp. 239-41.

29. Telegram to Gandhi, 21 August 1929, Gandhi Smarak Sangrahalaya, P. S. 15496.

30. 21 August 1929, *Collected Works,* vol. 41. p. 305n.

31. See, *e.g.,* V. Chattopadhyaya to Jawaharlal, 28 August 1929, AICC file.F.D. 1(ii), part I, 1929.

32. To President, AICC, 4 November 1929, AICC file, G-117 of 1929.

33. Gandhi's telegram, 6 November, and letter, 18 November 1929, *Collected Works,* vol. 42, pp. 101 and 181, respectively; Ansari to Jawaharlal, 7 November 1929, Ansari papers, Jamia Millia; Motilal to Jawaharlal, 7 November 1929, Motilal Nehru papers.

34. *The Leader,* 20 November 1929.

35. See letters to Dr. Gopichand, 6, 10 and 14 December 1929, AICC file, G 100 of 1929-30.

36. *Young India,* 9 January 1930.

10

Action—and Anti-Climax

After the Lahore Congress, however, Jawaharlal could push aside these nagging problems of the gap between thought and practice and devote himself happily to action. He organized the celebration throughout India of 26 January as Independence Day, when everyone was called upon to take the independence pledge drafted by Gandhi and Jawaharlal.

The working committee authorized Gandhi to start civil disobedience as and when he desired, and advocated, once the mass movement had started, a boycott of law courts and schools. By now Gandhi had at last seen his way ahead, and decided to march to the sea and violate the salt laws. To Jawaharlal law-breaking was invigorating in itself, and his support for Gandhi now was without any mental reservation. He, with a few friends, went down to Gujarat and marched with Gandhi for one stage, and the impression left on him was profound and permanent. Over twenty-years later he "wrote :

> Many pictures rise in my mind of this man, whose eyes were often full of laughter and yet were pools of infinite sadness. But the picture that is dominant and most significant is as I saw him marching, staff in hand, to Dandi on the Salt March in 1930. He was the pilgrim on his quest of truth, quiet, peaceful, determined and fearless, who would continue that quiet pilgrimage regardless of consequences.[1]

After this experience it was perhaps to be expected that, whatever the ideological and temperamental strains,

Jawaharlal would never completely break away from his leader.

On 6 April, Jallianwala Bagh Day, Gandhi manufactured salt and Jawaharlal called on the country to go ahead with mass civil disobedience. He himself took charge of the campaign in Allahabad district. As there was no possibility here of manufacturing salt, technical breaches were organized for inviting arrest. On the 9th he sold packets of contraband salt in the city, and the next day he and his wife led a large procession and collected salt from a special kind of earth brought in for the purpose. Thereafter Jawaharlal organized the collection of salt in various parts of the city as well as in vehicles, making salt in them and selling it with appropriate songs. But more worrying to the government was his activity in the Rae Bareli district and the formation of associations among the tenants for non-payment of rent.[2] On the 14th, Jawaharlal was arrested at Cheoki, a few miles outside Allahabad, tried in Naini jail and sentenced to six months' simple imprisonment for assisting in the manufacture of salt on 11 April.

'Great Day!' Jawaharlal wrote in his pocket diary the day the prison gates shut on him. He was placed in solitary confinement in a barrack reserved for dangerous prisoners and surrounded by a circular wall nearly fifteen feet high. To Jawaharlal this gave a greater sense of captivity than any rectangular enclosure; for, apart from creating a feeling of being closed in, it cut off a good bit of the sky in the day and the stars at night—the sight of which was one of Jawaharlal's chief pleasures in prison.

Refusing any special privileges, Jawaharlal often went hungry. Worse than the hunger, however, was the boredom. To evade this ennui Jawaharlal organized his life to a rigorous schedule. Up with the dawn, after a run of about a mile beside the main prison wall and a brisk walk for the same distance, Jawaharlal spent the remainder of the day mostly in spinning, weaving and reading. Since at first he was not allowed a *charkha,* Jawaharlal, keen on some form of manual labour, took up *newar* weaving and continued it even later. But as a disciplined Congressman his main interest was in hand-spinning.[3]

Jawaharlal was allowed only six books at a time, and there was some uncertainty as to whether this included reference works and dictionaries, and whether a multi-volume work counted as one book or more. So Jawaharlal had to give up the idea of continuing his letters to Indira, tracing the history of man. In 1928, when she was in Mussoorie and he was wandering in the plains, he had written to her, giving in brief outline the origins of the earth, the beginnings of life and human prehistory. He had got as far as the formation of classes, the development of organized religion and the coming of the Aryans, when he had been forced by the stress of public affairs to discontinue.[4] Now, in prison, though time was not lacking, he needed more books and probably even missed the inspiration : 'my mind was too full of the making of history, as it was being made from day to day in India, for me to think of the dead past.'[5] But he read much and made copious notes.

Jawaharlal's isolation was never complete. It was broken from the start by the presence of numerous convict warders and orderlies, ostensibly intended to attend on him but also used to keep a watch on him, and he was not allowed to mix with other prisoners lest they carry messages. But in fact a large number of other warders and servants also came daily for *darshan* and to discuss swaraj. Convicts smuggled in flowers, and his *punkha* coolie, who was not a convict, brought him a few little mangoes almost daily. 'They are not up to much', wrote Jawaharlal, much moved, 'but the gift is worthy of the Gods. The man is very poor.'[6] Officials of the jail and the town also called on him frequently. A month after his arrest, another Congressman arrested for civil disobedience was placed in the same barrack. But it was the arrival of Motilal Nehru and Syed Mahmud on 30 June that disrupted the placid routine of Jawaharlal's life. Looking after his father became now his main preoccupation, till both father and son were soon drawn, even from within jail, into political negotiations.

Some slack statements to a British journalist by Gandhi and Motilal were picked up by the two leading Liberals, Sapru and Jayakar, as a basis for a settlement at a time when both civil disobedience and the government's attempts to crush it were in full swing. Armed with some general platitudes from the Viceroy, they saw Gandhi in Yeravda jail and found him in what they felt to be a cooperative mood. In fact, however, while Gandhi sounded accommodating on the constitutional issue, he had clearly not given his whole mind to it and insisted that Jawaharlal's should be the final voice.[7] So the peacemakers proceeded to Naini prison to interview the Nehrus. Despite a letter from Jawaharlal to Gandhi given them to deliver, in which Jawaharlal made clear that he and his father had not been persuaded by Gandhi's approach to the constitutional issue and that he himself wished to continue the campaign, Sapru persuaded the Viceroy to transport the Nehrus to Yeravda for consultations with Gandhi.[8] Though Jawaharlal had not been very keen, Motilal had said that they had no objection, and a special train sped them across the country to see Gandhi.[9] But the talks of Gandhi and the Nehrus with Sapru and Jayakar came to nothing.

A few days later, Motilal was released on grounds of ill health, and Jawaharlal's own term of six months was drawing to a close. But the UP government had no intention of leaving him at large for long.[10] Nor did Jawaharlal expect it. Released on 11 October, he promptly resumed the Congress presidency, thereby—as the organization had been outlawed—rendering himself liable to arrest; and he then directed all the provincial committees to launch a fresh offensive. In his own province, where agricultural prices had been on a steep decline throughout the year, a no-tax campaign would obviously meet with a favourable response; and Jawaharlal announced that the district and town Congress committees would shortly organize non-payment of land revenue, rent and income-tax.[11] Though, on the face of it, this involved all sections of society, landowners, tenants and professional classes, in the political struggle against the government it was basically a call to the peasant tillers not to pay rent to the landlords. Its explosive nature lay in its rousing class conflict and spreading it to the countryside. The next day he was arrested, tried for sedition and incitement to manufacture of salt and non-payment of taxes, and sentenced to two years' rigorous imprisonment plus five months in default of fines. He had been out of prison for less than ten days.

Denied the artistry of action, Jawaharlal reverted to the regular tenor of Naini life.[12] A pain in the shoulder prevented him from much spinning and newar-weaving. But the insatiable reading was taken up again. He also recommenced his letters to his daughter, basing himself on his memory and his notebooks, for by now it was clear that ahead lay many years in prison—indeed he would only be able to write in prison—and if he hoped for the help of 4 reference books he would never write at all. But his sense of wonder had led him to amass a great deal of odd information. Over these letters Jawaharlal took much trouble, collecting his thoughts on paper and then organizing them lucidly to suit a girl of thirteen. The handling of the language was easy, but his style had not quite settled down and occasionally there was a trace of affectation. The letters dealt with the history of man. Like Raleigh and Condorcet, Jawaharlal wrote a history of the world while sitting in prison. Each letter was devoted to one theme or development; and the whole, starting with Mohenjo-daro and ancient Greece and ending with the writer's own times, was spread over nearly three years. The letters showed, when published as *Glimpses of World History,* a unity of outlook and a command of fact which would have done credit to any professional writer. That they were written with no research assistance of any kind and as an escape from the monotony of jail made the work an astonishing achievement.

Jawaharlal also gave some thought to the future of the national movement. A revolutionary dynamic, even in politics, could only be maintained by the goal of an economic revolution and by the rousing of a mass revolt. From this point of view, a no-tax campaign was vital and some attention should be given to defining its objective. The battle-cry of an economic programme was a far more powerful one for the peasant than that of political swaraj alone, and the object of a no-tax movement should be economic advance and not the release of a few leaders. Even the idea of a constituent assembly to settle the political future of India, which struck Jawaharlal at this time, could not be expected to rouse the kisans. In May 1929 the national body, following in the steps of the UP Congress, had accepted that the poverty and misery of the Indian people was due not only to foreign exploitation but also to the economic structure of society which required 'revolutionary changes'. Thanks to Jawaharlal the Congress was acquiring, if not a socialist viewpoint, at least an economic dimension. But no thought had been given to these 'revolutionary changes'. The Congress, in the middle of a war, could not be expected to draw up a definite economic and agrarian programme, but it should at least formulate some tentative ideas. Jawaharlal thought of some, 'not', as he said, 'from a purely socialistic standpoint, but from a Congress viewpoint with some leanings towards socialism'. Big zamindaris should be acquired by the state, with compensation to all except those who had sided with the British and against the national movement, and replaced by peasant proprietorship and large state farms, where major experiments could be tried by the cultivators to whom they would be jointly leased. There should be also an inheritance tax and a land tax which would be at a flat rate of 25 per cent of the agricultural income above a certain minimum and up to a certain limit, and beyond that graduated like the income tax. Tenants should have rights of occupancy, purchase, transfer, improvement and inheritance, and a ceiling should be placed on rent. The time might not be ripe for a radical agrarian programme for the whole of India, and leading Congressmen would not agree to it; but the UP could take the lead. While there was no point in needlessly irritating the zamindars and the capitalists and adding to one's enemies in the middle of a great fight, where a choice had to be made between two positions the Congress should without fear back the masses—the kisans, the landless people, and the petty zamindars—for they were the vital groups. The Congress was wise in avoiding precipitation of the class conflict, but it should always be remembered that such a conflict was there and could not be wholly ignored. The ultimate ideal should be clear-cut in their minds; it need not be advertised but it need not be kept secret either.

These ideas, very similar to the UP manifesto of 1928, were, as Jawaharlal was well aware, by no means revolutionary; but even their attainment was poised in his eyes on the continuance of a revolutionary struggle, and to that extent he was racing far ahead of reality. Even from within prison he and his companions sought to resist, and for the first time Jawaharlal contravened the jail rules by organizing a three-day fast in protest against the flogging of political prisoners and their harsh treatment in other jails. He was vastly delighted, too, by the news of his wife's arrest on New Year's Day and by her message on that occasion : 'I am happy beyond measure and proud to follow in the footsteps of my husband. I hope the people will keep the flag flying.' But generally, as Jawaharlal was compelled angrily to recognize, spirits were flagging and there was a mood for compromise.

It was in this context of fatigue that the British government sent out seductive messages suggesting a settlement. The thought that these siren voices might strike a response in the Congress drove Jawaharlal almost frantic. All such statements, he pleaded with his father, even if they offered full independence, should be ignored and the fight carried on. Motilal, however, was dying, and could give no guidance to the working committee, whose members had now been released. Gandhi was unwilling to reject the government's overtures out of hand both because he sensed a kindred spirit in the Viceroy, and because he believed that the war-weariness was more widespread than Jawaharlal was willing to recognize. The latter was prepared to overcome the staleness in the towns by stirring up the rural areas, but this did not appeal to Gandhi. Out of tune, therefore, with the mood of his leader, and deeply stricken by his father's death on 6 February, Jawaharlal made no decisive contribution to the discussions.

The negotiations with the Viceroy, carried out by Gandhi on his own, and the settlement which resulted, seemed to Jawaharlal a total and unwarranted surrender. Gandhi had agreed to discontinue civil disobedience in return for a partial amnesty, limited to those not charged with violence, and permission to picket peacefully and to manufacture salt under certain conditions; and he committed the Congress to take part in the Round Table Conference to consider a scheme of federation and responsibility with safeguards 'in the interests of India' for such matters as defence, external affairs, the position of minorities, financial credit and the discharge of obligations. This was a far cry from the demand for independence and the right to secede, and even from the position taken up by the Congress in the talks with Sapru and Jayakar in the summer of 1930. Nor had Gandhi stood firm on the demands for a general amnesty, an inquiry into police excesses, which to Jawaharlal was preliminary to any participation in the Round Table Conference, the return of all immovable property which had been attached, and the unlimited right to collect salt.[13]

However, despite his disappointment, at the Congress session at Karachi Jawaharlal moved the resolution ratifying this settlement. It has frequently been suggested that Gandhi secured this by agreeing, in turn, to a resolution, drafted by Jawaharlal and revised by him, committing the organization to provide in any future constitution for not only the basic civil liberties, adult suffrage and free primary education, but also 'real economic freedom'. But the argument that in return for his acceptance of the political compromise Jawaharlal was given a recognition of socialist objectives is defeated by the list of fundamental rights incorporated in the resolution. In industry, economic freedom meant only a living wage and proper conditions of work, liberation from serfdom or conditions bordering on serfdom, decent treatment of women workers, prohibition against the employment of school-going children, the right to form trade unions and the establishment of machinery for settling disputes by arbitration. The state should control mineral resources and the key industries. These could not constitute part of the 'revolutionary changes' which the Congress had accepted in 1929 as being necessary. But in agriculture the position was even worse. The Karachi resolution stipulated no more than a substantial reduction of land revenue and rent, with total exemption only for necessary periods in the case of uneconomic holdings, a progressive tax on agricultural income above a certain level and a graduated inheritance tax. There was no reference to the abolition of landlordism or the socialization of land or even the annulment of at least a portion of the rural debt. On the other hand, much of Gandhi's eleven points of 1930 was included—reduction of civil and military expenditure, exclusion of foreign cloth and yarn, prohibition, abolition of the salt tax and lowering of the exchange ratio of the rupee.

Jawaharlal too was aware that this resolution did not go even as far as his earlier efforts, from 1928 onwards, at drafting an economic programme which would have some meaning for the peasants and workers of India—But he sponsored it as it formed at least one-more step taken by the Congress, however haltingly, not on the road to socialism but towards the recognition of the need for an economic policy.

So the resolution on fundamental rights in itself did not compensate for the loss of ground suffered because of the political settlement; and if Jawaharlal publicly supported the latter, it was because such conduct was in consonance with both his policy and his character. As Jawaharlal saw it, the settlement was undoubtedly a self-inflicted defeat; but no permanent damage had been done to Indian nationalism. Gandhi had not broken, but only ignored, the logic of the struggle for freedom. That struggle, in fact, could only end with the attainment of independence. So this was no peace but only a truce. The temporary phase was bound to pass sooner rather than later, and the fight recommence; and then once again the nation would require the leadership of the man who had called a depressed people to life and action. Till then, in the period of neither peace nor war, it was Jawaharlal's duty to keep the spirit of battle alive, to respect the cohesion of the party and to abide by the leadership of Gandhi.

REFERENCES

1. 30 June 1951. Foreword to Tendulkar, *Mahatma,* vol. 1 (Bombay 1951).
2. Hailey to Hirtzel, 8 May 1930, Hailey papers, vol. 19.
3. During this term of six months he spun over 30,000 yards of yarn on the *charkha* and nearly 750 yards on the *takli* (a hand spindle).
4. *Letters from a Father to his Daughter* (Allahabad, 1929).
5. Preface to second edition, October 1931.
6. Diary entry, 2 May 1930.
7. Gandhi to Motilal, 23 July 1930, *The Bombay Chronicle,* 6 September 1930.
8. 28 July 1930.
9. Sapru to Jayakar, 8 August 1930, Sapru papers, J. 16.
10. Hailey, governor, to Crerar, home member, 2 October 1930, home dept. pol. file, 257/III of 1930.
11. Speech at Lucknow, 18 October 1930, *The Tribune,* 21 October 1930.
12. Sec letter to Dhan Gopal Mukherji, 17 October 1930.
13. See his undated note, which clearly was written at this time, AICC file, G.6(KW) (i), 1931.

11

Agrarian Crisis in the United Provinces

Jawaharlal's speeches immediately after the announcement of the settlement were, somewhat to Gandhi's embarrassment, bellicose.[1] He called on Congressmen to retain the war mentality, for the time was sure to come when they would have to fight again; meanwhile, they should abide by the agreement which their leader had reached, and exploit it fully in such matters as picketing of liquor shops, manufacture of salt, boycott of foreign cloth and preaching of swadeshi.[2] There was also scope for more important activity in the sensitive areas of Gujarat and the United Provinces, where the movement of 1930 had developed into rural no-rent campaigns. That in Gujarat had been the more successful but it was also the more easily called off, for it had been primarily a political effort in a small area no larger than half a district in the UP, with relatively well-to-do cultivators responding to the call of Gandhi and Vallabhbhai Patel to pay nothing until the government cancelled a summary enhancement of the revenue. The authorities were forced to acknowledge that the assessment had been carelessly arrived at, and, after the settlement, the chief issues were the restoration of lands which had been confiscated and the reinstatement of officials who had been dismissed. But the situation was very different in the United Provinces.

Here, in March 1931, as the slump in prices continued and even the *rabi* (spring) crop was a failure, the whole scope of the movement was changed, as Gandhi described it, from one for nonpayment of rent to one purely for seeking economic relief.[3] Tenants were advised to pay what was possible, which in general appeared to be 50 per cent by occupancy tenants and 40 per cent by statutory tenants, provided the landlords gave receipts for the full amount. The Congress organizations in the tehsils acted as agents of the peasants in negotiations with the landlords, and Jawaharlal met some senior officials of the UP government, while the provincial Congress committee opened an office at Lucknow to deal with the government.

However, though the government recognized the economic distress and realized that there was nothing objectionable in the attitude of the Congress, they feared that its mediation would strengthen its hold in the rural areas and refused to recognize that the Congress had any role in this matter. Knowing Gandhi's keen desire to make the settlement a success, they sought to drive a wedge between him and Jawaharlal. In this they were not wholly unsuccessful. Gandhi, in fact, was frightened by the officials with the bogey of a class war being let loose by Jawaharlal. He liked the idea of Congress tehsil committees acting on behalf of the tenants, but disapproved of advice to withhold payment of rent even in part, the appointment of Congress *tehsildars* and attacks by tenants on zamindars.[4] He even, to the government's delight, practically withdrew the claim of the Congress to be an intermediary between the government and the people.[5]

Jawaharlal's health at this time being on the verge of collapse, he had to take a holiday, and while he was in Sri Lanka and southern India, Gandhi was in charge of the UP problem. Ignoring the resolution of the UP political conference passed a few weeks earlier that the rents should on no account exceed those prevailing at a time when agricultural prices were what they were at this time, Gandhi called upon the tenants to pay all the rent they could as early as possible. They were asked to pay in no case less than 8 annas in the rupee in the case of statutory and non-occupancy tenants, and 12 annas in the case of occupancy tenants—more than what the UP

Congress had recommended. He added that the tenants should certainly not listen to advice to pay no rent at all or resort to violence.[6]

Fortified by Gandhi's half-hearted support of the kisans, the government now forced the pace and, without openly denouncing the settlement, set about breaking up the alliance of the UP Congress and the tenantry as well as the Congress organization in the countryside. So when Jawaharlal came back to the UP in the middle of June, he found the situation and atmosphere much worse than in March. The talukdars were terrorizing the peasants with the help of the police, Congress volunteers were being beaten up in many places, and even activity such as peaceful picketing, permitted by the settlement, was in places banned by over-enthusiastic district authorities. Jawaharlal was too loyal to Gandhi to accept, even to himself, that his leader was weakening their case. But he took the view that what Gandhi had asked the tenants to pay was not the minimum but the maximum and this need not be paid if it entailed debt and sale of cattle and ploughs, or if the kisans were ill-treated.[7] The UP Congress set up commissions of inquiry to visit the districts and ascertain details of official and zamindari repression. For their part, the UP government claimed that they were prepared to grant no further remissions. Gandhi suggested to the Viceroy and his officials that the district authorities should fix the amount of revenue and rent to be collected after consultation with Congress workers, but, if this were not acceptable to the government, at least a detailed inquiry to enable temporary adjustments should be ordered. The Government of India were willing to consider this, but it was vetoed by the UP government. Jawaharlal met the chief secretary and urged that as the season for collection of rents was over and tenants had already paid 9 to 12 annas or more in the rupee, further collections should be suspended and coercive processes stopped. This would immediately relieve the tension and produce the proper atmosphere for an inquiry into future adjustments. But the government, on the plea that rents had earlier been deliberately withheld, insisted that the process of collection should continue longer than in normal years. So evictions continued, and attempts were made to secure new tenants for these holdings. Congressmen in particular were penalized for taking an interest in these matters, and such tenants as declared themselves against the Congress were given special remissions.[8]

Sensing that the Government of India were, at least as far as the UP was concerned, at this time less belligerent than the local government, Jawaharlal got Patel, as president of the Congress, to write to them to intervene.[9] But nothing happened, and meantime the general attitude of the Government of India also stiffened. Yet, under Jawaharlal's guidance the UP Congress committee did not consider the request of the Rae Bareli district committee for permission to start civil disobedience, but instead called on all its branches to refrain from any such action for the time being.[10] The committee appointed by the UP Congress to inquire into the agrarian situation, which also reported at this time, publicly denied that the Congress was opposed to the zamindars or wished to countenance a class war.[11] Jawaharlal had no wish to embarrass Gandhi, by this time in London for the Round Table Conference, or his colleagues in the working committee; nor was the organization on a war footing.

Touring the districts, Jawaharlal found the conditions varied, depending on the particular attitudes of the local officials. He was more interested in ascertaining the facts than in exploiting them. Even the UP government conceded that his speeches were 'less open to objection than usual.'[12] But, on the whole, the situation was grim; and Jawaharlal was at last forced to contemplate a no-rent campaign. He also brought the crisis to the notice of the Viceroy and of Gandhi. The Government of India merely referred his letter to the UP government, while Gandhi authorized Jawaharlal to do as he thought fit.[13]

By now the Government of India were prepared for a fight. But at this stage it was the UP government that hung back. The Congress leaders were invited to a discussion with the officials concerned. The talks came to nothing. The UP Congress committee, still reluctant to have a confrontation in which the tenants would obviously suffer most, offered to renew negotiations.[14] But there was not even a remote chance of these succeeding, for the authorities were determined to yield no ground; the only question for them was whether the charade of discussion should be gone through. The central and local governments believed that this would have the advantage of strengthening the forces within the Congress against Jawaharlal. In fact, this assessment was inaccurate as well as prejudiced. Jawaharlal was as disinclined as any other Congress leader to start a no-rent movement, primarily because of the absence of Gandhi. He now, unlike in 1921, understood the basic nature of the peasant problem; he knew that it was a part of the class war; but he preferred to project it as an aspect of the struggle against the British, and even in this he sought to avoid battle. But the option was being gradually removed.

On 6 December the district Congress committees in Rae Bareli, Etawah, Kanpur and Unao, in addition to Allahabad, were authorized to commence their no-rent campaigns.[15] Payment of rent in these districts came to an almost complete standstill, other districts were also lining up, and it was clear that once the movement started it would spread throughout the province.[16] The UP government secured the permission of the Government of India to arrest Jawaharlal if he toured any of these districts.[17] However, though Jawaharlal did visit some of these districts, nothing was done. To strengthen their case, the UP government lowered the water rates, introduced a bill to secure tenants from eviction if they paid two-thirds of the arrears due for the previous four years, and offered to consider immediate measures to protect tenants against debts which had become overdue owing to the fall in prices.

Then, at last, they decided to strike. Notices were served on Jawaharlal and other leaders prohibiting them from speaking or writing in support of the campaign; and Anand Bhawan, along with many Congress offices, was searched. Jawaharlal's own arrest was delayed because he was away on tour in Bombay and the Karnatak. On his return to Allahabad Jawaharlal was served with a notice not to leave the city without official permission and the UP provincial conference, scheduled to be held on 26 December, was banned. Still, the Congress struggled to avoid battle and postponed the conference.[18] But Jawaharlal himself was arrested on 26 December for violating the order restricting him to Allahabad. He was taken off the train at Iradatnagar. station, on his way to Bombay to welcome Gandhi, and sentenced a week later to two years' imprisonment.

REFERENCES

1. See the Viceroy's record of interview with Gandhi, 19 March 1931, *Collected Works*, vol. 45 (Delhi, 1971), p. 315.

2. Speeches at Lucknow, 8 March, *The Leader*, 11 March 1931; Allahabad, 9 March, *The Leader*, 12 March 1931; Bombay, 15 March, *The Bombay Chronicle*, 16 March 1931.

3. Letter to Emerson, home secretary, 23 March 1931, *Collected Works*, vol. 45, pp. 334-5.

4. Emerson's report of his interview with Gandhi on 6 April 1931, home dept. pol. file, 33/XI, of 1931.

5. Crerar, home member, to Hailey, 6 May 1931, Hailey papers, vol. 20.

6. Manifesto, 23 May 1931.

7. Speeches at Rae Bareli, 25 June, *The Leader*, 3 July and Soram, 5 July, *The Pioneer*, 8 July 1931.

8. Jawaharlal's letters to Jagdish Prasad, 29 and 30 July and 1 August 1931, AICC file, G. 118 of 1931, and 31 July 1931, AICC file, G40(KW)(iii) of 1931; report of UP government for the second half of July 1931, home dept. pol., 18/7/31.

9. Patel to Emerson, 15 September 1931, home dept. pol., file 33/36 of 1931.

10. *The Leader*, 23 September 1931.

11. *Agrarian Distress in the United Provinces*, pp. 49-50.

12. Fortnightly report of UP government for the first half of October 1931, home dept. pol., 18/10/31.

13. Jawaharlal to E.C. Mieville. private secretary to Viceroy, 16 October 1931, and Emerson to Jagdish Prasad, 21 October 1931, home dept. pol., 33/36 of 1931; Jawaharlal's cable to Gandhi, 16 October 1931, and Gandhi's reply, 19 October 1931.
14. T.A.K. Sherwani to chief secretary, 3 November 1931, home dept. pol., file 33/36 of 1931.
15. *The Bombay Chronicle,* 7 December 1931.
16. Fortnightly report of UP government for the first half of December 1931, home dept. pol., 18/12/31.
17. UP government's telegram, and reply of Government of India, 7 December 1931, home dept. pol., file 33/36 of 1931.
18. *The Leader,* 25 December 1931.

12

In and Out of Prison

Clearly this was going to be a long spell in jail for Jawaharlal and now, for the first time, prison life began to tell on him. He had trouble with his teeth, and his general condition was poor. His living conditions too were, at the start, such as made for relative discomfort. He was first placed in Naini jail, and then, after a few weeks, transferred to Bareilly where both environment and man were vile. His barracks were at least six feet below ground level, which meant that the surrounding walls were over twenty-four feet. Further, for the first time since Nabha, not only the ward but the barracks also were locked at night. The fortnightly interview with his family was spoilt by the close supervision of not only the jailor, but of a policeman who took notes. His companions also, with the exception of Govind Ballabh Pant, irritated him. So generally Jawaharlal fretted.

This malaise was worsened by other events. In April his mother was beaten in a lathi-charge and badly injured. Then, because, at an interview in jail with Ranjit Pandit, Indira had shown him a school report of his children, the jailor insulted Jawaharlal's mother and wife who were also present, and the government ordered that they could not interview Jawaharlal for a month. This roused Jawaharlal to bitter anger, and he declined to have any interviews even after the month was over; for on no account, as he put it, was he prepared to take the slightest risk of further insult to his mother and wife.[1] It was not till early in 1933, after a break of eight months, that he began, on Gandhi's persuasion, to see visitors again.

In June 1932 Jawaharlal was transferred to Dehra Dun jail. Here the climate was pleasant and the jail buildings not severe. The superintendent, an Irishman whose name deserves to be remembered, Captain Falvey, had been a pupil of de Valera, and he did what he could to alleviate conditions. Jawaharlal was even permitted to take his walks outside the prison gates. But all this could not diminish the inner turmoil. Indeed, on hearing of the savage treatment of political prisoners in other jails in the United Provinces, Jawaharlal felt ashamed of the better conditions of his own prison life, and he invited the government to give him the same treatment as the others.[2]

Jawaharlal was concerned, too, about his wife and mother roughing it out on their own and his two sisters languishing in jail; but it was the thought of his growing daughter that frequently came strongly to him and filled his mind. It was because letters to her brought her image close to him that he continued writing his neat little essays, taking her stage by stage through the human past, even though they could not be sent to her and had to be kept aside for a later date.

Jawaharlal was no professional scholar writing within a clearly defined and balanced framework. Taking, as he described it, centuries at a stride and seeing continents at a glance, he rushed past what he found dull and lingered at points where his interest was aroused. He was, for instance, fascinated by the great men of history—and not necessarily the men of virtue and idealism.

In the preface, written on 1 January 1934, he commented that 'even as I was writing the letters my outlook on life changed gradually. Today if I had to rewrite them, I would write differently or with a different emphasis.' But in fact he retained all his life the half-liberal, half-Marxist view of history which holds the book together. The story of man was one connected whole, and the only history that could be properly written was the history of the world. It was the product not of individuals or national peculiarities but of world forces, and developments in different countries told basically the same tale. History was not what was achieved by leaders or governments but what happened to peoples, and this was the result of the interplay of ideas, economic interests and social relations. Though he made no deep analysis, he broadly believed that the class which controlled the means of production was the class that ruled, and that the history of man was the history of class conflicts and social struggles. To grasp this was to secure the ability both to understand the past and to face the future with confidence and to be prepared for effective action.

The intellectual acceptance of history as the result of impersonal world forces for which no individual could be blamed or applauded led Jawaharlal to criticize the imperialist system rather than the British, and to strive to consider even issues pertaining to India impartially as a scientist examining facts. He was a sensitive Asian nationalist, but he was wary of nationalism as 'an unreliable friend and an unsafe historian', and dwelt on the shortcomings of his own people as much as those of their rulers.[3] He had, since his return from Europe in 1927, shown an acute distaste for institutional worship. He continued to admire the great Hindu scriptures. The Bhagavad Gita was 'that jewel of a poem'; and as for the Ramayana and the Mahabharata—'Who but the greatest of men could have written them?'[4] But they impressed him more as literature and historical testimony than as revelation. He disliked temple-going, was scornful of ritual and regarded prayers as morbid. But, writing in the early thirties when the memory of the Kanpur riots—in which his friend Ganesh Shankar Vidyarthi had lost his life—was still fresh, he was particularly concerned with the savagery committed in the name of religion. It was important to release India from the chains of the complex ideology of custom, convention and superstition. He was at pains to tell his fellow countrymen that Islam did not believe in religious persecution and a man like Mahmud of Ghazni, whom most Indians regarded as an archiconoclast, was in fact no more than a successful soldier. He had come to India to conquer and loot, and would have done so whatever religion he had belonged to. The best of Indian culture was a synthesis;

this had badly frayed and should be rebuilt on the securer foundations of freedom and social equality and in consonance with a better world order.

When Jawaharlal was too tired to write, there were always books. Fortunately there was no restriction this time on the number he could read and keep, and he was also allowed newspapers and journals without restriction. So Jawaharlal settled down to jail routine and was irritated by talk of the release of all political prisoners. He even turned roundly on a fellow prisoner who talked of parole for medical treatment. Gandhi's fast in 1932 in protest against the communal award treating the scheduled castes as a separate community for purposes of elections was a sharp shock. The thought that Gandhi might die, and for such a minor reason, and that the only remaining protective force in his life might be removed, knocked Jawaharlal for a time off balance. He wept, with mixed anguish of anger and love for a man who could precipitate such a crisis so wantonly, and with bitterness towards a people who could let their heroes risk death in such a way. Gandhi, amid his own travail, sensed this reaction and sent Jawaharlal a reassuring telegram, which helped, along with the news of the fast having been broken, to restore Jawaharlal's stability. However, the whole episode drove him further on his inner resources.

The next year, Gandhi undertook a purificatory fast and again plunged Jawaharlal, along with millions of his countrymen, into an emotional crisis. Gandhi realized this from afar, and wrote a chatty letter which was meant to soothe. The two telegrams Jawaharlal sent in reply indicate his bewilderment and dread of personal loss. 'What', wired Jawaharlal in his first mood of petulance, 'can I say about matters I do not understand. I feel lost in strange country where you are only familiar landmark and I try to grope my way in dark but I stumble. Whatever happens my love and thoughts will be with you.' But as the hours passed, he felt that he owed Gandhi a more cheerful message, and that evening he wired again : 'Now that you are launched on your great enterprise may I send you again love and greetings and assure you that I feel more clearly now that whatever happens it is well and whatever happens you win.[5]

At the commencement of the fast the government released Gandhi, who suspended civil disobedience for six weeks. This was a blow to Jawaharlal, but his mind, still numbed by the fear of Gandhi's death, accepted it. However, once the ordeal was over, Jawaharlal was able to see Gandhi with a much clearer vision than at any time before or since. For a short while the blinkers fell. He realized that Gandhi's attitude was sheer revivalism against which cool thinking had no chance. Gandhi's political actions were often guided by an unerring instinct, and, fortified by this, he did not encourage others to think. He himself, as he frequently asserted with pride, was satisfied with the next step and had given no precise thought to the long-term objective. The emphasis on God and faith, the acceptance of the existing social order, the stress on compromise, the reliance on lieutenants who were proclaimed reactionaries—all these jarred on Jawaharlal, and his love for Gandhi could not conceal from him that he was drifting further and further away from his leader. Obviously, a stiff battle between rival loyalties awaited him outside, and, not relishing this prospect, he did not look forward to his release. But coincidentally, just as he had finished the last of his letters to his daughter, he was transferred to Naini jail and, a week later, on 30 August, twelve days before he was due to be out of prison, he was released.

Jawaharlal's comment, on emerging from jail, that he attached little importance to the swadeshi and Harijan movements, the reports of his talks with his colleagues in the UP and his statements to the press that India's primary problem was economic and a new structure of society was inevitable, raised expectations that he would formally break away from Gandhi and the old Congress and form a new party with independence as its goal.[6] There was certainly little in common between the public attitudes of Jawaharlal and of Gandhi. The younger man, while in jail, had made a wide study of international affairs, and saw India as a part of the pattern of world forces. There was, as Jawaharlal saw it, an inevitable, universal swing, not necessarily to the Soviet model but towards the general lines of the Soviet conception. Fundamentally the choice before the world was between some form of communism and some form of fascism, and he was all for the former.

In India, the effort of the British to protect not merely their own vested interests but also those of their allies, the zamindars, the princes and the capitalists, had not to Jawaharlal a chance of success because it went against the broad economic forces determining the future of the world. But nationalists, on their part, could not possibly hope to confine themselves to a replacement of foreign by home interests and seek to avoid the disturbance of class divisions and the social status quo. A socialist state was a concomitant of independence, and, if an Indian government took the place of the British and kept all the vested interests intact, this would not even be the shadow of freedom. The Congress, as the spearhead of the Indian nationalist movement, needed a new ideology which was oriented to economic priorities and world conditions. There had to be a fundamental change of regime, politically, economically and socially, and the three were inextricably linked. British imperial rule had to be destroyed, the autocracy of the Indian states had to be ended, the whole land system had to be changed, industry brought under public control and all wealth shared. Each was a part of a total problem.

These ideas were all far removed from the outlook of Gandhi, who was seeking to renew peace negotiations with the British and to convert his countrymen, through fasts, to better social behaviour. His were the politics of intuition, requiring no argument or logic; Jawaharlal followed the path of reason, applying the laws of history and change. The break seemed inevitable, and as Jawaharlal went to Poona to confront his leader, also just released from prison, even he probably prepared himself for it. But he could not forget that, intermeshed as was the crisis, the most important front was the political one; and till the British had been expelled there could be little advance towards socialism. To combat economic wretchedness with the state power obstructing them was a hopeless waste of energy. But in this political struggle Gandhi's leadership, however wayward, still seemed indispensable; and Congress was still the most militant organization in India. So both leader and party were necessary to him, and it was not just the springs of personal loyalty and affection which proved once again too deep to permit release. Jawaharlal, face to face with Gandhi after two years, publicly affirmed his continuing acceptance of Gandhi's leadership, and letters were exchanged in which Jawaharlal stated his position in terms which were easy for Gandhi to approve.

Once he had decided not to break with Gandhi and the Congress, it was out of character for Jawaharlal to lead a rebellion from within. However sharp his expression of disagreement in private conversation, to the outside world he was determined to accept Congress policy and decisions and interpret them in as favourable a manner as possible.[7] It was idle to expect the Congress as constituted to become a full-fledged socialist organization, but there was every hope of it becoming more and more socialistic. A time might come, sooner rather than later, when the new ideas might cause a split in the Congress; but till then advantage should be taken of the national movement and it should be pushed as far as it could go. The Congress should be led out of the backwaters of pure politics by socialist elements who, rather than forming independent and sterile study centres, could exploit the Congress programme of mass action.

Jawaharlal expected to return soon to prison, but, while he was out, he sought to keep up the struggle, even if at a lower pitch, for the only alternative was a compromise with imperialism, and this was unacceptable not only to him personally but manifestly to the Indian people. Travelling round the country, Jawaharlal was convinced that never, at any rate since 1857, had there been such extraordinary bitterness against the government and such a passionate desire to be rid of it. So he refused to be distracted by such sideshows as village uplift and the Harijan movement. The national fight had to continue, and it would be strengthened by making it a social and economic fight for the masses and purging it of Hindu and Muslim communalism.

Jawaharlal had till now deliberately ignored the growth of the communal evil in Indian politics in the hope that public attention could be diverted from it by emphasis on the positive aspects of the national struggle. Hunger, poverty and exploitation had nothing to do with religion. But the time now appeared to have come for a frontal attack on communalism as a cover for political reaction.[8] In language which even Gandhi regarded as too fierce,[9] he condemned the Hindu Mahasabha for its reactionary and anti-national policy of co-operation with the government and support of vested interests.[10] The Hindu communalists wanted no basic change of the political and economic structure, and sought official favours to augment their own position. This criticism applied equally, of course, to Muslim communal organizations, and Jawaharlal recognized that they were as anti-national and reactionary in every sense of the word.[11] But he rebuked them in milder terms. Fear was justified, or at least understandable, in a minority community which was economically and educationally backward; and communalism born of fear had to be exorcized and not just brushed aside : 'Honest communalism is fear; false communalism is political reaction.' He always, like Gandhi, took the line that it was for the Hindus, as the majority community, to make concessions while the communal problem lasted. This in itself, despite the call to magnanimity, assumes a communal approach, however subconscious. The argument is based on the belief that the majority community is a privileged one, and the minority community has reason to be communal. It was true that Jawaharlal had not carefully probed this issue, and was irritated by the Mahasabha's criticisms of Gandhi and the Congress and its open wooing of the government. But even so, the implication that there was something to choose between

Hindu and Muslim communalism was dangerous in its possibilities.

However, all these public activities were not to be for long. All local governments were authorized by the Government of India to arrest him if opportunity arose, not on some minor issue but on a serious charge which would involve a substantial sentence.[12] What worried the government now was not so much Jawaharlal's efforts in the rural areas as the impact of his writings and speeches on the lower middle classes. These were in grave economic distress and might well respond to his call for a new revolutionary ideology. Ultimately, it was the Bengal government which agreed to bell the cat. On his visit to Calcutta in January, Jawaharlal had in forthright terms condemned the vulgarity of imperialism and stressed that there was no half-way house between nationalism and imperialism. He had also sharply rebuked the terrorists for adopting a futile and out-of-date policy. But the government had no use for such an ally against terrorism. Jawaharlal was arrested at Allahabad on 12 February and brought down to Calcutta, tried for sedition and sentenced on 16 February to two years' simple imprisonment.

Back for a 'rest cure' in his 'other home', this time the central jail at Alipore in Calcutta, Jawaharlal reverted to the routine of prison life and adjusted himself to living in a small cell and bare barrack yard, with a clerk sentenced for embezzlement as his only companion.[13] The Bengal authorities did not encourage reading and writing, and for some time, after he had exhausted the novels in the prison library, the only book Jawaharlal had was a German grammar. This was later set right. But he never settled down in Alipore and was relieved when, early in May, he was transferred to the familiar barrack in Dehra Dun jail.

Throughout these months the news from outside was depressing. The ill health of his mother and wife was a constant source of worry; and political news was no more cheerful. Gandhi's statement in April withdrawing civil disobedience was a heavy blow. An undated, incomplete note obviously written at this time indicates that Jawaharlal was being driven once more to the recognition that he had come to a parting of the ways. There was hardly any common ground between himself and Gandhi, and he had been wrong in subordinating their differences in a larger loyalty to the cause of national freedom : 'Our objectives are different, our ideals are different, our spiritual outlook is different and our methods are likely to be different.' The Congress was now aggressively anti-socialist and, in its acceptance of constitutionalism, politically more backward than it had been even in the heyday of the Swarajist party. Gandhi's statement withdrawing civil disobedience, the reasons given and the general outlook displayed 'seemed to me to be an insult to the nation, to the Congress and to any person with a grain of intelligence. I felt with a stab of pain that the cords of allegiance that had bound me to him for many years had snapped.' The concentration on non-political issues and the personal and self-created entanglements which led Gandhi to desert his comrades in the middle of the struggle were amazingly casual and likely to be fatal to the movement.

In August, when Kamala's condition took a turn for the worse, the UP government let Jawaharlal out of prison, and he took this opportunity to pour out his heart to Gandhi. Apart from this private letter, which Gandhi did not take seriously,[14] Jawaharlal responded to the government's gesture and took care to keep away from political activity. The proclaimed socialists in the Congress, who in May, as a counterblast to the milk-and-water programmes of the parent body, had formed the Congress Socialist party, had not concealed that they sought and drew inspiration from him. They believed that they were echoing his ideas in hailing the Congress as potentially the greatest revolutionary force in the country and seeking to combine the national struggle with socialism.[15] The decision to keep the Socialist party within the Congress was also modelled on Jawaharlal's precedent of the Independence for India League. Yet Jawaharlal refused, while out of prison, to give them any encouragement.[16] He considered the step premature and likely to divert attention from the immediate issue of political independence. The socialists had no support among the people, and it was more important to push the Congress as a whole, however slowly, towards acceptance of economic objectives than to nurture the doctrinaire views of a handful of individuals. Jawaharlal had a radical rather than an ideological mind. The precedent of the Independence for India League was not a happy one. It can be argued that Jawaharlal was giving up too easily, that while he had a socialist vision derived from Europe he lacked the stamina to formulate specific programmes suited to India and promote the strenuous work of forming cadres and establishing an organization—in other words that he lacked a 'revolutionary perspective.'[17] Such criticism is balanced by the fact that, however disappointed with Gandhi and the Congress, Jawaharlal was still certain of their indispensability in the struggle to expel the British; nor could he regard the motley crowd of Marxists, Fabians, Gandhians and orthodox Hindus who led the Congress Socialist party with anything but 'amused contempt.'[18]

After eleven days, when his wife's health slightly improved, Jawaharlal was taken back to prison. But this time he was lodged in Naini jail, and allowed out once or twice a week to see Kamala. Then, in October, when she was moved to a sanatorium at Bhowali, Jawaharlal was transferred to the nearby jail at Almora.

The illness of his wife pushed all else to the background. Over the years their relationship had matured from indifference to a deep attachment. Often in jail his mind wandered to her, and he sat waiting for her letters and looking forward to her interviews. 'Felt greatly cheered', runs a characteristic diary entry, 'at seeing her. I am much too fond of her!'[19] Now, with her at death's door, he became a bundle of nerves, and, more to take his mind off the crisis than anything else, he set to work feverishly drafting the work which was to be his greatest literary achievement. He began in June 1934 the writing of his life story and finished it on 14

February 1935. So a massive manuscript of 976 pages was dashed off in less than nine months.

The treatment at Bhowali did Kamala little good and it was decided that she should go to Europe. For the first time, Jawaharlal had to worry about money. He had an annual income, derived from book royalties and such shares as were still left to him, of about nine thousand rupees, and with this he had to run a large establishment at Anand Bhawan, pay heavy medical bills and arrange for the passages by sea and the stay in Europe.[20] It was probably at this time that a member of the Birla family, the wealthy financiers hearing of his difficulties, offered to pay him a fairly substantial monthly allowance, such as they provided to many leading Congressmen; but Jawaharlal expressed his surprise at the suggestion and sharply declined the offer.[21] He mustered such savings as he had and made the arrangements, and Kamla sailed, with Indira and a doctor in attendance, in May.

REFERENCES

1. To the superintendent, district jail, Dehra Dun, 11 July 1932.
2. Letter to the superintendent, district jail, Dehra Dun, 16 November 1932.
3. Letter, 14 December 1932, *Glimpses,* p. 457.
4. *Letters from a Father to his Daughter* (1972 edn.), p. 80.
5. Telegrams, 8 May 1933.
6. Statement at Kanpur, 1 September, *The Leader,* 3 September 1933; interview in the *Pioneer,* 1 September 1933; statement to the press, 4 September, *The Leader,* 6 September 1933; report of Banaras correspondent, 11 September, *The Leader,* 13 September 1933.
7. See, for example, letter to Kapil Deva Malaviya, 10 September 1933.
8. Interview in *The Leader,* 21 November 1933; to S.A. Brelvi, 3 December 1933.
9. To Jawaharlal, 27 November 1933.

10. Speech at Banaras, 13 November, *The Hindu*, 14 November 1933; statement at Allahabad, 22 November, *The Tribune*, 24 November 1933.

11. Interview in the *Pioneer*, 18 November 1933.

12. Home secretary to all local governments, 26 September 1933, reprinted in *The Civil Disobedience Movement 1930-1934* (Govt. of India confidential publication, 1936), pp. 88-9.

13. See telegrams to Gandhi and to his daughter, 13 February 1934.

14. 'Jawaharlal's explosion is not so dangerous as it sounds. He only exercised his right to let off steam. I believe he is now quiet.' Gandhi to Patel, 19 August 1934, quoted in K. Dwarkadas, *India's Fight for Freedom* (Bombay, 1966). p. 444.

15. Acharya Narendra Deva's presidential address at the first session of the Socialist party conference, reprinted in *Socialism and the National Revolution* (Bombay, 1946), pp. 5-29.

16. To Sampurnanand, 22 August 1934, Sampurnanand papers, National Archives of India.

17. Subhas Bose, *The Indian Struggle* (Calcutta, 1964), p. 336.

18. Sampurnanand, *Memories and Reflections* (Bombay, 1962), p. 72

19. 9 April 1934.

20. See note on income and expenditure, 14 May 1935.

21. Letter to U.N. Dhebar, 7 June 1957, Nehru papers.

13

Death of Kamla Nehru

On 2 September the doctor cabled Jawaharlal as well as the government that Kamala's condition was critical, and his sentence was suspended to enable him to proceed at once to her bedside. 'So this is the end', he wrote in his diary; but even at this moment his dignity did not fail him. He asked for clarifications, and was told that his movements would be unrestricted in India till his departure as well as in Europe, but if he returned before his sentence expired in February 1936 he would be imprisoned again.[1] He was also requested not to make any political speeches before departure. On these terms, which did not infringe his honour, Jawaharlal left Almora for Allahabad and took the first available flight to Europe.

Kamala was in a clinic in Badenweiler in the Black Forest in Germany, and Jawaharlal found her condition changed very much for the worse. In addition to the physical ravages of her illness, she was also giving way to the psychological strain. She was anxious to get back to Switzerland and Jawaharlal therefore moved her early in 1936 to a clinic in Lausanne. Her condition fluctuated daily, and Jawaharlal clutched at momentary glimmers of recovery. But there was really no hope, and at 5 a.m. on 28 February she died.

Kamala's short life—she was not thirty-seven when she died—was overcast with acute pain and suffering. Born in a social milieu much humbler than that of the Nehrus, she was faced from the start with the resistance of some of her husband's family, who treated her as an intruder from the outside world into their exclusive relations with Jawaharlal. Nor, in these early years of tension and repression, were Kamala's relations with Jawaharlal cloudless. Different in temperament and upbringing, deliberate adjustment was required from both sides and a special effort from Kamala to raise her personality to his level, if their marriage was to succeed. But from the start she was dogged with sickness. Their daughter, Indira, was born in November 1917; but thereafter her health slowly slid downhill. Tuberculosis was first diagnosed in 1919 and, despite varied treatment and a long stay in Europe, took firm root. In 1925 a son was born prematurely and died after two days; and three years later she suffered a miscarriage.

Added to this were the strains of national politics, with the family often scattered, Jawaharlal for long stretches in prison and the House frequently searched and property attached. Yet, despite all these stresses and disadvantages, Kamala's life was, in its own way, one of happiness and achievement. Never a simpering consort, she slowly rose above her surroundings and grew in mind and character till she could derive joy and companionship from her married life. The moody self-pity and death-wish, induced by being bedridden for months at a time, were shaken off. Illness was no longer stagnation but an impetus to energy. That she had not received a regular education was a handicap she felt sorely : This disadvantage too she surmounted in her own life; but the education of women became to her a part of the struggle for freedom.

It was more than mere faith in God and works of charity in the Ramkrishna Mission and similar institutions which gave her strength and scope for service. Social action of a more exciting kind called her, and she trained herself not only to endure the separations from Jawaharlal but to participate in the struggle. Though ill, her courage never failed. One of Jawaharlal's keenest experiences of satisfaction was when she was arrested in 1931 and went to jail with a statement which was an unconscious blend of self-confidence and commitment to him. Gradually, as time passed, their relationship had matured. His early lack of serious interest was replaced first by a light-hearted, protective loyalty and then by a commitment which was stronger than passion and warmer than consideration. In Sri Lanka in 1931 they had discovered each other again, and realized that their marriage had neither broken nor tarnished. Stricken by his past neglect, he allowed Kamala to move slowly from the fringes towards the centre of his life, till, by the end, as even the unimaginative police department recognized, he was a 'devoted husband'.[2] Many women, drawn by his charm or driven by snobbery, made claims on him and, especially after Kamala's death, sought to thrust themselves into his life; and he did not always firmly resist their gross ardours. Yet, despite occasional dalliances, Kamala was the only woman who ever meant anything to him; and he kept her image unsullied.

The publication of Jawaharlal's *Autobiography* in the spring of 1936, only a few weeks after the death of Kamala, gave the world an inkling of his nature and enabled it to share his sorrow. All the reviews in Britain, including those in Conservative journals, immediately recognized the book's importance and quality. The life, the man, the witness, all seem to have imposed a paralysing humility on the critics. It was an essential document of the period, a key to the ideas and politics of a whole new world. Here was a man who spoke and thought in the language of modernity and reason, whom, unlike Gandhi, the West could understand, a man like themselves who happened to find himself on the other side. His individual vision was of general interest and universal value. In this, the first important first-hand account of the modern phase of Asian nationalism, Jawaharlal showed that in India it was a civilized, responsible movement that owed as much to the principles of European revolution and the liberalism and nonconformity of Britain as to the Indian context. So the *Autobiography,* despite being a long and serious book, became a best-seller and within, weeks ran into many editions.

The book was characteristic of Jawaharlal. It was honest and introspective. Standing almost outside himself he commented frankly on the society and age in which he lived, on the people he had known and on his own mental development. The book is not a wooden narrative of events; nor is it, like Gandhi's autobiography, a part of confessional literature. Jawaharlal was too undemonstrative, too repelled by any trace of exhibitionism, to interest the world primarily in himself. Indeed the *Autobiography* is in one sense a *tour de force* in that, after over 600 close-knit pages, his privacy remains unbroken. If a portrait of a personality, wistful, complex and of indrawn tension, caught in its own integrity, is gradually built up, it is almost as a by-product. But what Jawaharlal did set out to tell was of the Indian condition and of British rule, which hurt both his feelings and his intelligence by forcing the large majority of his countrymen to live in sordid and brutal circumstances. The reader found himself in the presence of great moral and historical issues as seen through the eyes of a refined and humane man.

What further helped to gain a wide audience for the *Autobiography* was its prose style. It was a clear, fluent book, written with terse, nervous elegance and control of phrase, and with a wide knowledge of English writing, old and new. It showed a mind of intellectual and moral quality, free of cliche emotions, but attractively replete with half-tones, subtleties and diffidences. In later years, Jawaharlal often spoke of the *Autobiography* as having 'dated'. It has, of course, 'dated' in the sense that it deals with a period that is dead. But the book has not lost its freshness as a piece of craftsmanship and as the expression of a sensitive human being.

Moreover, Jawaharlal wrote with detachment. There was self-scrutiny and self-criticism but no self-pity. The hardships he had opted for were taken for granted. The attempt was not at self-justification but at justification to himself. Estranged from his own people by being soaked in the exploiter's culture, he was a mixed-up being, yearning for roots and struggling to work out his own destiny. Tortured by doubt, impressive in his indecision, agonizing over all sides of every question, always asking to what end was the long, wearying struggle, he provided a picture of warm and vulnerable humanity. Jawaharlal made no claim to be exceptional; rather, he was a natural disciple with a taste for heroes. He clung to those who would determine his intellectual uncertainties. Motilal and Gandhi are the chief characters in the book, and he recognized how much he owed to them and depended on them, even while he was clear-sighted, especially about Gandhi's limitations. The bond of mutual confidence between him and Gandhi was also seen as an iron corset, supporting but confining. He confessed to his repeated display of weakness at critical moments, to his frequent surrender of judgement to personal loyalties, to his dedication to purpose and principle rather than to doctrine and definition.

Jawaharlal was not strong in analytic thought and the book provides no profound ideas or philosophy. Such ideas as he had were intellectual impulses rather than logical constructions. Even his Marxism was vague and confused, for his ideology was to a large extent based more on sympathy than on conviction. But he bore witness to a passionate commitment to nationalism, though in no narrow sense, to an awareness of world forces, and to a total personal integrity. Born to wealth and an easy life, he had been forced by the situation into the world outside. A heterogeneous character with great inner resources and of infinite mood, aware of natural beauty and in love with mountains, capable of responding to every side of life, yet he had preferred to spend years in prison. Fastidious and lonely by instinct, he had taken to politics and become indifferent to all else because he cared about the human scene and was disturbed by the ugliness and stupidity of the world. The deep personal affections he could give he had almost stifled. His sense of the essential pushed private life to the background, and led to a conscious withholding of emotion. Out of the pages of the *Autobiography* rises, almost it would seem against Jawaharlal's will, the story of the slow development of what was by the end a happy marriage; and its tragic close was revealed in the six brief words of the dedication, 'To Kamala, who is no more'.

The whole book was written in jail at a time when writing was at once a discipline, an indulgence and a solace. But there is no bitterness against the British. Jawaharlal's quarrel was not with the foreign ruler but with systems—with imperialism, with capitalism, with the social evils of religion. Such bitterness and contemptuous wit as he does disclose he reserves for some of his fellow Indians. The Liberals who, as he thought, concealed behind platitudes and compromises a low-minded opportunism, came in for sharp derision. But most Indian readers, drawn from the middle classes, were able to identify themselves with Jawaharlal in his expression of the hopes and obstacles of a whole generation.

After his wife's death Jawaharlal returned to India, resisting, on the way, the blandishments of Mussolini who sent a personal message of sympathy and sought to inveigle Jawaharlal into an interview while in transit at Rome airport. Jawaharlal sought to smother the inner emptiness in work. But the emotional strain was never far below the surface.

REFERENCES

1. Press statement, *The Bombay Chronicle*, 5 September 1935.
2. Note of H. Williamson, director, intelligence bureau, 27 September 1935, home dept. pol., 4/7/35.

14

Leading the Party

During Jawaharlal's absence in Europe he had been elected president of the Congress for 1936. The decision was, as usual, primarily that of Gandhi. The main issue before the Congress was whether they should contest the elections and accept office in the provinces under the new Government of India Act. Jawaharlal's views on the subject were well known. He regarded the Act as deliberately designed, to strengthen all the vested and reactionary elements in India, and acceptance of office under this Act would be a retrograde step which might well lead to the disintegration of the Congress and obstruction of a civil disobedience campaign at any early date. Gandhi too seems to have been of this view and therefore was keen that Jawaharlal should once again accept the responsibility.

In Europe, Jawaharlal's hostility to the Act and his radical tendencies had been strengthened. It so happened that at Lausanne Jawaharlal met by chance Ben Bradley, who was also a patient at the clinic, and Palme Dutt, who had come to see Bradley. Palme Dutt and Jawaharlal spent three days together, and the British Communist found the 'Professor', as Jawaharlal was known in Comintern circles, very receptive. He ageed that the Congress was, on the whole, moving towards the right, but was himself willing to work in close collaboration with the Communists. He hoped that some variation of the political and economic systems prevalent in Russia would extend to India, but he was not prepared to have this by coercive methods. Civil liberties were to Jawaharlal of absolute value, and the Communists had to reckon with this. Jawaharlal was not a Marxist in the normal sense of the word. He accepted the Marxist interpretation of history and its vision of a classless society, but he certainly did not believe in revolutionary dictatorship. Conditioned under Gandhi, he hated violence even if he did not in theory reject it, and stood for democratic and peaceful though not for constitutional means. But with these reservations, Jawaharlal, according to Palme Dutt, promised that he would, as president of the Congress, do all he could to promote the Communist party in India, and he even gave a series of specific undertakings is to what he would try to do.[1]

The Communists, of course, were now in a mood to co-operate with the Congress. By the summer of 1935 there had been a shift in Soviet and international Communist policy. The call was now for popular fronts. It was conceded that the Congress was the principal mass organization of diverse elements seeking national liberation in India: but it was not yet the united front of the Indian people. Workers' and peasants' unions and other such organizations should be brought into the joint struggle either in a united front or by collective affiliation to the Congress. The constitution of the Congress should be amended to permit such collective affiliation at the local, district, provincial and national levels, and joint bodies should be set up immediately. There should also be provision for greater initiative of the rank and file within the Congress in place of the hierarchical structure dominated by the working committee. The dogma of non-violence was a weakness which should be omitted from the Congress creed; but while a sharp ideological struggle should be conducted on this question, it was not so important that it should be allowed to split the national front. The elections should be fought jointly by the front in such a way as to provide sufficient representation for the left-wing elements and to enable the demands of the masses to be clearly expressed. The chief demand, the positive slogan of the front, would be for a constituent assembly freely elected by universal suffrage.

Now the Congress awaited Jawaharlal's guidance. Meeting Gandhi and senior Congressmen before the session at Lucknow, Jawaharlal found considerable support for office acceptance; and he was isolated in the working committee.[2] But embarrassment to him was avoided by shelving any firm decision on an issue which would only arise after the elections. Meantime, reflecting Jawaharlal's new ideas derived in Europe, the working committee agreed that it was desirable to develop closer association between the masses and the Congress organization so that they might take their full share in the shaping of Congress policy. It was also decided that the Congress constitution should be revised to make it a joint front of all anti-imperialist elements and enable closer co-operation with organizations of peasants and others.[3]

In his presidential address Jawaharlal, as was now to be expected of him, analysed the world situation and India's place in it. Two vast groups faced each other : decaying capitalism, imperialist and fascist on the one hand, and the progressive forces, socialist and nationalist, on the other. British imperialism in India also, though still powerful, was showing signs of decay and, in its desire to hold on, was developing an increasingly fascist mentality. But in the national movement itself there was a spirit of disunion, a malaise, a stress on petty, internal conflicts. Middle-class leadership was inevitable, but it easily tired if it did not draw strength and inspiration from the masses. The Congress should be not only for the masses but of the masses; only then would it really be for the masses. So Jawaharlal argued for the forming of new links which would permit the growth of mass consciousness within the Congress, and the revision of the party constitution for this purpose. The real problem was to join together all the anti-imperialist forces in the country, to forge a broad front comprising the mass elements as well as the great majority of the middle classes. There was no near prospect of direct action or civil disobedience, and the elections could be used to carry the message of the Congress to the people. To accept office under the Act which they had rejected was to stand self-condemned. The sole purpose of entering the provincial assemblies should be to create deadlocks so as to kill the proposals for federation and make the working of the Act impossible.

The speech, as a whole, mirrored the contradictions in Jawaharlal's outlook and the weaknesses of his political position. He affirmed his Marxist approach, his recognition of the Indian problem as a part of the world problem of capitalist imperialism. The only key to the solution of the world's problems, and of India's problems, lay in socialism, 'and when I use this word I do so not in a vague humanitarian way but in the scientific, economic sense'. But immediately, in the very next sentence, he moved away from the precise Marxist attitude : 'Socialism is, however, something even more than an economic doctrine; it is a philosophy of life and as such also it appeals to me.' The socialist approach in India would have to be adapted to the Indian conditions and speak in the language of the country. He was a libertarian Marxist, whose idea of socialism encompassed at every stage a large and irreducible measure of civil liberty. A belief in democracy was the core of his socialist attitude. He rejected any mechanical view of human nature and looked forward to a socialist society which, by removing economic and social inhibitions and obstacles, would provide greater scope for individuality. It was this understanding of socialism which underlay his presidential address; and immediately after the Congress session he established an Indian Civil Liberties Union on non-party lines, with members of all shades of political opinion and even from outside politics.

Powerful as the presidential address was as an attack on imperialism, the government felt that they would be unable to sustain a prosecution on it. In the months that followed, while Jawaharlal toured the country addressing scores of meetings and 'simultaneously carrying on war at various fronts',[4] the authorities, regarding him as 'a potential danger of the first magnitude',[5] followed him round with their notebooks seeking carefully but in vain for any statement that would justify his arrest and ensure a long sentence. Instead, they had to console themselves with the thought that his preaching of socialism was weakening the Congress and this would be reflected in the elections.[6]

Jawaharlal started what was virtually a country-wide election campaign in Bombay with a bang. The Congress was contesting the elections and entering the assemblies in order to combat the Act and render it unworkable. As to how this should be done, there was as yet no agreement; but he himself was convinced that acceptance of office would weaken their movement. The first and immediate issue was political, the development of a revolutionary mentality for the attainment of independence. He believed that socialism was inevitable for the solution of India's prime problem of poverty and degradation, but he had no wish to force the issue. If he talked about it now, it was solely to educate the people so that they would be in a better position to decide when the issue came up.

Such unhesitant exposition of his intellectual and emotional commitment to the socialist ideal naturally roused resentment. The more intelligent among the businessmen realized that to promote a public debate with Jawaharlal was to invite humiliation. It would be obviously far more effective to strengthen the opposition to Jawaharlal within the Congress. Patel, Rajendra Prasad and Rajagopalachari objected as strongly to Jawaharlal's speeches in Bombay as any of the capitalists, and appealed to the grand master, Gandhi, who called on Jawaharlal for an explanation.[7] They could not openly object to his crusade for socialism, but they criticized his underrating of khaddar and his suggestion that the responsibility for not including women in the working committee was not his. Jawaharlal replied that, though technically he was responsible for the decision, the committee as it took shape was not of his making, and Gandhi retorted that he was not satisfied with the answer.[8] Yet, on the main issue, Jawaharlal was unrepentant; and he toured the Punjab making the same points with equal vehemence.

The public response was enthusiastic. But when the working committee met in the first week of July, Jawaharlal was plainly rebuked by Gandhi and the others. Rajendra Prasad, on behalf of the right wing, wrote to Jawaharlal criticizing him severely, and the latter offered to resign and submit the dispute to the AICC for discussion. But Gandhi pulled him up for arrogance, intolerance and lack of a sense of humour. Jawaharlal meekly submitted. His speeches were thereafter all in a lower key. He now gave greater emphasis to the part which the Congress had played in involving the peasants in the national movement, and made claims for the party and its leader which he himself could not have seriously believed. The Congress was not, of course, socialistic, but it no longer ignored economic issues; and whenever a conflict of interests emerged it was always willing to sacrifice the interests which clashed with those of the masses. The socialist outlook, which the Congress had been stressing since Gandhi took it over, helped in the political struggle by clearing the issues and strengthening the role of the masses.

By now Jawaharlal was as indispensable to the Congress as the party was to him. He commanded, even before his election tours gave him a wide popular appeal, the support of large sections of radical youth who, but for him, would have left the Congress for left-wing parties. Even the Congress Socialist party might have broken away from the parent body. Throughout India there were men and women who, along with nationalist feeling, had developed a conscience on economic matters, who saw in Jawaharlal the spokesman of their viewpoint, and who, because of him, followed the lead of the Congress even if they did not belong to it. He was, too, the only Indian politician who had an international audience, and it was he who secured for the party recognition on the world stage. Had Jawaharlal, therefore, insisted in the summer of 1936 on resigning the presidency, it is difficult to believe that Gandhi and his followers would have been short-sighted enough to let him do so. But it was not just that it did not lie in Jawaharlal's nature to precipitate such a conflict and to safeguard his political chastity at the price of weakening the nationalist organization. The psychological hankering to follow Gandhi and the ingrained loyalty to the party were only part of the explanation. Jawaharlal knew that there was no working-class leadership or even an alternative elite leadership available; and so long as this was the case, it would be disastrous to weaken the Congress. And, as ever, his colleagues took advantage of this.

Jawaharlal now threw all his energies into the winning of the elections. This was the first of his national campaigns, covering the Indian village network by train, plane, car, bicycle, cart and steamer, on horse, elephant and camel, and on foot. Once he even ran for half a mile to reach a meeting-place, the crowd following him.[9] On another occasion the audience was so packed that he had to walk on their shoulders, and later felt ashamed for having done so with his shoes on.[10] But such actions had little effect on his popularity. His frequent losses of temper were short-lived and patently without malice. There was a degree of spontaneity and aggressive vitality in his behaviour which endeared him to the people.

Day after day the programme began at dawn and went on till late at night, and on one occasion without a break for twenty-four hours. Jawaharlal's speeches were impersonal, with little reference to individual candidates. He talked about the common problems of the Indian people—poverty, debt, foreign rule—made them think of India as a whole, explained the party manifesto, and promised nothing except unceasing struggle till freedom was won. He spoke in simple terms but treated his audience as mature. Many of them were little interested in all this, and camp merely to see for themselves the god-like figure of whom they had heard so much. Gandhi was one of them, but Jawaharlal was the glamorous prince.

It was obviously senseless to make a change in the Congress presidency in the middle of the campaign, and Jawaharlal was re-elected to preside over the Congress session at Faizpur in December 1936. He reiterated in his address what were by now familiar views—that the primary issue was political freedom, that socialism helped to analyse the situation and provided the only future solution to economic problems, and that the Indian struggle was but part of a titanic conflict which gripped the world. He felt the latter even more strongly than before, for the civil war in Spain, which had broken out since the Congress last met, was to Jawaharlal, as to so many intellectuals in the West, a matter of personal involvement. But, on the other hand, deep in the throes of electioneering, he tended to give less urgency to socialism. It was world peace and free democracy in India which were now the prime objectives.

Jawaharlal believed that there had been a change in Congress thinking since the Lucknow session. Then, acceptance of office was a certainty: now it seemed a very doubtful proposition. But, to his chagrin, immediately after the declaration of the results many Congressmen thought and spoke in terms of ministries. Such behaviour seemed to him not merely an abdication of purpose but so foolish and lacking in self-respect and political sense that he took hold of the debate in the UP and forced through a resolution in the provincial Congress committee against acceptance of office. Then, moving to Delhi for the crucial meetings of the working committee and the convention of legislators, he asserted that what the electors had said was in effect, 'To hell with this Constitution.'[11] Gandhi's own inclination was to support Jawaharlal, but he responded to the overwhelming mood of the party. The working committee described the results of the elections as a condemnation and rejection of the Act, impressed on all Congressmen that the fundamental policy of the party was to combat and seek to end the Act, and then, without a trace of logic or embarrassment, authorized acceptance of office if the leaders of the party in the assemblies were satisfied that while the ministries acted within the constitution the governors would not interfere.

Jawaharlal did not, it is needless to say, resign, but, with his firm sense of discipline, accepted defeat. While he had not changed his views he would, 'like a humble soldier', loyally abide by the resolution which had been adopted. The time might come when he would wish to resign, for no man could lead an army who did not know the way; but that time was not yet, and till then the Congress should 'hold together, push together, fight together and win together'.[12] It was theoretically feasible to accept office not in order to co-operate but to work for revolutionary change. However, Jawaharlal still thought it possible that the assurances sought from the governors would not be given, and, therefore, Congress ministries might not be formed.[13] But the working committee, overruling Jawaharlal, decided that even though no assurances had been given the Congress should accept office. The majority were so anxious for a quick decision that they were unwilling even to refer the matter to the AICC. As Jawaharlal ruefully commented, the question was being considered the wrong way—not what are the reasons for accepting office, but office must be taken and therefore reasons have to be found for it.[14]

REFERENCES

1. Palme Dutt's interview with the author, 20 November 1969.
2. To Syed Mahmud, 5 May 1936.
3. Resolutions to be placed before the Lucknow Congress, *The Bombay Chronicle,* 26 March and 8 April 1936.
4. To Ellen Wilkinson, 15 June, 1936.
5. Home secretary to all local govts, 19 August 1936, home dept. pol., file 4/15/36.
6. Home dept. pol., files 4/4, 4/6, 4/14, 4/15, 4/23, 4/32 and 4/34 to 4/38 of 1936.
7. See Vallabhbhai Patel to Rajendra Prasad, 29 May 1936, Maharashtra govt. records—intercepted letters.
8. Jawaharlal to Gandhi, 25 May and Gandhi to Jawaharlal, 29 May 1936.
9. *The Bombay Chronicle,* 26 January 1937.
10. Lal Bahadur Shastri's article in Zakaria, *A Study of Nehru,* pp. 150-1.
11. Speech at Delhi, *The Bombay Chronicle,* 15 March 1937.
12. Speeches at the convention of legislators, 19 March, *The Bombay Chronicle,* 20 March 1937.
13. Letter to K.T. Shah, 27 March 1937.
14. Proceedings of the working committee, 5 to 9 July 1937, AICC file 42 of 1936.

15

Out of Tune with the Congress

Again, Jawaharlal loyally accepted the decision. But such loyalty could not conceal that in his heart he hated it all. The Congress had moved away from almost everything that it had stood for in his eyes, and had become a responsivist, constitutional organization, avid for the minor loaves and fishes of office. So Jawaharlal virtually went into retreat. Though still the president of the party, he did not serve on the parliamentary board which sought to guide and co-ordinate the working of the ministries. He took no serious interest in the composition of the governments, not even that in his home state, the United Provinces. It is necessary to state this, because years later the charge was made by Maulana Azad that the leaders of the Muslim League in the UP had agreed to co-operate with the Congress in return for two seats in the cabinet, but Jawaharlal had whittled down the number to one and thereby destroyed the agreement reached by Azad.[1]

However, the facts are very different. When Jinnah took up again in 1936 the leadership of the Muslim League, he was still a nationalist who had no wish to support, or rely on, foreign rule. But Jinnah had no use for mass politics. His idea was to revert to the pre-Gandhian period and to form once more an alliance of elite politicians acting together as representatives of Hindus and Muslims to wrest concessions from the British. Yet Jinnah's tactics had never a chance of success. Certainly the Congress, which had mobilized the masses in a series of campaigns and established itself as a broad nationalist front, could not now be expected to agree that it was primarily a Hindu organization and would not seek to enlist the Muslim and other religious minorities in India. To Jawaharlal, in particular, critical of vested interests and emphasizing the basic problems of poverty and hunger from which the vast majority of the Indian people, whatever their religion, suffered, the religious elitism of Jinnah appeared medieval and obscurantist.

The election results had their own lessons for both Jawaharlal and Jinnah. While the Congress had done spectacularly well in the general constituencies, in the 482 seats reserved for Muslims it had put up only 58 candidates and won in 26. To Jawaharlal this suggested that the Congress had not done enough work among the Muslims, and that in the new 'mass contact' programme a special effort should be made to reach the Muslims. There was a widespread anti-imperialist spirit in the country and, apart from a microscopic handful at the top who were fearful of social changes, the Indian people as a whole were with the Congress. The party had therefore erred in not setting up more Muslim candidates. The elections had gone some way to lay the ghost of communalism, and the Congress should follow this up by working among the Muslim intelligentsia and masses and rid India of communalism in every shape and form.

Jinnah's diagnosis was very similar, but the lesson he drew was the opposite. The Muslim League had made a mistake in not organizing itself better for the elections and contesting all the seats reserved for the Muslim electorate. The Congress was becoming increasingly a mass party and striking out in new directions. Were its approaches to the Muslim masses to prove effective, Jinnah and the League would be left high and dry. So, if the Congress were to take him seriously, it would be necessary to strengthen the communal feelings among the Muslims. The only possible answer to the Congress 'mass contact' programme was to make the Muslims submerge their economic interests in religious zeal. Then the Congress would be forced to deal with the League. The hold of Islam on the Muslim masses should be strengthened to provide the sanction for the demand of the Muslim upper and middle classes for jobs and security.

It is against this general background that developments in the UP fall into place. In the elections, the chief opponent of the Congress was not the Muslim League but the National Agriculturist party, an organization of landlords promoted by the government to challenge the influence which the Congress had gained over the tenants. So the Congress and the League reached an informal, unspoken understanding in this province, avoided a conflict as much as possible and made a joint effort to defeat the government and their puppets.

After the elections Jinnah was in favour of a coalition with the Congress. Now that the Congress was willing to accept office if it were satisfied on certain points, there seemed to him to be no substantial difference between the two parties. He was right to the extent that the Congress no longer even claimed to be a revolutionary organization and there was no difference on that score between it and the League. But the main hitch still remained, that any coalition with the League implied the Congress accepting a Hindu orientation and renouncing the right to speak for all Indians. This the Congress was not prepared to grant. When, towards the end of June, it became clear that the Congress would take office, Khaliquzzaman and Nawab Ismail Khan, the leaders of the League in the UP, again suggested a coalition. Khaliquzzaman seems to have gone even further and informed Azad that the League would accept any terms provided he and Ismail Khan were included in the ministry.[2] Jawaharlal was not enthusiastic, for a Congress ministry should undertake land reforms and he did not wish this to be precluded by any agreement with the League, which was influenced by zamindari interests. But Azad was attracted by the possibility of the League ceasing in the UP to exist as a separate group. He consulted Jawaharlal, Pant, Kripalani and Narendra Deva and it was decided to offer ministerships to Khaliquzzaman and Nawab Ismail Khan in return for acceptance of the Congress programme and the winding up of the Muslim League group and the UP parliamentary board. All Muslim League legislators should become full members of the Congress party and abide by its discipline; no Muslim League candidates should be set up in by-elections, and they should resign their offices or vacate their seats whenever the Congress decided to do so.[3] Jinnah rejected these terms.

This account makes clear that while Jawaharlal was never happy about these opportunist, unprincipled bargainings with the League which had now, in the UP, become a narrow upper-class organization, he had allowed Azad, Pant and Rafi Kidwai to do what they thought best. Certainly the discussions had not broken down on the question of one or two representatives of the League in the ministry, nor had Jawaharlal decided unilaterally that it should be one and not two. Whether, if the negotiations had succeeded, the country and the Congress would have benefited in the long run is debatable. Any agreement would in effect have accepted that politics were a matter of alliances between upper-class groups, betrayed all Muslims who thought in non-communal terms and abandoned the economic programme on which Jawaharlal had been laying so much stress. No such agreement could have endured, for the League had no long-term economic or social objectives. The only incentive where its leaders were concerned was the hope of office, and once this was fulfilled the cracks were bound to widen. Indeed, the negotiations were throughout hollow and unreal, for alongside the parleys of Azad and Khaliquzzaman a by-election was being fought in a Muslim constituency where the new strategy of Jinnah was finding full play. Both the Congress and the League set up candidates, converting it into a test election. Jawaharlal himself spent two full days in the constituency, speaking as usual of economic and national interests, while the League raised the cry of 'Islam in danger'. It was the beginning of a new phase of Indian politics, in which communal rancour was to spread and embitter all relations. For the first time in his career, Jawaharlal was the object of a hostile demonstration. On his way to a meeting in the constituency his car was pelted with stones.[4]

A few months after the formation of the first Congress ministries the party also took office in Assam and the North-West Frontier, and all these ministries functioned for over two years. The eight ministries had to their credit considerable achievements. But, on the whole, the record of the Congress ministries was, as Jawaharlal realized soon enough, static if not counter-revolutionary.[5] Jawaharlal's general attitude, to the great disappointment of the left wing, was to stand up loyally for the ministries in public and protect them from petty and petulant criticism : 'we cannot agitate against ourselves'.[6] But though he tried consistently to develop an atmosphere of friendliness towards the ministries, he made it clear to them privately how much he disapproved of their conformism.[7] The whole atmosphere in India was alien to him—the semi-loyalist activities of the ministries, the quarrels for jobs, the refusal to handle agrarian problems boldly, the suggestion that British troops might be necessary for the maintenance of internal security,[8] the justification by Congress members of the Central Assembly of the dispatch of Indian troops to China.[9] His main objection to federation as envisaged in the Act of 1935 was the inclusion of the feudal and autocratic elements in the Indian states, and he wished the Congress to support the popular movements in the states. But Gandhi himself objected to this and pulled up Jawaharlal in public permitting a resolution in the AICC criticizing the government in Mysore. Jawaharlal drafted a sharp rejoinder but refrained from publishing it. All this, however, jarred. So he virtually opted out of the day-to-day activities of domestic politics and was happier visiting the remote areas of Assam or the Frontier province, writing a long tract on the language problem or indulging in an anonymous attack on the latent dictatorial tendencies in himself.[10]

Jawaharlal was more at ease and fully integrated in dealing with developments outside India. The growing tension in the world sharpened his views. Fascism and imperialism were blood brothers and the freedom struggle in India was part of the general confrontation in the world. Freedom, like peace, was indivisible : 'The frontiers of our struggle lie not only in our own country but in Spain and China also.'[11] His own lot was cast in India, and he could work most effectively there; but he always thought in terms of the larger world issues, tried to fit India into them and taught his audiences to do the same. Such interest and commitment would also enable the Indian people to play a part, however small, in international affairs and give them a voice in the councils of the world.

With this deep involvement in world issues, it was natural for Jawaharlal to think of a trip abroad in the summer of 1938. His mother had died, after a long illness, in January 1938; and, with his daughter at Oxford, he had no strong domestic attachment to hold him to India. The national movement was in reverse gear and at Haripura Subhas Bose had taken over the Congress presidency. Jawaharlal was pressed hard to become the general secretary but refused. He had even wished to step out of the Working Committee. He had been prevailed upon not to do so, but his interest was elsewhere, and in June, gleefully turning his back on India, he sailed for what to him were the vital centres of activity in Europe.

His own attitudes to the European crisis were clear. He felt that the dictators would have to be halted in their aggression and a world war was inevitable; but, on no account would India help in such a war even against the fascist powers. The policy of appeasement was less of a surprise to him than to his friends abroad, for India saw more of the imperialist than of the democratic face of the British government. Though baffled and concerned, like any other left-wing sympathizer, by the trials in Russia, he declined to lend his name to an appeal for an inquiry.[12]

En route to Europe Jawaharlal met Nahas Pasha and the leaders of the Wafd party at Alexandria, and then, on landing in Italy, set off immediately on the pilgrimage to Spain as the guest of the Republican government. He spent five days at Barcelona on the eve of the Battle of the Ebro. He had his first experience of air raids, visited the front and was captivated by the charm and self-confidence of General Lister, Success, he thought, was bound to attend the armies of the Republic, created in the stress of war, with their informality, comradeship and dedication. They would triumph over the professionals and experts of the rebel troops, despite German and Italian support and superiority in heavy armaments and aircraft, if only the British and French governments did not deny the Republic food and munitions. An afternoon with the British and American battalions of the International Brigade filled him with longing to join them : 'something in me wanted to stay on this inhospitable looking hill-side which sheltered so much human courage, so much of what was worth while in life.'[13] Meetings with President Azana, Alvarez del Vayo, the foreign minister, and 'La Pasionaria' rounded off the trip.

In England this time Jawaharlal was, thanks to the *Autobiography* and the success of the Congress in the elections, an even better-known figure than before. He attributed the greater interest in him to the importance that attached to what India might do in a world crisis; she had a tremendous nuisance value.[14] But the fact was that he now commanded greater stature in the world. He was accepted as the true representative of the Indian people and he moved in the mainstream of world opinion. This time Jawaharlal, unlike on his previous visit to Britain, was willing to meet figures in the government. Apart from talks with Halifax and Zetland, he met Linlithgow, then on leave in England. The conversation was general and there was no detailed discussion of Indian politics.[15] But as Jawaharlal recorded later, he told Linlithgow then 'that I gave England at the outside ten years before India was independent. I was not so far out.'[16] All that the Viceroy could retort, as they parted, was that a wide gap separated them and they would look . at each other across it.[17]

From London Jawaharlal went to Paris to address an international conference on the bombing of civilian populations. The Nazi government made informal approaches to Jawaharlal in the hope of inducing him to visit Germany as their guest.[18] In fact, Jawaharlal spent two days in Munich but as a private tourist and declined to meet any Nazi officials. He then went on to Prague, met Dr. Ripka, the Communist leader Clementis and, accompanied by Werzel Jaksch of the German Social Democratic party, visited the border areas. All his sympathies were with the Czech government in their resistance to Hitler; and the encouragement given to him by the British government, with its own class sympathies and leaning towards fascism, nauseated Jawaharlal. He made it clear that when war came, as it was bound to, the Indian people would not allow the British government, whom they utterly distrusted, to take any decision for them. India would willingly throw her entire weight on the side of democracy and freedom; but Britain should first establish her *bona fides* by eliminating empire from India.[19] To add weight to his opinion, he urged the Working Committee to pass a resolution condemning Nazi attempts at aggression and stating emphatically that in event of war India could only be committed by a decision of her people.[20]

In September, at the height of the crisis, Jawaharlal was at Geneva and was caught up in the tension. Back in London he was fitted with a gas mask which he later presented to the Allahabad municipal museum, heard and was sickened by Neville Chamberlain's broadcast, and was present in the House of Commons to hear Chamberlain announce that he was flying the next day to meet Hitler and Mussolini at Munich. Jawaharlal shared the general relief that war had been postponed. But he had no illusions about the attitude of the British government, their anxiety to abandon Czechoslovakia and isolate Russia, their fear not of defeat but of victory, for that would have been a victory of real democracy. The weakness of England and France was their imperialism, and so the ending of imperialism was necessary even from the wider international viewpoint. Collective security could not function effectively so long as it had an imperialist base; and this made the freedom of India a vital factor in world politics.

Unable to secure in time a visa to visit Russia, which might have enabled him to fulfil an old desire to take the overland route via the Central Asian republics, Jawaharlal returned to India by the end of the year, and was drawn again into domestic politics. No one in Britain, even when discussing India, had referred to Hindu-Muslim relations or regarded them as of great importance. But in India they could not be ignored. The refusal of the Congress to form coalitions with the League seemed to Jinnah to be a betrayal born of arrogance, and since then his policy had been clear. Acceptance of office by the Congress made it an easy target. He attacked it as a Hindu fascist body which was out, with the assistance of a few Muslim 'traitors', to destroy the Muslim minority. When Jawaharlal and other Congress leaders asked him repeatedly to specify instances, Jinnah, now fast beginning to show the mastery of obstructive tactics and skill in avoidance which were to dominate Indian politics for the next ten years, steadily refused. The Congress was baffled. Jawaharlal was willing to go so far as to consider, in any scheme of provincial redistribution, the grant to important groups and minorities of territories within which they could feel that they had full opportunities of self-development, without which a creative life was hardly possible.[21] He disliked the term 'communal provinces' but his scheme contained the germ of territorial redistribution on the basis of religion. But to concede Jinnah's main demands, that the Congress should not approach the Muslim masses but should recognize the League as representative of Muslim opinion, was unthinkable. However, so long as the Congress was in office it could not ignore even uncorroborated allegations of partisanship. One way out of this dilemma was to approach the Muslim peasantry over the heads of the leaders of the League with a programme of economic change; but here Jawaharlal found that, with the Congress ministries not proceeding fast enough, the communal approach was successfully hampering efforts to draw the Muslim masses into the Congress. The other alternative was to take advantage of the League's decision to widen its base and precipitate a conflict between the reactionary outlook of its leaders and the needs of the Muslim masses. So Jawaharlal encouraged the holding of Muslim mass meetings demanding debt relief and abolition of the talukdari system in the interests of the Muslim kisans.[22] But these were long-term projects which hardly gathered any momentum in the context of extreme communal propaganda and violence.

Weakened by office and punched continuously by an enemy on whom it could get no hold, the Congress was now stricken by infighting at its highest level. Subhas Bose had, through long years of prison and exile, earned the succession to Jawaharlal as president of the Congress in 1938. When he announced early in 1939 that he would seek re-election, Gandhi encouraged the right wing of the Congress to set up its own candidate. But Bose won decisively and Gandhi acknowledged it to be his own defeat. Realizing that, despite Bose's electoral victory, the majority in the Congress still preferred Gandhi's leadership with its moderation, twelve leading supporters of Gandhi resigned from the Working Committee and then carried a resolution at the Congress session in Tripuri that Bose should nominate the new committee in consultation with Gandhi and accept his advice. Gandhi, however, declined to cooperate, with the result that Bose had to resign the presidency. Then followed, step by step, his ostracism, his setting up of a new party, and his lone path, away from the Congress, during the war.

In all this Jawaharlal's attitude was individualistic and unwelcome to both sides. He disapproved of the manner in which Bose was being hounded out after winning an election, but he could not bring himself to support Bose. So he declined to sign the letter of resignation of the twelve members of the Working Committee, but resigned on his own. Although some of his statements tended to be critical of Bose, at Tripuri he remained almost silent, tried in private discussions to patch up a compromise and urged Bose not to resign. When Bose insisted, Jawaharlal, while making clear his dislike of Bose's action, declined to serve in the reconstituted Working Committee till the outbreak of war changed the situation. Such ambivalence Bose could not understand and this, more than the direct offensive of Gandhi and the others which drove him out of the fold, he found most difficult to forgive.

To suggest that Jawaharlal had allowed Bose to be destroyed is, of course, to exaggerate absurdly. Bose had really destroyed himself. The logic of his attitude demanded his expulsion from the movement, and there was no way back. But Jawaharlal's seemingly erratic attitude certainly cries out for explanation. The quarrel between Bose and Gandhi was not, as Bose sought to make out, a straight fight between the Left and the Right. He had been tardy in condemning Germany, Italy and Japan, had in December 1938 met the German consul in Bombay,[23] had criticized Jawaharlal for supporting all lost causes such as China and Spain; and was not enthusiastic about welcoming Jewish refugees from Europe. In fact, Jawaharlal was right in suspecting a weakness in commitment to anything broader than nationalism; nor could one have confidence in Bose's judgement even in this narrow field.

Jawaharlal, therefore, could not be expected to side with Bose when battle was joined. With his image of the Congress as a broad anti-imperialist front, he had never been in favour of homogeneous committees in a sectarian sense; his idea of the Working Committee was of men with different views working together with mutual confidence. So he resented Bose's aspersions against his colleagues, but he also disliked the efforts to displace Bose, and in consequence refused to attach himself to either side.

In this cheerless atmosphere two developments gave Jawaharlal comfort. He was president for this year of the All-India States Peoples Conference, and he planned to co-ordinate the agitation in the various states and involve the rest of India as well. This should become the major issue in the struggle against the British, transcending the wrangles in the Congress and the controversy with the League, underlining the total unacceptability of federation as envisaged in the Act of 1935 and perhaps even leading to the resignation of the Congress ministries.[24] Though he was considerably hampered by Gandhi's very different approach of overtures to the rulers and acceptance of British arbitration, this was a field of action which Jawaharlal welcomed.

The second congenial task was national planning. The concept of a planned economy was, even in Europe in the late thirties, still vague and ambiguous. But it was felt that only in Soviet Russia was there national planning in the real sense, with the whole economy geared to the production of plenty for human welfare and not driven by the profit motive or intended for efficiency in war. In other words, planning was a part of socialism.[25] Jawaharlal agreed with this. He believed that India too had much to learn from the Soviet example. But to apply these lessons in a colonial economy and to consider planning in a country which was not yet free showed a bold and pioneering mind. This was the kind of work, long-term, adventurous and leading to socialism, which excited him. At a meeting of ministers of industry from the Congress provinces, it was decided to set up a National Planning Committee with Jawaharlal as its chairman. He took up the work with enthusiasm and constituted a committee with not only Congressmen but scientists, economists, businessmen and industrialists as well. A long questionnaire was drafted and widely distributed and nearly thirty sub-committees were constituted to make detailed recommendations on specific subjects.

Jawaharlal's own contribution, apart from holding the assorted crowd of planners together, was a clear statement of the general objectives of planning in India. To him planning was inevitably connected with a socialist economy within a democratic structure, but he had no wish to frighten away people by stressing the socialist aspect. The Congress had taken up planning because any vital national movement was bound to interest itself in all aspects of national life, but the Congress itself was not committed to socialism. So what Jawaharlal hoped to do was to lead his party and the Indian middle classes generally to socialism without their knowing it. Any attempt to dispense with the middle classes and bring about a premature conflict on class lines would lead to chaos and possibly to prolonged inability to build anything. He was, therefore, deliberately imprecise in formulating the aim of planning :

The ideal of the Congress is the establishment of a free

> and democratic state in India. Such a free democratic state involves an egalitarian society in which equal opportunities are provided for every member for self-expression and self-fulfilment, and an adequate minimum of a civilized standard of life is assured to each member so as to make the attainment of this equal opportunity a reality. This should be the background or foundation of our Plan.[26]

A year later he was more forthcoming and acknowledged that the overall objective was to socialize national life in all its many sectors.[27] Private enterprise was not ruled out but it would have to be strictly controlled and co-ordinated to the general plan. The emphasis placed by the Congress on cottage industries did not exclude large-scale industries and any plan should provide for and increasingly the Congress would realize the importance of the latter. He rejected the Gandhian viewpoint that machinery was evil in itself and resigned from the executive committee of the All-India Spinners Association.[28]

While planning, in its full dimension, should be for a free India, steps could be taken immediately to develop national resources, increase the national wealth between two and three times within ten years, raise the standards of the Indian people and prevent the creation of fresh vested interests. This emphasis on concrete short-term steps such as improved nutrition, more clothing and better housing for every Indian over the next ten years had the further advantage of bypassing the theoretical and ideological differences among the planners. The immediate national objective was stated to be self-sufficiency, planning for which might, apart from other benefits, help to weaken economic imperialism even before the British left India.

By the summer of 1940, despite the tremendous disadvantages of lack of a common viewpoint among the planners, paucity of statistics and other data, and no immediate likelihood of implementation, seventeen sub-committees had presented final or interim reports. These covered not only technical programmes of production but also wider issues of distribution, social justice and social welfare. The subcommittee to which Jawaharlal probably attached the most importance was that on the condition and rights of women. The second stage of planning had now been reached. A comprehensive report, based on the suggestions of the various sub-committees, was taking shape. The committee met daily for a fortnight in May 1940 and again in June, under Jawaharlal's presidency, and approved the general framework. Though there were various inconsistencies and frequent ambiguities of phrasing, the broad trend was in favour of state ownership or state control or a blend of the two.

However, political developments now took command. The Congress ministries, which had given the Planning Committee a purchase on the state, were gone. Jawaharlal himself was removed from the scene in October 1940 and the government refused to permit him to deal with matters concerning the Planning Committee while in jail. Jawaharlal's contribution to planning before 1947 has, therefore, to be considered a mere torso. Even so, it was path-breaking. The plethora of plans drawn up in various quarters during the war years and the setting up by the Government of India in rivalry of a department of planning with an industrialist from Bombay in charge all had their genesis in the work of the National Planning Committee. Jawaharlal had made India plan conscious.

REFERENCES

1. Maulana Azad, *India Wins Freedom* (Calcutta, 1967 edition), pp. 143-5.

2. Jawaharlal to Rajendra Prasad, 21 July 1937. In Khaliquzzaman's account of his meeting with Azad, he states that discussion centred only on two points : whether the League would resign office along with the Congress if at any time the Congress resigned (to which he agreed), and whether he would agree to another Muslim in place of Nawab Ismail Khan (which he refused). *Pathway to Pakistan*, p. 160.

3. Jawaharlal to Rajendra Prasad, 21 July 1937; Khaliquzzaman, p. 161.

4. *The Bombay Chronicle,* 14 July 1937.
5. To Govind Ballabh Pant, 25 November 1937, *A Bunch of Old Letters,* pp. 256-7.
6. Note on The AICC and Congress ministries, 4 November, *The Bombay Chronicle,* 11 November 1937.
7. See, for example, his letters to Rajagopalachari, 1 October and 4 November, to Subbarayan, 21 November, and to Pant, 25 November 1937.
8. See Jawaharlal's letter to Asaf Ali, 5 August 1937.
9. Statement to the press, 25 August 1937; Jawaharlal to Bhulabhai Desai, 12 September 1937.
10. 'The Rashtrapati', by Chanakya, *Modern Review,* November 1937.
11. Article in *National Herald,* 24 January 1939. This newspaper was started by Jawaharlal at Lucknow in the summer of 1938.
12. See letters to Krishna Menon, 22 May and 11 November 1937.
13. Article in the *National Herald,* 7 July 1939, reprinted in *China, Spain and the War* (Allahabad, 1940), p. 78.
14. Note to the Working Committee, 30 July 1938.
15. Glendevon, *The Viceroy at Bay* (London, 1971), p. 101; Jawaharlal's , note for the Working Committee, 30 July 1938.
16. Note written on 24 October 1955, Nehru papers.
17. Jawaharlal to J.B. Kripalani, 27 July 1938.
18. Message of German Consul in Bombay conveyed through Shankar Rao Deo, see Jawaharlal to Shankar Rao Deo, 26 May 1938; J.G. Stundnitz, German newspaper correspondent, to Jawaharlal, 25 June and 5 September 1938.
19. Letter to the *Manchester Guardian,* 8 September 1938.
20. To J.B. Kripalani, Secretary, AICC, 30 August 1938; note for Working Committee, 7 September 1938; cable to Kripalani, 26 September 1938.

21. See his draft concluding chapter written on 23 August 1937 for K.T. Shah's book *Federal Government*.

22. Jawaharlal's letter to Siddiq Ahmed Siddiqui, 8 September 1937.

23. I owe this information to Dr. M. Hauner who has found evidence in Nazi records.

24. Message to the 'States People', 3 February 1939; speech at Allahabad, 9 February, *The Bombay Chronicle,* 10 and 11 February 1939; presidential address at the All-India States Peoples Conference, 15 February 1939.

25. See G.D.H. Cole, *Practical Economics* (Pelican, May 1937).

26. Memorandum to National Planning Committee, 4 June 1939.

27. Note to National Planning Committee, 30 August 1940.

28. To Shankarlal Banker, 24 February 1940.

16

The War Crisis

When the war broke out, Jawaharlal was in China. He went to Kunming, Chungking and Chengtu but, before he could go to the north-west and meet Mao and the Communists, he had to cut short his visit and return hurriedly to India. On his return on 9 September, Jawaharlal found that Gandhi's immediate reaction to the war had been, apart from abhorrence at the triumph of violence, a spontaneous support of Britain. However, the Congress attitude to the war was formulated by Jawaharlal, and his approach was less emotional. It was for India to decide whether she would go to war. The Viceroy had now, without consulting representative opinion, taken that decision. But it was absurd for a subject India to fight for the freedom of Poland. If India were to participate enthusiastically in the war, she would have to be granted freedom. One had to be free and democratic to fight for freedom and democracy. If Britian fought for democracy, her first task was to eliminate empire from India. The Indian people would not bargain or seek to take advantage of Britain's difficulty; but whatever they did would have to be in accord with India's freedom and dignity.

The resolution of the Working Committee was on these lines. The war was clearly going to be a long one which in time would probably extend beyond Europe and involve the United States. So what was required of the Congress was to state the general attitude not only of the Indian nationalist movement but of all colonial peoples, and wait for the British government to clarify their cause by appropriate action. But the Viceroy had made up his mind that his present duty was neither to move even at snail's pace along the path of constitutional progress nor to seek ways of harnessing India's enthusiasm for democratic principles. In this projection the Congress had no place; on the other hand, more importance should be given to the Muslim League.

The Congress, in fact, despite the insistence in the resolution for some action by the government to establish its *bona fides,* conveyed to the Viceroy that it would be satisfied with a declaration stating that India would be free to determine her own destinies after the war. Jawaharlal made clear, even if only indirectly, his anxiety to assist personally to the full in the war effort, and wanted the association of persons like himself, who were representative of public opinion, with some form of a National War Council. If India and Britain waged war together as equal partners, with no formal legal changes, but with Indian leaders being taken into confidence and associated with decisions on such matters as the extent of India's war effort, the raising of armies and industrial mobilization, this in itself would have removed most of the constitutional difficulties by the time the war had been successfully concluded. But it was hinted that Jawaharlal would not insist on even this.[1]

The government, however, were not interested; and the Congress ministries in the provinces resigned. Nor were overtures to Jinnah for a joint approach to the situation created by the war more fruitful. So the Congress decided to go its own way. But that way was not clear. The resignation of the ministries was the beginning of 'partial non-co-operation', but the next step was uncertain.[2] The Working Committee decided that the policy of non-co-operation should continue till the government ceased to maintain their imperialist domination in alliance with the reactionary elements in the country. For the present, wrote Jawaharlal, all of us have to go through the valley of the shadow.[3] But in some ways the darkness was much greater for him. He had never been happy about Stalin's alliance with Hitler, and did not expect it to last long. However, the partition of Poland had been bad enough; and now Russia had gone to war with Finland. Russia's strength in the outside world lay in her principles and her idealism. The principles, for all he knew, might still be there, but the idealism was wearing thin. In these circumstances, Jawaharlal looked to the United States. He had admired Roosevelt's attitude in the Czech crisis, and what now gave him confidence was the belief that the burden of the future would ultimately fall on the United States. But Soviet policy and action strengthened his acceptance of the Gandhian method. This example of violence and opportunism distorting objective impressed on him the necessity of relying on non-violence and ethical action in achieving a free India. It is difficult otherwise to comprehend his meek acceptance of the constructive programme as the next step to be taken after the abandonment of provincial office. He himself resumed regular spinning after a break of nearly four years. He does not seem to have expected anything much to happen immediately, and was almost in a relaxed mood. He took slow trains as a diversion and was considering a trip in the summer first to Switzerland to see his daughter and then perhaps even to the United States.[4]

Events in Europe took charge of developments in India. Jawaharlal had surmised that the war could not continue for long in its 'phoney' phase and the German advance in the summer of 1940 did not rattle him. It was decided, as a demonstration of coolness, not to summon an emergency meeting of the Working Committee; but the policy as formulated by Gandhi and Jawaharlal was stated in a resolution, drafted by Jawaharlal, of the United Provinces Congress committee. As the British government still thought in terms of empire and the picture of India was still one of British imperialism in action, so, whatever might happen in Europe and however deep the sympathy of India for the victims of aggression, there could be no change in India's attitude towards Britain.[5] But Jawaharlal opposed an amendment that civil disobedience should be started immediately on the ground that it was not worthy of the Congress to take advantage of Britain's difficulties.

The British authorities were unequal to this level of honour. They were incapable of the magnanimity of the Congress, which with every reverse suffered by the British became more generous and accommodating. In June the Working Committee announced its disagreement with Gandhi's faith in non-violence in all circumstances. While the struggle for freedom should remain non-violent, the committee felt unable to apply the creed to national defence and absolved Gandhi from responsibility for the programme and activity of the Congress. Meeting again in the first week of July, the Working Committee went even further. Setting aside on this occasion not only Gandhi but even Jawaharlal, the majority in the committee did not insist on a declaration about independence by the British but offered to assist in defence if a fully national government were established. Jawaharlal argued that to reduce acquisition of power to assumption of office and to seek to worm into it was to move along constitutional lines. Real power was the hold on the people, and this would be lessened by 'office power'. This form of power, secured on terms different from those laid down in earlier resolutions, would prove disastrous. But Rajagopalachari, the author of the proposal, won over Patel and Azad, and Jawaharlal agreed to abide by it. He was not convinced that this was the best way of serving India, but his concern for Britain swung him into acceptance.[6]

The Congress, having offered a way out of the stalemate without compromising its basic position, awaited official reaction. The situation was bringing matters to a head, and either the government accepted the co-operation of the Congress or the conflict would be intensified. The response of the government, when it came at last, was the usual stale anticlimax. They offered to appoint a few 'representative Indians' to the Executive Council and set up a War Advisory Council. The future constitution of India should be framed by a small body 'representative of the principal elements in India's national life'—and these elements included the princes and British commercial interests; and any decision of that body would be subject to the fulfilment of Britain's obligations in India.

As a result, the Congress resolutions died a natural death and there was no further need for intellectual debate as to when non-violence was obligatory and when it was not feasible. The Congress had been pushed back into the mood of civil disobedience. It accepted again the leadership of Gandhi and prepared for conflict. The Government of India, on their part, went ahead with the arrests of Congressmen and Jawaharlal expected to return at any moment to prison. As he cabled to his daughter in Switzerland, an early resumption of the old pilgrimage was likely.[7] He even courted it by wandering about the UP in the uniform of a Congress volunteer and advising the volunteer corps to continue its activities. But again Gandhi moved away from a head-on collision, because it was not in his nature to press the British government at a time when they were themselves threatened in their home. All that he committed the Congress to was non-violence and a demand for freedom of speech to preach against participation in the war; self-imposed restraint could not be taken to the extent of self-extinction. The demand would be expressed by individual civil disobedience. The first to court arrest by making a public speech against support of the war would be Vinoba Bhave, and the second Jawaharlal.

Hastening to Wardha to dissuade Gandhi from undertaking a fast unto death in protest against British obduracy,[8] Jawaharlal was arrested on 30 October at Cheoki station on his way back to Allahabad and taken to Gorakhpur for trial. He declined to plead, stating merely that it was his particular function and privilege to spread disaffection against the British government in India.[9] But he read a long statement which, over twenty years later, still gave him satisfaction.[10]

> It is not me that you are seeking to judge and condemn, but rather the hundreds of millions of the people of India, and that is a large task even for a proud Empire. Perhaps it may be that, though I am standing before you on my trial, it is the British Empire itself that is on its trial before

> the bar of the world... Individuals count for little, they come and go, as I shall go when my time is up. Seven times I have been tried and convicted by British authority in India, and many years of my life lie buried within prison walls. An eighth time or a ninth, and a few more years, make little difference. But is is no small matter what happens to India and her millions of sons and daughters. That is the issue before me, and that ultimately is the issue before you, Sir.[11]

The district judge gave Jawaharlal what was intended to be a deterrent sentence of four years. The savagery surprised Whitehall and New Delhi as well as Sir Maurice Hallett, the Governor at Lucknow; but Hallett vetoed any change in the terms. However, Churchill directed the India Office to telegraph at once to the Viceroy expressing the hope that the actual rigour of the sentence would be modified and Jawaharlal not treated like a common criminal.[12] Even this hope was unanswered. After a week in Gorakhpur jail Jawaharlal was moved by stealth and under cover of night, in a railway compartment with shutters down and a car with curtains drawn, to his old quarters in Dehra Dun jail. There he remained, except for a week in Lucknow prison in April 1941, till his release at the end of the year. This time the government had no intention of easing in any way the harshness of jail life. In jail he was allowed one weekly newspaper and six books at any one time, and he could have one interview, send one letter without enclosures and receive one every fortnight. There were also many petty harassments. He was not for some time permitted a washerman or a barber, a warder was fined for allowing a prisoner who had been discharged to say good-bye to Jawaharlal, and the prisoner himself was not allowed to collect ten rupees which Jawaharlal had given him for his fare home. Friends from outside were not allowed to send Jawaharlal packed lunches, and he could only receive fruit if he happened to know the sender. On one occasion, fruit sent by an unknown well-wisher from Rawalpindi was sent back at Jawaharlal's expense. When Jawaharlal wrote home asking his secretary to make a public announcement that no parcels or letters should be sent to him, this passage was blotted out by the censor. As he was to buy everything he needed through the jail staff (who were not known for promptness) and get nothing from home, he was sometimes short even of toothpaste. He was directed, for the first time in his prison career, to give his thumb impression and he refused. He was, after a while, given all the letters received from his daughter abroad, but the others were piled up in the office for weeks before Jawaharlal was told of them and asked to pick one. Permission to deal with the business of the National Planning Committee was refused. Papers pertaining to the Kamala Nehru Memorial Hospital were, after many months, exempted, but this delay had so held up work that Jawaharlal resigned the chairmanship.[13] His plan for sorting out his father's letters was defeated by the authorities, insisting that they would first have to go through these letters before sending them to him; as they obviously would be unable to understand the significance of these letters, Jawaharlal dropped the proposal. The limit on the number of letters he could write was later withdrawn, but on condition that none of these was published in the press—which was absurd because, apart from Jawaharlal's known aversion to giving any kind of undertaking, he was obviously in no position to give assurances about the behaviour of the recipients of his letters. In fact, Jawaharlal virtually gave up letter-writing and depended on interviews for keeping in touch with the outside world. Indira, who returned to India in May, took a cottage near Mussoorie; and this in itself made life a little pleasanter for Jawaharlal.

He had sought no favours. On the other hand, after hearing reports of ill-treatment of political prisoners in the camp jail in Lucknow, he wrote to the jail authorities that even the few privileges he was receiving had become hateful to him and he might defy jail discipline and invite the consequences.[14] A lesser man might have become personally embittered. But Jawaharlal accepted all this as part of his life and work without worrying about it. A sentence which he jotted down in his notebook at this time and was fond of quoting was that one could enjoy life perfectly only after resolving not to count the cost. What he understood by this was something very close to the teaching of the Gita; one should face the risks and perils of the adventure of life without calculating either what it involved or what might be its results. By enjoyment he meant something much more than self-indulgence; it was doing what one had to. 'All we can do', he advised his daughter, 'is to face our job and do it as well as we can and to remain tranquil in spite of shock and disaster.'[15] The certainties of moral and ethical values which he had built around himself gave him serenity and strength. It is not surprising that though he had long ago moved away from the simple religious faith of the twenties and had now no anchorage of scriptural or secular dogma, he carried about with him a tiny edition of the Gita.

Half relaxed and half resentful, determined not to worry and yet driven to exasperation by inactivity in a cataclysmic situation, Jawaharlal frequently set aside the present for thoughts of the future. But even more often his mind wandered back into the past. It was during this spell in jail that he began his journey into the five thousand years of India's history. His election tours had woken him to the myriad aspects of India's diverse unity; and to this was added an increasing appreciation of India's thought and culture. Earlier he had wanted to change his country and bring her abreast of the twentieth century. This aspiration never left him. But with it was now blended a pride in India's achievement and a firm sense of his own basic Indianness.

Towards the end of the year the Government of India came round to the view that all Congressmen in jail, including Jawaharlal, could be released. So Jawaharlal was out again on 4 December.

His personal mood of bitterness against British policy seemed but a reflection of the general hardening of Indian public opinion. There was a widespread conviction that the British were not only alien oppressors but the greatest disruptive force in India and the champion of all reactionary elements. On the other hand, the involvement of Russia and the United States and the spread of the war in Asia had altered the nature of the conflict. Jawaharlal had no hesitation in expressing publicly his hope that the progressive forces, as represented by Russia, the United States, Britain and China, would emerge victorious. What was required to enable India to do what it wanted to do, join the war wholeheartedly on the side of .the Allies was 'a pleasant psychological shock'[16] establishing that the old order had changed in India as well; but of any such imaginative action the Government of India were wholly incapable.

Jawaharlal was, therefore, keen that the Congress should not waver in its refusal to change its policy so long as the British gave no indication of anything more than remote assurances. The party should hold together under Gandhi's leadership and present an unshakeable front to the British while keeping in line with international events.[17] But at Bardoli in Christmas week Rajagopalachari once again persuaded the Working Committee to set aside Gandhi and ignore Jawaharlal and offer the co-operation of a free India in the defence of the country on a national basis.

Jawaharlal attached hardly any importance to this resolution. As the British showed no sign of responding to the demand of the Congress, this was a mere theoretical exercise. No compromise was possible between imperialism and nationalism, and Rajagopalachari's persistent suggestions of a settlement only added to the confusion. Gandhi, unwilling even to consider freedom at the cost of non-violence, formally withdrew from the organization. But he commended the resolution to the AICC and utilized the occasion to designate Jawaharlal formally as his chosen successor.

> Somebody suggested that Pandit Jawaharlal and I were estranged. It will require much more than differences of opinion to estrange us. We have had differences from the moment we became co-workers, and yet I have said for some years and say now that not Rajaji [Rajagopalachari] but Jawaharlal will be my successor. He

says that he does not understand my language, and that he speaks a language foreign to me. This may or may not be true. But language is no bar to a union of hearts. And I know this— that when I am gone he will speak my language.[18]

REFERENCES

1. Haig's telegram to Viceroy, reporting conversation with Mrs Pandit, 19 September, and Desmond Young's report of conversation with Jawaharlal, 21 September 1939, Haig papers, vol. 7; Viceroy's note on interview with Gandhi, 26 September 1939, Zetland papers, vol. 18.
2. Jawaharlal to E. M. S. Namboodripad, 22 December 1939.
3. To Madame Chiang Kai-shek, 25 December 1939.
4. To Madame Chiang Kai-shek, 20 February 1940.
5. Resolution, 19 May 1940, UPPCC papers, Lucknow.
6. Discussions in the Working Committee, July 1940, Anand Bhawan papers.
7. 10 September 1940.
8. B.V. Keskar. 'Alone with Gandhiji and Nehru', *Illustrated Weekly of India,* 30 May 1971.
9. Report of trial in *The Hindustan Times,* 4 November 1940.
10. See letter to Mrs Dorothy Norman, 19 January 1962, Nehru papers.
11. Statement of 4 November 1940, reprinted in Nehru, *The Unity of India* (London 1941), pp. 395-400.
12. Amery to Linlithgow, 14 November 1940, Linlithgow papers, vol. 9.
13. See letters to the jail superintendent, 2 January, 4 February, 24 February, 19 March, 29 July and 5 August 1941; to the Inspector-General of Prisons, 16 February and 10 March 1941; Padmaja Naidu to Frances Gunther, 13 March 1941, home dept. file 3/31/40 pol. (I).
14. To the Inspector-General of Prisons, 23 August 1941.
15. Letter, 18 November 1940.
16. Message to the *News Chronicle,* 11 December 1941.
17. To Sampurnanand, 14 December 1941.
18. 15 January 1942, Tendulkar, *Mahatma,* vol. 6, p. 43.

17

The Cripps Mission

Meantime, the Japanese sweep drew closer to India's shores. Early in the year, Franklin Roosevelt thought that India was as good as gone.[1] In February Winston Churchill told the king that Burma, Ceylon, Calcutta and Madras as well as a part of Australia might fall into enemy hands.[2] Jawaharlal also realized that the British refusal to part with power was unrealistic in the face of the imminent fall of their empire in India. Satyagraha had been called off because of the desire not to embarrass the British, whose allies were Russia, China and the United States; but there was no question of being merely passive if the Japanese stepped into India. Congress workers should spread out into the countryside and organize towns, wards and villages for every eventuality. Small units of about fifty houses each should be formed, and the residents mobilized to prevent panic, prepare for air raids, maintain law and order when control slipped from British hands, set up local co-operatives to ensure food supplies, encourage khadi, cottage industries and village handicrafts to enable local self-sufficiency, and resist the Japanese as best they could. What Jawaharlal appears to have had in mind was a fragmented war of attrition such as was taking place in China. The British had spurned the offer of the Congress to co-operate in the war, but in no case would the Congress bow before a foreign invader. They might not be able to push back armies but these armies would have to pass over their dead bodies. India would never accept the fate of France.

In Calcutta Jawaharlal sought to allay fright and exodus, and in Allahabad he discarded his car for a bicycle to get in closer touch with the people. The elaborate black-outs and air raid precautions ordered by the government were not only out of date but likely to increase panic. The general alienation from the British bureaucracy increased when, after the fall of Rangoon on 7 March, reports came in of discrimination against Indian refugees on the long trek from Burma. At last the British cabinet woke up to the urgency of the situation. Attlee, strengthened by the entry of Cripps into the War Cabinet on 19 February, drafted the British proposals. Their main points were the convening after the war of a constituent assembly elected on a system of proportional representation by freshly elected provincial assemblies, the recognition of the possibility of Pakistan by conceding the right of any province that was not prepared to accept the new Dominion constitution to retain its existing constitutional position, and the request for the collaboration, while the war lasted, of Indian parties with the British government, who would continue to bear the full responsibility for India's defence.

Armed with this declaration, Cripps flew to India to secure its acceptance by the Indian leaders. He relied on his persuasive ability, his known goodwill for the cause of Indian freedom and, above all, his close friendship with Jawaharlal. What he failed to understand was that Jawaharlal liked him but had no high opinion of his judgement[3] and that the fate of India was not an issue which Jawaharlal would be willing to determine at a personal level.

The Congress disliked the provisions about a Dominion constitution rather than full independence, the representation of the Indian states in a constituent assembly by their rulers rather than popular representatives and, above all, the recognition of the idea of a partition. It was for the last reason that Gandhi opposed the declaration, Jawaharlal was away in Allahabad for the wedding of his daughter on 26 March; but Azad, speaking for the Congress, emphasized the importance of effective control of defence by Indian representatives. He stated that this was far more important than the provision for non-accession of provinces.[4] It was therefore clear that, however disappointed the Congress might have been with the long-term proposals and whatever Gandhi might think, its attention was concentrated on the need to mobilize the forces of the Indian people to meet the immediate crisis.

However, all depended on Jawaharlal. The latter was anxious to collaborate in the defence of India and if he were satisfied that the declaration enabled this, Gandhi could not have pressed his objection. So, on the eve of meeting Jawaharlal, Cripps secured Churchill's approval for rewording the paragraph on defence-arrangements, and it was now affirmed that the task of organizing the defence of India must be the responsibility of the Government of India with the co-operation of the peoples of India. But the Viceroy stepped in, and toned down the co-operation in the military effort to mean merely the designation of an Indian to some office connected with the defence responsibilities of the Government of India without in any way impinging upon the functions and duties of the commander-in-chief.[5] This was obviously inadequate and Cripps concluded that his mission had failed. As a final effort he suggested that Azad and Jawaharlal should meet the commander-in-chief, Wavell.[6] The Congress had already reached a decision rejecting the proposals not merely because of the objectionable nature of the long-term arrangements but for the failure to transfer responsibility for defence, to which the Working Committee attached the greatest importance; but Azad agreed that he and Jawaharlal would meet Wavell and the Congress refrained from publishing its resolution.

On this basis, the talks continued, Cripps suggested the transfer to an Indian of such functions of the defence ministry as the commander-in-chief considered could be handed over safely and practically. A further safeguard was that 'under the new arrangement whereby the executive council will approximate to a cabinet' all important matters would be decided by the council as a whole and not by any individual member.[7] It is clear from this letter that Cripps was thinking in terms of cabinet government in India as generally understood. He had also obviously spoken in these terms to

Indian leaders. There is no reason to doubt Azad's statement that at the very first interview Cripps had talked of a national government functioning as a cabinet, and the Viceroy's position becoming analogous to that of the King of England—a statement which Cripps never contradicted.[8] In fact, at his first press conference on 20 March, he had recognized that the executive council could be turned into a cabinet;[9] and on 4 April Azad wrote to Cripps that 'the effectual control of the defence of India should rest with the Indian National Government'—the first time that the phrase was used in the correspondence.[10] But Linlithgow secured authority to write direct to the British government on these matters, and made sure that Wavell would stand firm.[11] There is nothing in the published British documents to show what took place at Wavell's interview with Jawaharlal and Azad, and the Congress leaders also refrained from talking about it. But in fact it was a disaster, Wavell being totally rigid and prepared to concede nothing.

The Cripps mission was by now beyond redemption, and the Congress had nothing to do with its failure. Cripps had got out of his depth, and Churchill, Amery, Linlithgow and Wavell made sure that he could not scramble back to land. The War Cabinet informed him that the character of the Viceroy's Council could not be changed. The final agony was drawn out by the eagerness of the Congress to find some way of reaching a settlement and the arrival of Louis Johnson, Roosevelt's personal representative in India. A defence formula was drawn up dividing the functions of the Indian Member and the commander-in-chief. This approach recognized that the National Government would be responsible for the entire government of the country including its defence but, in view of the war, would delegate full control of military operations to the commander-in-chief. There was now general expectation of a settlement.[12] Jawaharlal himself said later that he at this time estimated the chances of success at 75 per cent.[13] But the cabinet, fortified by American assurance to Churchill that Roosevelt would not interfere,[14] directed Cripps to bring the whole matter back to its declaration with only agreed amplifications and wanted a precise definition of the term 'National Government'.[15]

The luckless Cripps now quibbled. He drew a distinction between national government and cabinet government, assuring the War Cabinet that he had throughout emphasized that the existing legal and constitutional position must remain unchanged, and described a National Government loosely as one 'mainly composed of representative Indians together with Viceroy and Commander-in-Chief.'[16] On the other hand, he informed the Congress that the Viceroy would doubtless do all he could by means of appropriate conventions. With a co-operative Viceroy this might have worked. Indeed, Jawaharlal thought that if Linlithgow had talked to the Congress leaders and discussed with them how the executive council worked, a settlement might have been reached.[17] But Linlithgow had no desire to see Cripps succeed.

In despair, Cripps appealed to Jawaharlal, as an old friend, to save him. But Jawaharlal's hands were bound—not by Gandhi or his colleagues in the Working Committee but by Cripps's own shifts of position. He told Cripps that there were limits beyond which he could not carry the Congress and the Congress could not carry the country. So Cripps informed Johnson with embarrassment that he had to revert to the text of the original declaration; and Jawaharlal and Azad were amazed, at their final interview with Cripps on 9 April, to find that all the searching for new formulae had been a waste of time and the phrase 'National Government' now meant nothing at all. It was to be neither a free nor a cabinet government.[18]

REFERENCES

1. W. D. Hassett, *Off the Record with F.D.R.* (New Brunswick, 1958), p. 28.

2. J. W. Wheeler-Bennett, *King George VI* (London, 1958), p. 538.

3. See Jawaharlal to Mahadeva Desai, 9 December 1939, *A Bunch of Old Letters*, pp. 402-3.

4. Cripps's account of interviews with Azad, 25 and 28 March 1942, *Transfer of Power,* vol. 1, pp. 479 and 514.
5. Cripps to Azad, 30 March 1942, *Transfer of Power,* vol. 1, p. 563.
6. Idem, 1 April 1942, *Transfer of Power,* vol. 1, p. 598.
7. Cripps to Churchill, 4 April 1942, *Transfer of Power,* vol. 1, pp. 636-9.
8. Azad to Cripps, 11 April 1942, *Transfer of Power,* vol. 1, pp. 7-13-5.
9. *Transfer of Power,* vol. 1. p. 547.
10. Azad to Cripps, 4 April 1942, *Transfer of Power,* vol. 1, p. 640.
11. Viceroy's telegram to Amery and Amery's reply 2 April, and note of Viceroy's secretary, 3 April 1942, *Transfer a Power,* vol. 1, pp. 614-15 and 623.
12. *The Hindustan Times, 9* April 1942.
13. Press Conference, 12 April, *National Herald,* 13 April 1942.
14. R.E. Sherwood, *Roosevelt and Hopkins* (New York, 1950), vol. 2, p. 102.
15. Telegram, 9 April, *Transfer of Power,* vol. 1, pp. 707-8.
16. To War Cabinet, 10 April 1942, *Transfer of Power,* vol. 1, p. 716.
17. Report of Sir E. Villiers of conversation with Jawaharlal, 5 July 1942, *Transfer of Power,* vol. 2 (HMSO, 1971), p. 690.
18. Johnson to state department, 11 April 1942, *Foreign Relations of the U.S. 1942,* vol. 1, p. 631; Azad to Cripps, 10 April 1942. *Transfer of Power,* vol. 1, pp. 726-30.

18

Collision Course

Denied the chance to form a representative government, Jawaharlal set about the second-best task of unofficial organization for self-reliance. He announced that the Congress would continue its policy of non-embarrassment of the British. War production should not be impeded. He was dissuaded by Azad from broadcasting over All-India Radio on these lines, but he promised Johnson that he would proceed to Calcutta to secure the termination of industrial strikes.[1] On the other hand, if the Japanese invaded India they would be met not only with non-violent non-co-operation but even, if necessary, with guerrilla warfare and a scorched-earth policy. In fact, he went further than merely demanding resistance to the Japanese, and declared that he would oppose even Subhas Bose (who had gone over to the Axis powers) and the Indian troops he had mustered.

Gandhi warned Jawaharlal that his attitude was likely to break up the Congress leadership. He even forced Jawaharlal to withdraw his suggestion about guerrilla warfare and publicly exulted over it.[2] The failure of the Cripps mission had by itself restored the influence, of Gandhi in the Congress command, and he was now convinced that the immediate step should be the withdrawal of the British from India. If Japan attacked India and the British had not withdrawn, the Indian people should offer complete non-violent non-co-operation to the Japanese and not place any obstacles in the way of the British forces. However, a scorched-earth policy should not go beyond the destruction of war material.

This was too much for Jawaharlal and he made his opposition clear. Even a toned-down version of Gandhi's draft, produced by his followers, was unacceptable to Jawaharlal, who resisted not an odd detail or assertion but the whole attitude of defeatism and sympathy with Japan which underlay this resolution. His own draft asserted, in consistency with the earlier position of the Congress, that while India had no quarrel with the people of any country, she was opposed to Nazism and Fascism as well as to imperialism. Britain should abandon her hold on India, but the Congress repudiated the idea that freedom could come to India through foreign interference or invasion. Any attack on India should be resisted by non-violent non-co-operation, for the British had prevented the organization of national defence by the people in any other way. A scorched-earth policy was not affirmed, but was implicit in the intention to fight to the last.

Jawaharlal had his way. One can only assume that he had persuaded his colleagues to give one more chance to his policy of support to the Allies. Nothing could be expected directly from the British; but Jawaharlal placed his faith in the United States and China. In February 1942 Roosevelt had sent Jawaharlal a friendly message through Edgar Snow and invited Jawaharlal to write to him.[3] When the negotiations with Cripps broke down, Jawaharlal wrote directly to Roosevelt in the hope of involving him in the Indian problem and stated that there could be no further talks with the British 'for the present',—thus hinting that the door was not completely closed.[4]

Roosevelt, however, refused to intervene. Fortified by this attitude, the Government of India became even more aggressive. These developments strengthened Gandhi's position, and he could with much justice contend, in the sharp and prolonged private debate that now went on between him and Jawaharlal, that the latter's support for the Allies evoked no effective response in any quarter and served only to expose the Indian people to the assaults of the British. So, when Jawaharlal met Gandhi at the end of May, he was in no position to withstand a policy for which he had no enthusiasm. It was, of course, still important to him not to harm the cause of Russia, China and the United States, and he argued for this, as Gandhi later told the Viceroy, with 'a passion which I have no words to describe'.[5] But he could invoke no argument more substantial than passion. Once Gandhi abandoned his pro-Japanese stance and conceded that after the British administration was withdrawn the Allied armies could remain in India and the first act of a national government should be the conclusion of a defence treaty with the Allies, there was no reason for Jawaharlal not to acquiesce in Gandhi's policy. Even from the international viewpoint, help to China and advancement of the Allied cause, a total withdrawal of British power was necessary, for only then could the Indian people shake off their passivity and be totally involved in the war effort.

Gandhi, as usual, had no clear ideas as to the way in which the British could be induced to quit India, Jawaharlal was against a mass civil disobedience movement, but Gandhi thought in terms of such direct action after the public mind had been prepared for it and in such a manner as not to aid the Japanese. But he had no wish to act precipitately and hoped for an interview with the Viceroy before taking any firm decisions.[6] At Bombay the AICC again appealed to Britain and the United Nations to end British rule in India and promised explicitly to throw all the resources of a free India into the war. This freedom should be the prelude to the freedom of all other dependent peoples, and countries occupied by Japan should not be restored to their former masters. Gandhi was authorized to start a non-violent mass struggle on the widest possible scale, a fight to the finish, but not immediately; and he announced that he would make every effort to see the Viceroy.

The response of the government was to round up the leaders of the Congress in their homes. A special train took them first to a station outside Poona where Gandhi and his entourage were asked to alight. Just when the Working

Committee had agreed that the British knew how to do this sort of thing well,[7] there was a hitch. At Poona itself, where the train stopped contrary to schedule because a signal was against it, the crowd on the platform recognized Jawaharlal and ran towards him. When the police tried to stop them with a lathi-charge, Jawaharlal, 'with remarkable agility', jumped through the corridor window on to the platform. At least four policemen were required to overpower him and get him back into the train. When they reached Ahmednagar, the police officer apologized for what had happened and hoped that, as he had only been carrying out orders, Jawaharlal bore him no personal animosity. Jawaharlal assured him that he did not, but was still very angry over the lathi-charge.[8]

This was Jawaharlal's longest term in prison, for 1040 days or over 34 months, from 9 August 1942 to 15 June 1945. The twelve members of the Working Committee lived together in Ahmednagar till March 1945, when they were split up and the members sent to jails in their own provinces. Jawaharlal, with Pant and Narendra Deva, was moved to Naini, then to Bareilly and then again to Almora. For the first few days after their arrest, Gandhi and the Working Committee were cut off from any form of communication with the outside world. No letters, newspapers or interviews were permitted, and the public did not even know where these leaders had been interned. This policy was later relaxed to the extent of allowing newspapers and two letters to, and four letters from, members of their families per week on strictly personal matters. This latter concession did not benefit Jawaharlal much, at the start, because his daughter and sister Vijayalakshmi were both in UP prisons, and the UP government, out of step with the central government for months, refused either to deliver letters from Jawaharlal which had been cleared by the Government of India or to forward letters which Jawaharlal was entitled to receive.[9] Later, the prisoners were allowed books, but, for fear that uncensored information would reach them, these books were scanned for invisible writing.[10] After Jawaharlal and his colleagues had been for over two years in jail, in October 1944 the government considered allowing interviews, but the prisoners of Ahmednagar firmly refused them. After so many months of isolation, no interview for a few minutes could be satisfactory; and there was also a question of pride involved.

Forced into close companionship, these Congress leaders, who had in common only dedication to a common cause and acceptance of Gandhi's leadership, frequently found themselves in heated discussion, and by the time of their release some were hardly on speaking terms. Isolation for so long a period, punctuated with reports of the deaths of those dear to them—Ranjit Pandit, Azad's wife—added to the normal rigours of imprisonment. To tone down these frictions and fraying of nerves, Jawaharlal organized a regular community life. Duties were allotted to each person and rotated every week. He himself did more than his share, supervising the cooking, preparing salads, nursing the sick, organizing badminton and volleyball and taking charge of the gardening. To the latter in particular he devoted, especially in the early months, a great deal of time, for it gave him a certain psychological satisfaction by providing activity for his hands and body at a time when his mind had of necessity to lie fallow.

When books and journals were allowed in, Jawaharlal had a fresh source of comfort, and on 13 April 1944 he took up again the writing of the book which he had begun at Dehra Dun jail in 1941. Less than five months later, on 7 September 1944, *The Discovery of India*, running into a thousand handwritten pages, was finished.

This is a great jumble of a book which bears the marks of haste and tension. It is repetitive, has many long quotations and, if Jawaharlal had had time to revise it on his release, would probably have been reduced to nearly half its length. There are some autobiographical chapters, written mostly in 1941. The account of Kamala's death is moving in its subdued yet intense sense of loss, but this section as a whole does not rise to the level of the *Autobiography*, if only because it is more impersonal, and weak in the attractively self-conscious nature of the earlier work. The chapters on the war years blend into a general, scathing account of British rule in India.

However, the core of the book is a long survey of India's culture before the coming of the British. The contrast with the *Glimpses* is striking. Jawaharlal is no longer primarily interested in social and economic change, in action and great men, or in Marxist analysis of class struggles : 'I have grown more contemplative. There is perhaps a little more poise and equilibrium, some sense of detachment, a greater calmness of spirit.'[11] He had not sloughed off his Marxism but there was now in his thinking an appreciation of the Vedanta, its idealism and its ethics. India's culture in particular engrossed him. He was fascinated by its continuity and seeming vitality and staying power. There appeared to him to be an unbroken chain from Mohenjo-Daro, which political fortunes could not destroy, and the result was a mellowness and a gentleness of the Indian spirit, a desire and a capacity to live and let live, an absorption of every fresh intrusion of foreign elements to form a new synthesis, a unity and stability which could only be explained by India's 'depth of soul'. So, in an astonishingly narrow nationalist tradition, he put together a version of India's cultural history derived from secondary sources and studded with testimonials from European observers. It was not just the hurry and the atmosphere in which the book was written but the theme itself which led to woolly writing.

Yet, if the book is lacking in analysis, elegance and clear thinking, it had a purpose. It sought to portray an emotional comprehension of Indian nationalism and to stress the necessity of revitalizing the Indian people. India's past could be so depicted as to draw lessons for its future. Its continuity could only be explained by the fact that while the form often remained, the inner content was always changing. However, these social forms, like caste, had a limit of expansion and the result was a growing, strangling rigidity. Social conservatism and poverty had been encouraged by alien rule and were the chief characteristics of contemporary India; but if India became free and was true to herself, there was no cause for despair.

The Discovery of India, written in the dark years of Indian nationalism, carried not a precise, scientific argument but a buoyant message.

REFERENCES

1. Azad, p. 58.
2. Jawaharlal's speech at Calcutta, 19 April, *The Hindustan Times,* 21 April 1942; Gandhi in *Harijan,* 26 April 1942.
3. 'When you get there and see Nehru, say hallo for me. I wish you would ask Nehru to write me a letter and tell me exactly what he wants me to do for India. You can send it through our diplomatic pouch!' E. Snow, *Journey to the Beginning* (London, 1959), p. 257.
4. 12 April 1942, *A Bunch of Old Letters,* pp. 469-70.
5. Letter of 14 August 1942, *Transfer of Power,* vol. 2, p. 705.
6. Jawaharlal to Louis Johnson, 4 June 1942, *Foreign Relations of the United States* 1942, vol. 1, pp. 667-9; Fischer, *A Week with Gandhi,* (London, 1943), pp. 78-9, 105 and 109-10; Jawaharlal's confidential note on talks with Gandhi, June 1942.
7. Mira Behn, *The Spirit's Pilgrimage* (London, 1960), p. 240.
8. Report of F. E. Sharp, deputy inspector-general of police, Bombay, 10 August 1942, home dept. pol. (1), file 3/21/42, vol. 42.
9. Home department pol. (1) file, 3/21/42, vol. 42.
10. See under secretary, home dept, Govt of India, to additional home secretary, Bombay govt, 29/30 September 1943, home dept. pol. 3/21/42. pol. I, 1942-3, vol. 2.
11. *The Discovery of India,* p. 24.

19

Post-War Prelude

Jawaharlal and his companions, after they emerged from prison at the end of the war in June 1945, were in a bitter mood. India had for nearly three years lain under virtually military rule. Collaborators, loyalist, communal and left-wing—all had had their heyday at the expense of the national movement. Deep famine in Bengal had been regarded as low priority. Corruption and black-marketing ravaged the land. All this infuriated Jawaharlal, and his speeches and interviews on release reflect this. India was to him comparable to the European countries freed from Nazi rule, with resistance movements emerging to the surface.[1] Though the Congress had not organized the 1942 rebellion, it delighted him that the people had not miserably submitted to repression but had, on their own, struck back. He demanded stern action against blackmarketeers and trials in open court of those guilty of atrocities against the people.[2]

Gandhi was at this time thinking in terms of another campaign of civil disobedience.[3] However, the Working Committee decided to permit its representatives to attend the conference summoned by Wavell at Simla to consider the formation of an interim government. Jawaharlal was not one of the invitees but was present at Simla, a town which he hated for its atmosphere of officialdom for part of the year. The outcome of the conference confirmed Jawaharlal's suspicions of British motives, for Wavell acted as a total partisan of the Muslim League. He not only conceded parity between 'caste Hindus' and Muslims and between the Congress and the League but, going back on his word to

Gandhi,[4] agreed not to select a Muslim belonging to the Congress. Thus was virtual refusal to regard the Congress as a non-Hindu, secular organization, and acceptance of Jinnah's contention that it was as much a communal party as the League. But Wavell was unwilling to let down the loyalist Muslims outside the League and particularly those who had helped so greatly in the recruitment of soldiers in the Punjab.

However, this was not acceptable to Jinnah, who insisted that all Muslim members should belong to the League and that, in an executive council so formed, the Muslim members should have a veto on all important decisions. These were demands which even Wavell could not accept; and, had he chosen, he could at this stage have deflated the League to manageable proportions. Jinnah was aware of this. Wavell, instead of seizing this occasion to restore Indian politics to an even keel, enabled Jinnah to gain the full advantage of his obduracy by promptly abandoning his own proposals and dissolving the conference. The offer of the Congress to join the executive council while leaving it open to the League to come in later was ignored.[5] Nothing could have made clearer that it was Jinnah's wishes that mattered above all else.

The League derived the fullest benefit of this in the elections for the central and provincial assemblies that were held at the end of the year. In the provinces where Muslims formed a majority, the League did not secure a majority of votes. For instance, its vote in the Punjab was 46.56 per cent, in Sind 45.75 per cent, and in the NWFP 37.19 per cent. But the seats gained by the League were far more than were warranted by its vote. Except in the NWFP, where the Congress had a clear majority of 30 seats, including 19 Muslim seats, and the League only 17, the League secured all or most of the reserved Muslim seats. In the central assembly too it won every Muslim constituency with 86.6 per cent of the vote. It had demonstrated that it had a considerable following, especially in the urban areas. However unpractical the concept of partition and imprecise the notion of Pakistan, they had struck a response in the minds of many middle-class Muslims.

Jawaharlal was still of the view that the League had not gathered real strength and was the creation of the wishful thinking of elderly British governors. When a test came, all Muslims would come flocking back to the Congress. But the results of the elections greatly strengthened the arguments for pandering to the League. Therefore, while insisting on the departure of the British and the summoning of a constituent assembly for free India, the Congress reluctantly recognized the right of any area to secede provided this was the clearly established will of the inhabitants of that area and it did not result in the compulsion of any group or community in that area. Jawaharlal hoped that, granted the right to secede, the Muslims would not exercise it but rather use it to shed their fears.[6] Given a sense of freedom, the Muslim masses, at any rate, would realize the absurdity of Pakistan. A plebiscite should be held after British authority was withdrawn from India and the Muslims would either not want to secede or, if they did, would quickly retract their decision.[7] But, especially after the elections, this was a forlorn thought. By the spring of 1946, with the government of India encouraging the League and the Congress reconciled to the principle of secession, the frost had settled on all hopes of a free and united India.

So, with the emphasis now on tactics, pace and procedure rather than on principles, events gathered momentum. The air was full of hate and passion, negotiations were the continuation of civil war by other means, and killing and rioting became the accepted instruments of political manoeuvre. There was probably a touch of escapism in Jawaharlal's concentration at this time on two other issues outside the mainstream: the Indian National Army (INA) and relations with the neighbouring countries of Asia.

The story of the INA is that of about 20,000 Indian officers and men taken prisoner by the Japanese, who had responded to Subhas Bose's call to form an army to wage war, alongside the Japanese, in the cause of India's freedom. When the war ended, Bose had died in an aircraft accident, and the British intended to treat the captured INA men as guilty of treason.

Jawaharlal himself had no doubt that the action of these men had been an error of judgement. Freedom could not be secured with the assistance of any foreign nation. However, the soldiers of the INA, some of whom he met, seemed to him the pick of the Indian army, who had, for the most part, been inspired by the noblest motives. When the Government of India decided to stage a public trial, at the Red Fort in Delhi, of three INA officers, Indian public opinion was deeply stirred to an extent that surprised even Jawaharlal. He organized relief for the INA men and their dependants, harried eminent men and women who did not normally take an interest in politics to express their concern, set up an INA defence committee of lawyers, and himself put on once more, after over twenty-five years, his barrister's gown and appeared in court.

The other issue, always important to Jawaharlal and in which his interest had not been dimmed by the years of isolation in prison and the tragic situation in his own country, was the condition of Asia. With the defeat of Japan, the pressure on China had been relieved; and in the civil war which followed, Jawaharlal, despite old friendships, strictly refrained from taking sides. Of more direct concern was the question whether the old imperialist powers—the British in Burma and Malaya, the Dutch in Indonesia and the French in Indo-China—would be able to restore their former dominance. This was a general problem and Jawaharlal was keen that the Asian countries should help each other. He welcomed the idea of an Asian conference suggested by Aung San of Burma[8] and was infuriated by the British use of Indian troops to support the French and the Dutch. Even worse was the attitude of the United States, which apparently, for its own purposes, was underwriting European imperialism in Asia. This could only ensure a continuing revolt of millions with a passion which even the atom bomb could not suppress, and end in a third world war.[9]

Jawaharlal himself wished to visit Burma, Malaya and Indonesia, to meet the nationalist leaders of these countries, plan co-operative endeavour and inquire into the conditions of the Indians settled there. On arrival at Singapore, Jawaharlal met Mountbatten, who, with anticipation and a sense of drama, had arranged for Jawaharlal's reception at the airport with all the courtesies due to a prime-minister-designate. There was at Singapore a small memorial to the INA, built in a prominent place by the INA personnel. This had been repeatedly destroyed by the British authorities and repeatedly rebuilt. Mountbatten was anxious that Jawaharlal should not visit this memorial. The only concession Jawaharlal made to Mountbatten was to avoid a public function. But he visited the memorial quietly and without announcement and placed some flowers there, and this was immediately known to the local population.[10]

In his tour of Malaya, Jawaharlal told the local Indian population, who were attached to India and anxious to retain their Indian nationality, that those who had made their permanent residence in Malaya should adopt Malayan nationality, till, as Jawaharlal optimistically hoped, the time came when there would be a common nationality for India and all these regions of South-East Asia. His own visit, he felt, had had a good effect in cheering up the Indian community, improving their organization, drawing the Malayans, Indians and Chinese closer, toning down any political action that might be envisaged against Indians and opening up scope for an improvement of their economic prospects.

REFERENCES

1. Interview to the United Press of America, 21 June, *The Hindustan Times,* 23 June 1945.
2. Press conference, 23 June, *The Hindustan Times,* 24 June 1945.
3. J.B. Kripalani, *Gandhi : His Life and Thought* (New Delhi, 1970), p. 224.
4. Wavell's account of interview with Gandhi, 24 June 1945, Wavell, *The Viceroy's Journal,* ed. P. Moon (Oxford, 1973), p. 145.

5. Jawaharlal's interview to the press, 11 July, *The Hindustan Times,* 12 July 1945.
6. See his draft note written at Gulmarg, 17 August 1945.
7. Interviews to the press, *The Hindustan Times,* 4 and 7 April 1946.
8. Letter from Aung San, 13 December 1945, and Jawaharlal's telegram, 26 December, and reply to Aung San, 27 December 1945.
9. Statement to the press, 15 October, *The Hindustan Times,* 16 October 1945; and presidential address to the All-India States Peoples Conference, 31 December 1945, *National Herald,* 1 January 1946.
10. Jawaharlal's report to President, AICC, on visit to Malaya, 28 March 1946.

20

The Cabinet Mission

The naval mutiny in Bombay in February 1946 finally convinced the British government that the raj was crumbling, and they sent out a special mission of three cabinet ministers to seek an agreement on the constitutional issue. Jawaharlal's own mind was clear on the objective. The basis of negotiations with the Cabinet Mission should be the independence of India. The exact relationship between India and Britain could be left over for future settlement, but it should be clearly understood that all such problems could only be considered on the present basis of independence. The final authority to determine the constitution would be a Constituent Assembly, composed of delegates elected by the provincial assemblies according to proportional representation. If any province refused to participate or to elect delegates, it could be bypassed and left out for the time being; there should be no compulsion. This Constituent Assembly would draft an all-India constitution, but such questions as Pakistan would be settled either by the consent of the parties or by a plebiscite, on a precise and defined issue, of all the inhabitants of the area concerned. But time was the essence of the whole problem, and there should be no delay in convening a Constituent Assembly and forming a provisional central government acting freely as a cabinet with no obstruction from the Viceroy or the India Office. The Congress should not get entangled in long discussions about details.[1]

With the League evasive on the precise meaning of Pakistan and the Congress unwilling to discuss long-term plans, the Cabinet Mission put forward proposals of its own. It suggested the establishment of a union government dealing with foreign affairs, defence and communications; two groups of provinces, one predominantly Hindu and the other predominantly Muslim, which would deal with all other subjects which the provinces desired should be dealt with in common; and the vesting of all residuary powers in the provinces.[2] To consider this plan, a conference of the leaders of the two parties was convened at Simla.

At the conference it was implicit in Jinnah's arguments that he was not thinking in terms of a sovereign state. He recognized that the union executive could deal with most matters referred to it though he felt there was no need for a union legislature; and he inquired whether the constitution of the union would be permanent or provision would be made for revision after a set period. Jawaharlal pledged the Congress not to exercise compulsion on the units to stay in an all-India federation. Jinnah stated that if the Congress would accept the groups, the League would accept the union. Jawaharlal said that while his position came near to that of Jinnah, any union would be futile without a legislature, and the provinces must decide for themselves about groupings; and to this Jinnah replied that he had fought for freedom; equally with Jawaharlal and would be very glad to sit with him to discuss matters.

Encouraged by this, the Cabinet Mission drew up on 8 May 'Suggested Points for Agreement' between the two parties. There should be an all-India government and legislature, both composed of equal proportions from the Muslim-majority and Hindu-majority provinces, and dealing with foreign affairs, defence, communications and fundamental rights. Residuary powers would vest with the provinces. 'Groups of provinces may be formed'. The Constituent Assembly would be elected by the provincial assemblies. The assembly 'will divide into three sections', representing the Hindu-majority provinces, the Muslim-majority provinces and the states.

That the Mission no longer insisted on groupings was clear. The Constituent Assembly should divide into sections, but provinces might form groups. The Viceroy recognized this concession to the Congress.[3] Jinnah, too, understood this clearly and promptly protested.[4] The Congress, of course, reiterated its position. All groupings should be optional, and this subject should be left open to decision by the Constituent Assembly. Constitution-making should begin with the federal union. If an agreement with the League favourable to the growth of a free and united India could not be achieved, an interim government should be formed at once and matters in dispute referred to an independent tribunal.[5] Immediately, Jawaharlal suggested an umpire, and he and Jinnah retired to consider the proposal. The Congress prepared a list of possible umpires who were neither English nor Indian, and Cripps made various proposals. But Jinnah soon denied that he had ever agreed to the principle of arbitration.[6]

After this, the two sides again reverted to rigid positions. Jinnah declared that the question of partition had been settled by the Muslim vote at the elections, but he was willing to agree to the sovereignty of Pakistan being 'delegated' to a union for three subjects provided that sovereignty was recognized in the form of a group. Even communications were now limited to those necessary for defence. To this Jawaharlal retorted that the Congress and the League were completely opposed to each other on the question of partition, and it was essential to have a strong centre with control of many more subjects than the three basic ones. The conference could make no further progress, and the Mission decided to issue its own plan. Partition, on the basis of either a large or a small Pakistan, was rejected. The Indian union would deal with foreign affairs, defence and communications, and have the powers necessary to raise the finances for these subjects. The idea of parity at the centre was dropped, but any major communal issue in the central legislature would require a majority of each community as well as an overall majority. All other subjects and powers would vest in the provinces, which would be free to form groups, and each group could determine the provincial subjects to be taken in common. Any province could by a majority vote of its assembly call for a reconsideration of the union and group constitutions periodically after ten years. The Constituent Assembly would be elected by the provincial assemblies, with each province being allotted a number of seats proportional to its population, and this number divided between the communities on the basis of their population. The members so elected 'will divide up into three sections'—Section A comprising Madras, Bombay, UP, Bihar, CP and Orissa; Section B Punjab, NWFP and Sind; and Section C Bengal and Assam. Each section would draw up provincial constitutions and, if desired, a group constitution. Any province could elect to come out of any group in which it had been placed after the first general elections under the new constitution. The framing of the constitution would obviously take time; but an interim government having the support of the major political parties and in which all the portfolios were held by Indians would be set up immediately.[7]

The Mission plan was intended as a compromise, yielding some points to the Congress and some to the League in the hope that both would accept the whole even if not wholly satisfied. The idea of Pakistan as a sovereign state was rejected, and at the level of the Indian union there was to be no weightage for the Muslims. Even in the elections to the Constituent Assembly the Muslims were not to have, as at the time, more seats than their numbers warranted. These were all concessions to the Congress. However, to make the plan palatable to the League, Sections B and C, comprising the five Muslim-majority provinces, were created in the Constituent Assembly. But there was one major internal contradiction in the Mission plan, which was to lead to disaster. Grouping of provinces was optional, but meeting of members of the Constituent Assembly by sections was compulsory. If a section met and decided on a group constitution, a province could opt out of the group only after the first general elections under the new constitution. In other words, grouping would in practice not be voluntary at all—unless the clause on optional grouping overrode that on compulsory forming of sections.

In fact, because of an assurance given by the Cabinet Mission to the League, of which the Congress was unaware,[8] that decisions in sections would be by a majority vote of the representatives of the provinces, it was the optional grouping clause which would be set aside; for the representatives of NWFP in Section B and of Assam in Section C would always be in a minority. Forced to clarify its understanding of its Plan, Pethick-Lawrence wrote to Azad that grouping was an essential feature of the scheme and it could only be modified by agreement between the two parties. As for the Constituent Assembly, there would be no interference with its discretion once it was formed and working on the basis of the various statements being made.[9] In other words, the sovereignty of the Constituent Assembly would be limited by the terms of reference under the plan.

All this was dispiriting to Jawaharlal. Hopes of a settlement, on the basis of independence not in the future but at once, had been bogged down in a morass of interpretation. There was also the whole problem of the Indian states, of special interest to Jawaharlal in his capacity, at this time, as president of the All-India States Peoples Conference. It was difficult to believe that the widespread instances of repression in the states could occur without the support of the political department, for the maharajas and the nawabs were but shadows cast by the paramount power. Jawaharlal was for a friendly approach, urging the rulers to abandon autocracy and, where the lack of viability of their principalities was obvious, to merge them in the neighbouring province. There would then be left about twenty large states, autonomous units in the federation and with democratic governments under princely figureheads.[10]

However, these sawdust autocrats, confident still of the support of the British, paid no heed. Reports continued to pour in from the various states of unwarranted firing, summary arrests, ill-treatment of prisoners and banning of popular organizations. These gave a touch of unreality to negotiations for British withdrawal from India. When

Jawaharlal defied a ban on his entry into Faridkot state, the local authorities quickly reached a settlement. But soon after, a crisis developed in Kashmir. There a strong, non-communal, political organization, the National Conference, had been built up by Sheikh Abdullah and other leaders, who, though Muslim by faith, shunned the Muslim League and were members of the Congress. After the failure of secret attempts in March 1946 to merge the National Conference in the communal Muslim Conference and associate the whole with the Muslim League, the Kashmir government arrested Sheikh Abdullah and the other leaders of the National Conference. This repressive action was specially provocative to Jawaharlal, for at the time of his arrest Sheikh Abdullah was on his way to Delhi to meet Jawaharlal at the latter's request. Jawaharlal's first impulse was to leave Simla for Kashmir to support his friends, but he curbed himself so as to give the Viceroy a chance to intervene.

By the middle of June, Jawaharlal felt he had waited long enough and decided to enter the state, along with some lawyers, to assist in Sheikh Abdullah's defence. Wavell asked Azad to dissuade Jawaharlal and himself urged him to desist, but in vain. The Viceroy then informed the Kashmir government that any untoward incident involving Jawaharlal during the next ten days would be highly embarrassing for all-India reasons, and suggested that the trial of Sheikh Abdullah be postponed, in which case Jawaharlal too might postpone his visit. But the Kashmir authorities refused and prepared to arrest Jawaharlal on the border. The maharaja offered to abdicate and his prime minister to resign if the government of India compelled them to take no action against Jawaharlal, and Wavell and the political department hastened to reply that no such pressure was being applied.[11]

Jawaharlal abided by his programme, and, on 19 June, was stopped by the Kashmir authorities at the state border. They served an externment order and organized black-flag demonstrations. Jawaharlal was in a high rage. He condemned the extreme discourtesy shown him and the Congress organization and expressed scorn for the maharaja's official and military minions. He waited for five hours to give the state government time to reverse their orders and then informed the magistrate that he was crossing into Kashmir. On doing so he was arrested; but the adjournment of the trial of Sheikh Abdullah and the insistence of the Working Committee led him to agree to return to Delhi on the clear understanding that he would be back in Kashmir.

Meanwhile, the discussions on the Mission plan had continued. On 6 June the Muslim League had announced its acceptance of the plan 'inasmuch as the basis and the foundation of Pakistan are inherent in the Mission's plan by virtue of the compulsory grouping'. Now it was for the Mission to win over the Congress. Wavell informed Azad that grouping was not compulsory, and it was for the representatives of provinces meeting in sections to decide whether or not they wished to form groups.[12] The Congress was, therefore, justified in adhering to its own interpretation of the plan, and was now more concerned with the inclusion of a Congress Muslim in the interim government. The Mission, misled by Azad and Rajagopalachari into believing that the Congress would not insist on this, blamed Gandhi for this development and rejected the demand. The Congress replied by refusing to join the interim government, while continuing to accept the long-term proposals as the Congress understood them.[13]

REFERENCES

1. Jawaharlal's confidential note on impending conversations with Cabinet Mission, 15 March 1946.
2. Pethick-Lawrence to Azad and Jinnah, 27 April 1946, *Papers relating to the Cabinet Mission to India* (New Delhi, 1946), p. 9.
3. 'I went to bed unhappy all the same. I sympathise with the Muslims rather than with Congress, and I am not convinced that our document is quite fair to them.' Diary entry, 7 May 1946, Wavell, pp. 260-1.

4. Jinnah to Pethick-Lawrence, 8 May 1946, *Papers relating to Cabinet Mission*, pp. 15-16.
5. Azad to Pethick-Lawrence, 8 May 1946, *ibid.*, pp. 17-19.
6. Jawaharlal-Jinnah correspondence, 10 and 11 May 1946, *ibid.*, pp. 19-20.
7. For full text of Cabinet Mission plan, see M. Gwyer and A. Appadorai, *Speeches and Documents on the Indian Constitution, 1921—47* (London, 1957), vol. 2, pp. 577-84.
8. V.P. Menon, *The Transfer of Power in India*, (paperback Madras, 1968), p.311.
9. Pethick-Lawrence to Azad, 22 May 1946, *Papers relating to Cabinet Mission*, p. 34.
10. Jawaharlal's presidential address to the All-India States Peoples Conference, 31 December 1945.
11. Pol. dept's telegram to resident, Kashmir, 18 June, resident's telegram to pol. dept., 19 June, and pol. dept's telegram, 19 June 1946, gov.-gen, sectt. file 295(4)-G/43.
12. Wavell to Azad, 15 June, *Papers relating to Cabinet Mission*, p. 42.
13. Wavell to Azad. 22 June, and Azad to Wavell, 25 June, and Congress resolution, 25 June 1946, *ibid.*, pp. 48-52.

21

The Interim Government

Seemingly satisfied with the response of the Congress, the Cabinet Mission left on 29 June, leaving it to the Viceroy to negotiate the formation of an interim government on the basis of the acceptance of the Mission plan by both the major parties. Soon after, Jawaharlal was elected in succession to Azad as president of the Congress. The new president summoned a meeting of the AICC in Bombay and secured its approval of the conduct by its leaders of the negotiations with the British government. Both there and at a press conference a few days later, Jawaharlal reiterated, in sharp and emphatic terms, the Working Committee's interpretation of the Cabinet Mission plan : "We are not bound by a single thing except that we have decided to go into the Constituent Assembly.'[1] The assembly would meet in sections but it did not follow that there would be grouping.

These statements were seized upon by Jinnah to withdraw the League's acceptance of the Cabinet Mission plan. It is unfair to blame Jawaharlal merely because Jinnah used this as the chance to break out of the cage of acceptance. Jawaharlal was not acting in a mood of pique. To make clear that these were not casual statements, he reiterated his views in the following weeks.[2] His utterances were deliberate and in line with Congress policy. Jawaharlal and the Congress believed that the League derived its main sustenance from the support of the British and without this its tissue would weaken. That support had been withdrawn by the Cabinet Mission and Jinnah was aware of it. The important thing now was to make it clear to the British that the Congress intended India to conduct herself as a fully independent, sovereign state. Fair treatment to the minorities was the obligation of a free India and not enforceable by the British.

From Bombay Jawaharlal set off again for Kashmir. This visit, unlike the previous one, passed off quietly. Patel and Azad persuaded the Viceroy to secure the lifting of the ban on the entry of Jawaharlal, who promised not to raise any major issues or address any public meetings.[3] He attended Abdullah's trial and had four long private interviews with him, but was unable to meet the maharaja, who pleaded illness.[4] Jawaharlal's honour was now satisfied, and Kashmir faded, for the time at any rate, into the background.

The Viceroy invited Jawaharlal as president of the Congress to submit proposals for the formation of an interim government, repeated his assurance that he would act constitutionally and asked Jawaharlal to consider an approach to Jinnah before submitting his proposals to the Viceroy.[5] The Congress accepted this offer but insisted on a public announcement of the Viceroy's invitation before they sought Jinnah's co-operation : 'We shall welcome that co-operation but, if this is denied us, we shall be prepared to go ahead without it.'[6] Such an announcement was made, and thereafter, armed with a resolution of the Working Committee that it accepted the Mission plan in its entirety but with its own interpretations to resolve the internal inconsistencies and fill the omissions, Jawaharlal met Jinnah. The talks failed, as expected. Now it really seemed as if the British would ignore the League and work with the Congress on the basis, as Attlee had once suggested, that they could not allow a minority to place a veto on the advance of a majority. But the government's alliance with the Congress went against Wavell's grain, and the killings in Calcutta in mid August saw him scurrying back to the policy of appeasement of the League. He told Jawaharlal, who was for firm action against gangsterism, that he wished to send for Jinnah, and it was only the threat of the Congress to refuse to form an interim government if he did so that led him to desist.[7] Jawaharlal wanted a ministry of fifteen—five 'caste Hindus', five Muslims, one scheduled caste and four minority representatives—but as Wavell insisted on the number being fourteen, the Anglo-Indian representative was dropped.[8]

Jawaharlal insisted that this ministry should function as a strong and stable government and not merely as a stop-gap arrangement till the League was willing to join. The Congress was anxious to have a coalition but this could not mean a surrender to the League. Jinnah could nominate his five representatives but not interfere with the nominations of the Congress, including a nationalist Muslim. Such firmness cowed the Viceroy for the time being. He announced the list of ministers and in a broadcast, associated himself with the offer of the Congress to refer to the federal court all questions of interpretation of the Cabinet Mission plan.

Jawaharlal was vice-president of the executive council and held the portfolios of external affairs and Commonwealth relations. Now at last he seemed to have come to the end of a long and irregular road and to be able to move away from conflict and struggle to constructive effort : 'Too long have we been passive spectators of events, the playthings of others. The initiative comes to our people now and we shall make the history of our choice.'[9] Jawaharlal organized his team to work as a cabinet representative of the people.

A major issue confronting the new government was that of the NWFP. Here the Congress party had a clear majority; and of the total Muslim votes cast in the elections, the Congress and Nationalist Muslim candidates had secured 208,896 and the League candidates 147,880. But so long as the Frontier Province, of which only about 3 per cent of the population was non-Muslim, was outside the League's control, Jinnah could not claim to be the unqualified representative of Muslim India, and Pakistan could be no more than a dream. So British officials set themselves to destroy the popularity of the Congress and rectify 'the bastard situation'.[10] Their first opportunity came when Jawaharlal decided to visit the NWFP. Tribal relations formed a part of his portfolio and he was anxious to make a first-hand appraisal. The Governor, Sir Olaf Caroe, came to Delhi to dissuade Jawaharlal from visiting the province till after the League had joined the interim government, but Jawaharlal refused to postpone his visit and toured the province and the tribal areas in the middle of October. The League organized demonstrations against him and throughout his tour Jawaharlal faced hostile receptions and stone-throwing, which Caroe had no doubt had been organized by the League. Bruised, but fortunate not to have been killed, Jawaharlal completed his programme with courage. But the officials had succeeded in exploiting this visit to begin the weakening of Congress authority in the NWFP.

Meantime frantic efforts continued to bring the League into the interim government. In this the Viceroy now had the full support of the cabinet in London. Working on the premiss that the convening of the Constituent Assembly was the prerogative of the Viceroy and not of the Government of India, he was unwilling to take action until agreement had been reached with Jinnah on both the long-term plan and a coalition government.[11] Now, once again, was revealed the pertinence of Jawaharlal's statements at Bombay in July on the sovereign nature of the Constituent Assembly and therefore the minimum amount of extraneous action in its procedures. The Viceroy started discussions with Jinnah who, having no wish to be left out of office, was willing to respond. The only point on which he now insisted was that the Congress should not nominate a Muslim in the government, and Wavell appealed to Gandhi and Jawaharlal to waive its right to do so for the sake of a settlement. To this appeal was added a threat that if the Congress declined, the Viceroy doubted if he could allow the interim government to continue as it was.[12] Pethick-Lawrence backed up Wavell and added that the League would have to be brought into the Constituent Assembly if that body was to be of any use.[13]

Resentful though they were of these pressure tactics, the leaders of the Congress realized that there would be some advantages in bringing in the League. If this were effected in such a way as to bind the League to a proper working of both a coalition government and the Constituent Assembly, it might lighten the tension in the country and put events back on an even keel. So Jawaharlal called on Jinnah on 5 October, and found him considerably toned down. He assured Jawaharlal that he would never side with the British and would in no event permit the Viceroy to function as an umpire in any coalition government. In return Jawaharlal offered to have any fresh appointments of minority representatives considered by the whole cabinet, to refer major communal issues, if necessary, to arbitration and, instead of rotating the vice-presidentship, to create an additional vice-chairmanship of the cabinet co-ordination committee.[14] These concessions seemed to satisfy Jinnah; but within hours he reverted to his usual attitude of refusing to reach any agreement with the Congress and relying on the British. He insisted on the exclusion of any Nationalist Muslim from the government. The Congress replied that it could go no further than what had been offered by Jawaharlal, who added that he could never be a party to disowning the Muslims in the Congress. This was to him a personal as well as a national question of honour.[15] But discussions with Jinnah were resumed by Wavell. He accepted Jinnah's nomination of five members including one person belonging to the scheduled castes, but without securing a precise commitment on the part of the League to the Cabinet Mission plan, a renunciation of the League's policy of direct action and a pledge to co-operate in the government. Indeed the deliberate choice (apart from Liaquat Ali Khan) of second-rate diehard members of his party, and of a Harijan who represented nobody, established beyond any doubt that Jinnah's sole aim was to share power and disrupt the interim government. But so eager was Wavell to destroy the control by the Congress of immediate authority that he brought the League in, despite Jawaharlal's repeated protests,[16] unconditionally. It was among the most serious of Wavell's many disservices to India.

The working of the Congress-League government must be unique in the annals of modern administration. Each group met separately before a cabinet meeting and they functioned in opposition to the other. This suited Wavell. He forgot the specific assurance he had given to the Congress that he would prevent any attempt to make the interim government a battleground of communal politics instead of an instrument for administering India.[17] He encouraged the League in its obstructive attitude by referring every major issue to the two sides for opinion rather than insisting on the government functioning as a team, and himself acted as umpire.

More vital, of course, were developments in the various parts of India. News of the slaughter of Hindus in Bengal percolated to Bihar and roused the local peasants to attack the Muslims. Gandhi and Jawaharlal urged the Congress ministry to deal sternly with the guilty, and in this received the firm support of the Viceroy and the League, whose concern for the sanctity of provincial autonomy was presumably reserved only for Bengal and Sind. Jawaharlal and one of the League ministers in the central government toured Bihar and helped to bring the province under control. The army was called in, and rioting crowds dispersed by fire and, on a few occasions, by aerial bombing. Such firm and decisive action was possible only because of Jawaharlal's initiative.

His intervention, however, was in his personal capacity. The interim government itself could do, and did, little. It was riven by dispute and powerless in action. Matters came to a head on the question of convening the Constituent Assembly. It was scheduled to meet in December but the Viceroy and his advisers wished to postpone it on the ground, that the League had not yet accepted the long-term plan rather than to press Jinnah to reach an early decision.[18] Jawaharlal insisted that as the League was making clear that it would not accept the plan it should not continue in the interim government.[19] Attlee now decided to intervene and invited the Congress, the League and the Sikhs to depute their representatives to London.

The talks in London in December confirmed the misgivings of the Congress and served to strengthen Jinnah's position. The British government declared that, according to the Cabinet plan, decisions in the sections would be by a simple majority vote. They urged the Congress to accept this view and suggested, as a sop, that it could be referred, along with other questions of interpretation, to the federal court by the Constituent Assembly. Jinnah was delighted. He had, with the help of the British, recovered much ground. The League had, after an initial setback, moved into the government and brought administration to a standstill without any commitment on the Mission plan; and now the Congress was being pressed to abandon its position and accept an unfavourable interpretation of the plan so that the League could be cajoled into attending the Constituent Assembly. Pakistan seemed to be in sight.

The Constituent Assembly met as scheduled, on 9 December, but adjourned repeatedly without taking any controversial decisions or breaking up into sections so as to enable the League to make up its mind. To provide Jinnah with no substantial argument for declining, to join, the Congress, while voicing its disapproval of the manner in which the British cabinet had elaborated its plan to suit the League, accepted this interpretation and gave up its proposal of a reference to the federal court. All that it now stipulated was that there should be no compulsion of a province and the rights of the Sikhs should not be jeopardized. If such compulsion were attempted, a province or a part of a province should have the right to take whatever action was required to give effect to the wishes of the people concerned.[20] But Jinnah was still in a grandiose mood. The Working Committee of the League declined to reconsider its decision, and asked the British government to declare that the Cabinet Mission plan had failed and to dissolve the Constituent Assembly.[21]

So, by the end of January 1947, it became clear that no further negotiations and compromises were possible, and the efforts of the Congress in this direction had only resulted in confusing its followers and dividing its leadership. With the League adamant and the princes taking their cue from it and avoiding a decision on joining the Constituent Assembly, with

India and Pakistan 1947

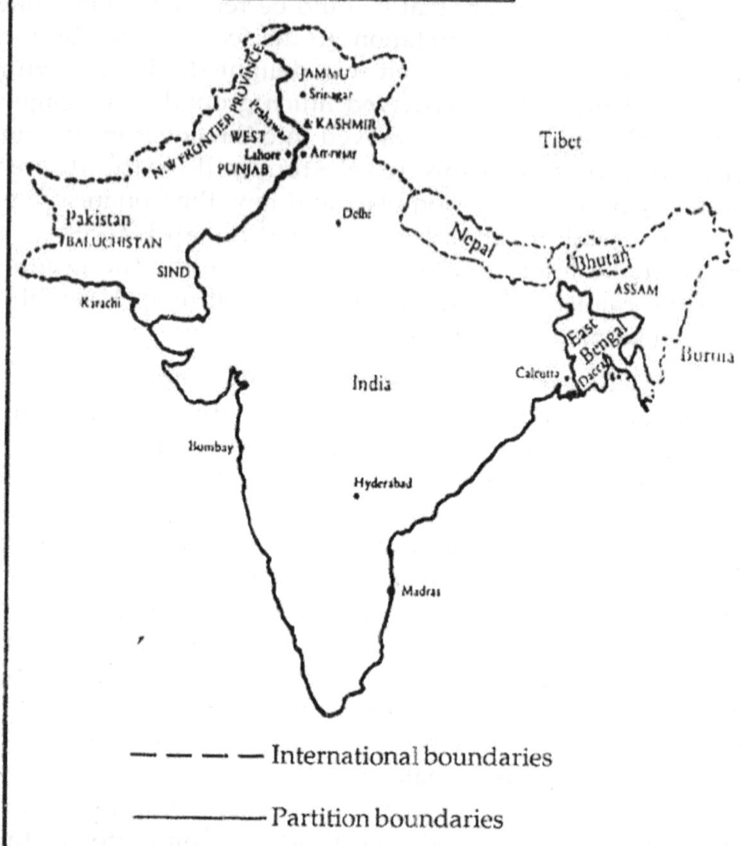

the virus of communal rioting spreading across the face of northern India and the interim government helpless to act, there was no purpose in still hoping and discussing.

On 5 February, nine members of the interim government—all except the five nominees of the League—wrote a joint letter to the Viceroy that in their opinion the League could not continue in the government. Jawaharlal followed this up eight days later by stating that if a quick decision were not given he and his colleagues would leave the government. The League, of course, had no intention of resigning and Wavell, instead of pointing out to Jinnah that he was having the best of both worlds, still wished to press the Congress for further—and futile—concessions. But the British government's decision was different. Attlee announced that the British would withdraw from India not later than June 1948, handing over, if there were no government established by a fully representative assembly, to the central government or in some areas to existing provincial governments. He added that Wavell would be replaced by Mountbatten.

REFERENCES

1. Speech at the AICC, 7 July, *The Bombay Chronicle,* 8 July 1946.
2. Speech at Delhi, 21 July, interview at Lahore, 30 July, and speech at Allahabad, 1 August, *The Hindustan Times,* 22 July, 31 July and 3 August 1946, respectively.
3. Patel to Wavell, 8 July, and Azad to Wavell, 9 July 1946. Gov.-gen. sectt. file 295(4)-G/43; Wavell to Jawaharlal, 17 July and Jawaharlal to Patel, 20 July 1946.
4. Jawaharlal's note on Kashmir, 12 August 1946.
5. Wavell to Jawaharlal, 6 August 1946.
6. Jawaharlal to Wavell, 10 August 1946.
7. Jawaharlal to Cripps, 18 August, and to Wavell, 19 August 1946; Wavell to Jawaharlal, 19 August 1946.
8. Jawaharlal to Wavell, 20 August, and Wavell to Jawaharlal, 22 August 1946.
9. Jawaharlal's broadcast, 7 September, *National Herald,* 8 September 1946.
10. The phrase is Lord Ismay's. A Campbell Johnson, *Mission With Mountbatten* (London, 1951), p. 54.
11. Wavell to Jawaharlal, 13 September 1946.
12. Gandhi to Wavell, 27 September 1946.

13. Krishna Menon to Jawaharlal, 26 September 1946.
14. Jawaharlal's notes of conversations with Jinnah, 5 October, and letter to Jinnah, 6 October 1946.
15. Jawaharlal to the Nawab of Bhopal, 10 October 1946.
16. See Jawaharlal's letters to Wavell, 13, 14, 15 and 23 October 1946.
17. See his own report of his interview with Patel, 12 June 1946, Wavell, p. 291.
18. Jawaharlal to PSV, 15 and 16 November and PSV's reply, 16 November 1946.
19. Jawaharlal to Wavell, 21 November 1946.
20. Resolution of the AICC, 6 January 1947.
21. Resolution of the Muslim League, 29 January 1947.

22

The Transfer of Power

On 24 March 1947 Mountbatten was sworn in as Viceroy. In the first few weeks, of the viceroyalty, while Mountbatten went through the motions of consultations and seeking to breathe life into the Cabinet Mission plan, Jawaharlal was consent to be a mere spectator. He first gave all his attention to the Asian Relations Conference. The idea of such a conference had been in Jawaharlal's mind from December 1945, and, after preliminary arrangements had been made, invitations were sent out in September 1946. It was to be a non-official conference representative of all shades of opinion in the countries of Asia (plus Egypt). Convened in the uninhibited times before India was free and Jawaharlal was restricted by the requirements of official policy, the conference could hear the views of both the Kuomintang and the Communists, of the Arab League as well as the Hebrew University. The Soviet Central Asian republics were represented; and in addition the Soviet Union, along with Australia, New Zealand, Britain and the United States, sent observers.

There was, in fact, an euphoric atmosphere about the conference. Its main purpose was to enable the leaders of Asia, on the threshold of a new world, to meet. Not only controversial issues involving these countries, but even matters like defence and security which concerned powers outside Asia were excluded from the agenda, which listed only such innocuous subjects as national freedom movements, migration and racial problems, economic development and the status of women. But the agenda was the least important part of the conference. For ten days, from 23 March to 2 April, Delhi saw itself as the natural centre of a resurgent continent, conscious of its glorious past and forging links for the future. Nothing came of the Asian Relations Organization set up by the conference, and no participant country acted on the resolution to set up national units of this organization or academics of Asian studies. There was not even a second session of the Asian Relations Conference, though one may trace its influence in the origins of the Asian-African Conference held at Bandung in 1955. Yet Jawaharlal was satisfied with the conference as the expression of an emotion which he personally felt deeply.

Even after the conference, Jawaharlal took no active part in the constitutional discussions. Mountbatten and his advisers drew up a 'Plan Balkan', whereby power would be demitted to the provinces and they would be left to decide whether they would form any groups.[1] The plan was not shown in detail to the Congress leaders, and Jawaharlal knew only the general outlines. He certainly does not seem to have known that power was being transferred to the provinces, and was assuming that partition would involve no more than a division of the Punjab and Bengal. Then, on 10 May, when Jawaharlal was Mountbatten's guest at Simla, the Viceroy wrote to him that instead of governor's rule or fresh elections in the NWFP, a referendum should be held on the issue of partition by an organization under the control not of the governor but of the Viceroy. 'I will tell Caroe [the governor] to tell Dr. Khan Sahib [the chief minister] that you are in general agreement with the procedure.' Jawaharlal promptly denied this and refused to be hustled. This was a matter on which the Working Committee felt very strongly and had specifically directed Jawaharlal to convey its feeling to the Viceroy. All that Jawaharlal had agreed to was that the people of the Frontier Province should be consulted before final decisions were taken, but it was very important when this was done and in what context, and any referendum would require the full concurrence of the provincial government.[2]

On the night of 10 May Mountbatten, acting on 'an

absolute hunch', gave Jawaharlal the complete text of the Plan Balkan as revised by the cabinet. Jawaharlal was so upset that he burst into Krishna Menon's room at 2 a.m., speechless with indignation.[3] The hastily written note which he sent to Mountbatten shows signs of excitement and is in places incoherent. But it made clear that the Congress would not accept the break-up of the Indian union and the transfer of sovereignty to the provinces. Any plan should start with the union and the opting out of certain areas rather than a number of sovereign units coming together if they so desired. To jettison the basic conception of India and denude the Constituent Assembly of its significance was to yield to the League and ignore the views of all other sections of opinion in India. The preposterous' suggestion to settle the future of Baluchistan in accordance with the wishes of a few nominated Sirdars, the insistence that the NWFP be given a fresh opportunity to reverse its decision to form a part of India and the refusal to apply to Sind the formula enforced on Assam that a Muslim-majority part of it should be attached to the contiguous seceding area were all intended as special favours to the League. The inevitable consequences would be to invite the Balkanization of India, provoke civil conflict and add to violence and disorder, ensure a further breakdown of the central authority and demoralize the army, the police and the civil service. The states would also declare themselves independent kingdoms, probably in subordinate alliance with Britain, and this would create an almost unbridgeable gulf between the peoples of India and Britain. The public assurance to the tribes on the frontier that they could have treaties with whomsoever they liked was to invite them to profit by internal difficulties in India.

After Jawaharlal's rejection of the plan, Mountbatten, hurriedly plastering over his cracked confidence, postponed his meeting with the Indian leaders scheduled for 17 May, and directed his advisers to recast the plan to meet Jawaharlal's main objection. The Constituent Assembly would continue to meet; and there would be a second Constituent Assembly for those areas which decided not to participate in the existing assembly. The Punjab and Bengal would be partitioned if the representatives of either the Muslim-majority districts or the rest of the province desired it, and boundary commissions would be set up later to demarcate the boundaries on the basis of contiguous majority areas and other factors. It would not, however, be possible to provide a separate state for the Sikhs. Though Sylhet district was a part of Assam, as it was predominantly Muslim and contiguous to Bengal, a referendum should be held there to determine whether it should also be divided. Sind would decide through its assembly which state to join, and an appropriate mechanism would be devised to enable British Baluchistan also to choose. The real problem was with the NWFP, the majority of whose representatives were already participating in the Constituent Assembly. Here democratic principles were frankly set aside to enable Pakistan to become a reality. If the Punjab decided on partition, a referendum would be held in the NWFP under the aegis of the Governor-General and in consultation with the provincial government. Agreements with the frontier tribes would be negotiated by the appropriate successor authorities. As for the Indian states, British policy would continue as before and the plan would not apply to them.

This plan was broadly acceptable to the Congress because it accepted the premiss that India was a continuing entity, with the separation of those areas the majority of whose inhabitants desired it. Jawaharlal and his colleagues were anxious too for quick and final decisions. Lahore was being gradually reduced to ashes while Calcutta prepared for another round of killings; but the administration was doing little to stem the spread and intensification of communal fury. The first thing to be done was to effect an immediate transfer of power out of British hands, for British officials seemed neither willing nor competent to deal with the situation.

Catching Jawaharlal in this mood, Mountbatten induced him not only, despite all his earlier reservations, to agree to a referendum in the NWFP, but also to accept Dominion Status. From the start the Viceroy's objective had been to achieve a solution which would retain the Indian parties within the Commonwealth, and Jinnah, at one stage of the negotiations, sought to promote the chances of Pakistan by offering to accept Dominion Status. But obviously the prime importance was attached to the attitude of the Congress. In December 1946 Jawaharlal had moved in the Constituent Assembly the resolution that India should be an independent sovereign republic. His speech on that occasion reflected his bitterness with the British authorities for their rejection of the interpretation of the Mission Plan put forward by the Congress. In the following months Mountbatten's personal friendship had made Jawaharlal less edgy but he had not altered his views on this subject.

In May, however, Jawaharlal's keenness for an early *de facto* transfer of power was exploited in favour of Dominion Status. In his note of 11 May he had suggested that even before the British withdrew, the interim government should be treated as a cabinet with joint responsibility based 'upon full Dominion autonomy'; and if the League refused to accept this, its representatives should be told to resign. Mountbatten at first agreed to this, subject to the Viceroy retaining his overriding power to safeguard the interests of minorities; but then, presumably because of Jinnah's objection, he withdrew his consent. The Congress strongly protested and there was a fairly heated argument. It was finally decided that, to enable a speedy transfer of power once partition was decided upon, there should be two dominion governments with a common governor-general or two separate governors-general; and the armed forces would also be divided in accordance with the territorial basis of their recruitment.

The British cabinet approved the plan as it stood, with only one major addition: that the date for the transfer of power could be brought forward from June 1948 by conferring Dominion Status on one or two successor authorities even in 1947. Mountbatten presented this plan to the Congress and the League, secured their agreement to work it, and asked Jawaharlal, Jinnah and Baldev Singh (as a representative of the Sikhs) to follow him and broadcast to the nation on the evening of 3 June. Jawaharlal's effort was one of his outstanding performances. He was normally no orator but could, with genuineness and spontaneity, rise to the occasion. He stumbled along on the plains but was at home in the heights. His rhetoric was never overblown, his prose never over-excited. He now spoke of the past nine months when the Congress had been in office at the centre, months of sore trial and difficulty, of anxiety and sometimes even of heartbreak. There was much on the credit side, for India had advanced nationally and internationally; but his mind was heavy with the thought of the tragedy and suffering which the Indian people had undergone. It was with no joy that he now commended the proposals for secession, though he had no doubt that this was the right course. It was an India united not by compulsion but by the free and willing association of a free people that they laboured for, and it might be that these proposals would enable them to reach such an united India sooner than otherwise and with a stronger foundation :

> We are little men serving a great cause, but because the cause is great something of that greatness falls upon us also. Mighty forces are at work in the world today and in India, and I have no doubt that we are ushering in a period of greatness for India. The India of geography, of history and tradition, the India of our minds and hearts, cannot change.

It was with that faith that they should bury the bad past and make a fresh start.

It now remained only to implement the plan, to ascertain the wishes of the people in the areas concerned and to arrange for separation if it were desired by the majority. Curiously, Jawaharlal expected little trouble. He regarded the communal frenzy as a fever which would pass once the decision about Pakistan had been taken. He had too noble an idea of his countrymen to believe that the desire to kill and torture, born of religious zeal, had any deep root in their nature. He was wrong, but so was everyone else in a position of responsibility at this time; and all were surprised and caught unprepared by the widespread and savage killings that disfigured India before and after partition. After 2 June, Jawaharlal, in the belief that the present had been settled, thought mainly of the future. It was a difficult time but India would muddle her way through, and once they had settled down to the new order they should move fast. In these summer months Jawaharlal, for the first time since his release in 1945, was not caught up in the rush of events.

In acting on the clauses of the plan creating Pakistan, the Congress was chiefly concerned about its betrayal of the NWFP. At the meeting of the Working Committee which accepted the plan, Gandhi and Abdul Gaffar Khan were the only regular members who spoke against partition, and Gaffar Khan asked his colleagues to find out, as a small mercy, if the plebiscite in the NWFP could include the third alternative of independence as well.[4] The president of the party wrote accordingly to the Viceroy, and Gandhi took Gaffar Khan to meet Mountbatten. But Mountbatten refused to consider the suggestion and silenced the Congress by pointing out that it was Jawaharlal himself who had strongly objected to the grant of independence to any province. Jawaharlal had agreed to a referendum in the NWFP, as in Sylhet, as part of a larger pattern of consulting the people of the areas concerned; and the Congress could not retract.

Jawaharlal urged the Khan brothers to abandon ideas of independence and to rally their forces to secure a majority vote on the straight issue of accession to India or to Pakistan. A number of officials from the governor downwards, who were antagonists of the Congress, had expressed their opinion that its chances were still fifty-fifty; and the party should be prepared to put it to the test. Even if the Congress lost by a small margin, it could renew the struggle later. Indeed, it is probable that if the Congress had accepted battle it would have polled a large vote. As it was, the provincial party decided to abstain. Despite this, out of an electorate of 572,798, only 289,244 (50.49 per cent) were in favour of Pakistan, with 2874 against. This hairline majority in favour of Pakistan justifies Jawaharlal's acceptance of a referendum, for the Congress might have won it or at worst lost very narrowly; and this would have exploded the case for Pakistan. In fact, the League was given a walk-over.

The other problems created by the transfer of power and the process of partition were sorted out, though not without acute bickerings. A partition committee representative of the two parties and boundary commissions with Sir Cyril Radcliffe as the chairman with the decisive voice were set up. But the relationship of the partition committee with the interim government, and the role of the interim government after the decision to divide had been taken, caused controversy. Jawaharlal proposed that the government work as two committees, each dealing with all subjects, one for India and the other for the future Pakistan. Mountbatten was willing to act on this sensible suggestion but Jinnah objected, and as the letter of the law was on his side nothing could be done and the administration continued to be ineffective. Jawaharlal was driven to offer his resignation, and this crisis was only averted by Mountbatten dividing the cabinet as soon as the Indian Independence Act had been passed.

Another cause of worry to the Congress at this time was the conduct of the Indian states. The political department had always, but with added emphasis since the formation of the interim government, been shoring up the princes in their autocratic pretensions and aspirations of sovereignty; and Jawaharlal had repeatedly to complain to Wavell and Mountbatten about this. But Wavell had refused to interfere; and the political department began to burn records, wind up the residencies and political agencies and transfer railways, cantonments and other government property. Hyderabad, a large state in the core of India, which since the thirties had been seeking to increase its viability by securing access to the sea, was now invited to acquire financial and industrial concessions in neighbouring principalities such as Bastar. Encouraged by all this, many of the princes openly prepared for independence, the expansion of their armies and the acquisition of modern arms. One of them, Travancore, declared that it would assume sovereignty on 15 August, nominated a representative at Delhi and appointed an agent to Pakistan.

Jawaharlal held strong views on this subject of the states. He detested the feudal autocracy and total suppression of popular feeling, and the prospect of these puppet princes, with the encouragement of the political department, setting themselves up as independent monarchs drove him into intense exasperation. The whole policy of the political department was one of 'operation scuttle', with the deliberate intent of breaking up the unity of India and introducing, anarchy by the back door; and Jawaharlal was prepared to thwart this even, as he hinted to Mountbatten, by using force if necessary.

To Jawaharlal the test case was Kashmir. Not only had he close personal links with this state and the National Conference under Abdullah; it irked him that, despite his two visits in 1946, Abdullah and many of his colleagues remained in prison. So he planned to go there again, and Mountbatten's effort to dissuade him made him only the more determined. In fact, he did not go, Gandhi and Mountbatten going instead; but the maharaja succeeded in evading a decision on accession to either India or Pakistan.

However, apart from Kashmir, Hyderabad and Junagadh, all other states acceded to one or other of the two new dominions before 15 August; and Mountbatten served India well in laying the bogey of independence. Patel's willingness to reach agreements with the rulers and to give lower priority to popular representation facilitated Mountbatten's task in securing the accession of the states on the three subjects of defence, external affairs and communications. It was Jawaharlal and his way of thinking which the princes and their advisers resented, and by setting him aside Mountbatten made it easier for the princes to accede. He even got Travancore to retrace its steps.

At midnight on 14 August the Constituent Assembly met to usher in the dawn of freedom. Jawaharlal once again made one of his most movingly appropriate speeches and, in the process, coined an undying phrase.

> Long years ago we made a tryst with destiny, and now the time comes when we shall redeem our pledge, not wholly or in full measure, but very substantially. At the stroke of the midnight hour, when the world sleeps, India will awake to life and freedom. A moment comes, which comes but rarely in history, when we step out from the old to the new, when an age ends, and when the soul of a nation long suppressed finds utterance. It is fitting that at this solemn moment we take the pledge of dedication to the service of India and her people and to the still larger cause of humanity.

REFERENCES

1. H.V. Hodson, *The Great Divide* (London, 1969). pp. 229-30.
2. Mountbatten to Jawaharlal, 10 May, and Jawaharlal's reply of the same date.
3. Mountbatten's speech on the occasion of the third Jawaharlal Nehru Memorial Lecture. London, 12 November 1970.
4. Proceedings of the Working Committee, 2 June 1947, AICC file G43 (part I), 1947; R.M. Lohia, *Guilty Men of India's Partition* (Hyderabad, 1970), p. 21.

23

The Living Truth

The mood of elation evoked by the achievement of freedom was wiped out almost within hours. As early as March 1947 communal rioting in what was to be West Pakistan had led to migrations of non-Muslims; and the collapse of the non-League government and the administration of the province by officials had added to communal tensions. Yet no one, neither the Government of India nor the leaders of the Congress and the League, had paid much attention to this gathering potential of tragedy. So when, on 14 August, trouble started on a large scale almost simultaneously in Lahore and Amritsar and spread out to West and East Punjab and even to Delhi, the reaction was one of surprise and helplessness. In the following weeks, a great number of people were killed,[1] and there were migrations, with attendant murders and abductions, of at least five to six millions each way. The boundary force of about 23,000 men not only proved inadequate to control the situation but was itself weakening in morale, and some of its members were believed to have participated in these massacres on both sides.[2]

Nothing was to be gained by delving for the initial responsibility. Horror had, whatever its origin, gained such momentum that it was futile to suggest at this stage that one side was worse than the other. Nehru moved tirelessly round Delhi, extending the protection of his personal interest to frightened Muslim families, and frequently jumped into mobs of fanatic rioters to scold and even to smite in order to quell. But more important than the maintenance of the public peace was the necessity to-exorcize the madness, born of fear, which had seized the Indian people. Nehru addressed meetings throughout northern India and broadcast repeatedly that they should build an India where no citizen felt insecure because of his religion. Secularism, always a principle of the Congress, was now rendered more urgent by the compulsion of events. Everyone seemed to be thinking in terms of retaliation, but the government would not adopt that as a policy.[3] If the people of India had not retaliated, the Indian army, instead of being occupied with subduing mob violence and guarding hospitals in India itself, could have marched into Pakistan for the protection of the minorities there. Butchering Muslims was not just a matter of personal degradation and communal fanaticism; it destroyed the dignity of India and the prestige of her government, betrayed the philosophy of Gandhi which had inspired the struggle for freedom, and threatened democracy and liberty by strengthening the forces of fascism.

Nehru, functioning in the eye of the storm as a man inspired, drew close once again to Gandhi and relied more heavily upon him than he had done in the two years prior to the transfer of power. Gandhi, back in Delhi on 7 September, supported Nehru's efforts to protect the minorities, shun vengeance, abide by the old ideals and resist the narrow outlook that appeared to be gaining strength at every level of Indian opinion. But Gandhi could lend no power to the prime minister in his role as head of the administration; and in this sphere Nehru recruited the services of Mountbatten, even though he was a constitutional head of state.

The problem of administration extended rapidly from preventing murders and organizing refugee camps and hospitals to the broader issue of relations with the new state of Pakistan. Nehru believed that the division of India was a short-term political solution which could not override cultural affinities and economic compulsions. So the Government of India disavowed any intention of harming Pakistan or treating it as an enemy and expressed their continuing hope that, when the current turmoil ended, the two states might unite by the free will of their peoples.[4] But events did not help to restore this goodwill and balance. Just as the fury in the two Punjabs was beginning to abate, a crisis emerged in Kashmir. On the eve of the transfer of power, the maharaja's government, unable to decide between accession to India or to Pakistan, proposed to sign standstill agreements with both countries. The Government of Pakistan agreed, but from the Government of India there was no response, because the maharaja's proposal reached them only long after the trouble started. In fact, the official Indian attitude was indifference as to the maharaja's decision. Nehru's advice to the Kashmir authorities was merely to invite Sheikh Abdullah, who had been released by the end of September, to form a provisional government and to announce fresh elections; nothing should be done about accession until then.[5] Abdullah too campaigned for democratic rights and did not publicly concern himself with accession.

More than Kashmir, the Government of India were at this time concerned with Junagadh, a small state with dispersed territory on the west coast. On 15 August 1947 its Muslim ruler, despite the fact that over 80 per cent of the population was of a different religion, declared the accession of his state to Pakistan. What happened to Junagadh would be important, as both the Governments of India and Pakistan recognized, not only in itself but because it would serve as a precedent in the larger issues, which were still pending, of Kashmir and Hyderabad. Mountbatten, though Governor-General of India alone and not of both dominions, inhibited his government's options. Concerned about his own position, he threw his weight against military action.[6] He persuaded Nehru to rule put war and commit himself to a plebiscite in Junagadh.

Pakistan, therefore, had gained considerable vantage on the question of Kashmir even before the crisis broke. On the night of 24 October, news reached Delhi that well-organized tribesmen had entered Kashmir from Pakistan and were marching on Srinagar. The defence committee, meeting the next morning, decided to send arms to the Kashmir government. Mountbatten was in favour of at least a temporary accession to India, but neither Nehru nor Patel attached any importance to this. Nehru was more concerned that the maharaja should associate Abdullah with the resistance.[7] The next day, when the prime minister of Kashmir saw Nehru and requested that Indian troops be flown into Kashmir, Nehru declined and was only persuaded by Patel and Abdullah to agree.[8] Clearly, therefore, whatever Nehru's romantic attachment to the mountains of Kashmir, it did not influence his policy, and the decisions on Kashmir were not, as has been frequently suggested, being taken by him alone in an overwhelming mood of sentiment.

At the meeting of the defence committee on 26 October, Mountbatten and the chiefs of staff advised against flying troops to Kashmir, but when Mountbatten saw that his ministers were determined to do so, he gave in. He was wise enough to discern that on this issue Nehru and the cabinet might have ignored his views, especially as Gandhi felt as strongly as they did and terminated what Nehru later termed 'a difficulty of the spirit' by telling Nehru that there could be no peace by submission to evil in Kashmir.[9] But Mountbatten succeeded in persuading Nehru and Patel to link military assistance to immediate accession and the offer of a plebiscite after law and order had been restored. The accession of Kashmir was accepted and Indian troops were flown out on the morning of 27 October, just in time to prevent the sack of Srinagar.

Nehru turned down Abdullah's suggestion that an ultimatum be given to Pakistan and war declared at the end of it;[10] but though he was not willing to launch into an all-out war with Pakistan, there was no slackening in the efforts to clear Kashmir of the invaders. Nehru had no thought of compromise. Kashmir had become to him a symbol of the basic conflict in India and on the decision there 'one might almost say, depends not only the future of Kashmir but the future of Pakistan and to a considerable extent the future in India. Thus we are playing for much higher stakes than might appear on the surface.'[11] However, Mountbatten succeeded in persuading him to refer the Kashmir problem to the United Nations by arguing that the only alternative was a full-scale war. Mountbatten would have preferred a general reference to the United Nations to stop the fighting and conduct a plebiscite; but the Government of India would do no more than make a specific reference with regard to Pakistan's aggression. Though India was committed to allow the people of Kashmir to decide their own future, Nehru was unwilling now to tie this up with the reference to the United Nations.

So the limited reference was made to the United Nations. Patel had not been in favour even of this;[12] and Gandhi too, whom Nehru consulted, consented to it with some reluctance. He saw the draft and revised it to remove the suggestion of an independent Kashmir as a possible alternative to accession to either state. It was unfortunate—and Nehru was later deeply to regret it—that Mountbatten, who had no clear understanding of international affairs, had succeeded in persuading Nehru to bring the United Nations into the picture. Having achieved this, he now set himself to prevent any extension of the war. Nehru, however, was determined to 'see this Kashmir business through. We do not believe in leaving things half-done.'[13] He insisted to Mountbatten, even after the decision to refer the matter to the United Nations had been taken, that expulsion of the raiders was still the first priority.

By the reference to the Security Council India stood to suffer in every way. To the Indian request on 31 December 1947 that Pakistan be directed not to participate or assist in any way in the invasion of Kashmir, Pakistan replied not only with a denial but with general allegations against India of hostility to Pakistan, 'genocide' against Muslims and securing the accession of Kashmir by fraud and violence. The Security Council under the guidance of the British delegate, Philip Noel-Baker, ignored the specific complaint of India and made clear its preference for Pakistan. It was assumed that India and Pakistan had an equal interest in Kashmir and therefore whatever was done should seem fair to the Government of Pakistan and the tribesmen as well as to the Government of

India. Further, in virtual acceptance of Pakistan's general charges against India and ignoring the fact that the United Nations had been approached on a limited issue, the 'Kashmir question' was replaced on the agenda by the 'India-Pakistan question'.

In Kashmir itself, while India was inhibited from a full-scale effort to drive out the invaders, there was no abatement in Pakistan's offensive. It was in this context that the Indian cabinet decided in January 1948 to withhold payment of Rs. 55 crores (about £ 30 million), due to Pakistan as part of the assets of partition, until a settlement had been reached in Kashmir, for it was clear to them that this amount would be used for the purchase of arms to sustain the fighting against India. Mountbatten, acting unconstitutionally, criticized the decision of his cabinet when Gandhi raised the matter and described it as both unstatesmanlike and unwise and the 'first dishonourable act' of the free Government of India.[14] On Kashmir, Gandhi had no doubt that the troops of Pakistan would have to be driven out. He would not accept the premise that Muslims should, by the mere fact of their religion, be regarded as not Indian. But the withholding of payment of money to which the Government of India were committed appeared to Gandhi to be on a different footing. This was one of the chief causes which impelled Gandhi to commence, on 13 January, a fast to quicken the conscience of the Indian people and improve relations between Hindus and Muslims. So the cabinet reopened the question and, while convinced that their decision had been right on merits, decided to make immediate payment if Gandhi wished it. When all the facts were placed before Gandhi he advised full payment and the cabinet announced a reversal of their decision.

The fast itself, which lasted five days, seemed to Nehru to have had generally a good effect even in Pakistan. He himself had tasted in sympathy for one or two days, eliciting from Gandhi, when he heard of it, affectionate concern. 'Give up your fast. . . . May you live long and continue to be the jewel of India.'[15] But the good effect wore out soon enough in both countries, the evil of religious hatred being too deep-set to be cured easily, and on the evening of 30 January 1948 Gandhi was assassinated. Death in the cause of human harmony was the perfect end to Gandhi's life, the last line of the sonnet. He himself would have seen it as the final accomplishment. As Nehru observed in one of his superb flights of English prose, Gandhi had unconsciously become the perfect artist in the art of living, and even in his death there was a complete artistry.

> As he grew older his body seemed to be just a vehicle for the mighty spirit within him. Almost one forgot the body as one listened to him or looked at him, and so where he sat became a temple and where he trod was hallowed ground.... Why, then, should we grieve for him? Our memories of him will be of the Master, whose step was light to the end, whose smile was infectious and whose eyes were full of laughter. We shall associate no failing powers with him of body or mind. He lived and he died at the top of his strength and powers, leaving a picture in our minds and in the mind of the age that we live in that can never fade away.[16]

This was written a fortnight after Gandhi's death; but Nehru's immediate reaction was almost identical. The personal blow was, of course, overwhelming. Rushing to Birla House on hearing the news, he 'bent his head down and began to sob like a child.'[17] But within a few hours of the murder, pushed by Mountbatten in front of the microphone, his voice was again contained, and he mingled his heavy sense of loss with thanksgiving and a fresh call to duty.

> Friends and comrades, the light has gone out of our lives and there is darkness everywhere... . The light has gone out, I said, and yet I was wrong. For the light that shone in this country was no ordinary light... that light represented something more than the immediate present, it represented the living, the eternal truths, reminding us of the right path, drawing us from error, taking this ancient country to freedom. . . . A great disaster is a

symbol to us to remember all the big things of life and forget the small things of which we have thought too much. In his death he has reminded us of the big things of life, the living truth, and if we remember that, then it will be well with India. . . .[18]

REFERENCES

1. Estimates vary. P. Moon (with whom Mountbatten agrees) reckoned the figure to be about 200,000 *(Divide and Quit,* London, 1961, p. 283); G. D. Khosla believed that it was about 400,000-500,000 *(Stern Reckoning,* Delhi, n.d., p. 299); Ian Stephens places the figure at 500,000 *(Pakistan,* London, 1963, p. 80) and M. Edwardes at 600,000 *(Last Years of British India,* London. 1963, p. 223).

2. R. Jeffrey, 'The Punjab Boundary Force and the Problem of Order, August 1947', *Modern Asian Studies* (1974), pp. 491-520; Kirpal Singh, *The Partition of the Punjab* (Patiala, 1972), p. 108.

3. Speech on 29 November 1947, Constituent Assembly (Legislative) debates 1947, vol : II, pp. 917-22.

4. See Nehru's statement to the press, 16 September, *Times of India,* 17 September 1947.

5. Nehru to M. C. Mahajan, prime minister of Kashmir, 21 October 1947.

6. See his report to the King cited in H. V. Hodson, *The Great Divide* (London, 1969), pp. 430-1.

7. Hodson, pp. 449-50.

8. M.C. Mahajan *Looking Back* (Bombay, 1963), pp. 151-2.

9. Speech in Parliament, 8 March 1949, Constituent Assembly of India (Legislative) debates, 1949, vol. II, part II, pp. 1225-36.

10. Nehru to Sheikh Abdullah, 4 November 1947.

11. Nehru to Sheikh Abdullah, 3 December 1947.

12. See his letter to Arthur Henderson, 3 July 1948, *Sardar Patel's Correspondence,* vol. 6 (Ahmedabad, 1973), pp. 386-7.

13. Speech at Jammu, 6 December, *Statesman*, 7 December 1947.

14. A. Campbell-Johnson, *Mission with Mountbatten* (London, 1951), p. 265; Pyarelal, *Mahatma Gandhi: The Last Phase*, vol. 2 (Ahmedabad, 1958), p. 700.

15. J. Nehru, *A Bunch of Old Letters* (Bombay, 1958), p. 499. Original in Hindi. The phrase 'jewel of India' is a reference to the name Jawahar, which means jewel.

16. Harijan, 15 February 1948.

17. D.G. Tendulkar, *Mahatma*, vol. 8 (Bombay revised edition, 1963), p. 288. Nehru approved this sentence, letter to Tendulkar, 12 October 1952.

18. Broadcast, 30 January 1948. Speeches, vol. 1, 1946-9 (New Delhi, 1949), pp. 42-44.

24

Nehru's India

By about 1950 it may be said that India had closed a chapter in her long history and opened another. The British had gone, the new regime had been successfully established, and outstanding questions left over from the past had been dealt with. The Congress had, with the exception of the loss of Pakistan, completed its programme, and the way was clear for India to chart a new course into the future. The events and developments since 1950 are therefore still contemporary rather than historical, since they relate to processes still under development and to policies not fully worked out.

The historical approach is thus no longer satisfactory since the materials for a considered historical judgement as yet exist only partially. Neither will a mere catalogue of events serve the purpose, since it would leave the reader bemused with information without any enlightenment on the trend of events. For there is obviously a trend even though it cannot be assessed with the rigour of historical analysis.

The form proposed for this chapter is therefore that of an essay on contemporary India. This form is particularly convenient in the present case since the years 1947-64 have a unity not often to be found in India's past.

That unity was provided by the figure of Jawarharlal Nehru. By a combination of circumstances he had a freer hand in moulding Indian policy than anyone since some of the great Mughals. Along with this opportunity went the ideas as to what should be done, the energy to do it, and the magnetism to maintain his hold over the country to an unprecedented extent. This chapter will therefore be an essay in the assessment of Nehru's India.

The personal supremacy of Nehru at first needs some explanation. Apart from his personality he enjoyed certain other advantages. He was the son of a brilliant father in the select circle of major leaders during the twenties and he came from the heartland of northern India and core of the modern national movement, the middle Ganges valley.

He was successively the disciple, favoured son, and lieutenant of Gandhi, the patron saint of the movement, so that much of the veneration attached to the Mahatma descended to him. He was the idol of the younger left wing Congressmen for many years. Finally, he had graduated with flying honours in the Congress school of national distinction, political imprisonment. He was, after the death of Patel, the only surviving founding father of the nation. He carried with him something of the magic aura of the Mahatma for the masses and all the prestige of a forward-looking nationalist for the classes.

He was thus, after 1950, the master of the Congress and so the master of India. His national prestige made him indispensable, a fact underlined by occasional threats of resignation, and his indispensability increased as the patriotic ardour of Congress decreased and abuses crept in. He might be the King who had evil advisers or the King who was deceived or wrongly informed, or the King who misunderstood, but he remained the King.

This unique position was supported by a striking personality. The slight spare figure with mobile face and Gandhi capped head contained an abounding energy which constantly astonished observers and a magnetic personality which attracted while it commanded.

Though an intellectual and an aristocrat to his fingertips his eloquence could move the masses and he derived strength as well as pleasure from contact with them. His lightning tours made him known throughout the country and his impatience was regarded as a kind of divine discontent. Even his short temper was relished by those who did not suffer from it. His integrity was outstanding and a matter for awe.

His catholic interest in all sides of life, from gliding contests to trekking in the hills, increased the sense of identification with the people. A westerner in outlook, in taste, a secularist who disclaimed the name of Hindu and disliked the title of Pandit, he remained acceptable both to the orthodox and the peasant because of his burning patriotism.

Thus Nehru not only had the national stage virtually to himself; with his antecedents and his gifts he was able to dazzle and dominate the national audience that watched him. With such gifts and such latitude of action, Nehru's views became vital in judging his government's policies. With few first ministers could the gap between personal desires and government policy have been so small. Nehru's outlook was essentially that of a democratic socialist of the nineteen-thirties. He proclaimed himself a socialist in the twenties but equally firmly rejected Marxist communism after a visit to Russia. Authoritarianism offended his sense of individual freedom; that and the secret police were to him an aggravated version of the British imperialism and the C.I.D. which he was fighting in India.

His sense of personal rights and values led him to oppose Hindu orthodoxy almost as vehemently as the foreign government. Equal rights for all meant not only the outcasts or Harijans as Gandhi taught, but the regular castes as well and women as well as men. He saw socialism as the control of capital in the national interest rather than as the imposition of authority on private enterprise.

He was thus an enemy of privilege of every kind and a believer in social control rather than dictation. His idea was a society Indian in sentiment and social habit, secular in its outlook, and democratic in its working. An essential element in his outlook was a war on poverty.

The effect of his first contact with starving *kisans* of Uttar Pradesh as a young man never left him. His insistence on raising living standards prevented him from accepting Gandhi's belief in village democracies loosely knit in a non-industrial society because he believed that the introduction of modern mechanized industry was the only way by which this could be done.

In foreign affairs, in which he was the chief Congress expert from the early thirties, he was a democratic internationalist. He believed in self-governing nationalities, and in an international order to bind them together. He was naturally an opponent of imperialism and had a deep suspicion of the designs of European powers in Asia and Africa. His ideas in this sphere may be said to have been influenced by President Wilson's Fourteen Points.

While Nehru had unusually clear ideas as to what he wanted to do and an unusually clear field for putting them into practice, it must not be supposed that he was an unfettered autocrat, a kind of nationalist archangel. A threat of resignation would give him his way with Congress and even lead to deputations of dissuasion, and a bang on the table would secure assent in the cabinet.

But there were powerful vested interests, social and financial, which distrusted some of his policies and practised more subtle methods of opposition than open dissent. Since to be outside the Congress was to be branded as anti-Nehru the conservative groups in particular carried on their opposition from within by means of obstruction at all levels. It is only recently that a conservative as distinct from a communal party has appeared under the name of the Swatantra party.

They could take advantage of his multifarious interests and lack of administrative flair, which inhibited sufficient delegation to trustworthy agents, quietly to undermine his decisions on one subject while his attention was occupied with another. On occasion public opinion itself would stir, as in the matters of linguistic provinces and China. But in general the opposition to his policies was covert in form and obstructive in character.

It is in the extent of Nehru's fortune in dealing with this obstruction that the general success of his administration must be judged. On the first issue of a strong central government he enjoyed general support. Text book stories of anarchy and the spectre of partition were too fresh in every mind for localism to raise its head.

Under this impulse the new constitution gave the centre wide powers and the princes were integrated into the new state structure. Thereafter occurred a development which is an interesting commentary on the extent of Nehru's power. In Andhra an agitation sprang up for a state on a linguistic basis (of Telugu) separate from Madras. Nehru preferred non-linguistic states in the interests of a strong centre. He feared that a linguistic state, giving political expression to a regional patriotism, like that of the Telugus or Marathas, might generate an emotional force which would jump constitutional limits and threaten the centre's authority.

For some time he resisted, but when in 1952 Potti Sriramulu died by hunger strike in the cause of Andhra he gave in. In 1956 there was a radical reorganization on linguistic lines, the two exceptions being the Punjab and Bombay states. But when Marathas and Gujaratis demonstrated he gave in again and recognized a division into the two states of Maharashtra and Gujarat. Later (November 1966), his daughter agreed to a division of the Punjab into the Punjab and the Haryana states.

Democracy was another issue on which there was general agreement at least in the open. Thus we find the principle enshrined in the new constitution with the two features of parliamentary responsibility and universal adult suffage. With the general dominance of the Congress in the state legislatures the principle of responsibility has not yet been seriously tested; the greatest struggles have been internal faction fights within the Congress parties.

But it is now clear that universal suffrage has had an effect as the low income groups became more aware of their power of electing or rejecting candidates. High caste monopoly of office has suffered a severe blow, for no Brahmin can receive election today without low caste votes. Caste groupings are in many areas being exploited as ready-made political machines with the result that the massive electorate of mainly illiterate voters has been showing unexpected life.

The process has been helped by the revival of *panchayats* or village committees which Nehru championed. But he showed curiously little enthusiasm for proceeding to the logical next step in democratic practice, from a mass electorate to mass education.

Seventeen years after independence seventy per cent of the population were still illiterate. But here again one suspects that it was not Nehru's desire but performance which fell short. If, conservative interests might argue, we can't prevent every peasant and low caste man having a vote we can at least hinder his getting education and so make it easier to fool him.

The attack on privilege extended from the princes, who were generally agreed to be moribund, to the *zamindars* of northern India, who enjoyed large proprietary rights in return for collecting the land tax for the government (and keeping some of it for their trouble). They were a classic example of the working of the principle of unearned increment in land and had long been the target of criticism.

But unlike the princes they had influential friends. The great *zamindaris* were ended but terms of compensation were such that it has been maintained that the tenants derived little benefit. In the sphere of industry Nehru was at first more radical, beginning with threats of nationalization which alarmed foreign business. But in practice socialist theory found expression mainly in heavy taxation, comparable with that of Britain, and in a division of industry into public and private sectors.

The great new industrial enterprises were under state control while existing industries went on much as before with a greater degree of control. With foreign business enterprise the government was stricter but this took the form of insisting on a dilution of foreign with Indian capital and management. Foreign enterprise has complained but the extent of its continued activity does not suggest that the restrictions have been penal.

We now come to the subjects perhaps closest to Nehru's heart, the modernization, welfare, and social programmes. The grand object was to bring the country materially on to a level with the western world, by radically raising the standard of living, and by bringing into her social system the principle of individual personal rights.

The first process was a material one and its aim generally approved, while the second was moral and intellectual, involving ancient social conceptions. No one but Nehru would have dared to attempt both at once. The project of raising the standard of living was a gigantic one, for it was complicated by the rapid and continuous rise in the population. In 1941 it was 389 millions. In 1951, after seventy millions had gone to Pakistan, it was 356 millions, and in 1961 it was 434 millions. The means of the rise of standards was to be a double movement of increased agricultural output and large-scale industrialization to increase production significantly.

This in turn involved the use of foreign capital if an already poor country was not to be subjected to intolerable hardship. The year 1950 was a key one in this respect for in this year Nehru set up the National Planning Commission. Without this body and the constitutional powers allotted to the centre the progress so far made would have been impossible.

The first plan, launched in 1951, placed special emphasis on agricultural production to free India from dependence on overseas supplies. This part of the programme was a great success, production increasing by twenty-five per cent over the five-year period.

At the same time the great power and irrigation projects of the Damodar valley scheme and the Hirakud dam were undertaken. Along with these three new steel plants were started, sponsored respectively by Great Britain, West Germany, and Russia.

All these were retained in the public sector, but the private sector of industry also made a meaningful contribution. The claimed rise in the national income was eighteen per cent, which, even allowing for the concurrent rapid increase in population, was a substantial advance.

A second and more ambitious plan was launched in 1956, in which the emphasis was on large-scale industrialization. The aim was to increase the national income by twenty-five per cent. The cost was nearly double that of the first plan, some four thousand million in the public and two thousand million pounds in the private sector. This involved raising two thousand million pounds abroad, with resultant credit difficulties.

These were overcome by outside loans, in particular from the United States. The plan was completed with some trimmings and shortfalls; though its success was less spectacular than that of the first plan the achievement was greater because of its larger scale.

India's third five-year plan outlived Nehru. This called for an outlay of about eight thousand million pounds, of which nearly five thousand millions would be in the public sector. This great project aimed at raising the national income by five per cent per annum, at radical expansion of the basic industries, and at making India self-sufficient in foodstuffs. It is claimed that during the decade 1951-61 the national income (at constant prices) rose by forty-two per cent, income per head by twenty per cent and consumption by sixteen per cent.

These are impressive figures and there can be no doubt of the magnitude of the achievement. They represent Nehru's bid to reduce poverty and meet the challenge of an exploding population. There is no doubt that he was aware of the seriousness of this latter problem, but so far no serious measures had been taken to meet it.

We now come to the social programme. Nehru's concept of the individual was that of the western liberals and he wished to extend to the people of India legal rights on those lines. This involved, though few perceived it, a direct clash with the existing social system, with its deep roots and religious sanctions.

The groundwork of attack on social tradition had already been carried out by Gandhi, with his attack on outcastism and the stricter caste observances. There was already a widespread disregard of caste practices among the upper classes, and there was no open opposition to the abolition of untouchability and of the legality of caste restrictions in the constitution. But behind this lay the fabric of Hindu personal law still largely based on the age-old Laws of Manu, nearly as ancient and as deeply rooted as caste itself.

In Hindu social law the group matters more than the individual, the woman is subordinate to the man. Nehru hoped to alter all this in a single session with his Hindu Code Bill. But in fact it took six years to pass the two most important measures, the Hindu Succession Act (1955) and the Hindu Marriage Act (1956).

The former gives women equal rights with men in the matter of succession to and holding of property. The latter gives monogamy a legal basis and provides for divorce with alimony and maintenance. Another Act provides for the maintenance of the Hindu widow and of separated wives. Such was the obstruction from within the ample Congress majority that the whole process of revision is not yet complete. But what has been so far accomplished is nevertheless a major achievement.

Education is an essential part of modernization and here Nehru was more successful at the top than lower down. There has been a great proliferation of universities and technical institutes; they have more than doubled since independence and now number about seventy. Standards of course vary but in sum this must be adjudged a major effort.

Less progress has been made in primary education. Some fifteen per cent of the population were literate before independence. The present claim is thirty per cent. The matter of the official language is also one on which Nehru encountered opposition. Himself an Urdu or Hindustani speaker, he was willing for Hindi to be made the official language in spite of the difficulties this produced in the south. But he wished to retain English along with it.

This involved him in a long-drawn-out contest with the Hindi enthusiasts. Nehru considered that their success would both tend to isolate India from the outside world at a critical time and seriously alienate the south. The disturbances early in 1965 in South India suggest that there was substance in his view.

In foreign affairs Nehru enjoyed almost complete freedom of action until the Hungarian crisis of 1956, and to a large extent after. The country wanted India to play a full part in international affairs and to be treated on equal terms by the great powers : the details they left to Nehru. His guiding principles may be summarized briefly as national independence, anti-colonialism, internationalism, and neutralism or non-involvement towards the great powers.

The doctrine of national independence was relevant to the sub-continent, for it was Nehru's view that the physical limits of India should be coterminous with the national state. France and Portugal had colonial enclaves at Pondicherry and Goa respectively. The French voluntarily withdrew but the Portuguese held on until forcibly ejected in 1961.

This act was the product of natural impatience, but it was a unilateral breach of international law and dimmed somewhat the Indian image in the western world. In this same context Nepal has been in a difficult position as being geographically part of India but politically independent. India has respected this independence but has sought to influence her internal affairs, with the result that relations, as with Ceylon and Burma, were not always happy. Since Nehru's death they have improved in all cases.

As an anti-colonialist Nehru tended to be suspicious of the ex-imperialist powers. They were, he seemed to say, at best ticket-of-leave men while communist or eastern powers were at worst first offenders. Thus he worked for the ejection of the Dutch from Indonesia and the French from Indo-China, he was more severe with Britain at Suez than with Russia over Hungary, and his peaceful patience was finally exhausted by the Portuguese foothold in India at Goa. It was China which has ended this phase. As an internationalist India took an active part in United Nations affairs and served with credit and distinction in a number of places including the Congo.

In high politics, as it were, Nehru had three preoccupations, Pakistan, relations with the great powers, and his position in Asia. With Pakistan relations were at first very complicated indeed. There were disputes over the sharing of the old government's assets, the settlement of refugee property, the supply and use of canal water, and of course Kashmir. Underlying them was the bitterness engendered by the massacres and mass migrations.

The payment of the assets to Pakistan was secured by Gandhi just before his death in January 1948. The dispute about refugee property went on for years but has now been settled, or perhaps we should say the matter closed. The canal water issue arose from the Indian control of headwaters supplying water to Pakistan canals as part of plans innocently made in the past for irrigating the undivided Punjab. The water being vital for Pakistan, this question might have led to war at any time if India had cut off the supply.

The issue became more tense when India announced new plans which would take virtually the whole of the Sutlej outfall for use in India. In this matter the World Bank came to the rescue; in an agreement signed in September 1960 a scheme was accepted by which Pakistan could construct transverse canals to supply the old system with water from the Pakistan-controlled Indus.

There remains Kashmir. The original Indian case was the legally watertight one of accession by the prince. But India's weakness was that she had already rejected this ground in the small case of Junagadh and was soon to do the same in the large state of Hyderabad.

Here the people's will was to prevail. To bridge the gap between the two positions Nehru offered a plebiscite but was never able to find any terms proposed by successive U.N. mediators acceptable. He later proclaimed the union of Kashmir with India and resisted Anglo-American attempts to find a compromise. Patel might have given up Kashmir on the principle of the fewer Muslims in India the better, but Nehru was adamant.

Why? He was not interested in the Muslim fringe to the north-west. His heart, it can almost literally be said, was in the lovely and fatal Vale of Kashmir. His motives were partly strategical (defence against China), partly those of prestige, but mainly his care for secular democracy in India.

A Muslim state voluntarily adhering to the Indian Union is a living witness to secular democracy. The other argument used was that cession would let loose Hindu communal feeling to the destruction of the large Múslim minority still remaining in India. One can only observe that Nehru here maintained his position with great tenacity and at heavy cost; no one can know whether the remedy of independence or Pakistan union would be worse than the present disease of troubled relations.

In the world at large Nehru's policy was the now famous one of non-alignment or non-involvement with the great power blocs. It was invented under the shadow of the threat of nuclear war and for a number of years served India well.

The more states, thought Nehru, who were uncommitted, the more careful would the power blocs be before committing themselves to war. This policy was undermined by two developments. The advent of the hydrogen bomb gradually brought the realization that nuclear war cannot now be, and China upset Nehru's balancing trick of relations with both power blocs.

This leads on to his relations with Asia. For a time he toyed with Asianism, but the idea was too nebulous to win much support. But he certainly hoped for the moral leadership of Asia outside China and for this he cultivated good relations with that country, expressed in the *Panch Shila* or Five Principles of co-existence agreed in 1954.

In Africa, Nehru's natural sympathy with anti-colonialism led him into sympathy with and encouragement of African aspirations. At one time it began to look as though he was to be the tacit leader of an Afro-Asian group. But hesitancy on his part, due perhaps in some measure to disillusionment and perhaps to some degree of African disenchantment, caused this dream to fade also.

Nehru's fortunes were at their zenith in the mid-fifties, when he seemed to be successfully modernizing and liberalizing his country and exercising an increasing influence in Asia and Africa. About then the first wisps of cloud drifted across his sun; gradually the shadows lengthened and darkened until night fell with gathering clouds. A decade later all India's ills were being attributed to his mistakes, not least by those who had done much to frustrate his designs. The blazing rocket of the fifties became the fallen stick of the sixties.

It was, as nemesis so often decrees, the field in which the victim seemed strongest that Nehru suffered the cruellest blows. A foretaste was his haste in judging the British action in Suez while showing reluctance to condemn the Russian action in Hungary. Non-involvement for all, said the critics, but more so for some than for others.

A more serious matter was the flight of the Dalai Lama to India. Nehru had advised him to live on terms with the Chinese and welcomed him with muted enthusiasm. But while Suez might have been a misjudgement, the Dalai Lama was an embarrassment. His presence both soured relations with China, and stimulated a public response in India. Though the Dalai Lama was a Buddhist of a distinctly unorthodox kind, many Hindus regarded him as a sort of extension of Hinduism in a Buddhist monk's robe. For them he was an *avatar* (incarnation of a god) from the Himalayas, the abode of the Holy ones.

Henceforth Nehru was not a wholly free agent in the conduct of Indian affairs. There followed the occupation of Goa, already mentioned, which suggested an ageing Nehru, amenable to internal pressure.

The sourness of the Chinese led on to the China incident of 1962. Mutual suspicions led to counter charges and an aroused public opinion allowed no private settlement behind closed doors. Nehru's former dexterity and firm grasp of essentials faded into alternate defiance and procrastination.

The nub of the problem was the discovery of a Chinese highway from Tibet to Sinkiang built across the desolate Aksai Chin plateau, which British foreign maps in the nineteenth century had alternately included and excluded from the Indian empire. The road involved prestige and this made settlement difficult.

To this was added an unnecessary advance beyond the Macmahon line near the Sikkim border which precipitated the actual fighting in impossible conditions for the Indians. Nehru never recovered from the rout which ensued and the revelations of cross purposes and incompetence which followed. Like Napoleon after Moscow, he recovered enough agility to fend off western demands for a Kashmir settlement and American urgings for the conversion of military aid into an alliance. But policy he had none, and soon after he had released Sheikh Abdullah for what might have been his independent bid for a Kashmir settlement, he died.

As with Gandhi, men said that the light had gone out, but they felt that it had gone, not in the first glimmerings of dawn but in the gathering shadows of night. For this there was some justification. Diplomatically, India was alone in the world, with a hostile China and Pakistan, an aloof Russia, a critical western world and a disenchanted third world.

Internally, the third five-year plan had run into difficulties, both of finance and achievement. Industrial expansion was flagging while the unexpectedly rapid increase in the population had overtaken the increase in the national produce. Development had given way to marking time, and hope to disillusionment and anxiety.

Any attempt to appraise Nehru's achievement must fall somewhere between the extremes of success and failure. His rule, notable both for length and achievement, had neither the heroic note of success against odds nor the doleful one of stark failure.

If there has been more dexterity than conflict, a tendency to compromise rather than fight to a finish, mere has nevertheless been solid achievement. Has it been the success for which he had been striving; is the present India the India of his ideal?

In most areas of endeavour we find an air of half-achievement, of a process stopped short. In the field of democracy we have a shiny machine on a western model but no party system to oil its working parts.

In education there is an impressive expansion of higher education and a distinct lag in the primary field. Industry has expanded in a big way, but not sufficiently to raise materially the standard of life in the country as a whole. The middle class has greatly grown with this expansion, but as between them and the peasant mass it is still a question of 'we' and 'they'.

In the secular field good progress has been made with the reform of the Hindu Code, but there are distinct signs of an orthodox reaction; Hindus cannot be restrained from blaming Muslims whenever relations with Pakistan are specially strained. In the control of population there was little progress, but where else has anyone done any better? In foreign affairs India played a distinguished part but gradually lost the halo of superior moral virtue which Gandhi bequeathed her.

Looking back on this survey I should say that Nehru's greatest success was his social legislation, because achieved with the greatest effort, and likely to influence the future most. His greatest failure was his inability to set up an educated social democracy above the poverty line. Instead he established an India with all the appurtenances of a modern state.

New industry called forth an enlarged middle class. The enlargement and enrichment of this class took up most of the increase in the national income produced by the five-year plans, leaving the remaining eighty per cent much as before. When we compare the state of modern India with its condition in only 1940, the achievement was great, but it was not the achievement on which Nehru had set his heart.

25

The Mahatma's Political Heir

Jawaharlal Nehru shot into prominence as one of the topmost leaders of the national movement and as the acknowledged representative of the left trend in the organisation when Mahatma Gandhi had him chosen as Congress President in 1929. He was again chosen for two successive terms of presidentship in 1936-38. Naturally, therefore, he was the obvious choice for the leadership of the interim government in 1946 for the Prime Ministership of India after independence.

Although he was thus known as the political heir of the Mahatma and continued to act as his disciple for seventeen years of his life as the first Prime Minister of free India, the teacher and disciple sharply differed on a number of vital political questions. These included the perspective which should guide Congressmen after their basic objective—the freedom of the nation—was attained.

Mahatma Gandhi was of the view that, the objective of the Congress having been realised, it should cease to be a political party, converting itself into a Lok Sevak Sangh. This advice was heeded and sought to be acted upon by a small band of confirmed Gandhians led by Vinoba Bhave who shunned electoral politics and organised themselves in the non-political Sarva Seva Sangh. It was heeded also by the socialists who cut their Congress tail, organising themselves into an opposition socialist party in free India. Nehru would have joined them and others who stood to the left of the Congress in a well-organised Left Party (in opposition to a right party led by Patel and others) if he had agreed with and acted upon the advice of the Mahatma. A two-party system with its left and right poles would then have been the national scenario.

Nehru, however, disagreed. Even earlier, in the 1920s and the 1930s, when he was the acknowledged leader of the Left in the Congress organisation, he was opposed to that right-left confrontation which was envisaged by the communists and socialists. He therefore allowed himself to be what the Mahatma had chosen for him—a left leader who would not transgress the limits set by the rightist leadership.

As a matter of fact, when an open confrontation took place before and at the Tripura Congress in 1939, he took an ambivalent attitude—the only occasion when he temporally faded out of Congress leadership.

Subsequent developments like the Quit India Movement and its leaders which culminated in the Mountbatten Plan of transfer of power to two (Hindu and Muslim) Indias leading to the biggest ever mass slaughter in history etc convinced him that the disbandment of the Congress as advised by the Mahatma would be a calamity. What was required, on the other hand, was, he felt, to use the prestige of the national organisation and the newly-acquired authority of its leaders as the new rulers of the country, to bring some order and cohesion into the chaotic state of affairs that followed the partition of India. It was with this idea that he began, two months after the attainment of independence on 15 August 1947, a more or less regular fortnightly correspondence with State chief ministers. He hoped in his first letter,

> to keep in touch with your province and keep you informed not merely of the more significant developments in the Centre but also of events in other provinces which have repercussions over the rest of India .... It is in times of exceptional stress like the present that it is more than ordinarily incumbent on us to keep in close touch with each other, so that we can put forth concerted effort to overcome the growing dangers facing us.

The practice of writing letters to chief ministers, which he continued right up to his death, helped him to unburden himself of the intricate problems—national and international—with which he was constantly faced. It was in fact a continuity of and break from his earlier exercises in that ideological cohesion at the national level which made him the national leader *par excellence*. It was a continuity in the sense that it sought to give an all-India outlook to those (chief ministers and others) who tended to look at problems from narrow (provincial, communal) angles. It was a break from the old practices because he was doing it at the level of central and state governments, rather than at the level of a mass movement of which he had earlier been the leader. He, who had made a mark as the inspirer and educator of the millions, was now acting as the co-ordinator and educator of governmental leaders. The organisation which he led had been transformed from a mass movement into the political machine of the new ruling party.

This is not to suggest that Nehru ceased to be a man of the masses. He did undoubtedly go out campaigning among the people and inspired and got inspiration from the people. But his mass contacts were centered round the projects and activities of his government for which he sought co-operation from the people. There being no alien force against which he was fighting, he did not want (as earlier he did) the masses to take matters into their own hands. He was in fact impatient of such forms of mass action as had been adopted earlier (satyagraha, demonstrations, hunger strikes, etc.) when they were resorted to by the mass organisations and political parties to realise the demands formulated by them.

Here, for instance, are a few of his pronouncements taken at random from Vol. I of his *Letters to Chief Ministers:*

Strikes : "I have been deeply distressed by the recent strike in the Tata collieries. The strike was illegal and without notice and has resulted in great damage to the plan. The strike is over. But this kind of irresponsible behaviour is exceedingly harmful not only to industry but to the community as a whole and it has become essential for us to devise means to prevent this happening."

Again, "there have been some strikes which can hardly be called economic strikes. A definite attempt to sabotage is to be seen in these strikes. Then there is a threat of posts and telegraphs strike and possibly a railway strike. Government have done everything in their power, having regard to their resources, to ease the situation for their employees. They just cannot do anything more. If, in spite of this, there is any strike, then the only course open to government is to meet it with all the strength it has."

Students : "One of the most deplorable features of the present day is the extraordinary mentality of some of our students. I do not mind exuberance among students or even aggressiveness. I like vitality but what I do not like is the demands made for lower standards in passes, for hunger strikes because fees have been slightly raised, for a demand that a student should be represented in examinations and the like. All this indicates not a desire to fit oneself for shouldering responsibility but somehow to get a label without necessarily having any qualifications for anything. We cannot permit this drift."

It should be recalled that the industrial workers and the students were two sections of the fighting people who made big contributions to the freedom movement. They cannot be expected to ditto everything that Nehru and his colleagues consider possible and necessary, just because they (Nehru and his colleagues) have become rulers. They may have other ideas. Out of this arise the "exuberance" and "vitality" of students, which Nehru "likes" but which might manifest themselves in ways other than what he prefers.

As for industrial workers, they have not pledged themselves only to "economic strikes" but are part of the political movement as much after as before independence. Consolidation of the political freedom won and its expansion into socio-cultural fields require collective action by all sections of the toiling people including the industrial workers and students. Furthermore, the organised political force which leads this class—the Communist Party—has become a point of attraction for all those who are trying to forge a political alternative to the Congress. This is what Nehru, the leader of the new government in free India, did not understand, in fact was opposed to it.

This negative approach to the militant movements of the toiling people made Nehru, the leader of the new ruling party, heir to the profound crisis of the system which dogged him at every step in his life and in the life of the entire country as such. That crisis turned the Congress into a minority among the people in the very first test (the 1952 election) and made it successively lose power in several states and in the end at the Centre. His successor and daughter, in her drive to keep herself in power, had to clamp the notorious emergency and her successor and her son is today following in her footsteps, though the concrete methods he is adopting are different from hers. "Nehru himself blessed the notorious anti-communist "liberation struggle" calling it "a mass upsurge" and used it to get the Kerala government dismissed.

This, however, was not a sudden development; six years earlier, reviewing the Travancore-Cochin elections where his party was humbled, he had envisaged a "future" where "clear single-party majorities might not be available in states" and therefore "some form of coalitions between like-minded groups or a fluid or unstable state of affairs". What surprised his admirers was that among "the like-minded groups", he found in Kerala were the Muslim League, the Christian clergy and the various caste organisations. The Mahatma's warning that, if the Congress continued to function as a political party in free India, it would have to compete with communal forces appears to have come true in the very lifetime of his "political heir".

26

The Nehru Era

I was elected to the Central Assembly in 1934 and was in it till 1946. In 1946 I came to the Madras Legislative Assembly and also as Minister of Education there. In 1951 I opted to the Parliament in Delhi first in the Lok Sabha and then in Rajya Sabha till 1964. It was as a Member of Parliament that I had the opportunity to know and move with" Pandit Jawaharlal Nehru, the first Prime Minister of India.

Nehru and Sardar Patel were the two mighty men in the freedom movement and so long as the Sardar lived, Nehru had to share power with the Sardar. Both had indomitable will and courage but were different in outlook and temperament, Sardar was not happy about Nehru's unqualified secularism, nor did he like his radical attitude towards social reforms. He was strong and swift, while Nehru was soft and considerate. It is said that in the final act for unification of India, namely the police action in Hyderabad, many in the Cabinet did not know about it, till it was over and that Nehru was informed about it only after it began. On many matters, they did not see eye to eye with each other and they had to get Mahatma Gandhi's help on many occasions for a smooth running of the. government. But, as Lord Mountbatten said, both were necessary for consolidating the gains of Indian freedom. But with the demise of the Sardar in 1950, there was none in the Congress Party or Parliament to equal his stature, strength, and following. So Nehru reigned supreme. Nehru had another great advantage, namely that all the governments in the states at the time were Congress governments. And so, he ruled not only in the Centre but also in all the States. His word was law. But it must be said as a tribute to his lasting greatness that in spite of the great power he wielded, he kept a balance and sobriety which won the admiration of the people.

Setting up of the Planning Commission

Jawaharlal Nehru was a great believer in planned development. In this he drew his inspiration from Russia. Therefore, one of the first tasks done in the first Parliament was the setting up of a National Planning Commission for India of which the Prime Minister himself was the Chairman. The Indian constitution has spelt out basic objective in the "Directive Principles of State Policy." Among those "directive principles" were : "The State shall strive to promote the welfare of the people by securing and protecting, as effectively as it may, a social order in which justice, social, economic and political, shall inform all the institutions of national life" Further, "the State shall, in particular, direct its policy towards securing :

(a) that the citizens, men and women equally have the right to an adequate means of livelihood,

(b) that the ownership and control of the material resources of the community are so distributed as best to subserve the common good, and

(c) that the operation of the economic system does not result in the concentration of wealth and means of production to the common detriment.

Planning involves development of the various aspects of national life and economy such as improved agriculture, setting up new industries, extension of educational facilities, improvement of the machinery of administration fit to take up the responsibilities of development, evolution of a tax structure which will ensure social justice, land reforms, abolition of social inequalities and special measures for the uplift of women, backward castes and tribes and eradication of the colossal poverty concentrated in a large measure in the villages throughout the country.

Community Development Programmes

And so, as a corollary to planned development, a Community Development Programme, mainly aimed at raising the economic, social, and educational status of the people in villages was also necessary. Therefore a massive rural development programme had to be taken up. A development programme to uplift more than thirty crores of people living in over seven lakhs of villages was indeed a great and difficult job costing a great deal of money and effort. Fortunately the Ford Foundation under the leadership of Dr. Douglas Ensminger came forward to help in a big way and a Community Development Programme was evolved and placed before Parliament for approval.

The live-wires of the newly started Community Development Programme were V.T. Krishnamachari, when he was the Deputy Chairman of the Planning Commission, and S.K. Dey who was the Minister of State for Community Development and who was largely responsible for the implementation of the Project. The former had carried out impressive work in Baroda in rural development and later as Chairman of the Grow More Food Enquiry Committee in 1952 had made valuable suggestions on the question of an infrastructure for rural development. The Grow More Food Enquiry Committee had observed that all aspects of rural life were interrelated and that while particular problems might call for special attention, "the plans for them should form parts of, and be integrated with those for achieving the wider aims". The recommendations of this Committee were responsible, to a very large extent, for shaping the extension approach which became an essential vehicle of the Community Development Programme in India. It was felt that if the central aim of Community Development was investment in man, an integrated extension service should be the principal means to that end and that scientific knowledge and techniques should be carried to the people through the extension agency. The first Five-Year Plan gave recognition to this new approach in the following words : "Community Development is the method and rural extension of the agency through which the Five-

Year Plan seeks to initiate a process of transformation of the social and economic life of the villages."

Development of Science and Technology

One of the major developments during Nehru's period was the development of scientific and technological institutions in India on a large scale. Nehru was convinced that a technological revolution was necessary for the progress of the country, for greater production in agriculture and industry, for improving the health of the people both by preventive and curative methods for bettering communication and transport facilities and giving more employment for people. Research leads to scientific knowledge on which area-based technological inventions for higher yields both in the fields and factories. And so the government set about setting up a large number of research laboratories and institutions in various disciplines.

With the object of fulfiling these aims, the government decided to offer good conditions of service to scientists, associate them with the formulation of policies and give them an honoured placed in national life.

In the first Five-Year Plan, attention was chiefly devoted to the building up of a chain of national laboratories and other research institutions. In the Second Plan, the available facilities were developed, research was made more broad-based and research facilities in universities and at other research centres were further extended. In the Third Plan the programme of scientific and technological research was devoted specially to :

(i) Strengthening of the existing research institutions and expanding the facilities for research over a wide field;

(ii) encouraging basic research in universities;

(iii) encouraging, in particular, research in engineering and technology;

(iv) training of research personnel and expanding the programme of research fellowships and scholarships;

(v) carrying out research in the development and manufacture of scientific and industrial instruments;

(vi) coordination of research work carried out in national laboratories, universities, technical institutions, laboratories of scientific associations and research wings of government departments; and

(vii) utilising results of research after establishing their validity through pilot plant protectior, full-scale field experiments, etc.

As a result of effort in the first two Plans, an extensive network of institutions engaged in scientific research has corns into existence and pure research, applied research, and research in specialised fields are being undertaken in a large number of centres.

The Non-Aligned Movement

One of the outstanding events during Nehru's period in Parliament was the formulation of India's foreign policy and the coming into existence of the non-aligned movement. The alliance of the United States and the Soviet Union to defeat Hitler's Germany did not last long after their victory in the Second World War. Each began to consolidate its position for world hegemony and there developed two power blocs inimical to each other, namely the NATO (North Atlantic Treaty Organisation) and the Warsaw Pact countries. India was an emerging great nation and both the blocs tried to persuade, cajole and threaten India to join them. But all honour to Jawaharlal Nehru, that he resisted both the power blocs in his determination to build a great and independent India. The United States had started the organisation of SEATO (South-East Asia Treaty Organisation) and had tempted Pakistan with money and military help to join it. President Eisenhower wrote to Nehru making the same offer to India. I remember when Nehru spoke in Parliament rejecting the offer saying that India has not become free to become a slave again by allowing military bases to a foreign power on our soil. All of us lustily cheered him and the world admired him and India for this courageous and outspoken statement. This paved the way for the emergence of the Non-Aligned Movement.

Explaining the non-aligned movement, Nehru said :

Having attained political freedom, we are earnestly desirous of removing the many ills that our country suffers from, of eliminating poverty and raising the standards of our people, and giving them full and equal opportunities of growth and advancement. I speak of India because it is my country. But many other countries in Asia tell the same story, for Asia today is resurgent and these countries, which long lay under foreign yoke have won back their independence and are fired by a new spirit to strive towards new ideals. To them, as to us, independence is as vital as the breath they take to sustain life, and colonialism in any form, or anywhere is abhorrent. The vast strides that technology has made have brought a new age, of which the United States of America is the leader. Today, the whole world is our neighbour and the old divisions of continents and countries matter less and less. Peace and freedom have become indivisible. The preservation of peace forms the central aim of India's policy. It is in the pursuit of this policy that we have chosen the path of non-alignment in any military or like pact of alliance.

Non-alignment does not mean passivity of mind or action, lack of faith or conviction. It does not mean submission to what we consider evil. It is a positive and dynamic approach to such problems that confront us. We believe that each country has not only the right to freedom, but also to decide its own policy and way of life. Only thus can true freedom flourish and a people grow according to their own genius. We believe, therefore, in non-aggression and non-interference by any country in the affairs of another, and the growth of tolerance between them and the capacity for peaceful coexistence. We think that, by the free exchange of ideas and trade and other contacts between nations, each will learn from the other, and truth will prevail. We, therefore, endeavour to maintain friendly relations with all countries, even though we may disagree with them in their policies or structure of government. We think that, by this approach, we can serve not only our country, but also the larger causes of peace and good fellowship in the world.

The non-aligned movement began in 1961, with twentyfive member-countries of which the chief architects were Nehru of India, Nasser of Egypt, and Tito of Yugoslavia. In over twentyfive years, the membership has expanded to more than a hundred and has developed to be a powerful force in international affairs. It has held its meetings in various parts of the world from time to time. It was held in New Delhi in 1983 and India's Prime Minister, Mrs Indira Gandhi, was elected its Chairperson.

With the passing of time, Nehru's first Ministry after Independence began with great hopes and prestige. Nehru himself was at the height of his glory commanding the admiration and adoration of the whole of the country and of the many countries in the world. The newly emerging Indian nation was considered to be the rising great power of Asia. The idealism of the freedom movement continued. Many who had participated in the freedom movement under Mahatma Gandhi and were of proven calibre, though some others who were experts in their fields, were also taken in the Cabinet. C.D. Deshmukh, a former Governor of the Reserve Bank of India was the Finance Minister, my friend V.V. Giri in charge of Labour, Lal Bahadur Shastri, Gulzarilal Nanda, Abul Kalam Azad, N. Gopalaswamy Ayyangar and T.T. Krishnamachari were there. Many continued in the later periods. One of the notable later-additions was Sri C. Subramaniam, who along with one of our greatest agricultural scientists, Dr M.S. Swaminathan, was responsible for initiating the Green Revolution in our country. With Congress Governments also in the States, Nehru's behests were willingly received and implemented in all parts of the country.

The Chinese Invasion

In the later part of my period in Parliament, one of the greatest tragedies happened to India which had far-reaching effects and affected the prestige of our country amongst the nations of the world. That was the Chinese invasion of 1962. On 20 October 1962, China launched a massive attack against India at the North-Eastern border. The politicians, the Services, the people were not only all caught unwares, but also in a state of utter unpreparedness. India's policy towards China had been a series of misplaced faiths, illusions, assumptions spread over more than ten years. In spite of warnings from Parliament Members, Nehru refused to see what was obvious to lesser people, because he had an exaggerated opinion about his capacity to succeed diplomatically, where military preparedness was the only answer.

Chiang Kai-Shek was friendly to nationlist leaders like Nehru, before independence. At the same time, he is said to have authorised publication of maps which showed Tibet, Nepal, Bhutan, and Sikkim and large areas in Assam and NEFA (North-Eastern Frontier Area) along the Brahmaputra river as Chinese territory. Despite Indian protests later, China never repudiated these claims. In 1950, Chinese armies invaded Tibet, thus forcibly establishing claim to Tibet. But unfortunately India had been weak and without knowing the consequences conceded Chinese "suzerainty" over Tibet. India was careless and callous in concluding the Sino-Indian treaty of 1954. In ceding Tibet to China it should at least have made it a pre-condition that China accepts the conventional and hitherto undisputed boundary between India and Tibet. China then would have gladly agreed to substantial concessions, and to a clearer and more effective demarcation.

But V.K. Krishna Menon, the Defence Minister and K.M. Panikkar, his adviser on Chinese affairs, blundered colossally by making an undisputed gift of an area as large as the whole of South-East Asia put together to China. They knew that for centuries the boundaries between India and Tibet had remained conventional and loosely defined. For more than two thousand years, India and Tibet had lived in peace and in a spirit of good neighbourliness, with only a few police posts here and there to regulate the incoming and outgoing caravans on the frontiers. To have suddenly surrendered such a buffer area to the sovereign control of an expansionist militaristic regime, whose predecessor government had even laid claims to vast areas of Indian territory, was a fatal and unpardonable blunder.

Soon after China's invasion of Tibet, the Chinese started building a road through Indian territory connecting Sinkiang with Tibet as they had no direct road link with Tibet. A major roadway through long tunnels, overbridges, precipices and difficult viaducts and culverts, rising from three to fifteen thousand feat, was a gigantic venture. In the case of China, it involved thousands of labourers all along the route working day and night. And yet Indian espionage remained blind about this situation for three years India knew nothing about this highway till in 1958 a small party was sent to find out the facts. Actually the first alert came from China itself when one of the Peking newspapers proudly announced that a highway connecting Sinkiang with Lhasa in Tibet had been constructed in three years, and claimed it as a unique feat of engineering. Even after this disclosure, India remained silent, hoping as Nehru said : "it might be easier for us to deal with the Chinese Government without too much publicity for this incident".

Nehru then realized that he had been fooled by Chou En-lai, that before signing the Sino-Indian Treaty recognising Chinese control over Tibet, he should have at the same time insisted on a clear acceptance and even demarcation of the erstwhile boundary between India and Tibet. According to him, Chou En-lai said in 1956 : "They had agreed to recognise the McMahon Line in so far as the Burmese frontier was concerned and the Sino-Indian frontier was concerned. That would take care of the whole of the McMahon Line". He said further : "When I heard it, I wanted to be quite sure that I had not misunderstood him. Therefore I went back to the subject three times and made him repeat it. And because the matter was of much importance, "I put it down in writing when I came away". A shrewd person like Nehru should have realised that the words spoken by politicians have no value, and that China most of all had treated solemn written commitments as scraps of paper. He should have obtained these assurances in writing even if they could not be made part of solemn treaty.

Something worse followed in July 1962 when the Indian Defence Minister V.K. Krishna Menon went to Geneva. There he met the Chinese Defence Minister, Marshall Chen Yi. When someone asked Menon if he had read newspaper reports of a massive Chinese concentration on India's frontiers, he dismissed the report and remarked : "Would I be here if such a development was likely?" On return from Geneva, when more reports appeared about Chinese instrusions into Indian territory, Menon complacently assured the people that army was strong enough to meet any threat from China. Nehru shared Menon's complacency. On 20 October 1962, the Chinese crossed over in massive waves from several points along the two-thousand-mile border stretching from Ladakh in the North to Walong in the East. India was rudely shaken out of the deep stupor of complacency. Few even in the government realised what had happened. The Chinese armies began to pour down the mountain ridges, through various passes, capturing one post after another, throwing bewildered Indian defenders into confusion. "Comrades, friends, and fellow countrymen", wailed shocked and disillusioned Nehru, "I must speak to you about the grave situation which has arisen on our frontiers, on account of continuing and unabashed aggression by the Chinese forces. We have to meet a powerful and unscrupulous opponent". He appealed to the citizens to muster strength and courage to meet the menace.

Parliament and the Congress party were justly angry at the mismanagement of our defences by Krishna Menon and demanded his resignation. When Nehru resisted, there were cries, "then you must go". That settled the matter. He went home and called for the resignation of Krishna Menon. In his place, Y.B. Chavan, the then Chief Minister of Maharashtra was appointed as defence minister.

The Chinese invasion started on the morning of 20 October and was abated on 1st November. The Chinese occupied threatening positions at points at strategic advantage all over the Indian frontier. Even though India's rich oil fields lay at their feet and the deserted city of Tezpur offering free entry into the Brahmaputra Valley and Assam lay practically undefended, the Chinese declared a cease-fire and beat a hurried retreat to the chosen strategic positions. No convincing explanation had been forthcoming for the unilateral declaration of cease-fire by the Chinese on 22 November. They might have realised that, after the first stunning impact, the four hundred and fifty million people of India, by and large, had been roused to a sense of danger and with the spirit of 'do or die' which two decades ago had inspired them to face the bullets and bayonets of the British. Added to this was the fear that in a few days heavy seasonal rains and snow in the higher altitudes may not only cut off supplies but would make even retreat difficult.

This invasion damaged the reputation of India in the world to an unimaginable extent. This episode affected Nehru as nothing else did. He did not survive this ignonimous defeat to the country for long. For, he died stortly after, on 27 May 1964.

Men of my generation who have grown with Nehru cannot forget how millions of people admired and followed him during the freedom movement and after it. I had occasions to observe him from near and afar. He captivated all by his courage and his ability to move with love and courtesy with all ranks of people. Next to Mahatma Gandhi, he was the most loved and admired amongst the leaders. With him ended an era in contemporary history of India when a single leader had undisputed leadership not only to India, but to the many countries in the world striving for freedom. As his daughter, Indira Gandhi has said : "The story of Jawaharlal Nehru is that of a man who evolved, who grew in storm and stress till be became the representative of much that was noble in his time. It is the story of a generous and gracious human being who summed up in himself the resurgence of the "third world" as well as the humanism which transcends dogmas and is adopted to the contemporary context". His achievement by its very nature was much greater than that of a prime minister.

27

Jawaharlal Nehru : The Ideal Democrat

We have read and heard a lot about Jawaharlal Nehru, the sophisticated idealist who battled for long for the freedom of his motherland; the only son of a great father rolling in wealth who courted suffering and identified himself with the poorest of the poor; a born democrat who fought many a battle even with Gandhi, his mentor, over socialism; who created order out of the chaos that resulted from the partition of our motherland; who put a primitive agricultural country of 500 million people in his day on the industrial map of the world in the face of heavy odds; a supreme patriot who yet was concerned deeply with the world-view of history; who gave a new meaning to secularism in a nation divided grievously by religious animosities; an incorruptible hero of a deprived nation whom neither money nor power could purchase; and who opted for non-alignment as between Super Powers then as now keeping the world of the oppressed waiting on their doorsteps for small mercies and thus giving moral dignity and hope to all the poor of the world. And, who always remained a democrat at heart and in action, in spite of the unchallenged power he enjoyed and the total affection and reverence he received from almost all his people.

Humility

All this is known, though appreciated only by the people in accordance with the needs of their personal ambitions and circumstances of the day. No one, however, has been able to deny him a place among the immortals of history. But what is less known about him is his sense of innate humility; his unswerving dedication to democratic and humanistic values; his religious spirit of forgiveness and compassion and appreciation of the other man's point of view; his identification with popular causes and his willingness to compromise even with the adversary.

What he achieved was indeed great, but what he didn't or couldn't was not because he did not try, but because he felt strongly along with Gandhi that the means is as important as the ends, that great ends could not be achieved by small means nor would stay long if brought about by dishonest tricks, falsehood, violence, or by hitting below the belt. How rare is the man of authority about whom one can say after he is gone : "He was great and powerful but more than that he was good".

Exciting

I came to know him in 1936 as President of the Punjab Students' Federation. We had gone on a 21-day strike in the only Sikh college in the Punjab, at Amritsar, in protest against the pro-British management who had dismissed a few of our nationalist professors and students. We succeeded only partially; the odds were far too many against us, though we won the point of hoisting the tri-colour Congress flag on the college building which we had made a point of honour with us. What gave a most exciting turn to our careers at that young age was the nearness we developed with the politically tallest in the land. The entire nationalist leadership of the Punjab and the Frontier province rallied to our support by visiting us and imparting some of their patriotic fervour to our young formative minds. But the most unexpected was the inspiration we received through a message from Jawaharlal Nehru, the beau-ideal of all the young in the land, which electrified the atmosphere as nothing else could.

He said (I am quoting from memory) : "We should not mind if we succeeded or not in our struggle immediately, but if our cause is just and we are prepared to sacrifice for it, we are bound to win in the long run." Though considered a firebrand, he asked us to observe the strictest discipline in our ranks and do nothing which might give a handle to the authorities to weaken our cause or resort to repressive measures.

Also we should do nothing which should cause damage to the property or life of anyone, or leave behind a trail of bitterness and should keep ready for a compromise on honourable terms at all times: He said : "Do not falter in your resolve or submit to repression, but also do not be obstinate before facts". I wish this message of his someone would carry to the multifarious agitators of today. How often we confuse our petty political feuds and ambitions with the first principles of life?

Came the partition of the country. The non-Muslim refugees were pouring in from Pakistan in an endless stream with harrowing tales of butchery, rapine and abductions, and severe reprisals against innocent Indian Muslims were being committed. But here was the noble Prime Minister of India visiting all the disturbed areas in Delhi personally, consoling, reprimanding, intervening, separating parties locked in mortal communal duels, in spite of the Partition of this nation on the basis of religion. So far from communalism was he.

We are aware that in spite of their acute differences, it was Jawaharlal Nehru who had offered a seat to Jayaprakash Narayan in the Central Cabinet in 1953, which the latter refused to take and put forth his socialistic 14-point programme, and negotiations for the merger of the PSP in the Congress fell through. But Jawaharlal had convinced the nation of his utter selflessness.

Selflessness

Master Tara Singh, once an honoured colleague of his in our fight for freedom, had taken a different path after and a little before Independence. He led many agitations, one of the worst being in 1959. He was arrested and lodged in the Dharmasala jail.

His younger brother, Niranjan Singh, a well-known nationalist and once my professor for chemistry, asked me to accompany him to Jayaprakash Narayan, the PSP leader, to use his good offices with Jawaharlal Nehru, for his release, as he had fallen seriously ill in jail. "JP is the only one he would listen to", his brother pleaded.

Soothing Touch

I could not understand why JP was opposed bitterly to Jawaharlal politically, though he was on the best of terms personally with him. JP agreed to intervene, and the very next day, Master Tara Singh was released to the surprise of everyone! And the plea JP had taken with Jawaharlal was : "Master Tara Singh is the tallest of freedom-fighters and one of the truest Opposition leaders. We must keep him alive and well".

A few months after, Master Tara Singh, true to his style, threatened to go on a fast unto death, because he thought he had been defeated to the office of President of the SGPC through the "machinations" of the Congress Party, and particularly of Jawaharlal Nehru.

He came to Delhi and announced his resolve. I saw Master Tara Singh (whose permanent critic I was for his communal policies and yet respected him for his sense of honour and integrity) and requested him not to undergo (his suffering for a grievance which might turn out to be ill-founded.

At my request, Master Tara Singh wrote a letter to Nehru setting forth his reasons for going on a fast unto death and (in spite of my persuasion) holding him responsible for his defeat at the Gurudwara polls. I called on Panditji the same evening and explained to him the whole background and requested him to soothe the injured feelings of the old Sikh chief who felt hurt over an imaginary grievance.

Nehru hesitated for a while saying : "You know it is impossible to deal with this man. He does not know his mind. He does not stick to his word. He invents grievances and promotes communalism in a community known for its nationalistic outlook and sacrifices in the cause of the country's freedom. He is hurting their interests more than the nation's". I could not agree with him more, and yet pleaded that an awkward situation he had created had to be averted.

Panditji yielded to my pleas and wrote a soothing letter in reply. When the letter was received by Master Tara Singh, the press wanted to know its contents, but Masterji would not divulge them, though he announced his decision to abandon his fast as soon as the letter was received.

It became the subject of all sorts of caustic comments and wild conjectures in the press and the people at large. But when Master Tara Singh showed the letter to me, it took my breath away.

While disowning any responsibility for his defeat and saying that fasts for political reasons were anti-democratic, that he had opposed even Gandhi's fasts as well, that he was willing to discuss any Sikh grievances Master Tara Singh would like to place before him, Jawaharlal had concluded in the end: "If, however, you still feel I have hurt your feelings by any chance, I ask your forgiveness."

Both Master Tara Singh and I were is tears, the old patriarch saying to me : "For this one sentence, I did not show this letter to the Press. Jawaharlal is so great in his humility that he asks my forgiveness for any hurt he may have caused me. Should I be so mean as to publicise it to the press?"

Over Sheikh Mohammad Abdullah's incarceration for many years, he was equally unhappy. And, his one last act of grace was his unconditional release and his invitation to the Shaikh not only to stay with him, but also later to go out to Pakistan as his personal emissary to bring about lasting peace between India and its intractable neighbour! Alas, however, that was not to be, and Shaikh Abdullah was still in Pakistan when Jawaharlal breathed his last! No one grieved over his loss more than Shaikh Abdullah did.

Only a man of his moral stature and idealistic temper could invite the last imperial Viceroy to become the first Governor-General of free India and agree to remain within the Commonwealth after having opposed the idea for about two decades. Within India also he opted for compromise and conciliation between various sections rather than conflict or subjugation.

I know of an incident connected with Hem Barua, PSP member of Parliament from Assam. He came to me one day (as MPs, we were neighbours in the South Avenue apartments) and started crying. I asked him what had hurt him so deeply that he should cry so unabashedly. He said he had committed a great sacrilege that day. When pressed further he sobbed : "You see, this morning I criticised Panditji in full fury, hitting right and left, on the floor of the House. But when I came out into the lobby, Panditji followed me and placing his band around my shoulders asked me, "Hem, how is your book on Assamese literature proceeding?' I felt the weight of his generosity so much on my soul that I wished the earth would give way and I sink to perdition at that very moment."

Krishna Menon was relieved of his post in the Cabinet late in 1962 under circumstances which we are all familiar with. He felt greatly hurt. He believed he was not to blame. The whole Cabinet had taken decisions which he had carried out.

But never did a word escape his lips even after the demise of his great leader against his person or policies, no matter what the temptation or provocation. Such was the loyalty Nehru evoked from the friends he trusted.

How Panditji brought to the fore illustrious intellectuals like Dr. S. Radhakrishnan, Dr. Zakir Husain, Dr. John Mathai, Dr. B.R. Ambedkar, Dr. C.D. Deshmukh, Sri Gopalaswami Ayyangar, Dr. Tara Chand and many others, who loved to serve him in any capacity is a testimony of his love for intellect and character.

A true democrat, he would bow before the Opposition

(though consisting of very weak and insignificant groups) whenever he found the ruling party in the wrong. And several times, he deliberately climbed down in order to keep the face of the Opposition, though he knew the weakness of their case. It was he who as Congress President in 1936 had written an article (anonymously) titled "Rashtrapati Ki Jai" in *Modern Review* of Calcutta, against himself, and warned the people against his being bocsted too much too soon, so that he may not become another Caesar or ride roughshod ever the wishes of the people! Where in history could one find an example as rare as this?

China had wronged this nation grievously, but he never abandoned support to its cause at the UN or elsewhere. Pakistan often tried to bully and blackmail him, but he remained the most formidable protector of the Muslims in this country and a true friend of the Arab world.

He pulled the womenfolk of this land out of their thraldom of centuries as no one else perhaps could. He used to say: "My main contribution as Prime Minister of India is the liberties and privileges I've brought to the womenfolk of this conservative and male-dominated society—the right to property, divorce, and public employment."

I myself enjoyed his friendship in ample measure and the correspondence we had over various public issues is my proudest possession in life. I asked for an interview and the courier was there the very next day at your doorstep to inform you that it had been arranged. And as I sat with him, it appeared you grew up in stature, for us brought out the best (not the worst) in you.

How calm and unruffled he was, how affectionate and delicate in his gestures, how generous to your demands on his time and sense of idealism ! He never said "no" to an intellectual whom he honoured for his intellect and integrity. I never saw him angry, though many stories were current about his short temper. And sometimes his sense of humility was so embarrassingly overwhelming that you wondered if he was a human being or an angel.

There was a whispering campaign during his last few years in office that he was grooming his daughter as his successor. But the world saw that he had done nothing of the kind in spite of the best efforts of some of us to see this happen. It was someone else who succeeded him.

And when later Indira Gandhi came to power, there was no other choice before the nation.

How repugnant to him was flattery became clear to me when after our reverses during the Chinese invasion in October 1962, a Rajya Sabha Congress MP from Karnataka leading the debate on foreign affairs in the House tried to preface his speech with fullsome praise for Nehru and his great father. Panditji was brimming over with rage and after about two minutes, asked Dr. Zakir Husain, the then Chairman of the House, to stop him. "The debate, sir, is on China, not on me or my family background."

The able parliamentarian, much thumbled and annoyed, sank, as if dead, in his seat. When I rose next to second his motion on behalf of the Congress Party, I spoke on the genesis of the conflict, of the effect of our humiliation on world opinion, (in isolating China), the vindication of our policy of non-alignment (in that the engagement ended only after ten days and both the US and the USSR came to our rescue).

It had also made of us a nation, I said, more mindful than ever before of her weak defences and which would henceforth take no nation on trust only for its slogans, etc. As I had done my home-task rather well, it wreathed the face of Jawaharlal Nehru with a rare smile of approval, which brought the whole house down with the cheers of my colleagues, led generously by the Prime Minister of India.

Someone has said : "He [Nehru] couldn't achieve more than what he did because he could not take hard decisions, that he took history and the world around him too much to heart, that he was an idealist, almost a saint strayed into politics." But such, indeed, are the salt of the earth.

Great men are far too many strutting about, clothed in brief authority, for a time, on the stage of life. But history has ultimately honoured only those like him, not the time-serving opportunists, or small-time tyrants who are feared or made use of, when alive, and thrown on the dungheap of history when dead. The earth shook twice the day his earthly remains were consigned to the flames!

And this is so for good reasons. Scarcely, as Einstein said of Gandhi, would the future generations believe that such a one as he ever trod upon this earth. Undoubtedly, he was one of the wisest statesmen and a great man of history, but what will put him on the pedestal for our posterity is that he was, in spite of it, a good eternal man and a true son of Mother India.

28

Jawaharlal Nehru : The Man Behind His Achievements

"Thou art greater than thy achievements", Tagore had said in a different context. But how appropriate it is of Jawaharlal Nehru! In a life which exceeded the biblical span of "three score years and ten" by a brief four years and a half, crowded with action, but isolated from it by prison walls for a total of nine years (less, twenty-three days, to be exact), Nehru left his impress on diverse fields of action. He was not only a valiant fighter for the freedom of his country, a model of, selfless devotion to a cause, and an indefatigable crusader for social justice but also a champion on the world stage of peaceful co-existence, of equality of nations, of dignity of the oppressed humanity, and of a world free of exploitation. In all these fields, he will be remembered for generations to come. But, behind all his work, stood a man who cannot be measured by his achievements alone.

By any standard, Nehru's achievements, both at home and abroad, were substantial. For, he contributed not only to the pace of progress, but set, the pattern for them in several directions. Next only to Mahatma Gandhi, he played the most significant role in the freedom struggle. In fact, he gave a new direction to it by integrating the Indian movement with the worldwide struggle against imperialism. Nehru also gave a social content to what had hitherto been a purely nationalist movement, though he was not and he himself disclaimed to be, a pioneer in introducing socialist thought to India. In his celebrated article "Whither India" written in 1933, he asked :

> .... whose freedom are we particularly striving for. . .. ? There is the feudal India of the princes, the India of big Zamindars, of small Zamindars, of the professional classes, of the agriculturists, of the industrialists, of the bankers, of the lower middle class, of the workers. There are the interests of foreign capital, and of those of home capital, of foreign services and of home services .... It is obvious that there are serious conflicts between the various interests in the country, and every law, every policy which is good for one interest may be harmful for another ....

Whether a pioneer socialist or not, there is no doubt that Nehru did more than any other leader for the struggle for independence to popularise socialist thinking and make it a part of the ethos of this struggle. Social forces have emerged after his demise which have retarded, if not reversed, the process of socialist development, and yet, the legacy of the freedom movement cannot be denied. Arguments, however strained, continue to be put forward to prove the legitimacy of current decisions in terms of socialism.

Another contribution of Nehru to the process of development was his concept of planning. His heroic effort to draw up a plan for India's development in the midst of his heavy preoccupations, and in spite of enforced interruptions imposed by long periods of incarceration, even before the country had acquired the power to implement a plan so framed, was an instance of his devotion to and faith in the concept of planning. Such an act of devotion and faith could not fail to inspire the contemporary generation as also the generations to come. And so it has. Planning, like socialism, continues to be revered as a concept essential to development with justice, even as vested interests rob it of its effectiveness.

But perhaps the most outstanding contribution of Nehru was to place India's national aspirations in a proper perspective in the world context. Nehru is generally regarded as having shaped India's foreign policy after independence, but this is only partially true, for foreign policy is not the brain-child of any individual, however eminent. Nehru's contribution lay in the fact that after independence, he projected into foreign affairs some of the basic urges and interests of the suppressed humanity, newly liberated, which, next only to Mahatma Gandhi, he had himself helped shape and articulate during the long years of struggle. He affirmed the dignity of all individuals, long denied to citizens of less favoured nations, irrespective of race and colour, and he worked fervently for world peace, so essential for all developing countries.

It was out of these urges and interests, articulated, not in parochial and chauvinistic terms for India alone, but for all suppressed humanity that the basic tenets of foreign policy were formulated. "Panchsheel" affirmed the sovereignty and equality of all nations with the corollary of non-interference in each other's affairs and was supplemented by the concept of peaceful co-existence of different social systems. It was, however, the doctrine of non-alignment which included the principles both of non-interference and peaceful co-existence, and which Nehru asserted, along with Marshal Tito, that caught the imagination of developing countries. The countries of Asia, Africa, and Latin America were no longer to be supplicants in the chancellories of Western Europe and North America. They resolved to pursue their collective interests as they perceived them, asserted their right to do so, and to judge every question that arose in international relations on its merits, without aligning themselves with one power bloc or another. It was a quiet, peaceful assertion of the inherent right of every nation to be free and independent, which lent dignity and added to the stature of all nations, big or small, strong or weak.

Many other contributions of Nehru to the country and to the world can be added to this essentially sketchy statement of the work of his many splendoured life. But it is not the object of this essay to list them or to assess their value. Nehru has passed into history and history will in the fullness of time assess his successes and his failures, taking into account the enduring nature, or otherwise, of the policies he initiated and the values he preached. Indeed, the process has begun already

That he was a valiant fighter for freedom is beyond question. But was he merely a visionary, a romantic, with little patience for the grassroot work of mass organisation? Did he subordinate himself unduly to the Mahatma and fail to lead and organise a socialist movement which he could have done more effectively than anyone else in the country? Was the partition of the country a failure of his mass contact movement? To what extent was he responsible for it? Should he have accepted partition when it was offered as the price for freedom?

These and a myriad other similar questions are being debated and will continue to be debated for years. But in the meantime, history marches inexorably on. Social forces dormant in his lifetime have gathered momentum since. They not only threaten his policies, but seek to reverse the values that he, and indeed Mahatma Gandhi, stood for. It is not merely that a policy of privatisation is creeping in to replace the socialist policy of public ownership of the means of production. What is worse is that self-reliant development is being replaced by growing dependence on foreign capital and foreign technology and the concept of social good is being replaced by the acquisitive instinct of private profit as the motive-force of development. The result is. corruption all around.

To what extent, in the circumstances, will Nehru's work endure? Time alone can furnish an answer to this question; but on one thing, there can be little doubt. The assessment of Nehru's work may vary with time, his work itself may or may not endure, but, to recall the quotation from Tagore at the beginning of this essay, the man behind it is greater than his work. Personality will remain undimmed for generations to come, as it has been with the Buddha. The teachings of Buddha are no longer officially accepted in the land of his birth and enlightenment. But Buddha still shines in all his glory through the centuries. Similarly, India may reverse the policies of Nehru and even discard the values that he taught and practised, but Jawaharlal Nehru will remain for generations to come, not only for India but for the whole world, an embodiment of the spirit of renaissance, the product of the best values, the most rational and the most scientific, of human civilisation, indeed the most civilised man of his time. It is worthwhile, therefore, to try and understand the man behind his deeds, his motivations, and his thought processes which were responsible at the same time for his successes and for his failures. Fortunately, Nehru was prolific in his writings, and in his moments of introspection, which were not rare, he has given us more than a glimpse of his mind and his thought processes without a trace either of egoism or of self-pity.

In the stillness of prison, Nehru penned his innermost thoughts. In the 1930s, isolated from the turmoil of the freedom movement outside his prison cell, Nehru wrote his autobiography. A decade later, in the closing years of the Second World War while in detention at Ahmednagar Fort, he recorded his thoughts in his *Discovery of India*. He was an older men when the latter volume was written, and as it happened, the book marked the end of his life as a fighter, a rebel, with another phase, that of a builder, still to begin. Nevertheless, there is a remarkable identity of outlook in both, though perhaps a deeper self-analysis in the latter.

What kind of a picture of the man emerges from these recorded thoughts? First and foremost is his moral integrity, his total dedication to his ideals which provided the motivation for the hard life he led. To him the joy of life, or the "fullness of life", as he put it in his autobiography, came "from attempting to fit ideals with action". And, he added, "we realised that any other life involving a renunciation of these ideals and a tame submission to superior force would have been a wasted existence, full of discontent and inner sorrow". No wonder, a little later, answering the question he put to himself whether all these years wasted in prison had been worthwhile, he wrote :

> There is no hesitation about the answer. If I was given the chance to go through my life again, with my present knowledge and experience added, I would no doubt like

> to make many changes in my personal life...but my major decisions in public affairs would remain untouched. Indeed, I could not vary them, for they were stronger than myself and a force beyond my control drove me on to them.[1]

A decade later, his outlook was no different in *The Discovery of India.* In the concluding chapter before the postscript he reflected.[2] "We can make no complaint that life has treated us harshly for ours has been a willing choice, and perhaps life has not been so bad to us after all. For, only those can sense life who stand often on the verge of it, only those whose lives are not governed by the fear of death. In spite of all the mistakes we might have made, we have saved ourselves from triviality and an inner shame and cowardice. That for our individual selves, has been some achievement." And he concluded by quoting from Lenin :

> Man's dearest possession is life, and since it is given to him to live but once, he must so live as not to be seared with the shame of a cowardly and trivial past, so live as not to be tortured for years without purpose, so live that dying he can say : 'All my life and my strength were given to the first cause in the world—the liberation of mankind.

These were the thoughts that motivated him, and he could truly say at the end of his life that he gave all his life and all his strength to the liberation of mankind. And for this mankind he cherished an abiding love, but no illusions. As he wrote in *The Discovery of India* :

> How amazing is the spirit of man! In spite of innumerable failings, man, throughout the ages, has sacrificed his life and all that he held dear for an ideal, for truth, for faith, for country and honour. That ideal may change but that capacity for self-sacrifice continues, and because of that, much may be forgiven to man, and it is impossible to lose hope for him . . . Plaything of nature's mighty forces, less than the speak of dust in this vast universe, he has hurled

defiance at the elemental powers, and with his mind, cradle of revolution, sought to master them. Whatever gods there be, there is some-thing god-like in the man, as there is also something of the devil in him.[3]

A product of the Age of Reason and deeply influenced by the progress made by Science in the West, Nehru was strongly attracted to the methods of science. This did not make him anti-religion, though he admitted frankly that "religion, as I saw it practised, and accepted even by thinking minds, whether it was Hinduism or Islam or Buddhism or Christianity, did not attract me". He recognised, however, that "religion had supplied some deeply felt inner need of human nature, and that the vast majority of people all over the world could not do without some form of religious belief." He referred to "the unchartered regions of human experience, uncharted, that is, by the positive knowledge of the day," "Science, with its magnificent achievements, knew little enough about it", he admitted, but added a little later :

> But the way to that understanding seems to me essentially the way of science, the way of objective approach ... if the subjective element is unavoidable and inevitable it should be conditioned as far as possible by the scientific method.[4]

Nehru was essentially interested, as he said, "in this world, in this life, not in some other world or a future life." He had little attraction for metaphysics, he said, in fact : "I have had a certain distaste for vague speculation". "And yet," he added, "I have sometimes found a certain intellectual fascination in trying to follow the rigid lines of metaphysical and philosophic thought of the ancients or the moderns. But I have never felt at ease there, and have escaped from their spell with a feeling of relief."[5]

Nehru longed for action, but "not action divorced from thought, but rather flowing from it in one continuous sequence," as he put it. Thus, while both thought and action attracted him, the former had to be free and open and not dogmatic, and the latter to flow from it. In his words, "... when, rarely, there has been full harmony between the two, thought leading to action and finding its fulfilment in it, action leading back to thought and a fuller understanding—then I have sensed a certain fullness and a vivid intensity in that moment of existence."[6]

"But such moments are rare, very rare ...", Nehru had said. This could well be so, for Nehru had a remarkable receptivity to new thoughts, and almost an obsessive aversion to dogmas. "The burden of thought is so often a hindrance", he wrote and thought it was a sign of age. He allowed his mind to roam freely, but realised the discomfort it created. In a passage, almost poetic in its beauty, he said :

> The vagrant mind, finding no haven, still wanders about restlessly, bringing discomfort to its possesser as well as to others, there is some envy for those virgin minds who have not been soiled or violated by thought's assault, and on which doubt has cast no shadow nor written a line. ...[7]

Discomfort indeed; perhaps more than discomfort, a hindrance to decisive action. Nehru's 'critics have accused him of indecisiveness. This is certainly an exaggeration. There was, for instance, nothing indecisive about his opposition to certain world phenomena of his days, such as imperialism, fascism, and racialism, but with his mind tossed between arguments and counter-arguments, between pros and cons, his action sometimes lost the sharpness which the situation warranted.

Here then emerges from his own stray thoughts on life, its philosophies and its values, the picture of a sensitive man, shorn of pretences and assumed postures, completely honest to himself, determined to be of use to humanity and to lead a life devoid of frivolity and triviality. He is a man who had imbibed the best values of the modern age, turned his back on irrationality and superstition, and made science and reason the main guides to action.

No wonder, he endeared himself to the people of his own

country and charmed all those he met, for bereft of artfulness, even his failings were human, for all to see. There was no room in his mental makeup for spitefulness or hatred. He was one of those who lived up to the classical dictum to hate the sin but not the sinner.

And yet, his openness, his catholicity may have been a cause of weakness in action. Was his life a success? "I do not know. Others will judge", he said. "By what standards do we measure success or failure?", he himself asked. "That too I do not know", he replied. But one thing is certain. Whether a success or a failure, the man towered head and shoulders over his work and his achievements. India in her long history has been fortunate in having a few such personalities. It would do well to treasure their memories, and live by the examples they set, even if not by the values they preached and practised.

REFERENCES

1. Jawaharlal Nehru, *An Autobiography* (John Lane, London), pp. 596-98.
2. Jawaharlal Nehru, *The Discovery of India* (Signet Press, Calcutta, 1946).
3. *Ibid.*, p. 22.
4. *Ibid.*, p. 15.
5. *Ibid.*, p. 15.
6. *Ibid.*, p. 9.
7. *Ibid.*, p. 582.

29

Nehru : The Greatest Humanist of His Age

If ever the pangs of conscience for fellow-brethren has compelled a man to forsake a life of affluence and prosperity to court prison with all its sufferance and that too in the name of humanity and for the sake of freedom of the fraternity, it has indeed been truly so in the case of the life and times of Pandit Nehru. His long career reveals that he sacrificed everything for the sake of liberation of his country from foreign domination and in that memorable role, he proved himself to be a humanitarian first and last.

In one sense human rights are as ancient as the civilization of man, as it moved from nomadic existence to that of urbanity. The very basis of a healthy community existence is recognition of human rights and our scriptures have not hesitated to emphasize the prime importance of the principles of वसुधैव कुटुम्बकम्—common brotherhood of mankind. The very heavens appeared to be centred in the ethics of the famous verse :

न त्वहं कामये राज्यं
न स्वर्गंन पुनर्भवम्।
कामये दुःख तप्तानां
प्राणिनांऽआर्त नाशनम्।।

(I seek no kingdoms nor heavenly pleasures nor personal salvation since to relieve humanity from its manifold pains and distresses is the supreme objective of mankind).

Nehru was moved by these very sublime considerations

when in his lifetime, he gave up his fortune to serve his own kith and kin in bondage. In this freedom struggle which symbolised the very highest objectives of human rights, Nehru's name came to be associated with characters of Indian history like Mahatma Gandhi, Sardar Vallabhbhai Patel, Lokmanya Bal Gangadhar Tilak, Lala Lajpat Rai, Rajendra Prasad, Subhas Chandra Bose, and other luminaries of great distinction that have lit our history. Nehru was a great patriot, an illustrious statesman, and a many splendoured personality whose place in the history of India's freedom struggle is unique. His life is a brilliant essay in perseverance and devotion to the jealous mistress that law is. He lives in modern Indian history as one of the most illustrious lawyers of his time, an outstanding parliamentarian, a great constitutionalist and an ardent freedom fighter, a genuine humanist and a true friend of the poor. Everyone respected him for his independence of thought and the courage with which lie expressed his views. I rank Nehru as the tallest of all the humanists as it was his effort to win independence for enslaved colonies that brought about the emancipation of millions under bondage. This aspect needs to be emphasised.

The history of mankind will record in golden letters all human efforts made towards achieving the great humanitarian task of liberation of colonies or dependencies and helping them to rise to sovereign independent status, which Nehru fought for so vehemently with such world-wide success. It is indeed noteworthy to observe today that Nehru's daughter Indira Gandhi, should have later kept the same torch so well lit as to help continue to liberate neighbouring people to independence,[1] and India's strong persistent voice can be heard against the apartheid in South Africa.

Furthermore, though the first nuclear explosion attributed to India dates to the time when Indira Gandhi was the Prime Minister of the country, there can be no doubt ever about her steadfast policy never to use that device except for purely peaceful purposes. That aspect has been reiterated by all the Indian Prime Ministers ever since 1947, which stands to the credit of India in giving full weight to the larger humanitarian considerations which cannot be ignored if the future of mankind is to have a meaning.

Nehru's words will ever echo in the annals of Indian history : "We want freedom of thought, freedom of action, freedom to fashion our own destiny and build up an India suited to the genius of her own people. . , ."

Nehru's Era for Humanity

If Negro slave trade and conquest and colonization constituted the greatest violations of human rights in the Albuquerque age which dominated the global history consequent on European expansion of the nineteenth century, it was the cyclonic wave of decolonization, which originated from the Indian shores in 1947, that changed the entire political geography of the world, radically altered some of the age-long traditional concepts and norms not only of international law but also of the fundamental law of mankind and revolutionized human thinking to usher in a new age based on oneness of the human race and solidarity of human rights. The Indian independence was by far the most momentous event of the current century. It was indeed a joint unparalleled exercise in which both the conqueror and the conquered collaborated to a peaceful transfer of power by a unique Act of Parliament at Westminster which gave India and Pakistan in 1947, and earlier Burma and later Ceylon, their cherished independence. Thus the British, in creating sovereign states in Asia out of the erstwhile colonies of the Empire, moved by the humanitarian spirit fostered by Nehru set the example for the other colonisers to follow. It was in the same praiseworthy, peaceful humanitarian spirit that France gave up its colonies of Pondicherry and Chandranagore in India, though Portugal resisted but in the end humanitarianism triumphed to establish a government in Lisbon which ultimately liberated Portuguese Africa in the 1970s of the current century. It is to the standing glory of those who had the vision and the foresight to appreciate the new trend and to change their time-hardened policies to welcome the dawn of a new era. The liberation of the three continents of the world, namely Asia, Africa, and the Carribean Latin America, which followed 1947, involved the freedom of more than half the human population and this did vitally alter the future of mankind for the better. It settled once and for all; *first,* that the abominable institution of slavery was to be totally eradicated; *second,* that no one country could hold another in bondage; *third,* the acquisition of territory by conquest could no longer confer a legal right on the conqueror; *fourth,* even the threat to use force was contrary to the UN Charter and derogatory to human civilization; and *fifth,* the acceptance of the principle of international law that coercion and compulsion of one state over another to sign a treaty vitiated the agreement ab initio. These are but a few illustrations of the changes wrought in the politico legal philosophy in the World Community of Sovereign States. It would thus not be incorrect to conclude that the recognition of the fundamental right of man to be free, which flowed from Indian independence in 1947 and synchronized with the UN Charter of 1946, ushered in a new era heralding a bright future for mankind. This was the era of Nehru which enunciated a humanitarian era of our century. Those who fought and struggled for our country's independence as well as those who shewed humanitarian considerations, had their own contribution to make, not only in the evolution of the concept of human rights but also in the building up of a better Asia and a better world striving to become free from any kind of discrimination whether based on race, colour, or sex.

Nehru's name thus stands immortalised not only in the annals of India but in the history of the human race.

REFERENCES

1. The role of India in the struggle for the independence of Bangladesh and Namibia is well known.

30

The Spirit of Jawaharlal Nehru

It is rare indeed that a single individual combines in himself such a wealth of talent and ability, such an enormous output of work, such outstanding achievements at all levels of life and attracts to himself such a galaxy of friends and admirers from all over the globe, as Nehru. The story of Nehru's seventy-four years is an epitome of modern India's birth pangs and growth to its present stature as well as to become an integral part of world history. Nehru was very characteristically an individual with a winning personality. He was a visionary with a winning personality. He was a visionary with a practical side to his vision.[1]

Scholars of history and the freedom movement will be the first to salute his memory in this centenary of his birth. Politicians and statesmen will want to commemorate Nehru's impressive debut at the Bandung Conference in 1955 or to hail the five principles of peaceful co-existence which he had enunciated the previous year and to eulogize him for the doctrine of non-alignment or "dynamic neutrality" which he bequeathed to the world thereafter. This stance was affirmed at the summit meeting of non-aligned nations in Belgrade in 1961 and subsequently endorsed by all the free African states in 1963. Today these attitudes are being recognised as foundation stones for world peace and prosperity. Gandhi's years in South Africa had lit the spark, but the organised battle against apartheid may be said to have started with Nehru raising his voice against this abominable policy which continues to plague the human race even today.

Commentators will also want to recall his staunch advocacy of democracy and his unflinching commitment to India as a secular state seeking to develop a socialistic pattern of society. Internationalists will be delighted to record that from the very dawn of independence, India, thanks to Nehru, rode onto the world stage like a colossus and played its role with a consummate, if unexpected, display of brilliance and effectiveness. Moving the world's largest democracy from its hoary past, along with its spiritual and cultural heritage, to the new age of the temples of science and technology at Trombay or Tarapur or the giant dams at Hirakud or Bhakra Nangal was no easy task. Those who recognize that there is an emerging pattern of Indian culture, which brings together the glories of the past, the inestimable gift of the Constitution and its Preamble serving as a bridge through which to pass to India's new age of science and technology will not fail to see our first Prime Minister as the main architect of this dynamic, ongoing process of change, and renewal for the true human betterment of all our people. Men of letters will take pride in referring to Nehru's years in prison and the gems of literature he sent to his daughter from time to time—*An Autobiography; Glimpses of World History;* and *The Discovery of India.* Written with scant resources at his disposal and hence not without blemish, these volumes have nevertheless been acclaimed for their vision, intellectual vigour, brilliance of scholarship, and literary grace and charm.

During his premiership, there were two trends that dominated Nehru's life and consciously so—feeling and keeping in touch with the pulse of the masses and the search for world collaboration and harmony.[2]

Nor can one forget Nehru's genuine affection for children and his love of the weak toiling masses of women who for ages have been carrying the burden of the heat and the day. "The influence of Nehru on Indian renaissance cannot be measured, says Abdul Karim, in terms of day-to-day achievements. The whole future of India seems to be in a process of being formulated by Nehru."[3]

Searching Beneath the Surface

The question that naturally poses itself is—what was the secret of Nehru's greatness? What was the leitmotif of the entire enterprise? What was the mainspring, the dynamo behind the scenario that shed so much light and lustre on the India of his day? I venture to suggest that it was the unifying "spirit" that governed his entire being and personality, his "spirituality", if I may put it so.

As a person, Nehru stands out as an enlightened, brilliant, strong and dynamic leader capable of rallying people to himself and to the cause. He has given us a portrait of himself—anonymously—in a ruthless piece of self-analysis : "He has all the makings of a dictator in him—vast popularity, a strong will, energy, pride...and with all his love of the crowd, an intolerance of others, and a certain contempt for the weak and inefficient. His overwhelming desire to get things done, to sweep away what he dislikes and build anew, will hardly brook for long the slow processes of democracy."[4] And yet he had a "heart" for the weaker ones of society—children, women, and the toiling, suffering masses. Whence the combination?

His deep affection for the members of his family finds expression in "Letters from a Father to his Daughter" and the other masterpieces in which he reveals his moods, his beliefs, and his compassion. This spirit of friendship and fellowship Nehru extended to those who collaborated with him in India's saga. Prince among men, he was magnanimous in outlook, lavish in hospitality, steadfast and loyal to his friends—even to a fault. Ever since his encounter with the peasants in 1920, Nehru lost his heart to India and its teeming millions of men, women, and children. Nothing could stop him devoting all his energies to dreaming, planning, husbanding available resources for lifting them up by the bootstraps so that Gandhi's dream of wiping away every tear might be nearer fulfilment. Whence the power and stamina for such a herculean task?

If Nehru loved the people of India, he was also enamoured

of India's landscape. In his *The Unity of India,* he describes in lyrical terms "the feminine beauty of river and valley and tall and graceful trees of his own Kashmir, as well as its masculine charm of bard mountains and snow-capped peaks and glaciers and cruel and fierce torrents rushing down to the valleys below."[5] Consciously or otherwise, India's age-old veneration of its mountains and rivers became a part of the new Nehru after he had come to terms with himself and his mission to mother India. The art, architecture and culture and the spiritual riches embodied in the people of the land became part of the patrimony of this great leader as he embarked on the supreme adventure of building a better India.

The greatness of Nehru's soul made him extend his hand of friendship to all India's neighbours. He never fully got over the betrayal of 1962 and Pakistan's kaleidoscopic shifts of policy. Living as he did on the level of the spirit, in the realm of truth, authenticity and courtesy, it ill became such a one to taint the art of the possible with insincerity and hasty diplomacy. Perhaps he was misled by local advisers on whom he largely relied, and that will be held against him in a realpolitik reckoning! Be that as it may, it is Nehru the upright, the noble, the gentleman par excellence that always comes through. That is the price that is often demanded for a life lived according to the claims of the spirit.

Gandhi recognized in Nehru a "forceful spearhead of fervent nationalism" and, given the latter's acquaintance with the West and his knowledge of world affairs, cheerfully left to the young leader the enunciation and conduct of India's foreign policy. And Nehru was quick to see that there was a close link between the development of India and the forces at work in the rest of the world. While he recognized the need and power of economic growth, at no time could he reconcile himself to the idea of material progress as being the supreme goal. He said in this context : "Apart from material development that "is imperative, I believe the human mind is hungry for something deeper in terms of moral and spiritual development, without which all the material advance may not be worthwhile. For, as soon as man gets the material comfort he desires something deeper inside him, hungers for— well, something deeper, something *spiritual* and ethical."

By the same token, if political independence for peoples everywhere became a passion with him and led to a spate of freedom movements in the countries of the third world, the idea of joining one bloc of nations instead of another was totally abhorrent to him. Born of this foundational spirit of human dignity, freedom and equality of each individual, and of the dignity and equality of all countries, he propounded the doctrine of non-alignment which today encompasses the vast majority of the nations of the world.

If his father's influence made Nehru a strong, intrepid character and if Gandhi's influence made him temper his rationalistic outlook with a mead of "faith" which he did not quite understand, it was the impact of Rabindranath Tagore that kept Nehru a humanitarian and universalist all his life. I suppose it was peculiar to this man who came on to the stage when circumstances were most propitious for his entry, that, great as he was, he always revealed an humble dependence on men older than himself.

The greatness of Nehru's spirit was never more in evidence than in his attitude to England and the English after independence. When Mahatma Gandhi decided that, war or no war, the time had come for the British to quit India, Nehru was very much with the All India Congress Committee when he moved the historic "Quit India" resolution on 6 August 1942. Not long afterwards, Jawaharlal extended the hand of friendship to the new Britain and opted for the sovereign republic of India continuing within this "new" Commonwealth which was in effect a device of his own creation. Even Churchill was constrained to admit to Nehru, coming back from the United States to London after independence : "I would have liked to be with you and introduced you to American audiences. Do you know how I would have introduced you? I would have said, "here is a man who has overcome fear and hatred!" In a speech on the 3 June 1947, Nehru paid tribute to the labours of the Viceroy "since his arrival here at a critical juncture in our history". In a broadcast from London in 1951, Nehru himself eulogised "the basic temper of peace, abiding understanding, and friendship with which England and India approached their problems."

Because of his deep understanding and compassion for "man" as the centre and focus of all activity, Nehru instinctively perceived the wisdom of whatever made for unity and collaboration in the interest of that "common good" with which society has to prosper. I suppose these efforts are intended to touch, in the first instance, the welfare of families of which a society is comprised and of the individuals it nurtures within its bosom. India's age-old family bonds have stood her in good stead until now. A new "socialistic" understanding of person in the first community of the family could do a lot to offset the ravages of current, cut-throat competitive individualism with its by-products of selfishness and greed. Gandhi's warning that there is enough in India and the world for everyone's need, but not enough for any man's greed is being ignored sedulously by the wave of consumerism which has overtaken the country.

Nehru's strident insistence, in season and out of season, not only on the loftiness of ends and goals but on purity of means as well is timely counsel valid for all times. He would be appalled at the behaviour patterns in India today.

The upbringing of Nehru in an aristocratic family and his years at Harrow and Cambridge had turned him into more of a Westerner than an Indian. He approached India, as he himself says, "almost as an alien critic, full of dislike for the present as well as for many relics of the past," "I am an uncanny combination of the West and the East." His affinity with the heritage of the Upanishads and the teachings of Buddha and an approach towards life and its problems as exemplified in Ernest Renan's "Life of Jesus" made for just the right combination for the role of a bridge-builder which was his destiny.[6]

The Bridge-Builder

His fierce and passionate love of India was given full play after his encounter with the peasantry in May 1920. That entanglement grew in later years and influenced his mental outlook greatly. It brought about his conversion to "Indianness" and he never turned back. It coloured his dealings with other countries as foreign minister of India and as the natural leader of the Third World.

The many strands in the temperament, character, and intellectual calibre of Nehru derived from India and Europe stood him in good stead in his unique position. For one thing, it gave him a better understanding of the changes taking place at the global level. The England of his period was being heavily influenced by H.G. Wells, and Bertrand Russell and their critical attitudes towards the arrangements of human society and by the new theories of economics sponsored by Harold Laski and his group. It was also at a time when Nehru was at Cambridge that was influenced by the first thoughts of Fabianism and socialism and particularly by Meredith Townsend's *Europe and Asia.* Similarly, this was an age of vast scientific progress not least in Cambridge with the work of J.J. Thompson. Thus Nehru developed his rationalistic approach to the problems of life and his scientific attitude of mind. The real struggle today in India is not, he wrote, between Hindu culture and Muslim culture, but between both of them and the conquering scientific culture of modern civilisation.

Among the first steps to meet the challenge was the launching of research institutes to deal in a scientific manner with the massive problems confronting the country. He dreamt of, thereby, revolutionizing the agricultural scene and, in the industrial area, of placing India in the forefront. It is no doubt due to his vision and planning that India today can export every year roughly ten thousand scientists and engineers to assist other Third World countries in their quest for economic and social independence. No, wonder, then, that Dr. Radhakrishnan wrote : "He does not spend much time in glorifying the past, but is always active meeting the challenges of the future."[7]

One of the most remarkable traits of Nehru's personality was his deep respect for others and their opinions—his acceptance of them, be they Hindu, Muslim, or Christian, and from whichever part of the country they came from. This openness to others and their opinions included those of the opposition. It also embraced a healthy spirit of dissent in the heat and tumble of party politics. In a spirit of sarvodaya, Nehru's compassion made him decide also to give a preferential treatment to the scheduled castes and scheduled tribes who had been sinned against by the rest of society for thousands of years. In the same spirit, he unabashedly sought to give religious minorities a feeling of security and a sense of belonging. This, in turn, generated trust and confidence in his leadership. He could be counted upon not to let them down, when narrow, communalistic voices were raised against them and the implications of India as a secular state were being put to test. Such magnanimity is imperative for the mosaic of peoples and cultures that go to the making of modern India, balancing carefully the rights of minority communities with the imperative need to build an integrated nation.[8]

Acceptance of others and their opinions leaves one exposed and vulnerable. It can be the occasion of much anguish and pain. The independence of India was brought about by the joint efforts of a spiritual pilgrim and constructive idealist like Gandhi, on unflinching down-to-earth realist like Vallabhbhai Patel, and as restless and catholic minded student of world affairs like Jawaharlal Nehru. This helped keep the State on an even keel. However, Nehru was often in disagreement with Gandhi on particular courses of action to be followed. Gandhi's dream was of a democracy from below as the masses have a better insight into their problems. This did not find favour with Nehru. His idea of the economy being built on satisfying the basic human needs of those at the lowest rung of the ladder and going on from there with them was repudiated by Nehru in favour of a pattern of development that would step up the GNP and hopefully thereafter see to the equitable distribution of the fruits of development. This policy has led to a sort of elitist, bureaucratic set-up with all power centralised either at the Centre or at the State levels, the untoward consequences of which are still at work in the country. Nehru never understood the Gandhian concept of "voluntary poverty" in the interest of the development of the many. He mistakenly thought that Gandhi stood for poverty for poverty's sake. Today, with the concept of "small is beautiful" continuing to gain ground everywhere, of development being understood as having to be by the people themselves and at the local levels, it is Gandhian thinking that is one again receiving attention, particularly in the West. Hopefully, India too will welcome his basic insights, valid as they are for the future.

With the current stress on economic growth as an essential priority for development of the country, it still remains to be seen how social justice will be built into the production process. Only by doing so is there a fair chance of an equitable distribution of the fruits of development taking place.

Nehru had a rather romantic approach to life and development. This made him unduly trusting of those charged with the implementation of his policies. Inadequate safeguards led to the beginnings of that corruption at the hands of an elitist group and those associated with them which is the bane of modern India today.

Nehru found Gandhi's religious outlook quite irritating, and yet, in deference to someone better versed in the ways of the spirit, Nehru subordinated his differences for the sake of a great call and a tremendous social and political advanture. Yielding to the magic spell of the Mahatma, Nehru gave the palm to a seer and sage who had an uncanny instinct for the right move at the right time. Some would call this discernment of spirits by one whose life was ruled by the Lord and his will.

The Gnawing Question

The gnawing question is—what was it that, through Nehru, brought to India and the world such a tremendous upsurge of life and energy as the sleeping giant, the world's largest democracy, rose to take its place in the sun? How did this amorphous multitude of people, stirred no doubt by the Father of the Nation, follow Nehru in the mighty sense of purpose and direction he sought to give the country as he guided the ship of state through the turbulent waters of the transference of power and the challenges of reconciliation and peace at the most critical moment of India's history? A close friend of Nehru wrote in the *Manchester Guardian* of 17 April 1942 : "By the time he went up to Trinity, there already burned in him the ideal of a united, autonomous, self-sufficient India."[9] How did Nehru help India weather the storm and enter with dignity and grace as a democracy the path to future progress and prosperity within the comity of nations?

Spirituality in Action

It is interesting to read Nehru's negative comments on religion and to see them balanced by positive insights that seem to reveal the man in a "spiritual light". He tells us, for instance, in his *Autobiography* : "The spectacle of what is called religion or at any rate organised religion in India and elsewhere has filled me with horror......Almost always it seems to stand for blind belief and reaction, dogma and bigotry, superstition and exploitation and the preservation of vested interests!" "And yet I knew well", he adds, "that there was something else in it [religion], something which supplied a deep inner craving of human beings and brought peace and comfort to innumerable tortured souls."[10]

In another passage, he bemoans the unduly other-worldly attitude of religion. "The usual religious outlook does not concern itself with this world .... It is far removed from what I consider *spirituality*—the things of the *spirit*."[11]

Going a step further in his diagnosis, Nehru ventures to add that "religion probably consists of the inner development of the individual, the evolution of his consciousness. Religion lays stress on this inner change and considers outward changes as but the projection of this inner development." However, with his keen mind, he saw the need for integration and therefore completed his analysis by adding that "obviously the outer environment also powerfully influences the inner development." And he illustrates from life : "A man who is the victim of economic circumstances and who is hedged and restricted by the struggle to live can very rarely achieve inner consciousness of any higher degree."[12] Thus, even for inner development, external freedom and a suitable environment become necessary.

To meet the danger of falling into the opposite excess and of attempting to gain this outer freedom and of changing the environment so as to remove all hindrances to inner development by any means whatsoever, Nehru issues what I consider a very "spiritual" caution—the means should be pure; they should be such as not to defeat the real object in view; they must lead to the end; otherwise, they are wasted effort and might even result in ever greater degradation, both outer and inner.[13]

This clear perception of the wholeness of life, of the integration of sacred and secular in the life of the individual and in our common responsibility to the common good was an insight which was much less in vogue in his time than it is today. He was perhaps unconsciously enunciating a spirituality which must be practised in relation to the central concerns of society. A dynamic and action-oriented spirituality must become the true driving force of contemporary society. To transform the disparate fragments of humankind into anew humanity, the spirit, the spiritual energies of the inner bonds of love and fellowship are required.

If I have quoted Nehru himself at such length, it is to suggest that Nehru, though not religious in one sense of the term, nevertheless applied religion to life and practised the spirituality of purity of means, of nonviolence, of positive mutual acceptance and respect for others and their opinions, a consistent consideration for others, even unselfish love, a great compassion for his suffering fellow Indians and fellow human beings, and an awesome sense of responsibility for improving the quality of life in society.

In 1979, at Princeton University, at the Third Assembly of the World Conference of Religion and Peace, persons of all living faiths had some sessions on their understanding of spirituality, and this is what they came up with : "Spirituality is present in all people of goodwill; in theists as they imbue life with their experience of the divine presence and in atheists (even though many may not admit it) with their concern for the destiny of humanity." Spirituality may be defined as the consciousness of responsibility (including responsibility for restructuring political and economic institutions) rooted in one's experience of the divine.[14]

The vertical and horizontal approaches converge in ultimate concern which is the *common call to responsibility*.

In this sense, Nehru could certainly be said to have practised "spirituality" of the highest order. He used to the fullest the gifts, talents, opportunities that came his way, not for self-aggrandisement but with a great sense of service and responsibility to society. He was a good example of a person constantly striving to be fully human and fully alive in the personal conduct of his life as well as in the great social undertakings with which he was associated.

Man : The Pathway to God

Christmas comes every year to remind the followers of Christ and all the world that God became man to teach us in an unforgettable way that the source of the eternal flows deep within his humanity, that in the thornbush of the human endeavour to become a real, full human person, the flame of the absolute burns, that man is a path to God, that service of man, and especially of the poor and lowly is true religion and that to be human in this way is to be godly.

Both Gandhi and Nehru had, in different ways, come

under the influence of Christianity. Even if the religious practice of the England of his day was not remarkable, the spirit of Christianity was what Nehru imbibed. This was noticeable in a great sense of fairplay and justice, in consideration for others and even unselfish love, in a certain nobility of spirit more to be caught than taught. The grace of God, Belloc had said, is in courtesy! The identification of service of God and service of man, so characteristic of Christianity, had made a lasting impact on him. Mother Teresa's exemplification of this truth is continuing to challenge the conscience of our brothers and sisters in all the five continents. "I sought my God and my God I could not find! I sought my soul and my soul eluded me. I sought my brother and I found all three."

When on his return to India, Nehru heard Gandhi enunciate the same teaching and proclaim that any effort for the betterment of the human condition is a "yajna": that taking water through a desert where trees are rare is a "sacrifice", he felt heartened and strengthened in his understanding of life and in his humanistic approach to its problems.

During his seven years abroad, Nehru had been heavily influenced by Tolstoy and had imbibed a lot of socialism and Marxism which appealed to him and lit up many a dark corner of his mind. He found the presence and example of the Soviets to be a bright and heartening phenomenon in a dark and dismal world. And the communist philosophy of life gave him comfort and hope. But perhaps he had also been made familiar with the scene of the Last Judgement in St. Mathew's Gospel and its implications for each and all of mankind. "I was hungry, you gave me food, when thirsty you gave me drink; when I was a stranger you took me into your home; when naked you clothed me; when I was ill you came to my help; when in prison you visited me. You have my Father's blessing; come, enter and possess the Kingdom that has been ready for you since the world was made."[15]

It was his encounter and continued contact with the peasantry of India that clinched the matter. With them there was a conscious,—even subconscious,—relationship with the Maker. Awareness of the presence was part and parcel of their make-up—in their very bones. Nehru's new-found spirit found an echo in their minds and hearts. This put the two Nehrus together, the Nehru of the West and the Nehru of the East, now one among his people. When Nehru first met them, he was strung with shame and sorrow at the degradation and overwhelming poverty of India. "A new picture of India seemed to rise before me, nacked, starving, crushed and utterly miserable. And their faith in us embarrassed me and filled me with a *responsibility* that frightened me."[16] His extraordinary rapport with every Indian, man, woman or child, had almost a physical quality. As Gandhi said : "It is not so much that they want to listen to him. They just needed and wanted to see him." The mutual "darshan" begot a profound sense of patriotism, as the spirit of responsibility grew stronger in Nehru and struck an ever more responsive chord in the hearts of the people. The spirit of Nehru became so identified with the spirit of the peasants of India that in his Will and Testament of 1954, he wanted the major portion of his ashes to mingle with the dust and soil of India and become an indistinguishable part of India. It was the same spirit that was enshrined in the gift of Anand Bhawan to the nation.

Nehru reveals his real self even more clearly when, he writes about culture and civilization. Civilization and culture bring out, he says, all that is best, finest, and grandest in the spirit of man. Two very spiritual traits he lists as basic to culture—restraint over oneself and consideration for others. "Does culture mean some inner growth in man? Of course, it must. Does it mean the way he behaves to others? Certainly it must. Does it mean the capacity to understand the other person? I suppose so. It means all that." And in another passage: "Culture is the widening of the mind and of *the spirit*. It is a narrowing of the mind or a restriction of the human spirit or of the country's spirit."

India at the crossroads would do well during the Nehru Centenary to search once again and to recapture the soul of

India and the spirit of age-old civilisation and culture. "A civilisation decays much more from inner failure, than from an external attack."

Fine buildings, fine pictures and books, and everything that is beautiful are certainly signs of civilisation. But an even better sign is a fine person who is *unselfish* and works with others for the good of all. To work together is better than to work singly, and to work together for the common good is best of all. That example and spirit of Nehru is his greatest legacy to his countrymen.

Nehru's most remarkable characteristic for which he will be long remembered was his *intense humanity*. He was a great politician and an intellectual path-finder. But he was also a man of the widest sympathies and tolerance, a convinced and constant humanitarian. He had learnt at the feet of Gurudev that "all the world is my brother", and like his master, he scanned the past while peering into the future.

He never fought shy of truth when it was dangerous, nor made alliance with falsehood when it would be convenient. That was Tagore's assessment and Gandhi felt proud and glad that this beautiful land of ours has produced such great men, endowed with such a wonderful "spirit" of service and self-sacrifice. Jawahar is a real jawahar—jewel.

Nehru is still recognised as an outstanding leader. The Centenary Year will make us all more familiar with his personality, achievements, and sterling contribution to the building of modern India. Nehru personified a patriotic stance for the preservation and enhancement of the unity of India, both in its cultural content and in its geographical areas. It was a passion with him. Greatness, whether for individual or nation, never comes from narrowness of mind but from a wide vision, a broad perspective, an inclusive outlook and a deeply human approach to life. Exemplifying all this, Nehru became an interpreter in India of the many great things the West has produced and an interpreter in other parts of the globe of India's rich cultural heritage. He thus became an ideal link between East and West and also between the various parts and groups in India. In Nehru, there was a conscious adherence to principles, a consensus approach to issues, and an intrepid spirit that has made a major contribution to effective democracy in the modern world. During his Centenary Year, Jawaharlal Nehru will once again impinge on the hearts and minds of the Indian people.

REFERENCES

1. C.P. Ramaswami Aiyar, *Biographical Vistas* (Asia Publishing House, Bombay, 1968), p. 230.
2. *Ibid., p.* 233.
3. Valerian Cardinal Gracias, "Jawaharlal Nehru : Man of Two Cultures and One World," in *Cardinal Cracias Speaks* (St. Paul Publication, Bombay, 1977), p. 811.
4. Lord Butler, *First Nehru Memorial Lecture, 1966.*
5. *Ibid.*
6. C.P. Ramaswami Aiyar, *Biographical Vistas,* p. 236.
7. Valerian Cardinal Gracias, "Jawaharlal Nehru: Man of Two Cultures and One World", p. 812.
8. V. Lawrence Sundaram, *A Great Indian Jesuit* (Gujarat Sahitya Prakashan, Anand, 1986), p. 160.
9. Lord Butler, *First Nehru Memorial Lecture, 1966.*
10. Jawaharlal Nehru, *An Autobiography* (The Bodley Head, London, 1955), p. 374.
11. *Ibid.,* p. 377.
12. *Ibid.,* p.379.
13. *Ibid.,* p.379.
14. Homer A. Jack, *Religion and the Struggle for World Community* (World Conference for Religion and Peace, New York, 1980), p.124.
15. Matthew, 25:35ff.
16. Jawaharlal Nehru, *An Autobiography,* p. 52.

31

Jawaharlal Nehru and the Rise of Non-Alignment

Jawaharlal Nehru was one of the great human beings to be born in India, or anywhere, in the last half of the nineteenth century. Indeed, few countries of the world could produce a Nehru (1889-1964) and a Gandhi (1869-1948) within one century. The only other country may have been Germany where both Albert Schweitzer (1875-1965) and Albert Einstein (1879-1955) were born within four years.

Jawaharlal Nehru was a man of many talents and achievements. He was successful both as an architect of national independence, a freedom fighter, and a consolidator of that independence, a nation-builder. He could make a revolution and also build a country. Two of Nehru's peers, Sukarno of Indonesia and Kwame Nkrumah of Ghana, succeeded brilliantly as nationalists, but both failed when they became heads of state or government. Nehru was successful before the independence of India and also afterwards.

During the years when Nehru was prime minister of India, he became a world statesman. His achievements in this field were many. He was the "father" of the nuclear test-ban movement which resulted in the partial test-ban treaty of 1963. He was one of the founders of the Bandung movement which resulted, if indirectly, in the establishment of a Third World caucus in the United Nations system known as the Group of 77. He was also one of the architects of the non-aligned movement which still remains a formidable force in the world community.

This essay is necessarily confined to Nehru's relationship to the rise of non-alignment. This movement took a solid form with the Summit of the Heads of State and Government of Non-Aligned States at Belgrade in September 1961. However, the path to the Summit was long and not straight. Other leaders, both independently and together, ascended to the peak, including Gamel Abdel Nasser of Egypt, Kwame Nkumah of Ghana, Sukarno of Indonesia, and Jossip Broz Tito of Yugoslavia.

For Nehru, the journey may have begun when he attended the Congress of Oppressed Nationalities at Brussels in 1927. He took several other steps towards developing the non-aligned position, especially in his beloved New Delhi. There, and elsewhere in India, with Gandhi and many others, he helped the Indian people gain their independence. He was also the first prime minister of independent India. Then he became one of the originators of the Afro-Asian Conference at Bandung, Indonesia, in 1955. This preceded by six years his preparation for and participation in the first non-aligned summit at Belgrade in 1961.

Each of these three conferences—Brussels, Bandung, Belgrade—will be remembered for a role played by Nehru. In this essay, an attempt would be made to describe these conferences and to attempt an evaluation of the achievements of non-alignment during Nehru's last years—he died in May 1964—and brought up to date. A brief consideration will also be given to the future of the non-aligned movement, one of several continuing legacies of Jawaharlal Nehru in his centenary year.

Brussels

When Nehru was 37 years old, in March 1926, he took his family to Europe. It was his first visit abroad after 1912 when he left England after a seven-year stay culminating in his being called to the bar. He took his wife, Kamala, and his daughter, Indira, from Bombay to Venice and thence to Switzerland where his wife might recover from a serious illness. They lived in Switzerland, but Jawaharlal was inquisitive and restless, and visited many European places and persons. In Berlin, he heard about the Congress of Oppressed Nationalities to be held at Brussels in February. He notified his colleagues on the All-India Congress Committee and they asked him to represent the Indian National Congress.

The Brussels meeting welcomed nationalists from Asia, Africa, and Latin America as well as friends of the oppressed from Europe and America. Asian delegates came from China, Dutch East Indies, India, Indo-China (Annam), Korea, Palestine, Persia, and Syria. Africans attended from Egypt, French North and West Africa, and South Africa. The states of Central and South America were represented as well as Mexico. Blacks and White liberals came from the United States and delegates arrived from many European countries. Well-known individuals present there included Roger Baldwin of the United States, Fenner Brockway of England, Mohammad Hatta who later became Vice-President of Indonesia, Ho Chi Minh who became the "father" of independent Vietnam,' George Landsbury of the British Labour Party, and Leopold Senghor who later was the longe-time President of Senegal. Messages of support came from Albert Einstein, Mahatma Gandhi, and Romain Rolland. The official languages of the Congress were those of the colonial powers: English, French, and German-Lansbury was elected President and Nehru became a member of the Presidium.

Nehru arrived at Brussels with a press statement, declaring that "there is much in common in the struggle which various subject and semi-subject and oppressed peoples are carrying on today."[1] Later, he delivered a long address, speaking in behalf of the Indian National Congress. He told the "distressing story" of how India "has been utilized, suppressed, and exploited by other people." He was applauded when he concluded that "the exploitation of India by the British is a barrier for other countries that are being oppressed and exploited." He felt it was an "urgent necessity" for other oppressed people that the Indians gain their freedom.

The Congress was conceived in Berlin with funds from Mexico and the Kuomintang in China. Apparently "the Russians approved the idea" of such a Congress, but at Brussels "Russia was conspicuous by its very absence." Delegates at Brussels decided to establish an ongoing organization, the League Against Imperialism. George Lansbury was elected President and Nehru was placed on its continuing executive. At the close of the Congress and when he returned to his Swiss mountain-top abode, Nehru wrote a highly political report about the Congress for his Indian colleagues. He called it "an event of first class importance... likely to have far-reaching results." He predicted, after talking to the Latin Americans present, that "the great problem of the near future will be American imperialism, even more than British imperialism."

Nehru was also impressed that the Asians at Brussels had a "strong desire" to form some "Asiatic federation." It was a recognition of a common bond uniting them", not "any feeling against Europe or America". In the end, Nehru felt that any such federation would be premature, but he encouraged the nationalist groups in Asia to exchange mailings and even visits Nehru urged the Indian National Congress to become affiliated with the League. He himself amended its executive meetings in Amsterdam and Cologne. In March 1927, Nehru wrote to Gandhi about his experience at the Congress. He did not think it "desirable or indeed possible for India to plough a lonely furrow now or in the future." Nehru added : "We are terribly narrow in our outlook and the sooner we get rid of this narrowness the better."

Nehru returned to India with his family in December 1927. He could only remain "in distant touch" with the League, but kept in contact with some of its personalities. By 1931 the League excommunicated Nehru "with bell, book, and candle" when the Indian National Congress made a truce with the British Government of India.

This brief experience with the Brussels Congress and the League did not put Nehru on the road to non-alignment. Nevertheless, it introduced the mature Nehru to the broader world of anti-colonialism. It also opened to him the workings of communism in Western Europe and the Soviet Union (which he visited briefly in November 1927) and the complex problems of international politics. The experience with the League demonstrated to him the power, outside India, of the "foreign and colonial offices of the imperial powers."

New Delhi

Non-alignment goes back at least to the Greek city-states. In our time, the term "non-alignment" may first have appeared, according to *Websters Dictionary,* in 1934. However, the 1976 supplement to the Oxford English Dictionary indicates that the word appeared in *The Times* of London on 5 May 1955—a few weeks after the Bandung Conference was held. Yet Jawaharlal Nehru used the concept, if not the full term, as early as September 1946. In a broadcast some months before the independence of India, Nehru declared : "We propose, as far as possible, to keep away from the power politics of groups, aligned against one another, which have led in the past to two world wars and which may again lead to disasters on an even vaster scale."[2] Here was a fully-developed concept, gained from Nehru's experience with pre-war colonialism and World War II, and in the political environment emerging after that war. Non-alignment evolved in Nehru's mind as a practical necessity for national survival in a post-colonial world where institutions of imperialism died slowly, not as an intellectual luxury concocted by exiled freedom fighters in Brussels, London, or Paris.

A few weeks latter, on 26 September 1946, Nehru spoke to a press conference in his capacity as member of the Interim Government in charge of external affairs. He declared that "in the sphere of foreign affairs, India will follow an independent policy, keeping away from the power politics of groups aligned against one another."[3]

Talking to the Constituent Assembly after Indian freedom in December 1947, Nehru reminded the delegates that "we have proclaimed during the past year that we will not attach ourselves to any particular group". He added that he had "nothing to do with neutrality or passivity or anything else". "We have sought to avoid", Nehru declared, "foreign entaglements by not joining one bloc or the other". He admitted that the result had been that "neither of these big blocs looks on us with favour" and indeed they think of us as "undependable, because we cannot be made to vote this way or that way".[4]

Nehru further declared in March 1949 that "we should not align ourselves with what are called power blocs" since "we can be of far more service without doing so". He also said that "obviously it does not mean that we should not be closer in our relations with some countries than with others."[5] In June 1952, Nehru in a debate in the Indian parliament used the word "non-align", three years earlier than recorded in the 1976 edition of the *Oxford English Dictionary*: "So far as our policy is concerned. ... we (India) have not swerved at all from our non-alignment with any group".[6]

Another step Nehru took in getting from Brussels to Belgrade was in March/April 1947 when he convened, even before Indian independence, delegates from twenty-eight Asian-nations. The Asian Relations Conference attracted representatives of both aligned and non-aligned Asian nations, many from Soviet Asia.

Nehru managed to bring Gandhi twice to these meetings. Gandhi urged, on 1 April 1947, that such meetings of Asians be held "regularly" and hoped that the delegates came together not to "wage war aganist Europe, against America, or against non-Asiatics". The next day Gandhi told these Asian leaders that "the message of Asia.. . is not to be learned through the Western spectacles by imitating the atom bomb". He asked them to go home "with the thought that Asia has to conquer the West through love and truth."[7] With this admonition, the delegates dispersed to their homes all over Asia. Within a year, Gandhi was assassinated.

Another step in Nehru's path towards non-alignment was

the creation of the concept of Panchsheel, the five principles. These first emerged at Beijing in April 1954. Called the Agreement on Trade and Intercourse between India and China, this treaty facilitated pilgrimage and travel to Tibet. The two governments inserted in the treaty five principles: mutual respect for each other's territorial integrity and sovereignty, mutual non-aggression, mutual non-interference in each other's affairs, equality and mutual benefit, and peaceful co-existence. When Prime Minister Chou En-lai of China visited New Delhi in June 1954, these principles were put forth by both Nehru and .the Chinese leader as "a solid foundation for peace". While they were not exactly rules for non-alignment, they were useful for several years in Asian relations.

In September 1954, when Indonesian Premier Ali Sastroamidjojo visited New Delhi, he recalled that President Sukarno also proposed five principles or Pantja Sila: nationalism, humanism, freedom, social justice, and faith in God. At a dinner honouring the Indonesian leader, Nehru said : "We talk also of another Panchseel or Five Principles." Thus the term Panchsheel was launched internationally. The Indian government later declared that Panchsheel as a "restatement, in more specific terms, of the principles embodied in the UN Charter".[8]

Bandung

In April 1954, Prime Minister Nehru met in Colombo, Ceylon, with his peers from Ceylon, Indonesia, Burma, and Pakistan : Sir John Kotelawala, Ali Sastroamidjojo, U Nu, and Mohammed Ali. They convened without a formal agenda. The Conference on Indo-China was in session at Geneva and Dien Bien Phu fell five days after their meeting ended. The five prime ministers discussed chiefly the Indo-China situation. A consensus communique was released. However, the decision most remembered from this meeting was to support a proposal, originally by Sastroamidjojo, to convene a conference of Asian and African state members of the United Nations.

Jawaharlal Nehru did not easily agree to participate, let alone sponsor, this Asian-African conference. He was juggling many international issues, including souring relations with the United States, delicate overtures to China, and always difficult problems with Pakistan. Also the Indo-China crisis remained volatile. Yet Nehru became slowly convinced that an Asian-African meeting, if it would not be confined to UN members, and if it would focus on major and not regional issues, might be very useful. Thus he went along with the other four prime ministers in favour of the proposal to convene a conference.

The five Colombo Powers next met at Bogor, Indonesia, in December 1954. Nehru attended that preparatory meeting for the conference. It was agreed to hold the meetings an Bandung, Indonesia, in April 1955. Sir John Kotelawala of Ceylon observed : "I do not think any of us claim the right to speak for Asia, but until such time as Asia can speak for herself, I think we have a duty to see that our views on Asian affairs do not go unheeded."[9] Nehru told the Bogor meeting : "The old balances are no longer there". He felt that the prime ministers must "place Asia and Africa in proper perspective in the world because the old perspectives no longer apply". Four purposes for the forthcoming conference were also spelled out, the last being "to view the position of Asia and Africa and their peoples in the world of today and the contribution they can make to the promotion of world peace and cooperation".

Most independent and near-independent Asian and African nations were invited to the conference, whether aligned to Washington or Moscow, or to neither. Thus such clients of the United States at the time as the Philippines, Liberia, Turkey, and Japan attended, as did such a client of the Soviet Union as the Democratic Republic of Vietnam. China was invited. A few countries (such as the Central African Republic) chose not to attend. Some were not invited: Israel, the two Korean states, and Taiwan. The five host countries could not decide whether to invite the Soviet Union. Was it an Asian country—or not? In the end, the Soviets were not invited.

Twenty-nine Asian and African nations came to the mountain city of Bandung. In addition to the five hosts, the Asian participants included Afghanistan, Cambodia, China, Iran, Iraq, Japan, Jordan, Laos, Lebanon, Nepal, Philippines, Saudi Arabia, Syria, Thailand, Turkey, Democratic Republic of Vietnam, State of Vietnam, and Yemen. The African countries present were Egypt, Ethiopia, the Gold Coast (soon to become Ghana), Liberia, Libya, and the Sudan

Jawaharlal Nehru was one of the founders of Bandung as well as one of its shining stars. His only rival at the conference was Chinese Prime Minister Chou En-Lai, although Col. Gamal Abdel Nasser of Egypt received much publicity since it was the first international gathering he attended. Nehru made no plenary address but spoke often in the closed committee meetings. He once observed : "I belong to neither (bloc), and I propose to belong to neither whatever happens in the world. If we have to stand alone, we will stand by ourselves, whatever happens. . . and we propose to face all consequences."[10]

Reacting to positions taken by Turkey and Pakistan, Nehru told the Political Committee: "if all the world were to be divided up between these two big blocs. . .the inevitable result would be war. Therefore every step that takes place in reducing that area in the world which may be called the unaligned area is a dangerous step and leads to war."[11] In his closing address to the Bandung Conference, Nehru reverted to the non-aligned theme: "If we are camp followers of Russia or America or any other country of Europe, it is, if I may say so, not very creditable to our dignity, our new independence, our new freedom, our new spirit, and our new self-reliance."[12]

In this Indonesian city, the leaders of Asia and Africa gave notice to the world that they wanted their "new" nations to be taken seriously. The unity and diversity of the Conference perhaps was best described by a black writer, Richard Wright :

> The despised, the insulted; the hurt, the dispossessed—in short, the underdogs of the human race were meeting. Here was class and religious consciousness on a global scale. . .What had these nations in common? Nothing. . . but what their past relationship to the Western world had made them feel. This meeting of the rejected was in itself a kind of judgment upon that Western world. . . .It was the kind of meeting that no anthropologist, no sociologist, no political scientist would ever have dreamed of staging; it was too simple, too elementary. . .There was something extra-political, extra-social, extra-human about it.. .They comprise princes and paupers, communists and Christians, leftists and rightists, Buddhists and democrats, in short, just anybody who lived in Asia and Africa.[13]

Bandung in 1955 was a forerunner of the first non-aligned conference at Belgrade in 1961, but it was not a direct predecessor. Indeed, efforts were made to convene a second Asian-African Conference, especially by Algeria and China in the mid-1960s. This effort to hold Bandung II in Algeria failed. One direct contribution of Bandung to Belgrade was to give confidence to some of the leaders present that they could convene successfully a world-class conference, despite widespread scepticism of the West, and many of its governmental leaders and press. Also the experience at Bandung made Nehru, Nasser, and Sukarno and their staffs close friends.

Bandung will be remembered as a hinge of history. Leopold Senghor, head of Senegal for many years and a fellow delegate with Nehru to the Brussels Congress, later called Bandung the most important event since the Renaissance that spelled "death to the inferiority complex of colonial people".[14]

Belgrade

After the Bandung Conference, President Josip Broz Tito of Yugoslavia invited Nehru and Nasser in July 1954 to his island of Brioni for political discussions. Yugoslavia was not, as a

European nation, invited to Bandung, but during this period Tito was developing his own foreign policy and maintaining a dialogue with his peers. In 1960, Tito, Nehru, and Nasser met again at the opening of the fifteenth session of the UN General Assembly in New York. Kwame Nkrumah of Ghana and President Sukarno of Indonesia joined them in discussing the mounting. Soviet-American tensions. Tito began advocating a meeting of non-aligned states. He travelled to nine African countries early in 1961 in his search for support for new machinery for world peace.

In April 1961, Tito and Nasser addressed a communication to twenty-two non-aligned countries suggesting a summit meeting before the opening of the sixteenth UN General Assembly in September. A month later, Nehru and Sukarno joined Tito and Nasser in asking appropriate countries to send representatives to a preparatory meeting at Cairo early in June.

Once again Nehru was a reluctant, not an eager, partner. Nehru had to be convinced that such a summit would be worthwhile. Krishna Menon, Indian foreign minister, hesitated to institutionalize the non-aligned position, fearing that it might only restrict the options of Indian foreign policy. But Nehru felt that, if a conference were to be held, India would have to participate. Also Nehru felt, that, India could influence the conference by helping in its preparation.

Fifteen countries, including India, attended the preparatory meeting in Cairo. Criteria were adopted as the basis for issuing invitations to states to attend the forthcoming Summit on a Heads of State or Government level. These included the following : "The country should have adopted an independent policy on the co-existence of states with different political and social systems and on non-alignment or should be showing a trend in favour of such a policy; the country should be consistently supporting movements for national independence; and the country should not be a member of a multilateral military alliance concluded in the context of great power conflicts."[15] A draft agenda for the conference was adopted and Yugoslavia was selected as the venue. Arabic, English, French, and Spanish were selected as the official languages.

The Non-aligned Summit opened on 1 September 1961 in Belgrade. Twenty-five states were represented. Delegates included one emperor, Haile Selassie of Ethiopia, the kings of Morocco and Nepal, and princes from Cambodia and Yemen. Also attending were the presidents of Cuba, Cyprus, Ghana, Indonesia, Mali, Somalia, Sudan, Tunisia, the United Arab Republic (Egypt), and Yugoslavia. Prime ministers were present from Afghanistan, Algeria, Burma, Ceylon, the Congo, India, and Lebanon. Three heads of delegations were the foreign ministers of Guinea, Iran, and Saudi Arabia.

At Belgrade, the twenty-five nations staked out the position of non-alignment in the post-colonial world where the two Super Powers were competing for supremacy. The definition of non-alignment was not perfectly made, nor was it easily accepted by outside sceptics and critics. Nehru succeeded in deflecting attention at the meeting from continuing colonial problems. As Professor Sarvepalli Gopal has written: "Nehru wrested the Conference out of the old ruts of ritual opposition to colonialism, imperialism, and racism and forced it to face the danger of nuclear warfare."[16] Indeed, the Conference composed and issued an Appeal to Peace, with Nehru and Nkrumah immediately afterwards visiting Secretary Khrushchev in Moscow, and Sukarno and President Keita of Mali visiting President Kennedy in Washington. The Conference also discussed a list of substantive world and regional issues and demanded a strengthened United Nations.

The Belgrade Conference did not know how to respond usefully to the resumption of nuclear weapons testing by the Soviet Union on the very eve of its convening. While many of the assembled presidents and prime ministers denounced these Soviet action in their speeches, the final declaration only weakly condemned the Soviets. However, Nehru told the Conference : "This danger of war comes nearer and nearer, has been enhanced and has become nearer to us, perhaps, by the recent decision of the Soviet Government to start nuclear tests... This decision makes the situation much more dangerous... I regret it deeply because it may well lead to other countries also starting this and, then apart from the danger inherent in nuclear tests...all this brings us to the very verge and precipice of war... It has become even more urgent that this process of negotiation should begin without any delay, without thinking of who is going to ask whom first. The person who asks first will deserve the credit, not the person who shrinks from asking others."[17]

An Assessment

Nehru, Tito, Nasser and the other leaders may or may not have fully realized the magnitude of the movement and indeed the institution they created at Belgrade. Nehru died only three years later, although preparations were already under way to convene the Second Non-Aligned Summit at Cairo in October 1964. Nehru's successor, Prime Minister Lal Bahadur Shastri, attended, with forty-seven countries participating. Nasser died in 1970 before the third Summit of fifty-four countries was held at Lusaka, Zambia. Tito lived through three more summits—Algiers in 1973, Colombo in 1976, and Havana in 1979—before dying in 1980. The seventh was held in New Delhi (1983) and the eighth and most recent in Harare (1986).

The Harare Summit coincided with the twenty-fifth anniversary of the Belgrade Conference and it was appropriately observed. Prime Minister Robert Mugabe of Zimbabwe in the keynote address declared in part : "The one question that today precedes all others is that, without an answer to it, answers to all other questions become pointless. (This) is the question of disarmament. Preventing the annihilation of mankind consequent upon nuclear war is the pre-condition of all our endeavours". Mugabe added : "May our deliberations today be attended with the positive spirit that inspired Tito, Nehru, Nasser, Sukarno, Nkrumah, and others to launch our movement a quarter of a century ago."

What did the movement initiated by Tito, Nehru, and Nasser accomplish over the years, as more than a hundred non-aligned states are already planning politically for their ninth Summit? Any balance-sheet of the non-aligned movement to date would have to recognize some disappointments.

After twenty-seven years, a blurred image in the world remains about the non-aligned movement. The leaders themselves have often failed to articulate simply the outlines of admittedly a complex entity. Deep ideological divisions have only given ammunition to the detractors of non-alignment--and there remain many. Also non-alignment remains a negative concept to many even if, Indians have been fond of noun with negative".[18] A positive, affirmative definition of non-alignment is still needed, one that goes beyond its institutional phase to denote national, regional, and global efforts for the goals of peace, dynamic social change, and social and economic justice. Equidistance and neutrality have been supplanted by less transitory strategies.

Another disappointment is that the non-aligned movement has so far not prevented the emergence of nuclear weapon states within its own family. Some members have caught the nuclear virus and feel that the acquisition of nuclear weapons might give them prestige and even security. Using the excuse that the non-proliferation treaty is discriminatory to non-nuclear-weapon states (because the Super Powers and the United Kingdom have not disarmed under Article VI), a few non-aligned states have got themselves pregnant with nuclear bombs. Although the gestation period is long and expensive, each of them one day might produce multiple births which can no longer be hidden from the world. The movement ignores this threat to its common security.

The non-aligned movement has never quite lived up to the hopes and rhetoric of its founders in being able to change history. The forces of history created non-alignment, but the movement has seldom, if ever, created history. Non-alignment has assisted history, at times has nudged it, but seldom caused significant changes. The favourite campaigns of the movement—against apartheid, for some kind of new economic order—have fallen short of success. Even if, since 1961, the

Super Powers did not go to war and indeed have engaged in detente of least twice, the non-aligned movement may have been only a marginal factor in their improved relations.

Another disappointment is the lack of an effective machinery of the movement. Given the hesitation of Nehru and its other founders to create another political bloc, the role of the chairman of the movement is imprecise. Some chairmen have performed better than others, but there is no continuing secretariat. Thus the impact of the movement has been uneven, especially within the United Nations community. The latest example is the role of the non-aligned at the Third UN Special Session on Disarmament in June 1988. Its foreign ministers met on the eve of the session and produced an impressive memorandum for the Conference. Yet, at the special session itself, non-aligned leadership was almost totally lacking.

A fifth disappointment is that the growth of the movement has slowed down considerably. New nations are emerging in this post-colonial era more slowly. Also there may be hesitations about growth within the movement. Should it extend its membership to such neutral but developed states as Sweden and Austria, if they would want to join? And what have been the factors, over many years, which have caused Mexico and some other Latin American countries to hesitate to become full members?

The non-aligned movement tries to bring peace to the world, but often finds it impossible to heal regional conflicts within its own ranks. The wars between Iraq and Iran and between Ethiopia and Somalia—these and others seem resistant to mediation within the movement itself. These conflicts, while troublesome, many have not injured the unity of the movement but may be tarnishing its reputation at least.

Still another disappointment relates to the fissures within the movement as it has multiplied fourfold in its membership. Some of its members are becoming economically developed, such as Singapore. Others of its members are the large bloc of least-developed countries, the so-called "fourth world". Still others of its members continue to be clients muted or otherwise, of one Super Power or another. Only with difficulty do they somehow fit within the rules of membership laid down before the Belgrade Conference. Also regional sub-caucuses have developed within the movement which take policy decisions for the whole, such as the African, Arab, and Central American groups. It takes strong leadership and stronger ideological glue to hold such a diverse group of states together.

A final disappointment is that the non-aligned movement appears more concerned about the violation of economic and social rights than of civil and political rights. The members demand food and housing and jobs more than freedom and democracy. They appear more opposed to poverty and disease than torture and imprisonment. Many have hoped, over the years, that the movement would act upon both sets of human rights simultaneously.

This litany of disappointments about the non-aligned movement, although real, does not overshadow the many accomplishments of the legacy of Nehru, Tito, and Nasser.

The non-aligned movement for almost three decades has prevented the further polarization of a bipolar world into pro-Washington or pro-Moscow allies. It has given legitimacy to the new nations, or old ones, which preferred to be independent and un-labelled politically. The very existence of the non-aligned grouping has given them political shelter, a clubhouse in which to gather.

The non-aligned movement has had the flexibility to endure and often thrive through almost three decades when the political landscape changed considerably, including the reputation of both the Super Powers. The movement has seen few defections—only Burma—and remains a source of solidarity for a majority of the independent nations of the world. More than a body of doctrine (the sum of its massive resolutions at eight summits), more than an ideology dating back to the break of Nehru and Nasser with London and Tito with Moscow, non-alignment remains a living faith for both rulers and their peoples.

The non-aligned movement gave much impetus to the process of decolonization. Credit must be given to the political forces unleashed by the Second World War and the rise of the United Nations, but the non-aligned helped greatly to lessen colonialism in our time. Decolonization was truly one of the successful revolutions of our era. Dependent territories remain, not only in Southern Africa, but elsewhere too. Yet much of the world is free—at least from old-fashioned colonialism.

The non-aligned movement has insisted that nuclear disarmament remains on the top of the world's agenda. It is wrong to assert that the "South" is unconcerned about disarmament, or about nuclear weapons. Beginning in 1961, but with Nehru even in 1954, the non-aligned have always put the ending of nuclear weapons tests at the very peak of their agenda.

The non-aligned movement has also insisted that the world community give high priority to Southern Africa—to ending apartheid and the occupation of Namibia. The pressures on Pretoria continue strong, but also on Washington and London to stop their equivocating. The non-aligned demand that racism must end, beginning with South Africa.

The non-aligned movement has become the best protector and defender of the United Nations system. The members of the non-aligned—mostly small states, but also some big ones such as India and Nigeria—need the world organization. The non-aligned, as the largest caucus in the United Nations, have come to dominate the UN agenda and, in the General Assembly, sometimes its voting patterns. Indeed, the UN caucus may be currently the most effective arm of the non-aligned movement.

What would the architects of Belgrade think if they could see their movement, and the world, today? What could Nehru think, months after the twenty-fifth anniversary of the signing of the partial test-ban treaty, about the tragic fact that a comprehensive treaty has not yet been signed? What would Tito think if he knew that the "new international economic order" has been shelved and that the gap between the developed and the developing countries continues to widen? What would Nasser think about the continued killings of West Bank Palestinians by the Israelis and the continued resistance to establish an independent Palestinian state?

The Future

Some observers believe that the non-aligned movement has a great future, that more states will become independent of political and military blocs, and that the size and effectiveness of the non-aligned movement will continue and even increase. Others feel that the movement may have already reached its zenith, but that it may take some years for its numbers and dynamics to fall off.

The polycentrism in the world community emerging during the past decades has cast some doubt on the future of the non-aligned movement. When there were only two Super Powers, both searching for clients or allies and when new nations were being born almost every month, the need for a "third force" seemed clear and welcome. Yet now that there are a third and a fourth and a fifth, and more, centers of economic and political power, non-alignment becomes a more politically complex choice. What happens when some of the non-aligned states, such as India, are also these new powers? Also when Beijing split with Moscow, non-alignment for some nations was to refuse to identify, not with Washington or Moscow, but with Beijing or Moscow.

The new turn of the Soviet Union under Gorbachev may also cause problems for the non-aligned movement. How will Moscow under perestrokia relate to the non-aligned? The Chinese for years have identified themselves with the non-aligned movement, but they have had the restraint not to ask for admittance. But what about Mr. Gorbachev? How will he and his new foreign policy relate itself to the non-aligned? On the other hand, will the new bilateralism between Washington and Moscow appear to be so much at the expense of other nations that they will rally ever closer around the non-aligned banner?

The Group of 77 also must be factored into any future discussion of the non-aligned movement. Established in 1964 to influence the UN Conference on Trade and Development (UNCTAD), today this caucus is a formidable lobby for the Third World in all UN economic bodies. It really has roots dating back to the Bandung and Belgrade Conferences. The future of this modest caucus, with perhaps more "machinery" than the non-aligned movement, bears careful watching. One day it could take over some of the functions of the non-aligned movement.

In the immediate future, however, the non-aligned movement will continue the legacy of Nehru, Tito, and their associates. It will continue to rally basically the developing nations of Asia, Africa, and Latin America—the poor and the oppressed under neo-colonialism.

Once Jawaharlal Nehru, while alive, proposed his own epitaph. He diffidenlty suggested: "If any people choose to think of me, then I should like them to say. . 'This was a man who, with all his mind and heart, loved India and the Indian people. And they, in turn, were indulgent to him and gave him of their love most abundantly and extravagantly.'"[19]

On the occasion of Nehru's birth centenary, it seems appropriate to internationalize and universalize this epitaph: "This is a man who loved the Asian and the African people." Perhaps neither John Foster Dulles nor *The New York Times* gave Nehru their love, but to this day the good people everywhere should be thankful for his legacy.

REFERENCES

1. Most of the material on the Brussels Gongress and the League Against Imperialism is taken from S. Copal, ed., *Selected Works of Jawaharlal Nehru* (Orient Longman, New Delhi, 1972), Vol. II, pp. 469. See also *Towards Freedom:*

The Autobiography of Jawaharlal Nehru (John Day, New York, 1941), pp. 445; 123-27.

2. Jawaharlal Nehru, *India's Foreign Policy: Selected Speeches, September 1946— April 1961* (Government of India.'New Delhi), p. 612; 2.
3. *Indian Annual Register* 1946, Vol. 2, p. 252.
4. Jawaharlal Nehru. *India's Foreign Policy,* pp. 24-25.
5. *Ibid.,* p. 47.
6. *Ibid.,* p. 63.
7. The *Collected Works of Mahatma Gandhi,* Vol. 86 (Government of India, New Delhi, 1983), pp. 586, 1983; 182-83.
8. G.H. Jansen, *Non-alignment and the Afro-Asian States* (Praeger, New York, 196), pp. 432, 51-75.
9. This and the next two quotations are from Homer A. Jack, *Bandung Toward* Freedom (1955), p. 37.
10. Sarvepalli Gopal, *Jawaharlal Nehru: A Biography* (Harvard University Press, Cambridge, 1979), Vol. II (1947-1954); pp. 346, 253.
11. George McT. Kahin, *The Asian-African Conference* (Cornell, Ithaca, 1956), pp. 88, 23, 66.
12. *Ibid.,* p. 74.
13. Richard Wright, *The Color Curtain* (World, Cleveland 1956), pp. 223, p. 12-14.
14. Richard L. Jackson, *The Non-Aligned, the UN, and the Super Powers* (Praeger, New York, 1983), p. 14.
15. Homer A. Jack, *Belgrade : The Conference of Non-Aligned States* (National Committee for a Sane Nuclear Policy, New Delhi, 1961), pp. 56, 5.
16. S. Gopal, *Selected Works of Jawaharlal Nehru,* Vol. III, p. 186.
17. Homer A. Jack, *Belgrade : The Conference of Non-Aligned States.*
18. K.P. Misra, ed., *Non-Alignment: Frontiers and Dynamics* (Vikas, New Delhi, 1982), pp. 512, 26.
19. Michael Brecher, *Nehru : A Political Biography* (Beacon Press, Boston, 1961), abridged edition, pp. 267, 254.

32

Nehru's *Creative* Response to Complex Challenges

Jawaharlal Nehru, was one of the most fascinating political leaders of the period from 1922 to 1964. In India, his position in the nationalist movement was next only to that of Mahatma Gandhi. When India became independent in 1947, Nehru became the Prime Minister, a position which he occupied until his death in 1964. Very few leaders of the national liberation movements of the post-1945 era have had such a long tenure in office. There were some striking potential personalities in Nehru's era. One was Lenin, who led a revolution in Russia in 1917 and who became the first important head of the ruling communist party of that country. Stalin succeeded him in the USSR. During the 1920s a colourful personality like Mussolini became the ruler of Italy and he was thrown out of power only after the Second World War. Germany saw the emergence of Hitler and Nazism in the nineteen-thirties. Sun Yet Sun and Chaing Kaishek were the important leaders of China in the first-half of the twentieth century. Mao Tse-tung, who dominated China after 1950, eclipsed both of them by his place in history. During the 1930s, Roosevelt became the most important political figure of the United States and the well-known saviour of capitalism from depression. During the Second World War, Churchill became the most important leader of Great Britain. After the war, Charles de Gaulle became an important figure in France and European community. In Yugoslavia, Tito became a dominating personality. Apart from Nehru, Asia and Africa had some important leaders like Nasser of Egypt, Nkrumah of Ghana,

Lumumba of the Congo (now Zaire) and Sukarno of Indonesia.

Among this group of political leaders Nehru stands as a class by himself. He was not famous for originating a new political party or for expounding a new political philosophy. But there were few political events and ideas of his times on which he did not express himself. His reaction to nationalism, imperialism, racialism, capitalism, socialism, and fascism were coherently expressed in many of his works and he influenced a large number of people in India and also those in other countries. After Nehru had become the prime minister and foreign minister of India, he also expressed himself on world political events. He became the symbol of Asian resurgence and he associated himself with the national liberation movements and antiracialism in Africa. As the head of government of India, he himself was associated with some of the wars India had with countries like Pakistan, China, and Portugal. But in a world in which many states were divided into two power blocs led by two Super Powers which had a very large number of nuclear weapons, Nehru became the champion of world peace and of the settlement of international disputes by conciliation and negotiation. In other words, he became the statesman of the nuclear age.

Liberalism and the Nationalist Movement

Nehru had a great share in the shaping of the nationalist movement. Of course, he was to some extent the product of the movement which preceded his role in it. He was also greatly influenced by Gandhi who became its most important leader from 1919 to 1945. But Nehru had some share in giving a shape to it even in this period.

The Indian nationalist movement was led by the Indian National Congress which was established in 1885, four years before Nehru was born. Even before the Congress was established, there was some political awakening in some parts of India. This arose from the Western impact and as a result of the social and religious reform movements which were establised before the Congress was founded. Referring to the impact of the West on Indian culture, a well known Indian scholar wrote :

> All are agreed that India entered into a new phase of life in the nineteenth century. The spirit of vitality came from the West through various channels like commerce and trade, increased facilities for communication, Western training, administrative unity etc. For the first time historians assert, an alien civilisation impinged upon every detail of Indian life, changed its patterns and created new values. Thus, India's wealth ceased to become treasure; money became capital, goods became commodities, land became a source of monopoly rent, and the self-sufficiency of rural economy was transformed into the interdependence of urban and world economy. Similarly, the vision of average Indian, so long closed like that of the frog in the well, was enlarged. Western philosophy and science introduced reason into daily habits and made Indians realise the meaninglessness of many ancient customs and prejudices.

Of course, only a small number of Indians educated in English were influenced by the Western thought. But many of them were leaders of social and religious movements and of the Indian National Congress in its first phase. They wanted cast reforms, caste abolition, equal rights for women, a campaign against child marriage, and a crusade against social and legal inequalities. In the religious sphere, many superstitious and hereditary priesthood were opposed. All these demands were related to the principles of individual liberty and social equality. This was the basis of political awakening also.

The specific demands of the Indian National Congress were at first connected with these principles. The wanted Indianisation of the army and civil source, the freedom of speech and representative assemblies, with the power of discussion of governmental actions. The leaders of the early Congress were constitutional agitators for the redress of grievance and were not inclined towards any rebellion. They were generally referred to as liberals. Jawaharlal Nehru's father, Motilal Nehru, was a very-active leader of these liberals. He was also an eminent lawyer with great respect for the rule of law. Jawaharlal Nehru was influenced by his father and his colleagues.

Nehru's early education in England also made him accept some of the ideas of European liberalism of the nineteenth century and the early twentieth century. He was a student at Harrow and Cambridge in England from 1905 to 1912. Later, even when he was influenced by Marxism, he wrote : "I am very far from being a communist. My roots are still partly in the nineteenth century, and I have been too much influenced by the humanist liberal tradition to get out of it completely. The bourgeois background shows and follows me around and is naturally an irritation to many communists. I dislike dogmatism and the treatment of Karl Marx's writings or any other book as a revealed scripture which cannot be challenged and the regimentation and heavy hunts which seems to be a feature of modern communism."[2]

There was no doubt that the liberalism of West Europeans, and particularly that of the Englishmen, influenced Nehru. Occasionally, during the nationalist movement, Nehru was unhappy with the so-called liberals of India who did not participate in the civil disobedience and other militant movements against the British government. Commenting on their basic attitude, he wrote : "But moderation, however admirable it might be is not a bright, and scintilating liberals have unhappily become a 'dull brigade'—sombre and serious in their looks, dull in their writings and conversations and lacking in humour."[3] And Nehru also noted that unlike the British liberals, the Indian liberals were without any economic foundation. Capitalism and industrialization had not led to the emergence of a powerful bourgeoisie in India or a particular ideology of individual freedom and civil liberties. Some of the Indian liberals were only mechanically repeating the ideas they had learned from European liberals.

But when India became free, Nehru did not have any resentment against these liberals. On the other hand, he associated them in a big way with the framing of the Indian constitution. A few years before and after 1947, India was also having rapid capitalist economic development. Apart from this, when once the militant, though non-violent, struggle against the British imperialism was over, Nehru returned to liberalism. It was easy for him to do so because India's struggle for independence, though militant in some respects, was essentially non-violent in form. Moreover, the transfer of power from British to Indian hands was peaceful.

Nehru never referred to the golden age of ancient India or to the so-called Hindu period of Indian history. This was because he did not want to associate himself with the narrow and exclusive-mindedness of any group in India. But he was a product of Indian, and particularly Hindu culture. And there was a tolerance and opposition to brutality which he inherited from this tradition. This is what helped his faith in liberalism.

Conflict and Harmony with Gandhi

Although Nehru obeyed Gandhi during the nationalist movement, he was no blind follower of the Mahatma. He often criticized Gandhi for his use of "fasts" as a political weapon and for his political style and idioms which made an appeal only to the Hindus. Nehru's commitment to non-violence was also not total. Commenting on the repercussions of Gandhi's fast, Nehru wrote in his *Autobiography* : "Again I watched the emotional upheaval of the country during the fast, and I wondered more and more if this was the right method in politics. It seemed to be sheer revivalism, and clear thinking had not a ghost of chance against it. All India, or most of it, started reverently at the Mahatma and expected him to perform miracle after miracle and put an end to untouchability and get Swaraj and so on and did precious little itself."[4]

But Nehru also realized the relevance of Gandhi and his method to free India. Unlike Subhas Chandra Bose with whom Nehru occasionally cooperated, he never rebelled against

Gandhi. And unlike M.N. Roy whom Nehru complimented occasionally, he never condemned the political record of Gandhi. He even said that the so-called Indian exiles, socialists and communists, were only splitting hair in arguments and quarrelling among themselves, while Gandhi was leading one mass movement after another in India.

Nehru understood Gandhi but he also misunderstood Indian traditions. Although Nehru tried to discover India through a book only late in his life and after he had glimpses of world history, he was broadly aware of Indian traditions even in his early life.

Nehru was never a mechanical and blind follower of Gandhi. He criticised not only Gandhi's use of fasts as political weapon but also his uncompromising advocacy of non-violence. Nehru maintained that coercion might be preferred to conversion on some occasions and that the ends must occasionally justify the means. But in the last phase of his life, he was moving towards the Gandhian views on this matter.

There were, of course, other matters on which Nehru took an independent line of his own. One was Nehru's preference for the extensive use of science and technology for the economic reconstruction of India. There was also a socialist rhetoric in many of Nehru's speeches and writings. And as the leader of the nationalist leader and head of the government of independent India, Nehru also put forward his international outlook and unlike Gandhi, linked India's problems with the then existing international problems.

In Defence of Complete Independence

None of these views, however, contradicted Nehru's basic liberal outlook. On the other hand, his complaint against the Westrn Europeans was that they compromised with the fascists, Nazis and the Japanese militarists and did not, in cooperation with the Soviet Union, take collective action against them.

The thrust of Gandhi's political movement was to

strengthen Indian nationalism. His idiom and style were traditional, but he clearly tried to promote the novel ideals. He stood for Purna Swaraj (complete independence) and Swadeshi (a national economy). Gandhi always emphasised mass action by political socialisation of the people and by organising civil disobedience. In many of these respects, Nehru went further and enriched Gandhism. He clearly stated that he stood for complete independence.

Nehru, like other Congress leaders and Gandhi, was in jail during 1942-45. They were all released from jail in 1945. Towards the end of 1945 and in the beginning of 1946, there were serious negotiations between the representatives of the British government and the Indian leaders on the matter of the transfer of power from the British to the Indian hands. By the time these negotiations took a concrete shape, Nehru was the President of the Indian National Congress and the chief negotiator on behalf of the Congress.

Loyalty in the Parliamentary System

When an interim government was formed at New Delhi in September 1946, Nehru became the Vice-President of the Viceroy's Executive Council. Ever since then, he began to function as the prime minister of liberal democratic India. He treated the Viceroy, who was the Chairman of the Executive Council, as the constitutional and nominal head of the Indian state and not as the head of the government. He appointed Krishna Menon as his special envoy to foreign countries to deal with foreign relations. He appointed India's representatives abroad and the delegates to the United Nations. In other words, Nehru was asserting himself as the virtual head of the government even before the transfer of power in 1947.

Nehru also made it clear to his colleagues that the prime minister was the leader of the Congress Party and the head of the government. Whenever there was a difference of opinion between him and Sardar Vallabhbhai Patel, who was the next important minister, Nehru maintained that the prime minister had to function as the leader.

Maker of the Modern State

After India became free, Nehru and his government had to fulfil another historic function to make a modern state. Even before 1947, India was not exactly a colony of the United Kingdom. In some respects, the British had left in India the rudiments of a state. The Indian Civil Service, known as the steel frame of the British empire, was pretty efficient. But its functions were primarily to maintain law and order to maintain the British rule in India and to collect revenues by different taxes for that purpose. But gradually the government had extended its functions and expanded its civil service. But there was no foreign service in India. There were no great development programmes before the government. Almost one-third of India was referred to as the native states and the princes, with a few exceptions, were autocratic and authoritarian. These states, again with a few exceptions, were socially and economically backward. One of the important tasks of the new government was to integrate these states with the rest of India. Sardar Patel was the minister of the states and he was primarily responsible for it. And he, with the help of senior civil servants, accomplished it within a short time. There was some resistance from states, particularly from Hyderabad which was the biggest state in the heartland of India. The Indian government had to take police action against the government of that state. The State of Jammu and Kashmir created a problem when its Hindu leader acceded to India. The Muslims were a majority of Muslims in that state and it was contiguous to Pakistan. It became an international issue. After a few days of Kashmir's accession to India, it was invaded. The invaders came from Pakistan and occupied some parts of that state territory. They are still holding to them. Thus it became an international issue. And Kashmir, which is now in India, had a special status in the Indian constitutional framework. But all other states were fully integrated into India. After the establishment of the Indian Republican Constitution in January 1950, a modern state emerged. In 1938 Nehru presided over the All India State Peoples' Conference. Explaining his views on the future of Indian native states,

Nehru wrote: "It is clear that these five hundred and fifty states cannot function separately as political and economic units. They cannot remain as feudal in a democratic India."

Nehru, as the prime minister, had a major role to play in these developments. Even before India became free, Nehru was taking active interest in the people's movements in the native states. Very few leaders from British India took as much active interest as Nehru had done in the native states. But the integration of those states with India was accomplished by the help of his colleagues and with the help of the police, army and the prestige of the Indian Government.

Shaping of Foreign Policy

In regard to the making of foreign policy, Nehru had to write on a clean slate. As the foreign minister and the prime minister of the country, he developed a foreign policy with an originality. It is no exaggeration to say that the formative phase of the foreign policy of independent India was largely Nehru's making.

Now India has emerged as a middle power in the international field. This was possible because of the foundations of independent India laid down by Nehru, of course, he made occasional blunders and met with some failures in international field. The most well-known failure of India was the military defeat of India at the hands of China in 1962. Perhaps Nehru could never regain the prestige he lost at that time. But India, built by Nehru, could gradually recover its prestige. And Nehru's non-alignment in foreign policy and his perspective on international relations stand fully vindicated by subsequent events.

It is significant that even when Nehru was in jail, he was planning the formulation of a foreign policy for India. His book, *The Discovery of India,* had a section entitled "The Congress Develops a Foreign Policy". Most of the revolutions adopted by the Congress on the subject were drafted by Nehru. When India became free, Nehru, as the foreign minister, had to provide leadership on formulating India's foreign policy.

And no other prominent leader of the Congress party was interested in international relations.

International Outlook: Statesman of the Atomic Era

When India was fighting for freedom, he was emphasizing the theme that freedom was indivisible. And he was always connected with the struggle of Indians for freedom and equality with similar struggles elsewhere. And even after India had become free, India did support the struggles for freedom in Indonesia, in Indo-China, in Algeria, and in many other African countries. It was India which brought the issue of discrimination based on racial differences in South Africa to the forum of international conference. Since then, it had remained as an international issue.

By the time India became free, an influential section of the States in the international community was divided into two power blocs—one headed by the United States and the other by the Soviet Union. On 7 September 1946, almost a year before India became formally free, Nehru, as the leader of the interim government of India, said : "We propose as far as possible, to keep away from the power politics of the groups, aligned against one another, which have led in the past to two world wars and which may again lead to disaster on an even vaster scale."[5]

Even after India had become independent in August 1947, it was not easy for Nehru to continue with India's independent foreign policy. Defending his position in the Indian Constituent Assembly on 24 February 1948, Nehru said :

> Now I am not talking in terms of this bloc or that bloc; I am talking independently of the blocs as they have appeared on the world stage. We have either to pursue our policy generally within limitations because we cannot pursue it whole-heartedly, nevertheless openly—or give it up. I do not think that anything would be more injurious to us from any point of view, but equally so from the point of view of opportunism and national interest in the narrowest sense of the word than to give up the policies

> we have pursued, namely, those of standing up to certain ideals in regard to...oppressed nations (instead of aligning) ourselves with this great power or that and becoming its camp-follower in the hope that some crumb might fall from the table.[6]

The people of India in general, and the leaders of the various political parties in particular, gradually accepted Nehru's basic approach towards international relations and Indian foreign policy. Even the government of a powerful country, like that of the Soviet Union, after Stalin's death, recognised the progressive aspect of Nehru's foreign policy. There were always some ambassadors and intellectuals in the United States who justified and explained Nehru's foreign policy. But there were powerful elements also in the Republican Party which did not do so. But for resolving many international disputes and implementing many agreements, like that of Korea, Indo-China and Congo, all important states accepted India's mediatory role. This was because, with development and proliferation of nuclear weapons, Nehru's view that world peace was indivisible found widespread acceptance.

Champion of the Mixed Economy

Another important aspect of Nehru's thought was his perception of the area of agreement between communism and capitalism that also meant the coexistence between the systems in the international field. On the national level this led to Nehru's attempt to give a sense of direction to Indian capitalist economy with some socialist features. Some important developments in the Indian economy such as increase in food production took place as the result of private enterprise. But after 1947 the heavy industries were at first built in the public sector with the help of the Soviet Union.

One important contribution made by Nehru to India was his popularisation of the use of science, and technology in the economic field. He organised the building of large dams and the extensive use of fertilisers and new seeds. These were very helpful to the private enterprisers in the agricultural field.

After some resistance, the Congress Party, under Nehru and others, also allowed the Communist Party to rule in some Indian states like Kerala, West Bengal, and Tripura. In some of them, land reforms legislations were implemented and lands, which originally belonged legally to the landlords, were distributed to the cultivating peasants and tenants.

Thus we see that although Nehru himself did not do anything basically to change the ownership of the means of production, he was comprehending the relevance of mixed economy for increasing production in a underdeveloped country like India.

Nehru always opposed some Indian communists who advocated bloody revolutions through the dictatorship of the proletariat and through India accepting the leadership of international communism headed by the Soviet Union or China, Nehru was not an advocate of the national and international crusades of either capitalism or of socialism against another.

Secular Ideas

In many respects, Indian society was medieval in structure when the British gradually conquered India and when they established one single central state in India after 1857. They followed a policy of divide and rule and retained the medieval and feudal structure in some parts of India. Some of the Indian movements against the British also drew sources of inspiration from India's past. Nehru was the first Indian bourgeois political leader who spoke the language of the scientific age and opposed the legacies of the past completely.

Nehru's secularism went beyond Gandhi's anti-communalism. He did not stop with saying that all religions were true, but maintained that religion had no part to play in public life in general and in politics in particular. The leadership of Nehru did give help to the making of the Indian nationalism, based on the political unity of the people on the basis of territorial integrity. Before Pakistan was created, Nehru was not a great success in mobilising Indian Muslims against the leadership of Jinnah and the Muslim League who preached Muslim communalism. But after 1947, Nehru had success in stopping the brutalization of the Hindus and in drawing a significant section of the Muslims to the Indian political and administrative life.

Scientific Temper

Apart from secularism, Nehru thought that India must imbibe the scientific culture of the New Age. He was convinced that the methods and approach of science have revolutionised human life more than anything else in the long course of history, and have opened doors and avenues of further and even more radical change, leading up to the portals of what has long been considered the unknown. "The technical achievements of science are obvious enough, its capacity to transform the life of scarcity into one abundance, its invasion of many problems which have so far been the monopoly of philosophy in becoming more pronounced."[7] Again he stated: "It is the scientific approach, the adventures and yet critical temper of science, the search for truth and new knowledge, the refusal to accept anything without testing and trial the capacity to change previous conclusions in the face of new evidence, the reliance on observed fact and not on preconceived theory, the hard discipline of the mind-all that is necessary; not merely for the application of science, but for life itself and the solution of its many problems."[8] From this viewpoint, Nehru popularised the scientific temper in the country and attacked superstitions and faith in astrology.

Modernization of Indian Society

But the Indian society was not so far modernized to the extent Nehru wanted it to be modernized. He had some limited success in reorganising the Hindu legal code. He was also responsible for shaping Indian politics on a secular basis. In spite of the widespread Hindu-Muslim riots in 1947 and scattered riots since then, the people of India are not brutalised. There was no hate-Pakistan and hate-China campaign in India inspite of the wars India had with them. This was due to the inherent qualities of the Indian people. And leaders like Gandhi and Nehru strengthened this balance of mind and tolerance of the Indian people. Gandhi, as a social revolutionary, made a tremendous impact on the people. But Gandhi's idioms and style could not make the same appeal to the non-Hindus of India as they did to the Hindus. Nehru had a cosmopolitanism—perhaps a spurious cosmopolitanism which never went deep among any section of the people. But it never antagonized or alienated any section of the people also. And it appealed to the educated people in all religious faiths.

A Meeting Ground of Different Views

To India of Nehru's era, he gave a shape. It was not by putting forward a clear-cut political philosophy or by a cadre of political workers. He did that but by his becoming a symbol of political unity. He could do so also by becoming a meeting ground of different ideologies and strands of thought. From 1920 to 1964, there were very few important national and international issues on which he did not express himself. On most of these issues, like Marxism, the Soviet revolution, fascism, collective security, democracy, scientific temper, and socialism, he was reacting to events and to the views of others. But he spoke originally on mixed economy in India, the convergence of advanced capitalist and communist states, international action against discrimination based on racial distinction and the Asian-African resurgence and on the reconstruction of world peace. Here we may note that India's gradual emergence as a middle power in the world is the result of Nehru's policies. So is India's refusal to become hysterical on national and international issues.

As Nehru predicted, the advanced communist societies and the advanced capitalist societies were discovering areas of agreement between them. And if this gathers momentum, the world will move from the first step of co-existence between the two systems to the next step of cooperation between them.

Nehru was a practising politician. But there were moments in his life when he dreamed like an ocean. And when he did so, he was like a thinker who would become relevant only after his times. In his centenary year, one can comfortably conclude that his thoughts have become valid now.

REFERENCES

1. D.P. Mukherjee, *Diversities* (New Delhi, 1965), p. 164.
2. Jawaharlal Nehru, *An Autobiography* (Allied Publishers, New Delhi, 1962) p. 591.
3. *Ibid.*, p. 411.
4. *Ibid.*, p. 373.
5. Norman Dorothy (ed.), *Nehru : The First Fifty Years Presented in His Own Words* (Asia Publishing House, Bombay, 1965), p. 249.
6. Jawaharlal Nehru, *The Discovery of India* (London, 1960), pp. 16-17.
7. *Ibid.*, pp. 16-17.
8. *Ibid.*, p. 525.

33

Tributes to Nehru

I did not know Nehru at all intimately; in fact, I did not even meet him many times. But his personality made an immediate impression at one's first meeting with him, and this impression did not change over the years. Nor was the effect he made just an impression; the word is too weak and too cold. "Captivation" comes nearer to the truth. Here was a human being who could win one's heart and keep it.

This would be something remarkable in anyone in any walk of life, but in someone whose position was humble and obscure it might not be so surprising as it was in a world famous statesman who has left a deep mark, and this on the whole world and not just on his own country. In this great statesman, the lovable human being was not smothered by the eminent public figure. I should say that, in Nehru, there was not even the faintest touch of pomposity or self-importance or self-consciousness. He retained the spontaneity and the buoyancy of youth after he had been carrying for years an unusually heavy burden of office. It was not till his last years that the unforeseen breach between India and China began to bow him down under its weight.

My first meeting with Nehru happened to bring out the essence of his personality in a way that was amusing but also illuminating and, above all, morally impressive. The date was one of the interwar years and Nehru had just finished serving one of his terms of imprisonment by the British Government of India. He had come out of prison and come to England for a holiday. An English lady invited me to lunch in her house to meet him. Nehru was already there when I arrived, but when the door opened for the next guest, it was a British general in uniform, and when the general saw Nehru, his jaw dropped. Apparently he had been implicated in some way in the sentence that Nehru had just been serving. (I never could discover whether our hostess' act in inviting the general and Nehru to meet each other had been deliberate or inadvertent. I dare say it was inadvertent. Her husband's family had a long-standing connection with India, and she may have thought vaguely that two men who were both connected with India in some way or other would probably fit well at the same lunch party).

I wondered how Nehru was going to take the situation. During the few minutes of conversation before the general's arrival, Nehru had left us in no doubt about his militancy. Manifestly, he was going all out to win India's independence from Britain; he was in the battle up to the hilt. Would his reception of the embarrassed British general be stiff? Would it be grim? This question was answered instantaneously by a twinkle that came into Nehru's eye. The situation had struck him as being funny, and he entertained us by teasing the general ever so gently—making him become more and more nervously conciliatory at each sly poke. This incident, though trifling in itself, was a revelation. I was in the presence of a human being who could fight with might and main—without hating his human opponents. There was plenty of fuel for resentment in Nehru's experience at British hands. Terms of imprisonment take painful bites out of a brief, human life, and the fighters for India's independence were being imprisoned by the British for acting under the inspiration of ideals to which the British themselves officially subscribed and which they took seriously, for their own benefit, at home. Here were grounds for bitterness, but Nehru showed none. I had known that fighting without hating was one of Mahatma Gandhi's principles. Here, in one of his chief companions, I was seeing something out of the Sermon on the Mount being practised in real life, and this without any smugness and without any apparent effort. That bowled me over, and the memory of that lunch is as vivid in my mind today as if it had happened yesterday and not thirty years ago.

Another personal memory of mine involves an incident which was still slighter, but it too is revealing. One day in 1956 the University of Delhi was doing me the honour of conferring a degree on me, and I was still far from the university precincts when the hour fixed for the ceremony overtook me. The university is in the old Civil Lines, at the opposite end of the seven (or is it fourteen?) Delhis from the Ashoka Hotel, and we had been held up by the traffic in the crowded streets of Shahjehanabad. When we were at last within about a quarter of a mile of the university (but about three quarters of an hour late) I was taken aback by the sudden appearance of Nehru running toward us. How could the Prime Minister have made the time to honour and please me by taking a personal part in the academic proceedings? And why was it he, of all people, who had set out in search of me? I had wasted an additional three quarters of an hour of his time, but he was not cross. The sufferers were his security men. When we arrived together at the university, we found them in a flap at having failed to prevent the Prime Minister from darting out through their cordon. That anxiety was well justified. Had not Mahatma Gandhi been assassinated? And was not the Prime Minister the man on whom Gandhi's mantle had fallen?

The last time that I met Nehru was in 1960, and it was sad to see him, not changed in spirit, but now visibly labouring under his load. He had asked me to come and visit him, and at our meeting I tried to keep off the subject of China, since this was, I knew, what was most tormenting him at the time. It was no use. He raised the subject himself and was evidently harrowed and almost obsessed by it. It was a striking contrast to previous meetings, but then, as each time before, came the human act that took one by surprise. I was in New Delhi to give the second series of Azad Memorial lectures (Nehru himself had been the first lecturer). I had just got to my feet to begin my first lecture when the Prime Minister came into the hall. Once again, he had made the time to take a personal part in academic proceedings, in order to give pleasure to a guest. This was generous in a Prime Minister, but it was also most moving on a day on which he had suffered a grievous personal loss. It was the day of Lady Mountbatten's death. Lady Mountbatten and Pandit Nehru had been particularly close personal friends. And, for Nehru's warm heart, close friendship counted, I should guess, for even more than they count for most of us. Again, I was deeply touched.

It seems certain that, for ages to come, Nehru will be remembered as a historic figure, but what is the future picture of him going to be? The lovable human being whom his intimate friends knew much better than I did—made his impression on one through one's meeting him in the flesh. At second or seventieth hand, this vivid personal impression will be dimmed, at best, and in time may be almost effaced.

Will Nehru be remembered as a great statesman? Unquestionably he was that. But I have suggested, and here I believe I am right, that his eminence in public affairs was not the distinctive thing about him. One must be thankful when a noble soul takes on itself the burden of political leadership, for politics are always in need of redeeming. They are a backward field of human activity in which our average standard of behaviour is decidedly lower than it is in family life or in our professional vocations. A noble soul goes into politics at its peril, for politics are as difficult to redeem as they are in need of redemption. Politics are intractable. They cannot be redeemed in one short lifetime, even by one of those rare spirits that combine high idealism with practical genius. The noblest-minded statesman cannot altogether escape becoming a bondsman of his imperious circumstances. To be caught on the sorrowful wheel is part of the personal price that the statesman-idealist has to pay. It is more blessed to be imprisoned for the sake of one's ideals than to imprison other people, incongruously, in the name of the same ideals. Nehru lived to have both experiences. This was the nemesis of taking over the responsibility for the government of a great country.

For Nehru himself, his political career, eminent though it was, was not, I believe, the most important thing in his life, because for him it was not an end in itself. For him it was a means of serving his fellow human beings— his Indian fellow countrymen in the first place, but not them alone, for his feeling for his fellows embraced the whole of mankind. Nehru has virtually said as much in more than one of his public utterances. He did care intensely for mankind's welfare and destiny, and his vision of this will be the thing in him for which he will be remembered by posterity if the verdict of history faithfully reflects the fundamental truth about him.

I find it difficult to pigeonhole this human personality in any of those impersonal categories in which historians deal. But if constrained to try my hand at this, I should say that Nehru served his fellow men most fruitfully and most characteristically by taking his place in a series of interpreters and mediators between the civilisation of the West and the other living civilisations. In modern times the West has been making a revolutionary impact on the rest of the world. The impact has been so potent that non-Westerners have been confronted with the choice of coming to terms with it or being hopelessly overwhelmed by it. Conversely, the West is now finding that it, for its own part, has to come to terms with the non-Western majority of the human race. We seem, in fact, to be in the birth throes of a new society embracing the whole human race, with all the manifold and contradictory traditions of its formerly segregated sections. This seems to be the goal toward which the last four or five hundred years of world's history have been leading. If this diagnosis is correct, the role of interpretation and mediation is the key role in the present age. It is a more important role than the mere statesman's; and, in fact, some of the most effective of the interpreters have done their work outside the political arena. They have done it as scholars, writers, artists, poets and prophets. Nehru was one of those who have played this part on the political stage, and, among the statesmen-interpreters of one civilisation to another, one can distinguish more than one type. There is the ruthless sergeant-major who dragoons his troops into putting themselves through the excruciating process of cultural mutation; and there is the seer who inspires his followers to tread the same painful path voluntarily. Famous representatives of the first of these two types were Peter the Great, Mohammed Ali, Mustafa Kemal Ataturk, and in a rather more deft and lighthanded way, the authors of the Meiji Revolution in Japan.

Jawaharlal Nehru is evidently a representative of the type that moves mankind, not by coercion, but by persuasion; and the other representatives of this kind of leader who first come into my mind are all Indians, like Nehru himself. One of them is the Emperor Ashoka, who was converted, by his experience of life, from being a coercionist into becoming a missionary, but who did his lifework, throughout, on the political stage. The other two whom I think of first are Ram Mohan Roy, the founder of the Brahmo Samaj, and, of course, Jawaharlal Nehru's master and mentor, the Mahatma Gandhi.

This is the company to which Nehru belongs, and in which he deserves to be remembered and to be immortalised.

MARTIN LUTHER KING, JR.

Jawaharlal Nehru was a man of three extraordinary epochs. He was a leader in the long anticolonial struggle to free his own land and to inspire a fighting will in other lands under bondage.

He lived to see victory and to move then to another epochal confrontation—the fight for peace after World War II. In this climactic struggle he did not have Gandhi at his side, but he did have the Indian people, now free in their own great Republic.

It would be hard to overstate Nehru's and India's contributions in this period. It was a time fraught with the constant threat of a devastating finality for mankind. There was no moment in this period free from the peril of atomic war. In these years Nehru was a towering world force skillfully inserting the peace will of India between the raging antagonisms of the great powers of East and West.

The world needed a mediator and an "honest broker" lest, in its sudden acquisition of overwhelming destructive force, one side or the other might plunge the world into mankind's last war. Nehru had the prestige, the wisdom, and the daring to play the role.

The markedly relaxed tensions of today are Nehru's legacy to us, and at the same time they are our monument to him.

It should not be forgotten that the treaty to end nuclear testing accomplished in 1963 was first proposed by Nehru. Let us also remember that the world dissolution of colonialism now speedily unfolding had its essential origins in India's massive victory. And let it also be remembered that Nehru guided into being the "Asian-African Bloc" as a united voice for the billions who were groping toward a modern world. He was the architect of the policy of non-alignment or neutralism which was calculated to give independent expression to the emerging nations while enabling them to play a constructive role in world affairs.

The third epoch of Nehru's work is unfolding after his death. Even though his physical presence is gone, his spiritual influence retains a living force. The great powers are not yet in harmonious relationship to each other, but with the help of the non-aligned world they have learned to exercise a wise restraint. In this is the basis for a lasting *detente*. Beyond this, Nehru's example in daring to believe and act for peaceful coexistence gives mankind its most glowing hope.

In this period my people, the Negroes of the United States, have made strides toward freedom beyond all precedent in our history. Our successes directly derive from our employment of the tactics of non-violent direct action and non-cooperation with evil which Nehru effectively employed under Gandhi's inspiration.

The peculiar genius of imperialism was found in its capacity to delude so much of the world into the belief that it was civilizing primitive cultures even though it was grossly exploiting them.

Satyagraha made the myth transparent as it revealed the oppressed to be the truly civilized party. They rejected violence but maintained resistance, while the oppressor knew nothing but the use of violence.

My people found that Satyagraha, applied in the United States to our oppressors, also clarified who was right and who was wrong. On this foundation of truth as irresistible, a majority could be organized for just solutions.

Our fight is not yet won, just as the struggle against colonialism is still unfinished, and above all, the achievement of a stable peace still lies ahead of and not behind us.

In all of these struggles of mankind to rise to a true state of civilization, the towering figure of Nehru sits unseen but felt at all council tables. He is missed by the world, and because he is so wanted, he is a living force in the tremulous world of today.

K. NATWAR SINGH

When Jawaharlal Nehru became Prime Minister of India on August 15, 1947, I was in my mid-teens. Thus my testimony is useful perhaps in terms of my own generation.

My generation—the interwar—was totally captivated by the person of Jawaharlal Nehru. Even more than Mahatma Gandhi, he influenced and altered our lives. He was our mentor and hero. In him our dreams and destiny coincided, and "he drew these tides of men into his hands and wrote his will across the sky in stars."

The vision of India that I and millions like me have is his gift. The idealism that we possess is of his doing. That India and her people continue to receive the world's attention and affection in such large measure is a tribute to his life and work.

He rid us of fear, superstition and cant. He taught us to be modern without ceasing to respect our ancient past. He gave us at once pride and humility. By his example and disarming candour he raised the level and quality of national and international dialogue and proved to us that private decencies can be transmitted to public affairs. A politician, he never cared to tidy his past. There was nothing to tidy up. He was his own most intelligent and unsparing critic. His character was complex and there were contradictory elements in it but this is not the time or the place to analyse his character or catalogue his mistakes

He had courage, wisdom, learning, compassion, charity, simplicity, style, grace, a deep sense of loyalty, wit, goodness and tolerance. He loved poetry, books, birds, mountains and nature. He loved challenges. He loved children. He was exquisitely sensitive. His interest in literature was very deep. He read widely, particularly when he was in prison. He cared for the arts and was happy in the company of writers and creative people. He could be impulsive. He also had great restraint. He was beautiful and he was the most civilised of us all. Rightly did we give our hearts to him. That we did not always follow him is his tragedy and our indignity.

I was never intimate with him personally. There are thousands who were closer to him, many more who knew him before I was born. But I did have the great privilege of being in his "presence" many many times. I have stood in pouring rain and ankle-deep mud—one of half a million to listen to his Red Fort speeches. I have also been alone with him—the last time in a Manhattan hotel. At least on one occasion I caused him some annoyance. But each time, regardless, I felt that my own young life had been enriched, enlarged and uplifted. He did that to people who came into contact with him. His books have the same effect.

Mankind will pause before his unique achievement. After him there are certain things which simply cannot be done, and his life remains his best testimonial. I end this memoir by recalling two incidents which I treasure and which show what a truly gracious and big man he was.

It was the lunch hour on a hot summer day in 1961, and as if by magical coincidence, Prime Minister Jawaharlal Nehru and I met in the corridor of the Ministry of External Affairs. I greeted him with folded hands with a book between my two palms. He stopped, returned my greetings, and asked me what the book was. I handed it over to him. It was Amaury de Riencourt's *The Soul of China*.

Mr. Nehru said, "I have read his *Soul of India.*"

"So have I, Sir."

The Prime Minister took a few steps towards the majestic staircase of the Foreign Office and remarked, "Rather Spenglerian, I thought."

I gave a nervous smile, and having never read Spengler, did not say anything.

He then walked on and as he was walking down the steps he looked around and said with a beautiful smile and a twinkle in his eyes, "Nehru Imperator, *hm!*"

This was Jawaharlal Nehru at his spontaneous best. The great man was sharing a little joke with me, as I had read *The Soul of India,* which carries a chapter entitled "Nehru Imperator."

Since Mr. Nehru was in such a pleasant mood, I dared to catch up with him and ask him whether he had seen a book on him by Mr. X. He said he had, but did not care very much for it. I was glad the book existed, for after all "it was a labour of love."

"Talking of a labour of love," he said, "reminds me that Dorothy Norman has been working on a book on me for several years. She has a huge amount of material and has almost everything that I have ever written or spoken."

I asked if the book was likely to be published in the near future.

Mr. Nehru said, "I don't know how far she has got with it."

I vaguely remember mumbling to myself that she had obviously a long way to go as it was difficult to keep up with the Prime Minister's speechmaking. I don't think he heard, although he did give me an enquiring but entirely lovable look and stepped into his car.

Mr. Nehru last visited New York in November 1961. He had just celebrated his seventy-second birthday, but his schedule would have and did exhaust those twenty years younger. Still he found time to see the musical *Camelot*. After the show he went backstage and Mr. Richard Burton introduced him to the other members of the cast. They all enjoyed meeting him and he them. When he got back to the hotel, it was past midnight. He asked me to call his secretary. I called but there was no response from his room. The Prime Minister had every reason to be annoyed, and I expected an explosion but none occurred.

Instead he said, "Don't bother. The poor man must be tired and has probably gone to bed."

"Could I do anything?" I asked.

He smiled, put his hand on my shoulder, and speaking softly said, "Young man, you too have had a long day, so run along and get some sleep. I will go up and look after myself, but tell them to have my breakfast ready at eight in the morning."

Thus ended an evening full of splendour yet free of formality. I felt deeply moved, and still wonder if only we all could be so considerate, wouldn't life be a little less gray!

The news of his death was so unexpected. A week earlier he had told a press conference in Delhi : "My life is not coming to an end so soon."

I was overwhelmed with grief and unashamedly I wept. The world suddenly lost some of its glow and much of its sanity. He is not there anymore but his noble and fragrant memory endures and I feel that his concern for us, in so many ways, follows us beyond the funeral pyre.

BERTRAND RUSSELL

Nehru was a man of rare dedication who devoted himself to his country from the time of his earliest years. It is not often appreciated that through the long years of struggle which occupied the greater part of his life he had to live under the shadow of potential imprisonment or brutality. Westerners are not sufficiently aware that Mr. Nehru spent fourteen years in prison because of his passionate belief in the emancipation of his country from the indignity of foreign subjection and of poverty, ignorance and disease. Fourteen years is an inconceivable time to be separated from one's family and friends when it is, as it were, in one's own hands to secure release by abandoning the struggle under the pretext of conducting it in a milder manner. During the years that I was President of the India League in London I knew of the invaluable leadership and direction which Jawaharlal Nehru gave to India.

In the years subsequent to independence it was an astonishing thing that Nehru was without the faintest suggestion of bitterness toward the nation which subjected his country and imprisoned him. It is a great tribute to him that he insisted that India should be non-aligned in the insane struggle for power which has preoccupied the United States and the Soviet Union at the expense of the welfare of mankind. Faced with overwhelming difficulties and pressures, Mr. Nehru insisted upon the role of media or where he could have secured financial and military aid from whichever side he might have chosen to use. This decision was responsible for the possibility of a third force of neutral and non-aligned nations, and as such may be a decisive factor in the survival of humanity. Had India foregone non-alignment, it is seriously doubtful that other nations could have maintained it, and the areas of conflict would be many more and the sources of mediation non-existent.

There is a further achievement of the utmost importance which is not sufficiently appreciated. Every conceivable argument has been available to tempt Mr. Nehru to forego democratic institutions in India. Illiteracy and poverty, disease and ignorance, a great subcontinent to govern, severe differences between Muslim and Hindu, many scores of languages and varied cultures reflecting a tendency toward a breaking up of the Union—all of these serious political facts could have induced him to say that they were too difficult to permit the rule of democracy with its instability.

Had Nehru made this decision, it is doubtful that the rule of law or of representative institutions would have any chance among the emergent nations. To the extent that they do is the achievement of Nehru. Had this decision been made, the varied and rich Indian culture would be subjected to uniform control in the name of security and political unity.

Nehru himself was responsible for an understanding of the magnitude of the contribution made to human knowledge by India and her peoples. His writing has been a primary source of knowledge for the peoples of other countries.

I do not think that the ease with which he might have taken more tempting paths is understood. I do not believe his greatness is fully appreciated, but I have every confidence that if mankind is allowed to survive he will be recognised in a manner adequate to his stature.

Looking back I agree with those who say Nehru made a mistake in not dividing the Congress Party into its socialist and non-socialist components by retaining Congress as his political vehicle. After the struggle for independence had been won, Nehru was hampered by the power of the right wing which increasingly came to dominate the Congress Party. This domination was only held in check by his own leadership and command over the population of India. The price, however, of having to reconcile the powerful economic forces which Congress comprised with his hopes for democratic socialism was the emasculation of the latter programme. India has a slow growth rate and remains stricken with poverty and disease. Nehru's own efforts to alter this would have succeeded more had his party been forthrightly socialist, with an opposition in Parliament representing the very forces which now dominate Congress. It came to be that these forces sought to imprison Nehru even where his policy of non-alignment was concerned, and no small part of Nehru's reluctance to negotiate with the Chinese was owing to his knowledge that the right wing of Congress prevented him from doing so. Nehru himself came to realise this, and perhaps the greatest tragedy of his death—caused in no small part because he carried the burden of India's development on his shoulders- was that he was only now taking forthright steps about his right wing.

A few weeks before his death Nehru announced to Parliament that he was prepared to negotiate with the Chinese on the basis of proposals advanced to him by my representatives last summer. A year ago it was impossible for Nehru to speak openly of negotiating with China. He was on record saying there was nothing to negotiate but a matter of slight adjustment to an already determined boundary.

Nehru wrote to me saying that he had made this announcement to Parliament, and days before his death he informed the Central Committee of the Congress Party of his intentions.

Up to the very last, Nehru had in mind to bring peace to his troubled boundaries with Pakistan and China, and he had to struggle against chauvinist and right-wing groupings in his Congress alliance. Nehru embodied throughout his life the policies for which he had to fight, ironically most desperately within the political party he forged.

Nehru, after his stroke, knew that if he retired his chances of survival were good. He also knew that only he could make peace with the Chinese and with Pakistan or defeat the right wing in the Congress alliance. He worked to excess, went to Bombay for political meetings when he was advised to rest. He held meetings with party caucuses and took major steps such as his announcements to Parliament and the Congress Central Committee of his intentions with regard to the

Chinese. He planned to come to the Commonwealth Conference and wrote to me of this. He likely knew he was courting death. It is not possible now to discuss his political battle and the vigour with which he conducted it despite his precarious physical condition. What is evident is that Nehru's death has removed serious hopes of negotiations with China and of settlement over Kashmir. Hopes of peace in Nagaland and of defeat for the right are also lessened. Nehru's absence will teach us how much we owe him.

PEARL S. BUCK

There are a few people in each century of human life upon this earth who affect the lives of all of us. Such a one was Jawaharlal Nehru. For more decades than any other one person in his time, he influenced us, East and West, and always for good. Even when he was unjustly criticized by those who did not know him, he exerted this influence. The result was that he became a figure universally respected for his independence and loved for his integrity and personality.

He was always a leader. I remember that my own admiration for him began in the days when he was a young follower of Gandhi. I admired Mahatma Gandhi, but I know very well the power of such a man as Gandhiji, and I was amazed to see how Jawaharlal Nehru, though young, maintained his own mind and will while according to the older man every sign and depth of affection and respect. This ability to defer and yet not to submit was a symbol of the greatness that was to show itself so plainly and forcefully as the years went on.

I have deplored, certainly, the lack of understanding that the leaders of my own country at times showed towards Prime Minister Nehru. Again, however, I have seen his greatness when he never retaliated or exhibited bitterness. Meanwhile the years have shown the correctness of his political stand. Under his leadership India remained a pivot nation between East and West, her people able to speak the language of both. Through the most troubled times that human history has ever known, Jawaharlal Nehru was able steadfastly to hold his people together and to weld their variety into a whole—a nation strong enough to stand firm, I believe, for centuries to come.

I do not forget other aspects of Jawaharlal Nehru's nature, his charm, his brilliance, his grace of manner and bearing. I know that had our times been more peaceful he could have found a high career as a creative writer, for his style of writing was distinguished and his imagination alive and quick. I regret the loss of the books he might have written had he not devoted his talents to his country in political life. I am grateful for the few important books he wrote, all of them basic in their importance. Yet I suppose it is true that India needed the active daily leadership that he provided more than she needed books.

At all events, Jawaharlal Nehru is unforgettable. He began his life in the shadow of Gandhi, but he soon emerged into the full light of his own day, and there he lived and will live forever, not only as the greatest figure of modern India, but also as one of the very few truly great men in all the world. I count it as one of my most treasured experiences that I met him face to face and heard his living voice.

CLEMENT R. ATTLEE
Nehru in Retrospect

My first encounter with Jawaharlal Nehru was when I was on the Indian Statutory Commission in 1928. He was standing with a number of young men shouting, "Simon, go back." We next met just before the Second World War. We met at Sir Stafford Cripps' house and discussed the Indian problem. We worked out and agreed to a scheme for the summoning of a Constituent Assembly to decide on India's future. This was in fact the proposal which Cripps carried to India on behalf of the wartime Cabinet on the so-called Cripps Mission. It would have succeeded and might well have resulted in a united India, but unfortunately failed owing to the opposition of Mahatma Gandhi.

Indian independence had to wait until I was Prime Minister. I sent out the Cabinet Mission whose well-intentioned plan failed of acceptance owing to Hindu-Muslim tension which had much increased in the interval. I invited Mr. Nehru and Mr. Jinnah and the Viceroy, Lord Wavell, to come to London to discuss the matter with my colleagues and myself, but once again no agreement could be reached. I was much impressed by Nehru's wide outlook, charm and reasonableness.

Thanks largely to Lord Mountbatten, but at the expense of dividing India, I was enabled to introduce and carry through the Indian Independence Bill.

When Nehru and I next met, we were both prime ministers at a Commonwealth Conference. There I could admire the ability of the Indian Prime Minister to hold his own with such men as Field Marshal Smuts, Mr. Curtin of Australia and Mr. Peter Fraser of New Zealand. At these conferences, though much of importance occurs at the formal meetings, a great deal of work is done at informal talks, especially on problems of internal moment to a particular dominion.

I can recall many, many long discussions with Mr. Nehru on the vexed question of Kashmir, sometimes between the two of us, sometimes with other prime ministers, but they proved fruitless. Although we proposed every possible variant in order to have a fair plebiscite, to which he had already agreed in principle, we could not get acceptance from Mr. Nehru. I have always considered this the blind spot of a great statesman. Whether it was due to his being a Kashmiri Brahmin by descent or to some other cause, Mr. Nehru so wise in other matters, was quite adamant on the question of Kashmir, though always courteous and patient. Apart from this he had shown high statesmanship in deciding that India should remain in the Commonwealth, a statesmanship matched by that of the King and the other Commonwealth Prime Ministers in accepting the desire of India to be a republic.

Henceforward over many years, with frequent meetings, I became more intimate with Mr. Nehru and much admired the way in which he piloted his country through the transition period and the difficulties of a country emerging into full independence. He had the inestimable advantage of being equally versed in Indian and European cultures. He could, therefore, while fully aware of his problems and those of Asia, also understand European and antipodean outlooks, as well as that of the United States. He was of course a strong supporter of the United Nations and gave his support when the UN decided on intervening to oppose aggression in Korea, and sent an ambulance unit to cooperate with the Commonwealth Division in that country.

I recall too that my last meeting with him in India was when we spoke together in support of World Government in New Delhi. It was natural that he and I, as fellow believers in democratic socialism, were in close sympathy. I understood the enormous task which he had to undertake in seeking to raise the standard of life of the people of India. Though of course rejoicing in the attainment of freedom by the Indian people, he was far too broad-minded not to recognise the good work which had been done over the years by British administrators, and was far too wise to fall into the error of some nationalists in seeking to destroy everything which had been introduced or belonged in any way to the former ruling power. I recall his advising a statesman of an undeveloped country just emerging from colonialism not to be too hasty in getting rid of the British elements in the administration, knowing how great a service the new India owed to Indians in the services trained under British rule.

Naturally as a disciple of Mr. Gandhi, he desired to follow a policy of non-alignment and to avoid taking sides in the ideological struggle between East and West though he was far too good a democrat to accept the philosophy of Communism. Indeed one of his greatest titles to fame is having kept India on the democratic path and to having created the most populous democracy in the world. Equally he withstood extreme regionalism which might easily have prompted fissiparous tendencies, for he recognised that unity was one of Britain's greatest gifts to India.

He was, I think, like other strong pacifists, too prone to judge others by himself. It must have been a great blow when he found that imperialism was not just a voice of white capitalism, but could be found in full force in Communist China. Aggression against Tibet was followed by armed attack against India, and Nehru himself had to resort to armed force to repel it. Having many pacifist friends, I could understand his point of view, but I was unable to share his optimistic outlook on world affairs. But it is, I think, to his credit that when faced with the fact of aggression he did not shirk the issue but took a realistic view. He thus showed one of the attributes of a statesman in having the power to learn from experience.

Nehru was of course a great moral force. He was selfless and never fell into the error of seeking to make himself a dictator or of assuming superiority to other men. It has been said truly that power corrupts, but it is also true that not all holders of it are corrupted by it, nor did he fall into the error of seeking to get quick results by adopting undemocratic methods. It may be that he held on to power too long, but this was not, I think, from any ignoble ambition to continue in his high position but from a desire to serve India to the utmost of his power.

There are few, if any, parallels in history to the magnitude of Nehru's achievement, and whatever storms in future may blow up, India will be eternally grateful to the man who piloted the Ship of State on her maiden voyage with so few errors of navigation. He will rightly go down in history as one of the world's great men who lived up to the high ideals which inspired him.

NORMAN COUSINS

Man and Symbol : A Fragmentary Appreciation

He was not one man but a procession of men. In him you witnessed a national hero, statesman, philosopher, historian, author, educator.

He was also a triumphant assortment of paradoxes. He was a supreme rationalist who presided over a nation with the most pervasive and complex religious make-up in the world.

He was an intellectual product of Western civilization who was accepted as symbolic leader by many hundreds of millions of Asians and Africans who feared the West.

He was an accomplished logician who lived on intimate terms with the imponderables and intangibles.

He was an avowed optimist who found it difficult to keep from brooding.

He had sensitivities so finely attuned that he could be jarred by the slightest vibrations, but he was able to make history-jolting decisions.

He believed the highest function of the State was to help develop the individuality of the individual, but no nation in the world contained as many natural obstacles to the emergence of that individuality as the nation he governed for seventeen years.

With such a man, you cannot essay a full evaluation or appreciation. The best you can do is to pursue certain qualities and attributes.

First, the Courage of the Man

August 1947. With national independence and partition of the subcontinent between India and Pakistan, four hundred and fifty million people became caught up in a vast convulsion. Hindus and Moslems, with a long history of tension between them, became part of a chain reaction of violence and horror. No one knows how many died. But 12,000,000 people became homeless. Rumors of atrocities and actual atrocities interacted to produce a spiraling madness.

For a while, the situation was relatively calm in New Delhi, with its large Moslem population. Then, suddenly, the storm broke. Late one night a Hindu mob, inflamed by stories of

Moslem terror in the northwest, swept into Connaught Circle, the main shopping area in New Delhi. The rioters smashed their way into Moslem stores, destroying and looting and ready to kill.

Even before the police arrived in force, Jawaharlal Nehru was on the scene. He plunged into the crowd in the darkness, trying to bring people to their senses. He spied a Moslem who had just been seized by Hindus. He interposed himself between the man and his attackers.

Suddenly a cry went up : "Jawaharlal is here! Jawaharlal is here! Don't hurt Jawaharlal Nehru!"

The cry spread through the crowd. It had a magical effect. People stood still and dropped their arms to their sides. Looted merchandise was dropped. The mob psychology disintegrated. By the time the police arrived people were dispersing. The riot was over.

The next day, friends rushed to Nehru, admonishing him for exposing himself to a mob at the height of its frenzy.

"You could have been killed," one of them said. "Then what?"

"That's for you to determine," he replied quietly. "Many others could have been killed last night. Then what?"

The fact that Nehru had risked his life to save a single Moslem had a profound effect far beyond New Delhi. Many thousands of Moslems who had intended to flee to Pakistan now stayed in India, staking their lives on Nehru's ability to protect them and assure them justice. In years to come, this confidence of India's Moslems in Nehru was to become a major factor in building a nation and holding it together.

Not many weeks after the communal rioting subsided, the Prime Minister and a foreign guest were driving in his private car about fifteen miles south of Delhi. The traffic piled up behind a caravan of camels in a village preponderantly populated by Moslems. Only recently, this village had figured in mass violence.

The combination of the heat, the heavy chalky dust from the dry dirt road, temper of the camel drivers, and the screams of people in the stalled buses, trucks, wagons, and automobiles provided the combustible materials for a communal riot. 'Young Moslems from the village suddenly appeared with knives. They surrounded Nehru's car. One of them recognized the Prime Minister and shouted angry words at him.

Nehru stepped out of his car, walked up to the young man, spoke to him quietly. Suddenly, a cheer went up for the Prime Minister. The Moslems surrounded him, expressing their devotion and loyalty. Then some of them began to weep in shame for their action. Nehru spoke with them, answering their questions, telling them of his hopes.

On the drive back to New Delhi, his guest expressed concern for the Prime Minister's personal safety. Mr. Nehru agreed the risk might be real, but he said he could not let it get in the way of things that had to be done.

The Human Polity of the Man

January 1951. Sunday. The desk clerk at the Imperial Hotel in New Delhi handed us a message. It was from Miss Sindhi at the Prime Minister's House. The P.M. was having some people over that afternoon and hoped we could come. Nothing special. Just relaxed talk.

Primed for a long bull session on philosophy and politics, we arrived at the P.M.'s house at about three o'clock. Mr. Nehru was at the door, greeting his guests. He seemed to be in excellent spirits. We were ushered to a large enclosed veranda. We looked around the room and recognized Dr. Sarvepalli Radhakrishnan, the eminent philosopher and Vice-President of India; also, Shiva Rau, prominent author and long-time friend of the Prime Minister. Among the other guests to whom we were introduced were two Cabinet Ministers and a Justice.

Mr. Nehru came into the room, his young grandson riding his shoulders, kicking Grandpa's ribs and demanding more speed.

"The gallop comes later," Mr. Nehru said, hoisting the boy over his head and placing him on the floor. He told the youngster he had a surprise for him. "In fact, I've got a surprise for everyone. This afternoon we shall all have a good time. I've arranged for entertainment."

The entertainer was a magician who went through a bewildering assortment of tricks. He caused long knives to turn into short knives, wine to turn into milk, and he made a chicken emerge from a paper cup. Then he demonstrated his accuracy with a bow and arrow, hitting a vertical thread at about twenty feet. Finally, he invited a member of the company to step forward. Mr. Nehru, enjoying himself hugely, prodded the Finance Minister into joining the act.

As soon as the Finance Minister discovered he was to be a living prop in a latter-day version of a William Tell episode, he seemed to waver somewhat. Mr. Nehru gently chided him into going on with the act. The Finance Minister was seated in a chair directly above which, six inches from his head, a circular wreath was suspended by several thin threads.

The magician announced that with one arrow he would sever all the threads, causing the wreath to fall around the Finance Minister's distinguished shoulders. Almost as an afterthought, he added that he would perform this feat while blindfolded.

Mr. Nehru spoke up.

"They tell me that good finance ministers are hard to find these days." he said. "I don't know whether we ought to allow him to go through with this."

The magician clapped for silence, put on his blindfold, picked up his bow, tested its tautness, and inserted the arrow. Then he paused and, still blindfolded, paced off the steps to his target, groping and stumbling on the way. Finally, he retraced his steps, assumed his battle station, and raised the bow and arrow.

"No, no," Mr. Nehru cried. "You're aiming at the wrong man! You're aiming at the Justice. We can't afford to lose him. The man you want is about sixty degrees to the left."

Suddenly, the magician let fly. The arrow pierced the strings and the garland fell neatly over the shoulders of the Finance Minister, who, suddenly released from his encounter with nonfiscal suspense, joined in the general laughter.

After a while, the group exchanged stories. The Prime Minister presided over the ice cream and punch bowl, the youngster at his side tugging at Grandpa's pants and asking when he could have a fast horseback ride.

The closest anyone got to serious talk was when Mr. Nehru told of a visit he had had the previous day from an old school chum who was now a wealthy industrialist.

According to the Prime Minister, the industrialist came up to him and complained that things had gone much too far. Taxes were crippling him and something had to be done about it. He said he had to pay a stiff tax on his private house in New Delhi. He also had to pay a tax on his hunting estate. As if this were not enough, he had to pay a tax on a house he kept in Bangalore. But worst of all was the tax he had to pay on his beach home in Juhu.

"Now I ask you, Jawaharlal, how do you expect me to keep up these houses with taxes like this?"

"Have you ever considered giving up a house or two?" Nehru asked.

"Now, what, kind of advice is this to give a life-long friend?" the man asked.

The group laughed.

"What makes the story so ironic." Mr. Nehru said, "is that here I am, fighting back legislation to confiscate luxurious property and this chap wants me to give him a tax refund. I suppose each man has to have his own dream world."

In this manner the afternoon passed. After the farewells, Dr. Radhakrishnan offered to drive us back to the hotel. Inside the car, Dr. Radhakrishnan said we had just seen a side of Nehru that few people knew.

"There is something eternally young, even boyish, about the P.M.," he said. "People tend to think of him as a man lost in brooding, nor even knowing how to laugh. Not so; he loves to laugh, as we have seen. It is very good for the nation that he can laugh. It helps to freshen his spirits. The important thing about Nehru is that he continues to think young. A man like this can never grow old. He will never look old, no matter how old he is. But he must take better care of himself. He works too hard."

The Man as Author, Poet, Historian, Philosopher, Thinker

He liked to write, felt incomplete when he was unable to assemble his thoughts and commit them to paper. He regarded writing as the most demanding, the most exhausting, but also the most satisfying of the creative arts. Writing enabled him to discipline his mind, to think sequentially and creatively. Being able to give life to a concept through words; using language as a vehicle of persuasion or as a voyage of intellectual exploration and discovery—these meant much to him.

At times he could write like the most detached and aseptic historian. At other times he would write with extreme sensitivity and grace. In describing a natural setting, he could be all poet. In his writing, as in his life, he was many men.

For many years, his writing, quite literally, kept him from losing his mind. This was during his various imprisonments as an agitator for Indian freedom. No one knows how many hundreds of thousands or millions of words he wrote while in jail. His autobiography came out of prison. He did a work on history, *The Discovery of India*. There were also, to be sure, the various pamphlets and tracts that made him the intellectual leader of the fight for freedom.

Of all his prison writings, however, perhaps none is more

remarkable than the collection of letters to his daughter Indira, later published under the title *Glimpses of World History*. The letters, running to almost a thousand pages in the book, constituted something of a liberal university education, ranging as it did over the whole of the human historical record—European, Asian, African, American, Australian. It took in not just the development of national and continental civilization but the creative thrust and splendor of mankind. Nehru's own insights and his appreciation of the human potential are in evidence throughout. What made the book unique in the history of literature was that his prison was totally bereft of historical materials. He wrote *Glimpses of World History,* with its thousands of facts and events and names, without reference books or notes of any kind. As a demonstration of human intellectual capacity, the book stands by itself.

It is doubtful whether any writer before or since has fused in one person more thoroughly the complex essences of East and West. He was a fascinating amalgam of two cultures; his formal education was English but his traditions were Indian. His intellect was rooted in the Enlightenment but his spirit in the Vedas. Few men of our time have been so avowedly rationalist, yet there were the strongest spiritual connotations in his feelings about India and her people.

> I have been attached to the Ganga and Jumna rivers in Allahabad ever since my childhood [he wrote in his will]. And, as I have grown older, this attachment has also grown. I have watched their varying moods as the seasons changed, and have often thought of the history and myth and tradition and song and story that have become attached to them through the long ages and become part of their flowing waters.... The Ganga reminds me of the snow-covered peaks and the deep valleys of the Himalayas, which I have loved so much, and of the rich and vast plains below, where my life and work have been cast. Smiling and dancing in the morning sunlight, and dark and gloomy and full of mystery as evening shadows

> fall; a narrow, slow, and graceful stream in winter, and a vast, roaring thing during monsoon, broad-bosomed almost as the sea, and with something of the sea's power to destroy, the Ganga has been to me a symbol and a memory of the past of India, running into the present, and flowing on to the great ocean of the future.

Intellectually, he could never quite comprehend, and sometimes he had difficulty in coping with, India's numberless castes. He disclaimed any affiliation with or affinity for the religious aspect of Hinduism, yet he presided over a nation that sensed and responded to a profoundly spiritual quality in him. Gandhi was a godhead; he easily fitted into a theology. Not so Nehru, a supreme logician. Yet when Gandhi's mantle passed on, it passed to Nehru. No one questioned its appropriateness. There might be all the difference in the world between the thought, style, and outlook of the two men, but there was a seamless connection between the two in their devotion to the Indian people and in the response of the Indian people to them.

> I have received so much love and affection from the Indian people [Nehru wrote] that nothing I can do can repay even a small fraction of it. Many have been admired, some have been revered, but the affection of all classes of the Indian people has come to me in such abundant measure that I have been overwhelmed by it.

The Leadership Capacities and Charismatic Quality of the Man

April 1955. The Asian-African Conference at Bandung. An event of profound importance for most of the world's peoples, symbolizing not just their freedom from outside rule but their full membership in the human race. Much of the drama flowed out of the juxtaposed presence of the two men who represented the two largest nations in the world—Jawaharlal Nehru of India and Chou En-lai of Communist China.

Both men knew that what was happening in their countries would have a great bearing on the way most of the newly independent nations would be developed.

Chou En-lai, speaking in English through an interpreter, was the first of the two to address the meeting. He identified China with the aspirations of Asia and Africa. He said that history was riding with China. This was done more in the form of an announcement than a claim. He invited the Bandung delegates to visit China and see the marked progress made under socialism. His manner was not bombastic or aggressive but matter-of-fact, austere.

When Nehru spoke some time later, the contrast between the two men couldn't have been more startling. It wasn't only that he spoke without a manuscript or without an interpreter. He had warmth, personal rapport. He became part of each individual, speaking to the best inside him. He was creating strength, awakening the individual's capacity and his hopes rather than attempting to convert a man to any large impersonal system. He held up no glorious certainties of historical determinism, only the saturating uncertainties of the human situation. But this was in the nature of freedom, which guaranteed nothing except a chance to do better; and freedom was within their reach.

At Bandung, the delegates may have been impressed by Chou En-lai, but they believed Nehru. And even when they did not agree with Nehru, they believed in him. This was the way it was with his own people. They might not have comprehended him at times, but they believed in him and knew that good would come out of such a man. Even though they were unable to connect themselves to his intellectuality, they never had trouble in understanding his integrity. And they knew that where he wanted to go was where India had to be.

At Bandung, Chou En-lai was surrounded by bodyguards, Nehru by men who wanted to talk to him—men from new nations who suddenly were obligated to make history and needed the kind of confidence that a Nehru could impart to them. He was Olympian but he was never aloof.

The morning before the last session of the conference at

Bandung, Nehru invited us to breakfast with him at his villa in the hills several miles outside the city. We sat on a veranda overlooking a flowering countryside. Nehru had already been down among the flowers, sniffing with satisfaction. His mood was deeply reflective. He spoke of the future of Asia with special reference to China and India. He said he had given the matter much thought. It was obvious, he said, that what happened inside India would have important effects outside India—not just in Asia but Africa. Here were two giant display cases for millions of people. The Indian display case, with all its complexities and difficulties, showed it was possible to have a progressive society without taking individuality away from the individual. The State should never subordinate the individual; rather, the State itself had the obligation to be infinitely inventive in trying to serve him and ennoble him. India had four hundred million people; most of them were poor. They needed jobs and food and medicine and schools and homes. It was precisely the kind of total need that the Chinese Communists said could never be met outside of a totally controlled society. They said what had to be done couldn't come fast enough or deep enough'without the machinery available to a total Marxist State.

These were the questions most of the world's peoples had to decide, Nehru said. And he believed that India, despite all difficulties, was making progress and could do even better.

We asked what he considered to be the main strengths and weaknesses in the development of Communist China.

He said, characteristically, that it was not for him to dispense such judgments; this was a task more appropriately done by history. But he added, also quite characteristically, that he would suppose that any leader of a State might have a certain caution in applying rigidly and literally economic or ideological doctrines that were based on the world as it was a century ago.

Was this a reference to the ideas of Marx and Engels?

Yes, he replied. There was much that was valid and valuable in Marx. But the world had undergone profound changes since Marx published his theories, and the attempt to pursue these doctrines as though they were natural law was itself retrogressive, in a sense.

Moreover, he added, Marxism provided too narrow a creed for the problems it had to meet. It gave so much emphasis to economic factors that it underestimated the power of all the other concerns of man. Life consisted of much more than economic growth. He was not at all certain, he added, that the Marxist ideas were completely understood by all those who attempted to apply them.

Then his eyes twinkled and he sat back in his chair and told of an incident at the conference involving Chou En-lai to illustrate his point.

"We were assigned to a subcommittee whose job it was to prepare a draft for a short statement for the conference. It was a simple statement that was required, and we were able to agree readily on the general substance. I invited Chou En-lai to write the first draft. He declined, saying he preferred that I do it.

I did—in English, of course, and then read it to him through his interpreter. He was appreciative but said there were several key words that tended to change the meaning from what he understood the statement was supposed to say.

Again we discussed the purpose of the statement in general and the troublesome words in particular. We had no difficulty in agreeing on the intended sense of the draft. All that remained now was to translate a few English words into Chinese. The attempt to do this took several hours—and even then, I was not completely satisfied that the translation was precise.

Do you know what came to my mind when I left that meeting? I said to myself : Good Lord, just imagine what Karl Marx must be like in Chinese!"

He laughed, then said : "I'm perfectly serious, you know."

There came to my mind a conversation with the P.M. in New Delhi some years earlier. Then, too, we were discussing what Stuart Chase called "the tyranny of words." In particular, words like "inevitability," "free will," and "determinism."

Imprecise though these terms were bound to be, I had asked Nehru whether he accepted the idea of implacable historical forces beyond man's reach.

In matters such as these, he had replied, it was well to avoid absolute judgments.

Even so, I had said, it was perhaps fair to ask how he reacted philosophically to the eternal debate over free will *vs.* determinism.

"I would still try to avoid absolute judgments," he had replied. "Actually, I think it possible to reconcile the two. Do you play bridge?"

"Very little and very poorly," I had said.

"No matter," he resumed. "Determinism is like the cards that are dealt you. Free will is how you play them. The interaction between the two determines what you are as a person—or even a nation."

The Man as Prophet and Politician

Jawaharlal Nehru may have been able to reconcile free will and determination, but he was never able to reconcile the conflict inside himself between prophet and politician.

As prophet, he had profound kinship with Mahatma Gandhi. Whenever you asked him about his innermost beliefs, he was certain to say that the most important conviction of his life—one taught him by Gandhi—was that good ends never justified bad means. Violence, even in a good cause, defeated the good.

"We must not appease evil," he had said in our recorded conversation in 1951, "but we must also remember that evil is not surmounted by wrong methods that themselves produce more evil. I have felt more and more that the basic lesson Gandhi taught was right, that means should not be subordinated to ends.

"I know these ideas cannot easily be translated into life. A political leader cannot function like a prophet. He has to limit himself to people's understanding of him; otherwise, he cannot function at all."

"What happens when the moralist becomes politician and is faced with the need to get things done?" we asked.

"I am not a moralist or even a very good politician. I have dabbled in various things because they interest me. The politician has to compromise. That is what makes him a politician. But it may make a difference if he at least begins with certain convictions or principles. Anyway, I think Gandhi was right about ends and means and about violence, I hope to come as close as I can to making this a working philosophy."

Some years later, in a letter, he returned to this theme.

> A leader must not only feel what is right [he wrote] but he has also to convince masses of people about it. Thus, he tends to compromise or else he would cease to be the leader. The only example I know in contemporary history of a leader who refused to compromise with what he thought was right is Gandhi--and Gandhi was assassinated in the end, as prophets often are.

Yet even Gandhi, faced with the terrible gravitational pull of events, could acquiesce in compromise, even if he was not an architect of it. Shortly after independence, armed raiders from the Northwest moved into the Kashmir. Nehru didn't hesitate. He ordered military action. He didn't wait to consult Gandhi.

Once having acted, Nehru told Gandhi he had decided to use force in the Kashmir because this was the only course open to him. He was sorry if what he had done had brought pain to Gandhi.

Gandhi put his arm around Nehru's shoulders. He didn't have to say anything.

The battle between politician and prophet inside Nehru never left him. Before he had the responsibility for governing a nation, he could define goals in terms of necessity instead of workability or attainability; he could move towards an objective without having to develop a consensus in order to achieve it; he could advocate rather than legislate. Once in office, he found himself plagued by some of the very tactics that had been so effective in gaining independence for India. Separatist movements sprang up throughout the country; this or that state would want its own language or cultural or political autonomy. The methods used to advance these objectives, naturally enough, were the same ones that had been used to such good effect against the British. In order to deal with these methods, it was necessary for Nehru to be tougher than his personal make-up would warrant.

We were in India in 1961 when the P.M. was having severe difficulties with Master Tara Singh, the Sikh separatist leader. In quest of his objectives, Singh went on a hunger strike. We asked Nehru how it felt being the target of this device, as contrasted to the time when he himself was an agitator identified with Gandhi, who made personal hunger and suffering into one of the most potent political weapons in history.

His face clouded over. I could tell it was painful for him to think about it.

"Frankly," he said, "I don't like it. I don't think this is the right way to go about persuading a government."

For the first time in the years we had known him, he seemed to stammer somewhat. Then he realized the irony of the situation. He smiled.

"I think I told you that a politician has to act in a certain way," he said. "What else is there to be done? I can't give into the man and allow India to become a mass of splinters."

"Do you feel the hunger strike is—well, hitting below the belt?"

"In a sense, yes."

"How did you feel about it when Gandhi used it?"

"To tell the truth, I didn't feel quite right about it even then. If I analyze my feelings, I suppose I felt rather awkward about it. But you don't have to try very hard if you want to catch me in an inconsistency. This is the occupational disease of any philosopher who finds himself in the position of an operating leader."

It was at that 1961 meeting that I discerned for the first time the visible evidence in Nehru of physical deterioration. One side of his seemed rigid, as though he had suffered a stroke. His posture was no longer as erect as it had once been. The fatigue came through in his voice. For more than a half century he had made India his life and work. Thinking he might be looking forward to a time when he might lay down his burden and return to his writing and thinking, we asked what he would do if it became possible for him to be freed of his government responsibilities.

"You mean, what would I do if I retired?"

"Yes."

We had thought his face would light up at the prospect. Just the opposite. He looked as though nothing would be more unwelcome.

"Well, I suppose there are some things I might do," he said without any particular enthusiasm in his voice. "I like to walk. I would probably walk quite a bit, in the mountains. I might want to read a bit. But I really haven't thought much about it."

More than ever, we realized that Nehru loved his job and had no thought of leaving it; he loved everything about it, the contradictions, the inner struggle, the endless pressures and counter-pressures, the physical strain and the anguish and the multiple problems and complexities and the insolubles. Most of all, he loved the direct connection he had with the people of India and destiny of his nation.

Before leaving him, we had one more question to ask-even though we knew he was annoyed whenever it came up. But everyone was asking the question all through India, and, indeed, throughout the world : After Nehru, who? In talking to newspaper editors and members of the government, we had encountered considerable feeling, some of it bitter, because Nehru had not selected a successor. One editor said he couldn't understand why Nehru couldn't anticipate the chaos and disintegration that would afflict India upon his death in the absence of a designated successor. A prominent member of the Congress party told us that the battle for his successor might go on for months. He said Nehru was neglecting his responsibility.

We put the question to the Prime Minister. But we approached the subject somewhat gingerly.

"People say that the greatest part of Gandhi's legacy to India was you," we said. "Now, who is your legacy to India?"

He didn't hesitate a moment.

"Four hundred million people who are capable of selecting a leader for themselves. I am not going to do it for them. It would be insolent of me to do it."

"But suppose they don't have that capacity?"

"They do. Anyway, it is rather depressing to me to believe that everything we have tried to do about preparing people to rule themselves has failed. I don't believe we have failed, at least not in that respect."

"They say—even some of your friends say—that if you fail to designate a successor, the attempt to choose one would tear the country to pieces. They say that all your good work could be undone if you don't train a man to take your place."

"I think we will do all right. I think the country will do quite all right."

At that time, it is possible that he was the only man in India who held that view. Today, the Indian people know how right he was. They have been able to select a successor, a good man and a wise man. They have been able to do so without upheaval or disintegration. And they have gained in strength because of it. They have vindicated Nehru's confidence in them. They have also justified his highest aspirations. Nehru's death, in a real sense, marks the coming of age of a free and mature India. His legacy is what he wished it to be.

LINUS C. PAULING

The Contribution of India to the Achievement of World Peace

A great contribution to world peace was made by Prime Minister Lal Bahadur Shastri when he announced, in November 1964, that India would not respond to the nuclear explosion that had been carried out by the Chinese People's Republic by adopting a policy of obtaining or making her own nuclear weapons, but would instead continue with her peaceful methods and would strive to eliminate the menace of nuclear bombs from the world.

This policy, based upon the highest ethical principles, represents the continuation of the moral policy of the late Prime Minister Jawaharlal Nehru, which was in the spirit of Mahatma Gandhi. Jawaharlal Nehru had described war as the negation of truth and humanity, based upon the deliberate and persistent propagation of hatred and falsehood, and he said that he had no doubt that world government would come, bringing peace and progress to mankind.

The action of the Chinese People's Republic in embarking upon the programme of manufacturing a stockpile of nuclear weapons, as indicated by the nuclear explosion in October 1964, has changed the world in such a way as to lead to an increased danger of nuclear war and world destruction. In May 1961, the sixty scientists and other scholars from fifteen countries who participated in the Conference Against the Spread of Nuclear Weapons, in Oslo, stated that the acquisition of nuclear weapons by additional nations would constitute a grave risk to the world, for the following reasons :

1. Each addition to the number of nations armed with nuclear weapons drives its neighbours toward acquiring similar arms.
2. As nuclear weapons pass into more hands, the chance increases that a major war will be started by some human error or technical accident.
3. The spread to more nations increases the chance of deliberate initiation of nuclear war.
4. Increase in the number of nuclear powers would further increase the difficulty of achieving disarmament.
5. After it obtains nuclear weapons, a nation becomes a more likely target in any nuclear war.

The participants in the Oslo Conference also pointed out that preventing the spread of nuclear weapons is an essential part of the struggle to end war. For more than a decade, scientists have been in agreement that the development of nuclear weapons has made it possible for man to destroy civilization. There is no adequate defense against nuclear weapons that could not be overcome by increasing the scale of the attack. There is no way of arranging international agreements to limit war between the great powers to the use of conventional weapons or of "small" nuclear bombs. Over and over again the leaders of nations, scientists, students of international relations, and other informed people have said that the stockpiles of nuclear weapons must not be used and that the only future for the world is one in which war between nations is abandoned and disputes are resolved by recourse to law.

Yet despite the general recognition of the increased danger to the world that would result from the spread of nuclear weapons, little action has been taken to prevent this deterioration in the world situation. One significant step was taken in 1960, that of making Antarctica a nuclear-free zone. Proposals that the whole of Latin America and the whole of Africa be made into zones free of nuclear weapons have not, however, been adopted, nor has the extension of the principle of demilitarisation to central Europe—as proposed by Rapacki, Kennan, and others several years ago—been subjected to serious discussion. Moreover, although it has been evident to the whole world that the refusal to accept into the world community of nations the most populous nation in the world, the Chinese People's Republic, would inevitably lead to the development of a Chinese stockpile of nuclear weapons, no effective action was taken to avert this dangerous change in the world situation.

I do not believe that existing great nuclear powers will carry out any major stages in the process of disarmament unless the Chinese People's Republic is a signatory to the disarmament agreements; the Chinese People's Republic cannot be expected to participate in the discussion of major international treaties until she is accepted into the community of nations under conditions worthy of her stature.

It is essential for the preservation of humanity that the Chinese People's Republic be brought into the United Nations and given the seat on the Security Council that she deserves to have, as one of the greatest nations in the world.

India has made a valuable contribution to the world by resisting the pressure to acquire nuclear weapons. Her example and her influence may be acquire determinative in causing other nations, such as Australia, also to resist this pressure.

Moreover, India, as a great nation whose leaders have expressed their dedication to ethical principles and world cooperation and their rejection of selfish ideologies, could take the lead in a vigorous effort to bring the Chinese People's Republic into the United Nations under such conditions that the development of a great Chinese stockpile of nuclear weapons would be given up.

I believe that this goal can be achieved if the nations of the world will accept the principle that all disputes between nations and peoples should be settled by arbitration and that war should be abolished from the world.

The replacement of war by world law must include not only great wars but small ones. Small wars are dangerous, because a small war may grow into a great one that would be a world catastrophe. Moreover, small wars are often characterised by extreme savagery and a great amount of human suffering, so that their abolition would be a boon to humanity.

During recent years the great powers have followed a policy that can only be described as constituting an extreme of immorality. This policy is that of instigating and aggravating insurrections and civil wars in small countries, and increasing the savagery of the wars and the suffering of the people by providing weapons and military advisers. I believe that these actions of the great powers are associated with policies of militarism and national economic interest that are now antiquated, and that they should be replaced by policies compatible with the principles of morality, justice, and world brotherhood. The wars in Vietnam and the Congo are examples; instead of aggravating these terrible wars, the nations of the world should be cooperating in the effort of stopping them and of finding an effective and acceptable method of settling the disputes in a just and moral way. I believe that the pressure of world opinion could in the course of time force the great nations to abandon the immoral policies that they have been following, with respect to the aggravation of wars such as those in Vietnam and the Congo, and that India could take the leading part in this effort. I believe that this action by India would represent the continued application of the ethical principles of Jawaharlal Nehru and Mahatma Gandhi.

I am confident that we can achieve the goal of the abolition of war and its replacement by world law, and that the world community will thereby be freed not only from the suffering caused by war but also, through the better use of the resources of nature, of the discoveries of scientists, and of the efforts of mankind, to a large extent from the suffering caused by hunger and disease. I believe that, with war abolished from the world, there will be improvement in the social, political, and economic systems in all nations to the benefit of the whole of humanity, and that we shall in the course of time be enabled to build a world characterised by justice for all human beings, and a culture worthy of man's intelligence.

34

Prem Bhatia on Nehru

We had barely crossed the Domel bridge when Jawaharlal Nehru died on 27 May 1964 in New Delhi. although the news was not to reach us in Muzaffarabad until over an hour later.

At the head of the procession of cars entering "Azad" Kashmir was Sheikh Abdullah, determinedly bent to bring peace between India and Pakistan. The rest of the procession consisted of Pakistani officials, their professional and political cousins from the "Azad" territory and a few of us journalists from India. The Pakistanis and their cousins had been in the procession since we left Rawalpindi in the early morning.

Our journey lay through Murree, where we were served a huge breakfast of tea and cakes. The Sheikh made a speech from the steps of the local post office. There was friendship and expectation in the cool morning air and the Sheikh was at his oratorical best.

Over the Domel bridge the driver of our car, himself a genuine Valley Muslim who was born in Srinagar, told us how in 1947 our aircraft, in chasing Pakistani "raiders", had tried to bomb this strategic link with the "Azad" area, but instead had hit the British cemetery in Murree and caused a panic exodus down the mountain slopes to Rawalpindi. "Lucky for us", he added with a laugh, "we hope your airmen will always miss their targets." He was proved wrong in December, 1971.

We lost sight of Sheikh Abdullah as we entered Muzaffarabad, where he was taken away to the residence of the "Azad" Kashmir "President" and we to the ornate shamiana under which the tables bent double with the weight of "gushtawas", "yakhni" and "biryani". As we prepared to dig into this Kashmiri banquet which was to be our lunch, a man came running to the shamiana. "Panditji" has passed away", he cried in his handkerchief, and then again, "Panditji is no more". He was choked with grief.

Chaudhry Mohammad Shafi, at one time a member of the Lok Sabha and a loyal follower of the Sheikh, was the messenger who carried the bad news to us. He was an old friend of mine, and I felt the tight grip of his fingers as he held my hand. "Please go to the Sheikh", Shafi pleaded with me, "he is in a very bad state. He needs you." The Pakistanis and the "Azad" Kashmiris around us came up to express their condolence, and each embraced me in turn like we do in north India to convey our grief over the loss of a close relation or a dear friend.

Sheikh Abdullah was indeed in a shocking condition when I saw him five minutes later. He had shut himself in his room, drawn the curtains and put out the lights. He wept helplessly. Things would never be the same again without Jawaharlal, he said between sobs, but he himself must continue with his mission. The Sheikh was still far from fully composed when I left him half an hour later to drive back to Rawalpindi and from there on to New Delhi. The lunch under the shamiana remained uneaten; the hosts hung around not knowing what they were required to do next.

Things have certainly not been the same again since that unhappy afternoon in Muzaffarabad. Life has come full circle with Indira Gandhi in the Prime Minister's chair. Significantly perhaps, the chair itself in the Prime Minister's room in South Block is back to where it was when Jawaharlal Nehru occupied it. During the eighteen months that Lal Bahadur Shastri held the office of Prime Minister the chair had been moved against the wall which divides the Prime Minister's room from the corridor outside and forms a part of the office of the Private Secretary.

But not everything that identified Jawaharlal's personality

and politics has been restored, as indeed it could not have been. The situation has greatly altered, and with the situation the attitudes and values that belonged to him. Indira Gandhi lives in a much more challenging world. Her methods and attitudes are not an imitation of her father's. They are peculiarly her own and of her chosen and surviving advisers.

In the heat and tumble of the battles of today—battles against "garibi", political opponents and the shortage of food, power and water—there is no trace of what Jack Kennedy once described as the late Prime Minister's "soaring idealism". Its place has been taken by a tough and unrelenting matter-of-factness, the stuff that goes to make a go-getting commander in an emergency. But do we really miss the "soaring idealism" of Jawaharlal? There are some among us who will tell you that they do. Most of these idealism lovers abused Nehru in his lifetime for "soaring" above their petty calculations and pettier minds.

One remembers Nehru most for a quality which can only be described as "bigness". In this comprehensive quality were contained his capacity to forgive (and often to forget) and his tolerance for an honest difference of opinion, provided it was not expressed with offensive vulgarity. He worried too, about what others thought about him. He could be hurt by the discovery that he was disliked or distrusted. Great as these virtues were, they would almost certainly not have won the war against Pakistan. Bangladesh might well have died in the process of birth.

—*The Statesman,* 27 May 1973

A LIFE FOR INDIA

In London today, British Prime Minister Harold Wilson opens the Jawaharlal Nehru Memorial Exhibition at the Royal Festival Hall. The exhibition comes to Britain from New York two weeks after India observed the first anniversary of the death of Nehru with a full working day. This was a fitting tribute to the memory of a man who for 17 years as Prime Minister of India rarely took a holiday. The English translation of a slogan he made popular reads : "Rest is sin." Nehru used to say that for many years to come Indians should consider themselves "condemned to hard labour."

An uncommon awareness of the value of time made Nehru an unusual Indian. He kept neither his visitors nor his files waiting. On the night before he died he had cleared all the official papers which his secretariat had sent to him. Thousands in India still remember nostalgically the speed with which he replied to their letters. This was not only a manifestation of his tremendous energy but also of a careful discipline. Above all it was a recognition of the need for India to hurry and to make up for lost time. The country had to catch up after centuries of backwardness.

Impatience coloured his political and economic policies. India could not be kept waiting while the rest of the world was moving. It had to catch up with progressive political thinking in other parts of the world and look ahead rather than behind. Socialism as an economic and social philosophy had to be adopted here and now even if the process of change had to be made to suit Indian conditions. In the later years of his life, Nehru did feel the dead weight of conservative tradition but there was no surrender on principles.

It is wrong to think that Nehru saw the challenge of China only when India was invaded in the autumn of 1962. He was certainly late in appreciating the military challenge but the political and economic threat was seen 12 years earlier. Nehru thought that communism could be fought satisfactorily only through economic progress. Hence his emphasis on planning and heavy industry. The Chinese possibly saw through that and the military attack was intended largely to disrupt India's economic structure and thereby to weaken it politically.

Nehru's 17 years as Prime Minister may be divided roughly into three parts. The first eight years until the Bandung Conference were the boom period in his own and India's history after independence. The first Five-Year Plan, modest by comparison with what followed, held the promise of great possibilities. His prestige within the country had touched its peak. World statesmen sought his advice and support and even if some did not like non-alignment they could not ignore the gathering momentum of this new international slogan.

The next phase lasted until the Chinese invasion. Much of the disappointment that Nehru experienced in these years arose from his awakening to the Chinese danger. He had already been shocked by the occupation of Tibet but that unhappy event had already been allowed to be forgotten by the later development of cordiality with Peking. In 1956, the Dalai Lama on a visit to India, asked to be allowed to stay in the country, which gave Nehru his first direct evidence of China's policies in Tibet.

Three years later the Dalai Lama had to flee his country and take asylum in India. Then began the first real phase of acrimony between New Delhi and Peking which led to the armed conflict of October 1962. By this time Nehru's disillusionment with China was complete and he had to revise his assessment of 1954 that China would not think of a military adventure for 25 years. If India felt humbled by China three years ago Nehru was completely agonised. For him it was not only a military reverse but also the destruction of a faith.

From the cease-fire of November 1962, until May 27, 1964, when he died, Nehru was in the third and the final phase of his career as Prime Minister and leader of his people. Time was again an important consideration with him—the need for time to reorganise the country's defences. The third phase meant also vital adjustments in political and economic policies. There was an increased dependence on the West for military equipment and training with a simultaneous emphasis on continuing non-alignment and an inevitable slowing down of economic development.

It has been said that Nehru died a broken man. That would be a vast exaggeration of the disappointments he suffered. Nehru was not a defeatist and in spite of the economic shortfalls and military inadequacy the country did not get the impression of being allowed to go under. One knew that Nehru was tired and sick and yet one had faith in his capacity to see the country through. Even a few days before his death he had started a reassessment of India's relations with Pakistan. Only Nehru could have permitted Sheikh Abdullah to go to Rawalpindi in May 1964 to seek a solution on Kashmir.

Nehru had many critics in his lifetime and their number has not decreased, but his death has by no means affected the reverence in which he was held while he was alive. Visitors to the Nehru National Museum still weep as they look at his working desk in what was his study. Shanti Vana (Forest of Peace), where he was cremated, has become a place of pilgrimage like the next-door site of Gandhi's cremation. Nehru memorials are springing up all over the country although the principal monument to his memory will be located in New Delhi.

One unfailing sign of India's love for Nehru is the esteem in which his only child, Indira Gandhi (now Minister of Information and Broadcasting), is held by the people. She has a claim to fame in her own right—for her overpowering charm, nimbleness of mind, and a greatly matured political sense. But to millions of Indians she is primarily Nehru's daughter. Admiring mobs greet her wherever she travels.

A final assessment of Nehru's life remains to be made but there is already agreement that this was a life lived for India. Some recall his mistakes but few deny him the status of the greatest Indian after Gandhi. Nehru did not want to be deified, but this is a wish which not everyone is likely to respect. It will not be long before his image appears in a few temples. That would only be a physical translation of a popular feeling.

—*The Guardian,* 10 June 1965

INDIA'S SELF-QUESTIONING

India enters the seventeenth year of independence with less than the certainty of previous anniversaries. China has much to do with the present national mood of introspection and self-criticism, but the fear of further aggression can be exaggerated as a cause. So can the continued friction with Pakistan.

Most of the criticism against the Congress—within the party and outside—is finally directed at Mr Nehru. Apart from the lunatic fringe who find nothing right in the Prime Minister's policies or actions, the majority of his critics find him guilty of one major fault. They say he is not strong enough to deal ruthlessly or even firmly with undesirable colleagues and followers. This fault is admitted by Mr Nehru himself but not with any sense of guilt. He is proud of his democratic ways and his liberal approach. Some time ago he said with unbecoming sarcasm that he would rather leave "firmness" to "editorial writers." The result of all this generosity of spirit is a leniency of outlook and a reluctance to take unpleasant decisions which have harmed himself as well as the Government and the party.

With this leniency of manner Mr Nehru has combined all these 16 years a curious incapacity for sharing responsibility. This is due partly to a genuine belief in his own superior judgment and partly to an inner fear of building up a rival leader. Perhaps the two reasons are mixed. Possibly because he believes in his own better judgement he finds it dangerous to share power with people who may turn out to be rivals without the capacity to shoulder responsibility. Genuine admirers and time-serving sycophants have also helped to build up a picture of an indispensable Nehru. There is little doubt that with all his objectiveness and intellectual honesty Mr Nehru has been influenced by such adoration, and has come to acquire more than a great man's normal dislike of criticism.

While age has brought an unmistakable mellowness to his personality, China has created a disillusionment which has become progressively bitter. Acutely aware of India's military limitations, and simultaneously deeply unhappy about the possibility of war, Mr Nehru today is mentally as desolate as a man of his great sensitiveness and patriotic purpose can be. Few in India realise the task he faces, and because he is not given to cheap slogans his critics accuse him of inaction. He is unhappy also because he sees in his declining health a danger of leaving to posterity the unsolved problem of relations with China. Deep inside him he feels hurt by the knowledge that he is constructively responsible for the present situation.

It is difficult to see what another leader could have done for better results against China if he had accepted the premises which India's foreign policy was built from the start. But another leader would probably have trained a cadre of well chosen and dependable lieutenants. Today Mr Nehru has hardly anyone he can lean upon.

Mr Jawaharlal Nehru shows no sign of total trust. He still keeps his counsel to himself.

Considerable disbelief persists about the Prime Minister's capacity to be thorough. The country misses his old dynamism. Everyone knows that the China problem will be a lasting anxiety, and it has to be faced. Relations with Pakistan will probably get even worse before they can get better. But anxiety on this score is by no means overpowering. Indian eyes are today turned inwards in a search for faults and remedies. Mr Nehru seems to have lost his vital spark, and yet it is hard to think of India without Nehru.

—*The Guardian,* 15 August 1963

TIMELESS QUALITY OF THE NEHRU LEGEND

Seeing him in the midst of hard work or unusual strain, many have been heard to say that Prime Minister Jawaharlal Nehru looks "tired".

This is not surprising for a man who at 68 works as hard as he did at 58 and who, despite his increasingly exacting preoccupation with affairs of State, is still willing to shoulder endless petty burdens which others could handle, though less spectacularly. There is no visible diminution in his responsiveness to such things as have always stirred his enthusiasm or provoked his displeasure.

Whether the occasion is a political mass meeting, a newspaper editors' conference, a wedding or a funeral, Mr. Nehru continues to be his own chief of protocol, adding importance to the situation by his presence and fatigue to his body. If others around him suffer by comparative neglect, the fact goes to prove that he himself remains, after his long period of leadership of the country, India's top hero, its principal dispenser of privilege and patronage and the centre of popular attention.

In this collective national attitude of adoration and loyalty, who except those habitually given to worrying about the future have the time or the desire to think about a successor? For the country at large, the Nehru legend has a timeless quality, and his own eternal youth gives to that quality a degree of perpetuity which deceives as well as pleases.

Despite his externally visible abruptness and impatience, the evolution of Mr. Nehru's personality has been practically an invisible process. This was natural for a person who gives away very little of his inner self and remains fully known only to himself so that one wonders if there is anyone "close" to Mr. Nehru. In the spiritual isolation in which he has lived for many years, even those who are known to the outside world as his "friends" and "confidants" have received only a strictly rationed quantity of his favours and intimate opinions.

That is why not one of the Prime Minister's colleagues and companions can honestly claim that sense of exclusive proprietorship which other great men, equal to or smaller than the Prime Minister of India, may have given to those around them in the long history of human eminence.

Yet a change does appear to have occurred in the past year or so in Mr. Nehru's overall attitude to the national situation as a whole. It is not a change in essentials but a marginal alteration in his approach. He has seen, perhaps more clearly than ever before, the magnitude of India's undertaking and his personal share in its accomplishment.

The result is a slightly greater willingness to accept imperfection both among people and situations, now being faced over the anxiety for rapid development. A more patient attitude may have resulted also from the realization that, making allowances for common failings and distractions, it is a more practical approach to concentrate on fewer targets rather than to attempt a solution of all problems at the same time.Two principal objectives remain in the focus of the Prime Minister's consciousness—the unity and solidarity of the nation and the country's economic advancement.

Steps for the achievement of these two ends have been marked by much success but also by occasional disappointment. Full accomplishment will probably come as slowly as Mr Nehru's advancing years. One can only hope that it will also be as purposeful and gracious as Mr Nehru's own life. If the country has deserved his wisdom and guidance for these many years, its need for those qualities is even greater today than when Mr Nehru was 67.

—*The Statesman*, 12 November 1957

35

Nehru—The Man

Nehru has long been dead. Yet today we hardly know anything about his personal life that we did not during his lifetime. In fact his total dedication to the job in hand hardly left him any time for a personal life.

In any profile of Nehru, his courage must get pride of place. Reflecting on the ups and downs of life he wrote. There is only one thing that remains to us that cannot be taken away: to act with courage and dignity and to stick to the ideals that have given meaning to life..."

And, "...only they can sense life who stand often on the verge of it, only they whose lives are not governed by the fear of death. In spite of all the mistakes that we might have made we have saved ourselves from triviality and an inner shame and cowardice."

In a quarter century of political activeness from 1920-1945, Nehru spent more than one third of this period in prison. These were years of his youth and middle age, the most productive years of a person's life. Yet they left behind no mark of bitterness or rancour, nor dimmed his zest for life or faith in India's destiny.

Even while in prison, he rarely grumbled, felt peevish or lost his poise. And he never indulged in self-pity. "It seems to me" he wrote from the prison cell, "I am getting far too much sympathy from others and I do not deserve it. It is those who work and labour outside who deserve sympathy, not we who laze and eat and sleep." His innate sense of decency revolted at the special treatment given to him in prison, and he repeatedly protested to the authorities against this unjust practice.

It is difficult to find instances when Nehru was petty, vindictive or malicious. After Independence there were no reprisals, no witch-hunting, no settling of scores. The ICS officers, who had imprisoned the national leaders or ordered firings on the Congress demonstrators, were given all respect and trust due to their office, and bygones were treated as bygones. A smaller man would have harboured animus against the British. But Nehru attended his first Conference of Commonwealth Prime Ministers in 1948 as if the colonial era had never happened. Even Churchill, his old adversary, had to concede, "I have always admired your ardent wish for peace and the absence of bitterness in your consideration of the antagonism that had in the past divided us."

Once Ram Manohar Lohia made a very offensive reference to Nehru's ancestry in the parliament. Said he, 'The PM pretends to be an aristocrat. I can prove that his grandfather was nothing but a Chaprasi (peon) at the Mughal Court." Unruffled, Nehru replied, "I am most grateful to the Hon'ble Member. I have been trying for years to get him to accept that I am a man of the people. Now he has admitted it himself."

In case he came across an instance of ugly behaviour, he would try to apply a corrective without reprimanding the offender. At the 1961 Republic Day Parade where the Queen of England was the chief guest, some politicians got ruffled as they did not get seats owing to their late arrival. When volunteers requested them to sit on the ground like others, they went protesting to Nehru. "Nehru quietly got his daughter and the Speaker to leave the Queen's entourage and to lead the MPs away and to sit on the ground with them." At a reception at Constitution House some MPs threw banana peels on the ground. "Nehru, seeing this, pointedly got up, came along with a plate and, without saying a word, shamed them by picking up the mess himself."

For a person who was born in luxury and seen so much comfort, he was spartan in his habits, austere in his living and almost miserly where the spending of public money was concerned. In May 1954, Nehru spent three days in Madras on official business. In reply to a parliament question it was revealed that his stay cost the state exchequer Rs. 90,000. He was upset and wrote to the chief ministers to observe economy on his visits, and added, "I shall hesitate to go anywhere if I am so costly."

Describing Nehru's first visit to the United States, B.K. Nehru writes, "... his entourage consisted of Sir Girja Shankar Bajpai, who was Secretary General of Foreign Office, and M.O. Mathai, his private secretary, and that was all. The travel was by commercial airlines... The journey across the Atlantic... involved more than *(a)* full night of travelling. The plane had sleeping berths available on extra payment. The Indian 'delegation' had bought itself one sleeping berth in order to save money, and the Prime Minister insisted that Sir Girja and not he, should occupy that berth as he was senior in age."

Nehru overlooked laxity in his colleagues, but he was unsparing in his own conduct. As a measure of economy the Finance Minister, C.D. Deshmukh, wanted the ministers to downgrade the post of their private secretary. Dharam Vira was then the trusted Principal Private Secretary of Nehru. Finance Minister wanted the PM to give the lead. Nehru relieved Dharam Vira without demur and downgraded the post.

Much folklore surrounds the great wealth of Motilal and the luxurious life that the Nehrus lived. In fact Motilal was more large-hearted than rich, and once he gave up his legal practice after joining the national movement, the situation gradually became pretty tight at Anand Bhawan. In 1927 he had to think twice before leaving for Switzerland to join his son. Earlier, to finance his trip to Europe, Nehru "had to return to the distasteful practice of law, and for preparing a brief Motilal secured for him the large fee of Rs. 10,000..."

After his release from Naini jail in 1933, Nehru was required to pay closer attention to his household affairs. "I had ignored them completely so far, and I had not even examined my father's papers since his death. We had cut down our expenditure greatly, but still it was far more than we could afford. We were not keeping a car because that was beyond our means..."

However, the insistent demands of life do not wait. So, Nehru took recourse to the last resort which Indian families in distress do : "To improve the immediate financial situation we decided to sell off my wife's jewellery, the silver and other familiar articles that we possessed, as well as many cart-loads of odds and ends." Nehru's hectic political activity and long terms in jail left little time for family life. And whatever time he could steal to spend at home was clouded by domestic worries. "Eighteen years of married life!" he writes in *An Autobiography,* "but how many long years out of them had I spent in prison-cell, and Kamala in hospitals and sanatoria?" When Nehru got married in 1916, Kamala was seventeen, "a slip of a girl, utterly unsophisticated," without much formal education. In the Anglicized Nehru household, she was a misfit. Referring to great "differences in our mental outlook," Jawaharlal writes, "I hardly realized that this delicate, sensitive girl's mind was slowly unfolding like a flower and required gentle and careful tending."

To be fair to Nehru, life did not give him enough time to work out a smooth equation with his wife. Occasionally, he refers to Kamala with a lot of feeling, and his memories of their togetherness are full of tenderness and remorse. "I thought of the early years of our marriage when ... I almost forgot her and denied her, in so many ways, that comradeship which was her due." And more pointedly, "I had taken from her what she gave me. What had I given to her in exchange during these early years? I had failed evidently and, possibly she carried a deep impress of those days upon her."

They came much closer when Kamala started taking an active interest in the freedom movement. "Our women came to the front and took charge of the struggle... In this upheaval Kamala had played a brave and notable part and on her inexperienced shoulders fell the task of organizing our work in the city of Allahabad."

This shared involvement in a great venture gave the Nehrus a new sense of companionship. "When I was arrested in February, 1934... Kamala went up to our rooms to collect some clothes for me. I followed her to say goodbye to her. Suddenly she clung to me and fainting, collapsed." With his stoic reserve and dread of showing personal emotion, this is the closest Nehru came to giving a glimpse of his conjugal intimacy.

Kamala's death was followed by his mother's two years later. His father had died earlier in 1931. His daughter Indira was pursuing her studies abroad. This left Nehru lonely and forlorn. "I would return to my home from my wanderings almost unwillingly," he writes, "and sit in that deserted house by myself." This was at least partly the reason for his turning into such a workaholic.

Nehru was forty-seven when he became a widower. He was not an ascetic. In fact his views on sex were rather unorthodox for those times. Writing about his student days abroad, he says, "Most of us were strongly attracted by sex and I doubt if any of us attached any idea of sin to it. Certainly I did not; there was no religious inhibition. We talked of its being amoral, neither moral or immoral."

Yet during Kamala's lifetime he remained loyal to her. After her death he did get involved with some controlled affairs. The one with Edwina Mounbatten is widely known. So ardent was his passion for her that even at a formal dinner given by Vijayalakshmi Pandit, the Indian High Commissioner in London, he disappeared with Edwina, leaving the guests high and dry. And the following we have on Pupul Jayakar's authority : "I asked Vijayalakshmi Pandit of Jawaharlal Nehru's relationship with Padmaja (Naidu). 'Didn't you know Pupul?' she replied, 'they lived together for years, for years.'

Questioned further as to why he had not married Padmaja, Vijayalakshmi replied, 'He felt that Indu had been hurt enough. He did not want to hurt her further'."

M.O. Mathai, Nehru's private secretary, who was privy to many a household secret, gives instances of Padmaja's extreme jealousy of Lady Mounbatten, and quotes Miss Naidu as telling him, 'Jawahar is not one woman's man.' Mathai also writes about Nehru's affair with one Sharada Mata, from whom he sired a son.

Physically, Nehru enjoyed excellent health and seldom suffered from any illness. His popular image is that of a robust, energetic and youthful person, always walking fast and with a springy gait. He was sixty-eight when he went up the Rohtang Pass, "mostly on horse-back, walked on top of the pass for one or two miles and came down on foot." As to his exhausting work schedule, H.V.R. Lyenger writes, "Having worked closely with him during a period of exceptional stress and anguish, I have come to the conclusion that no purely physical or physiological explanation is adequate."

Nehru spoke and wrote millions of words. His lively mind bubbled with ideas, and he had great faith in their potency. Men of action normally fulfil themselves through their deeds. For him, fulfilment came through articulation, philosophizing, conceptualizing. Even the launching of great schemes and projects were occasions for lighting sparklers of words and firing rockets of ideas.

This tendency becomes much more pronounced in his speeches. Most of them are too long and tedious. He is not only reflective in his speeches, but also discursive and rambling. His habit of soliloquizing or thinking aloud in public, though attractive at times, could prove harmful in a head of government.

"It would be a good thing for the world," said Nehru, "if all the Foreign Ministers remained silent for some time. More trouble is being caused in foreign affairs by the speeches that the Foreign Ministers ... deliver in their respective Assemblies or in the United Nations." And he himself provided the best example of this danger when he made so many hasty and ill-advised pronouncements about India's problems with China. As one observer remarked, "India's foreign policy was not in the files of the Ministry of External Affairs, nor even in the head of the Prime Minister but on his tongue."

Very often Nehru played with words as a child plays with marbles, and he enjoyed expansive talk just for the love of it. The German Chancellor, Adenauer, is reported to have felt exasperated when after a masterly expose of international problems, Nehru would not come down to earth but evaded specific questions of vital importance to the two countries. P.M.S. Blackett, the famous British scientist whom Nehru used to consult on India's defence production programme, said, "... he had too much intellectualism to solve any problem. He just chatted. He liked chatting about the world in general... When I was consultant to Defence Ministry, when I stayed with him, he just chatted. It was curious. I was surprised. He chatted."

This love of hearing his own voice and the unchallenged power he wielded for long gave Nehru an exaggerated notion of his own importance and made him somewhat insensitive to the response of others. Malcolm Muggeridge thought he was "rather a conceited second-rate person." Hugh Gaitskell said, "He is a very arrogant man; I think that is one reason he makes such long speeches. He really thinks everyone wants to listen to him."

At the Bandung Conference when Sir John Kotlewala described east European countries as colonies under communist domination, Nehru went up to him and asked with some heat, "Why did you do it Sir John? Why did you not show me your speech before you made it?" Sir John shot back, "Why should I? Do you show me yours before you make them?"

These stray instances of Nehru's arrogance are based on the perceptions of foreigners who never came close to him. But what does one say to this observation by Maulana Azad, his lifelong colleague and friend : "Jawaharlal is, however, very vain and cannot stand that anybody else should receive greater support and admiration than he." Raj Kumari Amrit Kaur, describing him as 'A Friend Without Friends,' said, "he is not averse to flattery and there is conceit in him which makes him at once intolerant of criticism and may even warp his better judgement."

Both during the freedom struggle and his tenure as prime minister, Nehru was occasionally faced with 'make or break' situations. Though at times he did come to the brink, he invariably retreated. "My outlook has always been against conflict," he told a journalist. In 1928 Nehru offered his resignation as General Secretary of the Congress owing to differences over the Simon Commission controversy. The Congress Working Committee did not accept it. "And again I agreed," wrote Nehru. "It was surprising how easy it was to win me over to a withdrawal of my resignation. This happened on many occasions ...,"

This penchant for resigning acquired much higher visibility during Nehru's years in power. In 1951 he threatened to resign over the Tandon controversy. In 1954 he desired to quit office as he was feeling stale. In 1957 he wanted to leave when he was outmanoeuvred in his attempt to replace Rajendra Prasad by Radhakrishan as the President of India. And in 1958 he created a furore by announcing his resolve to resign to a gathering of Congress MPs in the Central Hall of the Parliament. "I feel that I must have a period when I can free myself from the daily burden and think of myself as an individual citizen of India and not as Prime Minister." But again, instead of actually submitting his resignation, he left the decision to the MPs! Predictably, the MPs told him as to how indispensable he was for the country, and he faithfully bowed to the pressure from his party. So despite all his resolves and threats, he never actually submitted his resignation to the President.

When a journalist asked Nehru as to why he gave in to public pressure if he really wanted to resign, "His answer was that India needed him, that his constituency was the people of India." And just five days before his death when he was asked at a press conference if it would not be in the country's interest to solve the succession problem in his lifetime, he replied, "My life is not ending so soon."

Nehru was much bigger than the post he held. But power is an opiate, and it was pathetic to see its addictive hold over this colossus. His life's work was over by 1958, and he would have departed in a cloud of glory had he resigned then. And it "would have set the healthy precedent that the only exit route for a politician is not through defeat or death.

In the days of individual Satyagraha in 1940 when Nehru's arrest was imminent, he came to see Gandhi at Sevagram. As he was leaving Gandhi's wife gave her blessings and said, "God will look after you." Nehru replied, "Where is God, Ba. If he exists, he must be very fast asleep."

Nehru was not religious — not in the conventional sense. The strife, bigotry and intolerance that he saw practised in the name of orthodox faith gave him a 'horror of religion.' Moreover, his scientific, rationalist outlook could not come to terms with religious faith. Yet he recognized that religion, "... offered... a safe anchorage from doubt and mental conflict, an assurance of future life which will make up for the deficiencies of their life." He goes even further and says, "Whether we believe in God or not, it is impossible not to believe in something..."

Nehru's personal preference was for "the open sea, with all its storms and tempests." Traditional religion's straitjacket was distasteful to his eclectic mind: I was, somewhere at the back of my mind, a pagan, with a pagan's liking for the exuberance of life and nature, and not very much averse to the conflicts that life provides." Thus, 'The traditional Chinese outlook, fundamentally ethical and yet irreligious or tinged with religious scepticism has an appeal for me..."

In the strict, formal sense, Nehru was obviously not religious. But so far as the ethical and human dimensions of religion are concerned, he was as religious as any self-proclaimed man of God can be. After he asked Ba 'Where is God/Gandhi laughed and said, "While Jawaharlal always says he does not believe in God he is nearer God than many who profess to be his worshippers."

Nehru turned his face away from a life of luxury to serve his downtrodden countrymen. He suffered all sorts of privations and insults at the hands of the colonial rulers, and spent the best nine years of his life in jail. He was a man of deep compassion, a thorough gentleman, would not consciously hurt anybody, and was truthful in his dealings. He waged a lifelong struggle against injustice and oppression, and his sympathies embraced the whole of mankind. If such a person was not truly religious, who else could be?

But there is a terrain of human psyche which lies beyond the reach of logic and rationality where emotion, instinct and intuition hold sway. This is the terrain not accessible to the agnostic; this is the primordial soil in which religion is rooted. But Nehru was candid enough to observe, "It is all very well for the likes of Sapru and me... to talk pompously and in a superior way of our tolerance in matters of religion when neither of us has any religion worth talking about."

Nehru's more radical views about religion are contained in his *Autobiography,* published in 1936. His *Discovery of India,* published a decade later, shows a deeper understanding of it. He writes,

> ... religion had supplied some deeply felt inner need of human nature, and that the vast majority of people all over the world could not do without some form of religious belief... In the wider sense of the word, religion dealt with the unchartered regions of human experience... It was obvious that there was a vast unknown region all around us.

This unknown region did not interest Nehru very much. "I find the problems of this world sufficiently absorbing to fill my mind." And, "Essentially, I am interested in this world, in this life, not in some other world or a future life."

Thus, being a here-and-now person, his focus of attention is Man and the human condition. "God we may deny, but what hope is there for us if we deny man..." Consequently, the enlightened modern mind "is governed by a practical idealism for social betterment ... Humanity is its God and social service its religion."

Science had a decisive influence on Nehru's belief system: "It is the scientific approach, the adventurous and yet critical temper of science, the search for truth and new knowledge, the refusal to accept anything without testing and trial... all this is necessary, not merely for the application of science — but for life itself and the solution of its many problems." But a decade later he stated, "Scientists should note that they do not have a monopoly of the truth...Truth is too vast to be contained in the minds of human beings or in books, however sacred." And while addressing the annual session of the Indian Science Congress in 1963, he observed, "Without science there is no future for any society; but even with science, unless it is controlled by some spiritual impulses, there is also no future."

It is interesting to note that the above three quotations pertain to 1946,1957 and 1963. And they show how Nehru was gradually moving from a totally science-based, materialistic outlook to a science-tinged-with-spirituality position. In an interview to a journalist he said, "Yes I have changed. The emphasis on ethical and spiritual solutions is not unconscious. It is deliberate, quite deliberate."

In fact the science on which Nehru had built his worldview, had itself undergone a sea change. From Newtonian certitude, it had entered the probablistic realm of 'uncertainties' of quantum mechanics; and the three Euclidian dimensions had been pierced by the fourth one of space-time continuum. As a result of his vast reading Nehru was aware of these developments and this led him to discover correspondences between the modern science and Vedantic metaphysics. He wrote, ... "it is interesting to compare some of the latest conclusions of science with the fundamental ideas underlying the Advaita Vedantic theory. These ideas were that the universe is made of one substance whose form is perpetually changing, and further that the sum total of energies remains the same. Also that the explanations of things are to be found within their own nature, and that no external beings or existences are required to explain what is going on in the universe, with corollary of a self-evolving universe." Further, "All this upheaval of thought," said Nehru, "has led scientists into a new region, verging on the metaphysical." Of course, the process of Nehru's conversion to the Advaita philosophy was slow, and the changeover was never complete.

For Nehru, the ultimate test of a creed, a philosophy or a code of conduct was its social relevance. "The real problems for me," wrote he, "remain problems of individuals and social life ... of the adjustment of relations between individual and between groups, of a something becoming better and higher, of social development, of the ceaseless adventure of man... A living philosophy must answer the problems of today."

Going back to the roots of the Indian ethos, he says :

> The central idea of old Indian civilization... was that of *dharma,* which was something much more than religion or creed; it was a conception of obligations, of the discharge of one's duties to oneself and to others. This *dharma* itself was part of *rita,* the fundamental moral law governing the functioning of the universe.

Thus Nehru expects two things from any coherent system of belief and theory of statecraft: first, that it must answer the problems of today. That explains his aversion to metaphysics and transcendentalism. And second, it must have a sound ethical basis. Any approach which does not satisfy these two criteria cannot be the basis of a stable and just social order.

Nehru's contribution to the building of modern India is unique and enduring. He was handed a very messy slate, and he wrote on it an agenda of gigantic proportions. This made his task exceedingly difficult; but nothing short of it could have met the requirements of this newly liberated subcontinent. There could not be a greater tribute to the global vision of this man than the fact that none of his successors have been able to expand or modify his policy-frame in any significant manner. Perhaps no ruler in history conceived and launched so many and such massive projects for the welfare of his people, and that too in the face of such daunting odds.

In fact our quarrel with Nehru is not that he is not great, but that he was not greater. Especially when he had the capacity to be so. Thus, to borrow Dylan Thomas's phrase, ours has been a 'lover's quarrel' with Nehru.

It is also to be remembered that if several of his initiatives petered out after his death, the blame cannot be placed at Nehru's door. Programmes of social, economic and political reform, especially in the earlier stages, are not self-sustaining forces. The moment you neglect them or put them to wrong use, they lose their momentum and degenerate into empty rituals.

Perhaps none will deny that but for Nehru, India's modernist agenda could have been overwhelmed by forces of revivalism and communalism. When he assumed power, India was a rickety enterprise. It could have disintegrated into warring states, turned into a theocracy, or got saddled by a ruthless dictator. Nothing of the sort happened. To date Nehru has been succeeded by ten prime ministers in a row, and each succession has been completely peaceful and constitutional. This is the ultimate tribute to Nehru's leadership.

Nehru once wrote to G.B. Shaw, "There are too many questions which fill the mind and for which there appear to be no adequate answers, or if the answers are there, somehow they cannot be implemented because of the human beings that should implement them."

The situation in which Nehru found himself was bristling with myriads of such questions. And he was too civilized and eclectic a person to stamp them out with an autocratic flourish. A smaller person and a narrower mind claiming to know all the answers would have handled them with greater assurance and firmness.

When Nehru died on 27 May 1964, his old companion and occasional adversary, C.R. Rajagopalachari said, "Eleven years younger than me, eleven times more important, eleven hundred times more beloved by the nation... I have been fighting Sri Nehru all these ten years over what I consider faults in public policies. But I knew all along that he alone could get them corrected.... He is gone leaving me weaker than before in my fight."

And Arnold Toynbee wrote : "One must be thankful when a noble soul takes on itself the burden of political leadership, for politics are always in need of redeeming."

When Nehru left the scene, idealism and greatness walked out of Indian politics. Some of his successors were astute practitioners of realpolitik, but their concerns were much narrower and mundane. And ever since Indian politics has been in urgent need of 'redeeming'.

FOREIGN POLICY

For Nehru India was a part of the world. For Indira Gandhi, the world was an extension of India. Her thinking was not encumbered by any global vision or grand design. International peace and cooperation were integral to Nehru's view of foreign policy. Indira was not much fascinated by these nebulous concepts. She thought in concrete terms. Being an ardent nationalist, the country's honour, security and clout were the goals for which she strove. Also, by the time Mrs. Gandhi became Prime Minister, most of the colonies had won freedom and the old style colonialism and imperialism did not evoke strong emotions. Thus, hardly any great causes remained over which the world community could be mobilized. Non-alignment had its major appeal for the newly liberated countries. But as they got bogged down with their internal problems and were forced to seek aid from one super power or the other, it became something of an encumbrance.

In this ideologically sanitized environment, Indira's pragmatism served her well. Moreover, her foreign policy did not have to carry the burden of her domestic ambitions;

her obsession with personal power and her dynastic designs did not cloud her perceptions of the country's interests.

Pakistan

India's most immediate foreign policy concern has always been Pakistan. When Indira Gandhi came to power, the two neighbours had already fought two wars, the second one only four months before Indira's accession. The Tashkent Declaration did restore peace, though it would be more correct to call it a truce. Z.A. Bhutto, the then foreign minister of Pakistan, first rocked the boat by resigning in protest against the Declaration, and the following year launched his own People's Party of Pakistan.

In August 1968, Mrs. Gandhi offered to sign a no-war pact with Pakistan. President Ayub Khan agreed provided 'the countries could resolve the existing problems and those that might arise in the future.' This was a very tall order and put paid to any attempt to work out a durable basis for peaceful relations.

There are several critical factors which render normalization of relations difficult. First, the perennial Kashmir irritant, which has been getting worse with time. Second, India considers non-alignment as the linchpin of her foreign policy. It does not suit Pakistan at all. To her way of thinking she can ensure her security only by erecting a barrier of alliances around her. That explains her membership of the Baghdad and SEATO pacts, and her close alliance with the USA.

Thirdly, despite her much smaller size and resource base, Pakistan seeks parity with India. Thus it looks for allies and arms from wherever they are available. Fourthly, Pakistan occupies a crucial position in the United States' geopolitical calculations. With the Soviet attack on Afghanistan, Pakistan became a frontline state for America and reaped hefty rewards for her fealty. To these factors may be added the break-up of Pakistan as a result of the Bangladesh war. Both militarily and territorially, it was a deep wound suffered by her. She cannot live down this humiliation, but would love to return the compliment to India.

It was after the break-up of Pakistan in 1971 that Indira reached the peak of her power and crafted a foreign policy that bore her distinctive stamp. In pursuit of enduring peace she signed the Simla Agreement with Bhutto, the Prime Minister of Pakistan, on 2 July 1972. For her the most important part of this settlement was "that the basic issues and causes of conflict... shall be resolved by peaceful means," and both sides "will refrain from the threat or use of force against the territorial integrity or political independence of the other." Further, "all differences will be settled through bilateral negotiations" and "in Jammu and Kashmir the actual line of control resulting from the cease-fire line of 17 December 1971 shall be respected by both sides without prejudice to the recognised position of either side." This was the equivalent of a no-war pact based on the principle of bilateralism, and it rendered the UN observer group redundant.

Bhutto was careful to get the agreement approved by the Pakistan National Assembly. Pakistan's major gain was the withdrawal of troops from territories under each other's adverse possession. Bhutto was in no hurry to ask for the repatriation of 93,000 prisoners of war as their sudden arrival in Pakistan would have raised several awkward questions. A number of other agreements were subsequently signed to tie up the loose ends. Gradually trade links and travel facilities between the two countries were also resumed and ambassadors exchanged in July 1976.

There has always been a suspicion that some sort of secret understanding was also reached at Simla between Indira and Bhutto. This impression has been confirmed in an article by P.N. Dhar, who was present at Simla during the negotiations as Principal Secretary to the PM. According to Dhar, "Bhutto agreed not only to change the cease-fire into a line of control... but also agreed that the line would be gradually endowed with the 'characteristics of an international border' (his words). It was thought that with the gradual use of the LOG as the de facto frontier, public opinion on both sides would be reconciled to its permanence... when Mrs Gandhi finally asked Bhutto, 'Is this the understanding on which we will proceed?' he replied, 'Absolutely, Aap mujh par bharosa keejiye' (Please trust me)."

Looking to the credibility of the source, this report seems to be correct. Yet, as later events showed, to have 'bharosa' (trust) in Bhutto's oral assurance was like relying on a compact written on sand. Even when he took the agreement to the National Assembly, Bhutto stated that it did not prevent him from raising the Kashmir issue in the UN. He also said "... if people of Kashmir start a freedom movement, we will be with them."

Large arms supplies by China had enabled Pakistan to recoup the heavy losses suffered in the war. Whatever little chance there was for the survival of the Simla spirit was blasted by India's explosion of a nuclear device in 1974. The reaction in Pakistan was violent and Bhutto swore to catch up with India 'even if the people of Pakistan have to eat grass.' He also used it as a pretext to convince the USA to lift the embargo on arms supply clamped after the Indo-Pak war of 1965.

The imposition of Emergency by Mrs. Gandhi in 1975 and the subsequent Janata rule marked a relative lull in Indo-Pak relations. In July 1977 General Zia-ul-Haq staged a military coup in Pakistan, arrested Bhutto and hanged him in April 1979. Tension again started building up when the US resumed large supplies of arms to Pakistan consequent on the Soviet attack on Afghanistan at the end of 1979. When Indira returned as PM next month, General Zia was sitting atop a growing mountain of armaments. He pursued a two-track policy. On the one hand he signed an agreement with America in September 1981 for military and economic aid worth US $ 3.2 billion, yet the very next month he offered a no-war pact with India. Indira vacillated and missed a good opportunity to call Zia's bluff. After some diplomatic exchanges, Mrs. Gandhi offered to sign a treaty of peace and friendship with Pakistan. But in view of the wide divergence in the perceptions of the two countries on almost all issues, these efforts were stillborn. Ultimately, when General Zia visited India in March 1983 to attend the seventh Non-aligned Summit, an agreement to set up an Indo-Pak Joint Commission was signed.

The second track that Zia followed was to steadily beef up Pakistan's defence capability and concentrate on developing the atom bomb. By the early eighties it had become clear that Pakistan had acquired the capability of manufacturing atomic weapons. China rendered the greatest help in this matter, and sensitive devices were also secretly procured from Holland, West Germany, and some other countries. The American Democrat senator Alan Cranston alleged that Pakistan had clandestinely expanded its uranium enrichment facility at Kahuta.

A more insidious plot was the incitement and help that the Sikh militants in Punjab received from Pakistan. Training camps for the terrorists were set up across the border, and they were helped liberally with arms and ammunition. Some extremist Sikhs living abroad were welcomed and encouraged by the Pak rulers to escalate terrorist activities against India.

On her side, Indira Gandhi supported the violent agitation that erupted in the Sindh province of Pakistan in 1983 for the restoration of democracy. Pakistan accused India of fomenting this trouble and interfering in her domestic affairs. Thus, during the closing phase of the Indira era Indo-Pak relations were quite tense.

China

Mrs Gandhi was well aware that India's relations with China, her second most important neighbour, must improve. She consistently tried to follow this line, did not react to provocations, and did nothing to give offence to China. She adhered to the traditional Indian approach of endorsing China's stand on Tibet and Taiwan, and supported her admission to the UN.

Although China also saw no advantage in following a

collision course with India, she did not refrain from making hostile moves if these served her purpose. Here, her growing closeness to Pakistan and later with the USA proved inimical to the restoration of cordial relations. In 1969, she helped Pakistan build a road linking the occupied Kashmir with Sinkiang. This not only posed a security threat to India, but the entire road passed through territory which India claimed as her own.

China also lent open support to insurgent forces in India. She trained and armed Naga rebels to create trouble in the North-Eastern States. She projected the Naxalites as the vanguard of resurgent peasantry trying to overthrow a reactionary feudal order and gave official recognition to the Communist Marxist-Leninist Party which treated the Chinese revolution as its model.

Despite having developed her own nuclear arsenal China toed the Pak line in condemning India's testing of an atomic device. And when Sikkim was integrated into India, the Chinese reaction was fierce. She was strongly opposed to the Indo-Soviet Friendship Treaty and described it as an attempt at encirclement of-China.

Some of this hostility was symbolic, some an expression of solidarity with an ally, and some a reaction to acts of perceived unfriendliness. But a large part of it also stemmed from China's hegemonic outlook and her strategy to prevent India from emerging as a strong rival.

However, China also realized that chronic hostility to India was not in her interest. The first indication of change in the Chinese mood was given by Mao Zedong when, at the May Day parade in 1970, he chatted with the Indian charge d'affaires (the ambassador was withdrawn after the India-China war) and expressed his hope for the restoration of traditional friendly contacts between the two countries. India was uncertain about her response, and perhaps, let slip a good opportunity for early improvement in relations through over-caution. In 1975 a Chinese pingpong team led by a Vice Minister visited India. He again harped on the theme of traditional friendship between the two countries. Next year India appointed K.R. Narayanan as Ambassador to Beijing and China reciprocated the gesture.

After Mao's death in 1976 Deng Xiaoping emerged as the leader following a longish power struggle. His pragmatic approach marked a turnaround in China's attitude towards India. He held the view that the border problem can be solved through peaceful negotiation if both countries make concessions, 'China in the eastern sector and India in the western sector on the basis of actually controlled border line.' He suggested that the two countries should start improving relations in economic and cultural fields and the prickly boundary issue could be tackled later.

In concrete terms, China agreed to the Indian proposal to adopt a sector by sector approach to the settlement of the border issue. But hardly any progress was made on this front. Several agreements were signed between the two countries on cooperation in the economic and cultural fields, and visits by delegations and experts were exchanged. On balance, the closing phase of the Indira era saw some improvement in India-China relations.

Bangladesh

India had played a decisive role in the creation of Bangladesh, and then taken good care to underplay her contribution. One expected a long spell of good neighbourly relations between the two countries, and the start was quite promising. Mujib signed a Treaty of Friendship with India in 1972, and Indira Gandhi extended generous aid in the form of credit, foodgrains, fertilizers, crude oil, etc., to tide over the drought.

Mujibur Rehman was a great demagogue, but an incompetent administrator. As things got out of hand, he declared emergency in 1974, and introduced the Presidential system by amending the Constitution in January 1975. But the situation steadily worsened. Encouraged by Pakistan and, probably the USA, the army staged a coup on 15 August 1975, killing Mujib and his family, as also most of the prominent leaders of his party, the Awami League. General Zia-ur-Rehman became the new ruler, but was killed in another coup in May 1981, when General Ershad became the Martial Law Administrator.

There was always a strong anti-India lobby in Bangladesh, and it became more vocal after Mujib's assassination. The country was beset with all sorts of problems, and India was blamed for most of them. But the greatest irritant between the two countries was the sharing of the Ganga waters on the completion of the Farakka dam. For India, adequate discharge from Farakka was crucial to save the ports of Calcutta and Paradeep from silting. But Bangladesh felt that withdrawal of large quantities of water, would hit her interests. As the controversy sharpened, Bangladesh approached the UN. The issue was temporarily resolved by the two countries signing a Memorandum of Understanding.

With the stabilisation of the military regime, relative normality returned to India-Bangladesh relations and in January 1976 the two signed a trade protocol to step up bilateral trade. But the main focus of Bangladesh gradually shifted from India to the US, China, Saudi Arabia and Pakistan. As America became the largest aid giver and trading partner of Bangladesh, it naturally came to exert more and more influence over her policies. Yet, surrounded as it is by the Indian landmass, the two countries have to interact, negotiate and cooperate on several issues. By and large it has been an uneasy relationship.

Nepal

India's relations with two of her important smaller neighbours, Nepal and Sri Lanka, illustrate the constraints that beset cooperation between two unequal parties. Towards the close of the Nehru era, King Mahendra of Nepal was trying to establish closer links with China and Pakistan to acquire greater elbow-room against India. He was also upset at the activities of Nepali Congress rebels who had sought asylum in India. In a bid to assert Nepal's sovereignty, the king asked India to withdraw the Indian Military Liaison Group and the personnel manning the check posts. India conceded these demands without any fuss.

Indira Gandhi maintained a low profile and kept up the usual flow of assistance to Nepal. But to send King Mahendra the right signal, India imposed several trade restrictions and discontinued the supply of petroleum above a certain quota. The Nepali leaders realized that it would be counter-productive to push matters beyond a certain point. India too was wary of tightening the screw too hard. As greater sobriety and realism returned to mutual relations, a new Treaty of-Trade and Transit was signed in Kathmandu in August 1971.

Subsequent developments helped harmonize Indo-Nepalese relations to a large extent. In 1972 King Mahendra was succeeded by his son King Birendra. He understood better the value of Indian friendship and Indira Gandhi also enhanced aid to Nepal. Another factor that helped normalization was India's decisive victory in the Bangladesh war and her testing the atomic device. These happenings induced her neighbours to take her more seriously.

India is not only the largest aid donor to Nepal, but also her major trading partner. Her contribution in setting up irrigation dams, power plants, industrial units and construction of roads is quite substantial. More than six million Nepalese live in India. Above all, the lifeline of this land-locked country passes through India. Thus, Nepal's economy is deeply integrated with that of her big neighbour. Though Indira Gandhi had been quite sensitive to Nepali susceptibilities, the unequal relationship created its own strains. Whereas India has always disapproved of Nepal's ambition to be declared a zone of peace, the latter has incorporated this concept in her constitution framed in 1981.

Sri Lanka

With twenty per cent of Sri Lanka's population comprising Tamilians demanding autonomy, there is an inbuilt discordance in the Indo-Sri Lankan relations. Not that the two sides have not tried to cultivate good neighbourly contacts. The most notable achievement towards promoting friendly relation was the signing of an agreement in 1974, defining maritime boundary between the two countries and India's recognition of Sri Lankan sovereignty over the tiny island of Kachchativu.

But despite all goodwill on both sides, the problem of Tamil immigrants fouled up mutual relations. Whereas the Tamilians wanted autonomy, the Sinhalese looked upon them as interlopers. Several militant outfits, and especially the Liberation Tigers of Tamil Eelam, LTTE, resorted to increasingly violent means to assert their rights and, at times, the Sri Lankan government adopted severely repressive measures. Owing to the emotional involvement of Indian Tamilians with their Sri Lankan counterparts, the Indian government felt constrained to espouse the cause of the latter. It is also a fact that these militants received arms from India, and training camps were set up for them in Tamil Nadu. This was naturally much resented by the government of Sri Lanka.

Matters came to a head in 1983 when Sri Lankan forces inflicted heavy casualties on the Tamil militants. Thousands of victims fled to Tamil Nadu in panic and loud protests were raised in India against this carnage. Apprehending retaliation by India, Sri Lanka approached several countries for help and charged India with encouraging insurgency before the UN. India conveyed her firm opposition to involving foreign powers in this affair and offered her good offices to normalize the situation. The two countries set up an All Parties Conference for this purpose, but it failed to produce results.

USSR

Indo-Soviet relations, always cordial, were further strengthened by two new developments. One, the increasing estrangement between the USSR and China, which led to border clashes along the Ussuri river in 1969. Secondly, the signing of the Friendship Treaty in 1971 on the eve of the Bangladesh war. India was now the only large and dependable friend that the USSR was left with in the whole of Asia. And India, faced with the hostility of Pakistan, China and America needed Soviet friendship more than ever before.

But the relationship was not free from occasional hitches. In 1968 when the Soviet troops marched into Czechoslovakia, it became difficult for India to avoid openly criticizing her friend in the UN. The Soviet attack on Afghanistan at the end of 1979 faced Mrs. Gandhi with a tough choice when she returned to power a month later. Her considered stand was that the situation in Afghanistan required a political rather than a military solution, and withdrawal of foreign troops should be accompanied by stoppage of arms supplies to that region. Gradually her stand stiffened. When the Soviet Foreign Minister, Andre Gromyko, came to Delhi seeking endorsement of his country's action, Mrs. Gandhi replied, "On this I cannot help you." Later, during her visit to the USSR in 1982, she publicly demanded withdrawal of Soviet troops from Afghanistan.

But these minor differences notwithstanding, relations between the two countries continued to grow. A Joint Declaration at the end of the Soviet Party Chief Brezhnev's visit in November 1973 gave a fresh impetus to economic co-operation. Assistance in the fields of petro-chemicals, metallurgy, power and engineering was enhanced. Under a new five-year trade agreement for 1976-80, areas of co-operation were further expanded and the Soviet Union overtook the USA as India's largest trading partner. In May 1980, the USSR signed the biggest arms supply contract with India. The most attractive part of these trade agreements was the Soviet willingness to accept payment in rupees.

USA

Just ten weeks after she became Prime Minister, Mrs. Gandhi paid a five-day visit to the USA. This was her most serious bid to mend fences with the States. India badly needed foodgrains and foreign exchange. The response of the American President, L. Johnson, was effusive and patronizing.

At a party in her honour, he announced his resolve to ensure that "no harm comes to this girl." Later, he told the Indian Ambassador, B.K. Nehru, "We must get her elected. You tell me what to do...send her food, attack her. I will do whatever you say."

As to the actual American approach "Johnson believed that India had to be pressurised for its own good to make significant changes in her economic policy. He used pressure (to ensure this)." Pressure was applied in good measure to persuade Mrs. Gandhi to devalue the rupee and refrain from "publicly criticizing US policies in South East Asia." She was also persuaded to use part of the accumulated PL-480 funds for setting up the Indo-US Foundation to "promote progress in all forms of learning." Later an agreement was signed to supply 3.5 million tonnes of foodgrains and give a loan of $48 million to finance some projects.

Back home, Indira was severely criticized for compromising India's sovereignly. Whereas she went ahead with devaluing the rupee, the proposal to set up the Indo-US Foundation was dropped. Subsequently, the activities of the US Peace Corps were also curtailed. The USAID mission and, except in Delhi, the US Information Service libraries, were also closed. What hurt the US the most was a reference to "imperialists in Southeast Asia" in a joint communique that Indira Gandhi signed in Moscow in July 1966.

Lyndon Johnson, having failed to get his way, dragged his feet on the release of aid to India. Each shipload of foodgrains was cleared by him personally and India was made to live from 'ship to mouth' during a period of acute drought. This taught Mrs. Gandhi the hard lesson that India had to acquire self-sufficiency, especially in foodgrains, if she was to retain her self-respect.

Indira paid two more visits to the States. In 1971, she went there as part of a wide-ranging public relations exercise to awaken the international community to the problems created by the vast refugee exodus from East Pakistan.

President Nixon's response was cold. Her third visit in July 1982 was in response to an invitation from President Ronald Reagan. She tried hard to put across India's concern at the enormous arms supply to Pakistan. As she told the National Press Club, "Against whom would Pakistan use this military hardware? They cannot be used against Afghanistan because the Soviets are there, and they cannot be used against the Soviet Union." The only concrete gain of the visit was an agreement on the supply of enriched uranium to the Tarapur Atomic Plant. As the USA was not prepared to make it available, it was agreed that France would supply it in future.

At the conceptual level there was no reason as to why the largest and the strongest democracies in the world should not pull together. But India not only did not fit in the global strategic plan of the US, she stood out like a sore thumb. She criticized the American action in Vietnam, recognized the Heng Samrin government in Kampuchea and backed the Palestinian Liberation Organization against Israel. America found this stance offensive. In earlier years the US was one of India's major aid givers and the largest trading partner, and she found India's response singularly lacking in any expression of gratitude.

For India, the most provocative of US actions were the frequent delivery of arms to Pakistan which India considered far in excess of her legitimate defence needs. President Johnson had placed an embargo on the supply of arms to both countries after the 1965 war. In October 1970 President Nixon made a one-time exception to this embargo, and more exceptions were made later. In 1975 President Ford lifted the embargo altogether. In reply to India's protest, Henry Kissinger said that she had been importing 'nearly a billion dollars worth of arms every year, and it was necessary to set the balance right for Pakistan.' Later, in 1981 Pakistan and the USA signed an agreement for $ 3.2 billion for the provision of arms and economic aid.

Whereas politically the relations between the two countries have been seldom very smooth, on the economic and trade front it has been business as usual. Though US aid to India declined substantially, America again overtook the USSR as India's largest trading partner in 1983-84.

Southeast Asia

Indo-China was Nehru's main focus in Southeast Asia. His strong diplomatic support of the Vietnamese nationalist struggle was aimed at keeping it free from big-power rivalry. Indira Gandhi pursued the same line and promptly gave recognition to unified Vietnam and Kampuchea, much to the annoyance of the USA.

Other Southeast Asian countries, small and vulnerable, but strategically located, wanted security and aid. This the United States could provide best and, after the Vietnam debacle, was most interested in doing. These countries, therefore, drifted towards the United States. Also, common interest impelled six of them to form the Association of South East Asian Nations (ASEAN) in August 1967. This was primarily an economic union and, coupled with American aid, helped them grow into prosperous nations.

However, Mrs. Gandhi was able to create a more friendly environment in this region, particularly in relation to Indonesia and Malaysia. Bilateral trade was upgraded and an agreement for some joint ventures signed. India completed the demarcation of the continental shelf with Indonesia, and the latter also lifted restrictions on the immigrant Indians imposed by President Sukarno. But the gains were nominal and Southeast Asia has mostly lived and, grown apart from India.

West Asia

Compared to Southeast Asia, India has much heavier stakes in West Asia. Her large Muslim population makes India specially responsive to Islamic concerns. Most of her oil supplies come from this region. An increasing number of Indians have sought employment there, and several private and public sector companies have undertaken a number of construction projects in this region. Pakistan has repeatedly used her Islamic card to create ill will towards India, and the task of countering this propaganda throws up tough challenges to the Foreign office.

India has taken a consistently pro-Arab stand. When the Arab-Israeli war broke out in 1967, Indira Gandhi fully supported the Palestinian cause. The close personal friendship between her and the PLO leader, Yasser Arafat, was the outcome of this support. However, whether as a result of communal riots in India or Pakistani incitement, most West Asian countries have opposed Indian policies at one time or the other.

Two critical developments in West Asia produced shock waves in India. One was the quadrupling of the price of crude by OPEC in 1973-74. In a major effort to restructure her relations with the Gulf countries, Mrs. Gandhi succeeded in ensuring three-fifths of her crude supplies from Iran, Iraq and the United Arab Emirates on medium-term credit at stable prices. Much of this payment was made through the earnings of Indian workers and professionals employed in the Gulf, whose number in 1983 stood at three-quarters of a million. Indian companies also secured a number of contracts in these countries, and the Indian entrepreneurs considerably increased the range of their products exported to West Asia.

The second shock came with the start of the Iran-Iraq war in 1980. These two countries were then supplying more than two-thirds of India's requirements of crude. Also, several Indian projects were being executed in Iraq. India had to buy crude on the spot market and diversify her sources of supply. Indian exports to the Gulf countries were also affected. Large payments to Indian companies working in Iraq were held up and it took the country quite sometime to absorb the shock.

Non-alignment

For six years after Nehru's death not a single Non-aligned Summit was held. This is some indication of the change in the global political environment. Colonialism and the Cold War no longer excited the people very much. Politics was being subsumed by economics all over, and the European Economic Union best signified this change.

Indira Gandhi first met the two stalwarts of non-alignment, Nasser of Egypt and Tito of Yugoslavia, at the Tripartite Conference held in Delhi in November 1966. The three leaders expressed concern at the sufferings of the Vietnamese people, and highlighted the problems of economic growth faced by the newly liberated nations.

The emphasis of the Non-aligned Movement, NAM, also shifted towards economic issues, and it was at the Non-aligned Summit held in Algiers in 1973 that the idea of a New International Economic Order was first mooted. The seventh Non-aligned Summit, originally scheduled to be held in Baghdad, was shifted to New Delhi at short notice owing to the Iran-Iraq war. The conference was held in March 1983, and Indira Gandhi as the chairperson made a magnificent job of it. Not only had the movement lost its drive, there were highly contentious issues like Afghanistan, Kampuchea and the Iran-Iraq war which could rock the Summit. Mrs. Gandhi conducted the proceedings with great skill and ensured that there were no serious snags or ugly controversies. No sharply focussed statement could be expected from such a heterogeneous assembly, but it did help revive the sagging image of NAM.

Commonwealth

Whereas NAM did occasionally pay lip-service to political issues, the Commonwealth began skirting them altogether and focussed on matters of economic cooperation and development only. Indira Gandhi was much less enthusiastic about this organization than her father. She skipped several Commonwealth Heads of Government meetings (CHOGM). At one time there were rumours about India withdrawing from the Commonwealth when Britain was actively considering arms supply to South Africa. When the CHOGM was held in Delhi in 1983, she criticized the wastage of huge funds on arms race, when the same money could be profitably used to help the developing countries. Earlier she had regretted that the North had 'pushed aside' the Brandt Commission Report which had recommended that the countries of the North should set aside 0.70 per cent of their GNP for development aid to the South.

European Economic Community

Indira was quick to percieve that the real focus of economic issues had now shifted to the European Economic Commission, EEC, set up in 1958. India established full diplomatic relations with it the same year to settle matters regarding tariffs, trade quotas, etc. When the world trade was expanding rapidly, India was able to bring about a shift in her export to the EEC countries by increasing the proportion of finished products like engineering goods, garments, chemicals, etc.

In 1973 India and the EEC signed a General Trade Agreement to deepen and diversify economic relations, and a Joint Commission was also set up for this purpose. But worldwide recession in later years slowed down the tempo. Many EEC members imposed restrictions to protect their domestic market. China and Taiwan also offered increasing competition to the Indian products. Structural rigidity in India's manufacturing sector made rapid adjustments to fast-changing demands difficult. Yet EEC has become India's largest trading partner and figures prominently in her economic diplomacy.

Whereas Indira Gandhi's international outlook lacked the splendour of Nehru's global concepts and his deep concern for peace, she operated on a more down-to-earth plane. She correctly judged the changing direction for world trends and gave much greater economic content to India's foreign policy.

36

Will and Testament of Jawaharlal Nehru

I have received so much love and affection from the Indian people that nothing that I can do can repay even a small fraction of it, and indeed there can be no repayment of so precious a thing as affection. Many have been admired, some have been revered, but the affection of all classes of the Indian people has come to me in such abundant measure that I have been overwhelmed by it. I can only express the hope that in the remaining years I may live I shall not be unworthy of my people and their affection.

To my innumerable comrades and colleagues, I owe an even deeper debt of gratitude. We have been joint partners in great undertakings and have shared the triumphs and sorrows which inevitably accompany them.

I wish to declare with all earnestness that I do not want any religious ceremonies performed for me after my death. I do not believe in any such ceremonies, and to submit to them, even as a matter of form, would be hypocrisy and an attempt to delude ourselves and others.

When I die I should like my body to be cremated. If I die in a foreign country, my body should be cremated there and my ashes sent to Allahabad. A small handful of these ashes should be thrown into the Ganga, and the major portion of them disposed of in the manner indicated below. No part of these ashes should be retained or preserved.

My desire to have a handful of my ashes thrown into the

Ganga at Allahabad has no religious significance, so far as I am concerned. I have no religious sentiment in the matter. I have been attached to the Ganga and the Jumna rivers in Allahabad ever since my childhood, and as I have grown older this attachment has also grown. I have watched their varying moods as the seasons changed, and have often thought of the history and myth and tradition and song and story that have become attached to them through the long ages and become part of their flowing waters. The Ganga, especially, is the river of India, beloved of her people, round which are intertwined her racial memories, her hopes and fears, her songs of triumph, her victories and her defeats. She has been a symbol of India's age-long culture and civilization, ever-changing, ever-flowing, and yet ever the same Ganga. She reminds me of the snowcovered peaks and deep valleys of the Himalayas, which I have loved so much, and of the rich and vast plains below, where my life and work have been cast. Smiling and dancing in the morning sunlight, and dark and gloomy and full of mystery as the evening shadows fall; a narrow, slow and grateful stream in winter, and a vast roaring thing during the monsoon; broad-bosomed almost as the sea, and with something of the sea's power to destroy, the Ganga has been to me a symbol and a memory of the past of India, running into the present and flowing on to the great ocean of the future. And though I have discarded much of past tradition and custom, and am anxious that India should rid herself of all shackles that bind and constrain her and divide her people, and suppress vast numbers of them, and prevent the free development of the body and the spirit; though I seek all this, yet I do not wish to cut myself off from that past completely. I am proud of that great inheritance that has been, and is, ours, and I am conscious that I too, like all of us, am a link in that unbroken chain which goes back to the dawn of history in the immemorial past of India. That chain I would not break, for I treasure it and seek inspiration from it. And as witness of this desire of mine and as my last homage to India's cultural inheritance, I am making this request that a handful of my ashes be thrown into the Ganga at Allahabad to be carried to the great ocean that washes India's shore.

The major portion of my ashes should, however, be disposed of otherwise. I want these to be carried high up into the air in an aeroplane and scattered from that height over the fields where the peasants of India toil, so that they might mingle with the dust and soil of India and become an indistinguishable part of India.

—21st June, 1954

THE BASIC APPROACH

Reprint of a fortnightly letter which was addressed by Pandit Jawaharlal Nehru to the Chief Ministers on July 13, 1958, together with the note attached therewith. The said note was later published as "Basic Approach" in the AICC Economic Review, August 1958.

New Delhi
13 July, 1958

My Dear Chief Minister,

My fortnightly letter to you today will be a brief one, but I am attaching to it a note which is for the present incomplete. I may add to it later. It represents really some kind of loud thinking on my part and an attempt to clarify my own mind. I am venturing to share this with you.

2. More and more I have a feeling that in international affairs logic and reason have been pushed out by some kind of madness which is continually driving the world into dangerous directions. In spite of the abundance of goodwill and desire for peace that people in all countries possess, they are being driven to the brink of the precipice. Nearly all of us shout at each other and one country or group condemns the other, although it is obvious that this cannot lead to any peace or relief from the present tensions. Disarmament, so vitally necessary, seems a dream which has no reality.

3. In the Lebanon, a curious situation has arisen and is continuing. There can be little doubt that some kind of a civil war is raging there, a war in which the regular army has played

little part thus far. There is still talk of intervention which, if it takes place, will inevitably lead to the most dangerous consequences. Also, such intervention will mean a conflict and an attempt to suppress them. The United Nations Force of Observers and Secretary-General Hammarskjoeld have undoubtedly played a very helpful part in preventing dangerous developments. How far they will succeed in this, I cannot say.

4. In India, apart from the other great problems that face us, we are at the mercy of nature, that is, the rains. They have come in a large part of the country, but some of the drought-affected areas in Bihar, U.P. and some other places are still without rain. If adequate rain does not come within the next few days, we shall have to face a great disaster.

5. Some little time ago, the Prime Minister of Pakistan delivered a speech which was somewhat unusual for him. He talked in terms of peace with India and ruled out war. We welcome this. But his words have been belied by repeated attempts at aggression on the Indo-Pakistan border in the East. The actual incidents there cannot be considered major, but this tendency is a dangerous one and, obviously, we cannot supinely watch these incursions. We have to take steps to prevent them.

6. For the rest, I leave you to the note attached.

Yours sincerely,
Jawaharlal Nehru

Enclosure

We have many grave internal problems to face. But even a consideration of these internal problems inevitably leads to a wider range of thought. Unless we have some clarity of vision or, at any rate, are clear as to the questions posed to us, we shall not get out of the confusion that afflicts the world today. I do not pretend to have that clarity of thinking or to have any answers to our major questions. All I can say in all humility is that I am constantly thinking about these questions. In a sense, I might say that I rather envy those who have got fixed ideas and, therefore, need not take the trouble to look deeper into the problems of today. Whether it is from the point of view of some religion or ideology, they are not troubled with the mental conflicts which are always the accompaniment of the great ages of transition.

2. And yet, even though it may be more comfortable to have fixed ideas and be complacent, surely that is not to be commended, and that can only lead to stagnation and decay. The basic fact of today is the tremendous pace of change in human life. In my own life, I have seen amazing changes, and I am sure that, in the course of the life of the next generation, these changes will be even greater, if humanity is not overwhelmed and annihilated by an atomic war.

3. Nothing is so remarkable as the progressive conquest or understanding of the physical world by the mind of man today, and this process is continuing at a terrific pace. Man need no longer be a victim of external circumstances, at any rate to a very large extent. While there has been this conquest of external conditions, there is at the same time the strange spectacle of a lack of moral fibre and of self-control in man as a whole. Conquering the physical world, he fails to conquer himself.

4. That is the tragic paradox of this Atomic and Sputnik Age. The fact that nuclear tests continue, even though it is well recognized that they are very harmful in the present and in the future; the fact that all kinds of weapons of mass destruction are being-produced and piled up, even though it is universally recognized that their use may well exterminate the human race, brings out this paradox with startling clarity. Science is advancing far beyond the comprehension of a very great part of the human race, and posing problems which most of us are incapable of understanding, much less of solving. Hence, the inner conflict and tumult of our times. On the one side, there is this great and overpowering progress in science and technology and of their manifold consequences, on the other, a certain mental exhaustion of civilization itself.

5. Religion comes into conflict with rationalism. The disciplines of religion and social usage fade away without giving place to other disciplines, moral or spiritual. Religion, as practised, either deals with matters rather unrelated to our normal lives and thus adopts an ivory tower attitude, or is allied to certain social usages which do not fit in with the present age. Rationalism, on the other hand, with all its virtues, somehow appears to deal with the surface of things, without uncovering the inner core. Science itself has arrived at a stage when vast new possibilities and mysteries loom ahead. Matter and energy and spirit seem to overlap.

6. In the ancient days, life was simpler and more in contact with nature. Now it becomes more and more complex and more and more hurried, without time for reflection or even of questioning. Scientific developments have produced an enormous surplus of power and energy which are often used for wrong purposes.

7. The old question still faces us, as it has faced humanity for ages past : what is the meaning of life? The old days of faith do not appear to be adequate, unless they can answer the questions of today. In a changing world, living should be a continuous adjustment to these changes and happenings. It is the lack of this adjustment that creates conflicts.

8. The old civilizations, with the many virtues that they possess, have obviously proved inadequate. The new Western civilization, with all its triumphs and achievements and also with its atomic bombs, also appears inadequate and, therefore, the feeling grows that there is something wrong with our civilization. Indeed, essentially our problems are those of civilization itself. Religion gave a certain moral and spiritual discipline; it also tried to perpetuate superstition and social usages. Indeed, those superstitions and social usages enmeshed and overwhelmed the real spirit of religion. Disillusionment followed. Communism comes in the wake of this disillusionment and offers some kind of faith and some kind of discipline. To some extent it fills a vacuum. It succeeds in some measure by giving a content to man's life. But in spite of

its apparent success, it fails, partly because of its rigidity, but, even more so, because it ignores certain essential needs of human nature. There is much talk in communism of the contradictions of capitalist society and there is truth in that analysis. But we see the growing contradictions within the rigid framework of communism itself. Its suppression of individual freedom brings about powerful reactions. Its contempt for what might be called the moral and spiritual side of life not only ignores something that is basic in man, but also deprives human behaviour of standards and values. Its unfortunate association with violence encourages a certain evil tendency in human beings.

9. I have the greatest admiration for many of the achievements of the Soviet Union. Among these great achievements is the value attached to the child and to the common man. There the systems of education and health are probably the best in the world. But it is said, and rightly, that there is suppression of individual freedom there. And yet the spread of education in all its forms is itself a tremendous liberating force which ultimately will not tolerate that suppression of freedom. This again is another contradiction. Unfortunately, communism became too closely associated with the necessity for violence and thus the ideal which is placed before the world became a tainted one. Means distorted ends. We see here the powerful influence of wrong means and methods.

10. Communism charges the capitalist structure of society with being based on violence and class conflict. I think this is essentially correct, though that capitalist structure itself has undergone and is continually undergoing a change because of democratic and other forces. Still it is obviously true that there are class struggles and inequality. The question is how to get rid of this and have a classless society with equal opportunities for all. Can this be achieved through methods of violence, or can it be possible to bring about those changes through peaceful methods? Communism has definitely allied itself to the approach of violence. Even if it does not indulge normally in

physical violence, its language is of violence, its thought is violent and it does not seek to change by persuasion or peaceful democratic pressures, but by coercion and indeed by destruction and extermination in their grossest forms and, at the same time, it has no acceptable ideal.

11. This is completely opposed to the peaceful approach which Gandhiji taught us. Communists as well as anti-Communists both seem to imagine that a principle can only be stoutly defended by language of violence, and by condemning those who do not accept it. For both of them there are no shades, there is only black and white. That is the old approach of the bigoted aspect of some religions. It is not the approach of tolerance of feeling that perhaps others might have some share of the truth also. Speaking for myself, I find this approach wholly unscientific, unreasonable and uncivilized, whether it is applied in the realm of religion or economic theory or anything else. I prefer the old pagan approach of tolerance, apart from its religious aspects. But whatever we may think about it, we have arrived at a stage in the modern world when an attempt at forcible imposition of ideas on any large section of people is bound ultimately to fail. In present circumstances this will lead to war and tremendous destruction. There will be no victory, only defeat for everyone. Even apart from this, we have seen, in the last year or two, that it is not easy for even Great Powers to reintroduce colonial control over territories which have recently become independent. This was exemplified by the Suez incident in 1956. Also what happened in Hungary demonstrated that the desire for national freedom is stronger even than any ideology and cannot ultimately be suppressed. What happened in Hungary was not essentially a conflict between communism and anti-communism. It represented nationalism striving for freedom from foreign control.

12. Thus, violence cannot possibly lead today to a solution of any major problem because violence has become much too terrible and destructive. The moral approach to this question has now been powerfully reinforced by the practical aspect.

13. If the society we aim at cannot be brought about by big-scale violence, will small-scale violence help? Surely not, partly because that itself may lead to the big-scale violence and partly because it produces an atmosphere of conflict and of disruption. It is absurd to imagine that out of conflict the social progressive forces are bound to win. In Germany both the Communist Party and the Social Democratic Party were swept away by Hitler. This may well happen in other countries too. In India any appeal to violence is particularly dangerous because of its inherent disruptive character. We have too many fissiparous tendencies for us to take risks. But all these are relatively minor considerations. The basic thing, I believe, is that wrong means will not lead to right results and that is no longer merely an ethical doctrine but a practical proposition.

14. Some of us have been discussing this general background and, more especially, conditions in India. It is often said that there is a sense of frustration and depression in India and the old buoyancy of spirit is not to be found, at a time when enthusiasm and hard work are most needed. This is not merely in evidence in our country. It is in a sense a world phenomenon. An old and valued colleague said that this is due to our not having a philosophy of life and indeed the world also is suffering from this lack of a philosophical approach. In our efforts to ensure the material prosperity of the country, we have not paid any attention to the spiritual element in human nature. Therefore, in order to give the individual and the nation a sense of purpose, something to live for and, if necessary, to die for, we have to revive some philosophy of life and give, in the wider sense of the word, a spiritual background to our thinking. We talk of a Welfare State and of democracy and socialism. They are good concepts but they hardly convey a clear and unambiguous meaning. This was the argument and then the question arose as to what our ultimate objective should be. Democracy and socialism are means to an end, not the end itself. We talk of the good of society. Is this something apart from transcending the good of the individuals composing it? If the individual is ignored

and sacrificed for what is considered the good of the society, is that the right objective to have?

15. It was agreed that the individual should not be so sacrificed and indeed that real social progress will come only when opportunity is given to the individual to develop. Provided the individual is not a selected group, but comprises the whole community. The touchstone, therefore, should be how far any political or social theory enables the individual to rise above his petty self and thus think in terms of the good of all. The law of life should not be competition or acquisitiveness but cooperation, the good of each contributing to the good of all. In such a society the emphasis will be on duties, not on rights; the rights will follow the performance of the duties. We have to give a new direction to education and evolve a new type of humanity.

16. This argument led to the old Vedantic conception that everything, whether sentient or insentient, finds a place in the organic whole; that everything has a spark of what might be called the Divine Impulse, or the basic energy or life force which pervades the universe. This leads to metaphysical regions which tend to take us away from the problems of life which face us. I suppose that any line of thought, sufficiently pursued, leads us in some measure to metaphysics. Even science today is almost on the verge of all manner of imponderables. I do not propose to discuss these metaphysical aspects, but this very argument indicates how the mind searches for something basic underlying the physical world. If we really believed in this all-pervading concept of the principle of life it might help us to get rid of some of our narrowness of race, caste or class and make us more tolerant and understanding in our approaches to life's problems.

17. But obviously it does not solve any of these problems and, in a sense, we remain where we were. In India we talk of the Welfare State and socialism. In a sense, every country, whether it is capitalist, Socialist or Communist, accepts the ideal of the Welfare State. Capitalism in a few countries at least has achieved this common welfare to a very large extent,

though it has far from solved its own problems and there is a basic lack of something vital. Democracy allied to capitalism has undoubtedly toned down many of its evils and in fact is different now from what it was a generation or two ago. In industrially advanced countries there has been a continuous and steady upward trend of economic development. Even the terrible losses of World Wars have not prevented this trend, insofar as these highly developed countries are concerned. Further, this economic development has spread, though in varying degrees, to all classes. This does not apply to countries which are not industrially developed. Indeed, in those countries the struggle for development is very difficult and sometimes, in spite of efforts not only do economic inequalities remain, but tend to become worse. Normally speaking, it may be said that the forces of a capitalist society, if left unchecked, tend to make the rich richer and the poor poorer and thus increase the gap between them. This applies to countries as well as groups on regions or classes within the countries. Various democratic processes interfere with these normal trends. Capitalism itself has, therefore, developed some socialistic features even though its major aspects remain.

18. Socialism, of course, deliberately wants to interfere with the normal processes and thus not only adds to the productive forces but lessens inequalities. But what is socialism? It is difficult to give a precise answer and there are innumerable definitions of it. Some people probably think of socialism vaguely just as something which does good and which aims at equality. That does not take us very far. Socialism is basically a different approach from that of capitalism, though I think it is true that the wide gap between them tends to lessen because many of the ideas of socialism are gradually incorporated even in the capitalist structure. Socialism is after all not only a way of life but a certain scientific approach to social and economic problems. If socialism is introduced in a backward and under-developed country, it does not suddenly make it any less backward. In fact, we then have a backward and poverty-stricken socialism.

19. Unfortunately many of the political aspects of communism have tended to distort our vision of socialism. Also the technique of struggle evolved by communism has given violence a predominant part. Socialism should, therefore be considered apart from these political elements or the inevitability of violence. It tells us that the general character of social, political and intellectual life in a society is governed by its productive resources. As those productive resources change and develop so the life and thinking of the community changes.

20. Imperialism or colonialism suppressed and suppresses the progressive social forces. Inevitably it aligns itself with certain privileged groups or classes because it is interested in preserving the social and economic *status quo*. Even after a country has become independent, it may continue to be economically dependent on other countries. This kind of thing is euphemistically called having close cultural and economic ties.

21. We discuss sometimes the self-sufficiency of the village. This should not be mixed up with the idea of decentralization though it may be a part of it. While decentralization is, I think, desirable to the largest possible extent, if it leads to old and rather primitive methods of production, then it simply means that we do not utilize modern methods which have brought great material advance to some countries of the West. That is, we remain poor and, what is more, tend to become poorer because of the pressure of an increasing population; I do not see any way out of our vicious circle of poverty except by utilizing the new sources of power which science has placed at our disposal. Being poor, we have no surplus to invest and we sink lower and lower.

22. We have to break through this barrier by profiting by the new sources of power and modern techniques. But, in doing so, we should not forget the basic human element and the fact that our objective is individual improvement and the lessening of inequalities; and we must not forget the ethical and spiritual aspects of life which are ultimately the basis of

culture and civilization and which have given some meaning to life.

23. It has to be remembered that it is not by some magic adoption of socialist or capitalist method that poverty suddenly leads to riches. The only way is through hard work and increasing the productivity of the nation and organizing an equitable distribution of its products. It is a lengthy and difficult process. In a poorly developed country, the capitalist method offers no chance. It is only through a planned approach on socialistic lines that steady progress can be attained though even that will take time. As this process continues, the texture of our life and thinking gradually changes.

24. Planning is essential for this because otherwise we waste our resources which are very limited. Planning does not mean a mere collection of projects or schemes, but a thought-out approach of how to strengthen the base and pace of progress so that the community advances on all fronts. In India we have a terrible problem of extreme poverty in certain large regions, apart from the general poverty of the country. We have always a difficult choice before us; whether to concentrate on production by itself in selected and favourable areas, and thus for the moment rather ignoring the poor areas, or try to develop the backward areas at the same time, so as to lessen the inequalities between regions. A balance has to be struck and an integrated national plan evolved. That national plan need not and indeed should not have rigidity. It need not be based on any dogma; but should rather take the existing facts into consideration. It may and, I think, in present-day India it should, encourage private enterprise in many fields, though even that private enterprise must necessarily fit in with the national plan and have such controls as are considered necessary.

25. Land reforms have a peculiar significance because without them, more especially in a highly congested country like India, there can be no radical improvement in productivity in agriculture. But the main object of land reforms is a deeper

one. They are meant to break up the old class structure of a society that is stagnant.

26. We want social security, but we have to recognize that social security only comes when a certain stage of development has been reached. Otherwise we shall have neither social security nor any development.

27. It is clear that, in the final analysis, it is the quality of the human beings that counts. It is man that builds up the wealth of a nation, as well as its cultural progress. Hence education and health are of high importance so as to produce that quality in the human beings. We have to suffer here also from the lack of resources, but still we have always to remember that it is right education and good health that will give the foundation for economic as well as cultural and spiritual progress.

28. A national plan has thus both a short-term objective and a long-term one. The long-term objective gives a true perspective. Without it short-term planning is of little avail and will lead us into blind alleys. Planning will thus always be perspective planning and have in view the physical achievements for which we strive. In other words, it has to be physical planning, though it is obviously limited and conditioned by financial resources and economic conditions.

29. The problems that India faces are to some extent common to other countries, but, much more so, there are new problems for which we have not got parallels or historical precedents elsewhere. What has happened in the past in the industrially advanced countries has little bearing on us today. As a matter of fact, the countries that are advanced today were economically better off than India is today, in terms of per capita income, before their industrialization began. Western economics, therefore, though helpful, have little bearing on our present-day problems. So also have Marxist economics which are in many ways out of date, even though they throw a considerable light on economic processes. We have thus to do our own thinking, profiting by the example of others but

essentially trying to find a path for ourselves suited to our own conditions.

30. In considering these economic aspects of our problems, we have always to remember the basic approach of peaceful means; and perhaps we might also keep in view the old Vedantic ideal of the life force which is the inner base of everything that exists.

Yours sincerely,

Jawaharlal Nehru

Index